"I DIDN'T PULL ANY PUNCHES.
I DECIDED IF I WAS GOING TO WRITE A BOOK,
I WAS GOING TO GO ALL THE WAY WITH IT."
Cheryl Crane

DETOUR
A HOLLYWOOD STORY

"NOTORIOUS . . .
A four-course feast of nostalgia and nightmare."
Los Angeles Times

"SCANDALOUS . . .
Lana Turner's daughter tells her story
of a harrowing Hollywood childhood . . .
A real grabber!"
Kirkus

"SENSATIONAL . . .
Lana's daughter writes her own 'Peyton Place.'
Well written, well rounded, frank, open and direct."
Liz Smith

"LURID . . .
She tells us everything in exquisite Little Nell detail."
Newsday

"SHOCKING . . .
Cheryl Crane has come to grips with her dramatic saga
and written her riveting story."
Boston Globe

DETOUR

A HOLLYWOOD STORY

CHERYL CRANE

WITH CLIFF JAHR

AVON BOOKS ◆ NEW YORK

AVON BOOKS
A division of
The Hearst Corporation
105 Madison Avenue
New York, New York 10016

"A Belvedere Book"
Copyright © 1988 by Cheryl Crane and Cliff Jahr
Front cover photograph by Nat Dallinger
Published by arrangement with the authors
Library of Congress Catalog Card Number: 87-20914
ISBN: 0-380-70580-X

Published in hardcover by Arbor House/William Morrow and Company,
Inc.; for information address, Permissions Department, Arbor House,
William Morrow and Company, Inc., 105 Madison Avenue, New York,
New York 10016.

First Avon Books Printing: January 1989

AVON TRADEMARK REG. U.S. PAT. OFF. AND IN OTHER COUNTRIES, MARCA
REGISTRADA, HECHO EN U.S.A.

Printed in the U.S.A.

K-R 10 9 8 7 6 5 4 3 2 1

To JLR, MY CAVALRY OFFICER,

WHO'S ALWAYS RIDING TO THE RESCUE.

Contents

Acknowledgments

A number of people made enormous contributions to the creation and development of this book. I would particularly like to express my gratitude to Eden Collinsworth, Owen Laster, Floria Lasky, and Lou Valentino—as well as to two dear friends who are no longer with us, John Dodds and Stan Kamen.

My thanks too, for their friendship and memories, to Chief Clinton B. Anderson, Del Armstrong, Brenda Barak Nicky Blair, Sybil Brand, Charles William Brooks, William Crane (Uncle Bill), Evelyn Lane Dankner, Charles Graham, M.D., Herman Hover, Carol Kennoy, H. R. Lorenzo, Jeanette Muhlbach, Robert Osborne, Joe Perrin, Bob Perry, Liz Smith, Gene Stavis, and Bob Westbrook. In addition, I am grateful to the following institutions for their cooperation: the Academy of Motion Picture Arts and Sciences Library, the Doheny Library of the University of Southern California, the Kemper Military Academy, the Los Angeles *Herald Examiner*, Viacom International Inc., and the Woodstock Public Library.

I'd also like to give my special thanks and appreciation to my editor, Allan Mayer, for his excellent taste and judgment throughout—in particular, for contributing the title and for his help with the last two chapters.

Finally, I'd like to thank my mother (Mom) for her love and understanding, which I hope I shall always have. And I'd like to thank Josh for reliving with me all the good and bad times of my life, and for giving me a happy ending.

CHERYL CRANE

San Francisco
July 1987

I

GOOD FRIDAY

One

I had never seen Mother actually tremble before, not until that day. Staring at her hands made me sort of edgy myself, because the fingers were twitching as though they were troubled by bad dreams and I had no idea why.

It was very quiet inside our rented limousine as we stopped and started on our way through the Sunset Boulevard traffic. We were captive in a long line of cars all going to the same place.

A thought came to Mother's mind which put a tiny scoff on her lips, and she stubbed out a half-smoked Benson & Hedges to light another. The jaws of her gold lighter made an alarming snap, and I blinked while she just cast a distracted glance out the window. She had been chain smoking like this ever since she had returned the previous week from the Acapulco trip, inhaling deeply, as if trying to punish her poor lungs.

I could not understand about the jittery fingers and heavy smoking, and I could not make myself look out the window, either. Something was really eating Mother, but what?

I pondered the possibilities. It was true, of course, that this day, March 24, 1958, marked a new peak in her career. She and I and my grandmother, who was seated between us, had good reason to feel excited and even a little bit nervous. We were headed for the Academy Awards show. For the first time, Mother had been nominated for an Oscar—as best actress for her work in *Peyton Place*. If by some chance she won, there could be a big payoff. An

3

Oscar might restore her slipping name and win her back her old billing above the title in movies, in the way that winning one had done for Joan Crawford a dozen years before. Crawford's comeback in *Mildred Pierce* was masterminded by producer Jerry Wald, the very same man who made *Peyton Place*. Mother, however, was not favored to win, and she knew it.

I understood that she might have a mild feeling of dread about appearing at the Oscars as an award presenter. Though she had made thirty-nine movies and a thousand grand entrances, she had never braved live television. Tonight would be her first national appearance without the support of a memorized script, and while she could wisecrack with ease for the press, this was different. She'd have to "wing it" with only partial help from a teleprompter, and there would be more than 50 million people watching her out there.

But Mom, after all, was a trouper, and the prospect of appearing on live television would not explain her quaking like Marie Antoinette on the way to the block. She had displayed more composure when she played the wicked Lady de Winter marching to her execution in *The Three Musketeers* than she was showing now.

So here we sat in our golden coach, the three Turner girls—all gowned, coiffed, and lacquered to death. Carefully, we held in our bottoms so as not to wrinkle the dresses—just the way we held in our thoughts so as not to let out real feelings. You see, even when we were together, we were still alone. In this family, souls never touched.

While I would not dare to ask what was buzzing in her mind, as far as I could see, Mother had every reason to be ecstatic. She was the Oscar-nominated star of 1957's highest-grossing movie, a well-regarded actress at the zenith of her beauty. She looked tanned and sexy after larking away six weeks in Mexico with her boyfriend.

I could see something coming. Mother had glanced my way and was examining me with that quizzical look I was getting to know. Ever since *Peyton Place*, in which she had portrayed the mother of a troubled teenage daughter, she liked to play real life scenes with me that showed special maternal concern.

"Baby," she began, holding her hands still by clasping them together, "you won't forget what we talked about, will you? *Very* important. At the party tonight, when photographers come round to the table, I don't want a cigarette in your hand."

"Yes, Mother."

"No drinks either. I don't want to see pictures come out that show glasses on the table."

"Yes, Mother."

"You make sure there's nothing in front of you—I don't care if it's ginger ale. You're fourteen years old, and you know how that would look." One of her fingers pressed at a crease that had popped on her brow.

"Don't worry, Mother," I answered in my most grown-up voice, *"really."*

I was beginning to enjoy conspiring with her in these matters of keeping the star image pristine. She, Mickey Rooney, and Judy Garland had gone to high school together at M-G-M, where they had been drilled on how a child star behaved before the public: no booze, cigarettes, swear words, cleavage, or Grand Canyon smiles—just show the teeth, and so on. All three performers turned out to be hell raisers anyway, but Mother wanted to pass on to me that proper training and have me reflect it in public—for my sake as well as hers.

She still worked hard at glamour. At the age of thirty-eight, she'd rather lose a good earring than be caught without makeup, and she still resolutely discouraged photos that hinted at her fondness for vodka.

Sometimes, however, when she tried to shape me as an appendage of her image, I pulled away. Oh, I enjoyed the privileges afforded by her wealth and fame; however, inside me the true kernel of my being was struggling to sprout. I was the daughter of a movie queen, a Hollywood princess, but I was also *me,* whoever that was.

If my appalling childhood had bent the tree in strange ways, I was conventional, too, in the way of most teenage girls. I both hated and adored my mother, wanted to be like her but totally different and much, much better. If I needed her help, I also resented her for giving it. The main problem was that help did not come soon or often enough.

Although, as mother and daughter, we were alike in many ways, we were very different in physical appearance. I had been used in her publicity photos since birth, but I was no perfect little tintype of her, a fact people liked to discuss in front of me. ("Looks like her father, does she?" they would say.) Standing up straight beside her, which I avoided doing, I was then five inches taller. Her celebrated curves and golden hair only made me look flat-chested and mousy. True, I had been blessed with an *haute couture* frame and hubcap cheekbones, but at this point in my life, when I was still made to wear children's clothes, I regarded those assets as drawbacks to be endured with crimson blushes. I suppose I was bright and pretty enough, but coming out of an overprotected childhood, I had grown—one might say—*painfully* shy. At fourteen, I smoldered to break free.

The 1958 Oscar show offered a move in that direction. It would be the first time Mother and I were facing the world press without her holding tight to my little girl hand. Tonight I would be a woman, and one with a new name, Cherie. I had made my family promise to use the name Cherie from then on, pronouncing it "Sherry" and spelling it in the French way (even though, after all my tutoring, I still did not speak the language). Cheryl, I just hated. And to solemnize the debut of *Cherie Crane, Adult Person,* I had dressed accordingly.

My favorite color then was the lurid green of Prell shampoo. Mother's dressmaker had run up a chiffon party dress for me in that exact shade. Although the dress was nominally designed by Mother, the bodice wound up being contoured too ambitiously for my *haute couture* chest. I wanted strapless, Mother wanted sleeves, and we compromised on a halter. She was not pleased, but was gently amused about it, observing that its specially built-in bra had a small job to do.

Mother was dubbed the "Sweater Girl" when she was getting her start at Warner Brothers, but she saw the short life that such a nickname could have and thereafter underplayed her bosom. Bare cleavage bored her, anyway. She preferred clinging, impeccably tailored, high-necked dresses that showed off her perfect proportions and a bottom of which she was justly proud.

For tonight she had displayed admirable self-control by indulging me with my first grown-up dress. When she first saw me in it, she covered a frown. Her mouth dropped, though, when she saw the spike heels I just barely had on. The latest thing in dyed-to-match satin, these shoes—called "Spring-a-lators"—offered the engineering miracle of having no back or sides. You kept them on by curling your toes into a tonguelike contraption in the last. Practicing the day before, I paced the length of my grandmother's apartment a hundred times, driving her wild and having little more to show for it than red toes. I still wobbled.

What a vision I presented. My sonata in Prell green was topped off with a white ermine stole, as if the suds were rising. A relic from my childhood, the stole had originally been a winter coat that Santa gave me when I was three years old. For years it had shivered in Mother's fur storage rooms. In an uncommon moment of thrift, she had hauled it out and recut the ermine pelts along adult lines for me to wear tonight. Indeed, for this exciting night, I, too, had been recut along adult lines.

"Well, Lana my dear," sighed Gran, glancing out at Hollywood Boulevard (we were passing Grauman's Chinese Theater, where her daughter's handprints were pressed in cement), "win or lose tonight, you can be really proud of yourself. Maybe you'll win." She cleared her throat and rested her all-seeing eyes on Mother's hands. I thought Gran, too, was looking a little edgy.

"Oh, you know it's going to be Joanne Woodward," Mother said evenly. "Everybody knows that." A lovely smile began to flicker over her face. "She was sensational in *The Three Faces of Eve,* you know, Mom. A once-in-a-lifetime part. Joanne really deserves the Oscar." Her tone came off a shade too much of the good sport, and Gran pursed her lips. Maybe her daughter needed to work on delivery. She might have to use a lot of that humble stuff tonight.

Our car was among the last to draw up at the Pantages Theater on Hollywood and Vine. Fans on bleachers let fly with whistles and shrieks of "Lana! Lana!" Mother swept inside, and I turned to see Gregory Peck just behind us.

This was the thirtieth annual Academy Awards show, and it would be remembered as something of a landmark. Planned as a special tribute to old Hollywood, the event is said to have sparked the appearance of more household names than any other and is fondly remembered as the last one to be staged in an old, Art Deco movie palace. It was also the only Oscar show to be broadcast without commercials.

The evening started off with a big production medley of Oscar-winning songs sung by more than a score of stars. It ended with a sly little number that wedded the old and new. Mae West appeared and eased herself onto a silken divan, where she sang "Baby, It's Cold Outside." She sang it to Rock Hudson. He was thirty-three. She was sixty-six, and it was her first TV appearance ever. I had shivers.

Next on the program was Mother's presentation of an award. In a bid to make the opening of the show stronger, the producers had broken with tradition and scheduled one of the four major acting awards only twelve minutes into the show. Moments before, as she rose to go backstage, Mother lost one of her four-inch spikes. It made me giggle. "Okay," I whispered, "you want to borrow the Spring-a-lators?"

No one makes a grander entrance than my mother. Jimmy Stewart sang out her name, and she floated into the light looking as fans had never seen her. Poured into a skin-tight "mermaid" sheath in white lace over nude silk, she was obliged to walk in little mincing steps, which meant that the dress's "fishtail" kicked out below the knee. Sexy but covered-up, it was unmistakably Turner-esque. So was the big diamond necklace, a gift of her third husband, Bob Topping. (In presenting it to her, he had wrapped it as a collar around the neck of my dog.)

Fans puzzled over her deep Mexican tan, set off by hair snipped short, curly, slicked back on the sides, and silver as a dime. The applause was warm, though it wasn't quite the roar accorded a comeback. Mother had always been good copy, and the movie colony seemed curious to see her after more than a year's absence. I gathered there had been some kind of talk about her, and I could sense around us a more than usual rustle of whispers.

"Thank you so much," she said to Stewart, her voice quavering.

"Well, uh . . ." he said, starting to walk off.

"Oh, but Jimmy, don't leave, please."

"Why, y'nervous?"

"No," she lied. Then after a long, heart-stopping pause, she purred, "It's just that I like you."

"Well," he said, swallowing hard, "now *I'm* nervous."

It may have been coy, but it worked. You could see Mother's shoulders square back in relief. Her hands still trembled, though, as she opened the envelope showing Red Buttons as winner of the best supporting-actor award for *Sayonara*. After they bowed off, the next presenter (for a minor technical award) was forty-six-year-old Ronald Reagan.

Sure enough, Joanne Woodward took the Oscar for *The Three Faces of Eve*. When her name was read, Mother beamed with happiness for her. If she had some scrap of an acceptance speech in the back of her mind, Mother crumpled it up and switched roles. As 50 million folks watched Woodward accept the award ("I've been dreaming of this since I was nine years old," she gasped), many in the live audience at the Pantages were darting peeks at Mother, who was the only runner-up present. The other nominees, Deborah Kerr, Anna Magnani, and Liz Taylor, had stayed away (Taylor because her husband, Mike Todd, had been killed in a plane crash six days before).

The party afterward at the Hilton brought a lot of big stars to our table because Mother seldom table-hopped anymore. People came to her. To my blushing delight, everyone—including Cary Grant and Mother's costar in four pictures, Clark Gable—said how grown-up I looked. Until recently I had been allowed to see only cartoon movies, so if I knew of stars at all it was as visitors to our house, as everyday people. Only one leading man, James Mason, ever made me swoon. I had somehow managed to see *Odd Man Out*, and I spent all night keeping an eye out for him. Alas, he did not appear.

Sean Connery was seated at our table. He was twenty-seven, and I knew him because he had been Mother's handpicked romantic foil in a picture she had made the previous fall. I clung deliriously to his big shoulders as we whirled around the dance floor. The hardness of his back reminded me that he had once talked about winning a runner-up spot in the 1952 Mr. Universe bodybuilding contest.

He looked to be a gentle giant, Sean did, stuffed into his tuxedo—impish and soft-spoken, with a wee Scottish burr. He was not at all the dashing James Bond who would thrill everyone five years later in *Doctor No*. I might have practiced batting my lashes at his big brown eyes, but we were friends.

Sean was plainly awed by Hollywood and especially by my mother, with whom it had been rumored he'd had a romance that was destined to be brief because he was nine years younger than she. Mother was lately growing sensitive about having younger boyfriends. She was nearing forty—in those days a terminal age for movie queens—and she avoided anything that drew attention to the fact. She'd like to avoid showing off a too-adult daughter, for example, or getting involved in one of those May-September relationships that Hedda and Louella wrote items about. It was a good thing her current boyfriend was safely five years her senior.

The orchestra struck up the theme from the night's big winner, *The Bridge on the River Kwai*, but "Colonel Bogey" was a little hard to dance to and Sean and I wandered to the side. "Cheryl, luv," he whispered in my ear, "look over there at your mom. That's what I call a star." Across the floor, she was holding court at a ringside table. There sat the legend. She sparkled, she mugged, she listened intently. A steady stream of friends kissed the air near her cheeks, and she was astonished by the wicked things they said, tossing her head and laughing theatrically.

As we watched, Joanne Woodward appeared with Oscar in hand and bent beside Mother to hug for the cameras. She was trailed by her new husband, Paul Newman. Gregory Peck, his wife Veronique, and John Wayne stood chatting together behind them.

It seemed to me that the area glowed, as if unseen spots were bathing Mother in soft amber focus. She was not the biggest star in the room, she was not the most beautiful or most popular, but somehow she held sway at the side of the dance floor. It didn't seem to matter that stars of the New Hollywood were everywhere, including Woodward, Kim Novak, Sophia Loren, and Joan Collins. Or that her friendly rivals Rita Hayworth and Ava Gardner were both at home watching television and would soon retire from pictures.

The evening was a curious triumph for Mother. At a gala toasting Hollywood's old guard, she best epitomized its glamour, and everyone knew it. Her hands didn't tremble now. "I've never *seen* her this happy," I said to Sean. Twenty-five years would pass before I did again.

Two

The darkness was fragrant with night-blooming jasmine as Mother and I tiptoed our way along the garden paths of the Bel Air Hotel later that evening. She had invited me to spend the night at her bungalow at the Bel Air. We were barefoot; the Ferragamos and Spring-a-lators that had tortured our toes all night swung from our thumbs. I felt giddy from sneaking nips of Mother's champagne, and we both stifled giggles as we imagined the sight we must have presented—two tipsy females, all diamond-studded in brilliant green, ermine, and fishtails, and with sore feet.

With haughty disdain, we dropped our shoes inside her bungalow door, and, while I closed my eyes to inhale the night, Mother peered into the living room.

All was still. Seeing that a small table lamp burned as before at the room's far end, Mother shrugged a little sigh and led the way in. She poured a nightcap, loosened her dress, and snuggled into an overstuffed chair by the bay window, while I settled on the floor and rested my arm on her knee. This was a nice time for a mother-daughter chat. We almost never talked heart-to-heart, but all this evening I had felt so close to her, even protective. When they announced the best actress as ". . . Joanne Woodward," my anxious heart heard ". . . *not* Lana Turner," and I almost wanted to cry.

"Well, which boyfriend is it this week?" she teased fondly. Mother suspected she was seeing her own hopelessly romantic nature repeat itself in me, because I was dating two boys steadily at the same time. They were very

12

different from each other. One patterned himself on Pat
Boone and the other on James Dean. My switching back
and forth between a straight arrow and a nonconformist
reflected some growing light and dark in my nature, but I
didn't know it then. I just thought, as I could see by Mother's example, that it was fun to twist boys around. Her
eyes gleamed with such delight when I spoke of it that I
sort of laid it on to please her more.

"Oh, Peter and I are back together," I laughed. "I was
getting a little tired of Ziggy last week, with his thing
about leather and chains. But I don't know. Ziggy's awful
cute, Mother, and I give him such an *aw-ful* hard time."

"Mmm?"

"Oh, yes. Like I always remind him how Peter and I
go riding together on our own horses, but that he's too
young even to have a motorcycle and take me out riding.
He gets so mad. And other stuff, y'know?"

"Well, Baby," she said, patting my hand, "last year
you broke your back falling off a horse." She stopped,
glanced at her bedroom door, and listened. Silence. Re-
alizing her voice was too loud for the late hour, she continued more softly. "So we certainly don't need a
motorcycle accident, do we? And do you really mean to
say that Ziggy likes leather and . . . what? Chains? Peter
is beginning to sound better to me every day."

We rambled on for a while about boys, horses, school,
and whom we had seen at the Oscars. She had never spoken to me about her work before, but she allowed as how
she might accept a role opposite Jimmy Stewart in an Otto
Preminger film called *Anatomy of a Murder*. The part reminded her of the mankiller she played in *The Postman
Always Rings Twice*.

Show business was a muddle to me then, and my mind
began to drift. In the soft glow of the lamp, the suntanned
skin of her face seemed to fade into the tan wall behind
her, leaving her silver hair and white teeth floating in
space. Her necklace sparkled like a fiery constellation. I
saw disembodied lips that moved in sync with words about
Preminger's toughness and the way Bill Holden had embraced her tonight. Mother, I thought, this is my mother.
Here we are. A face on a wall, a face on a screen, the

whole world's Lana Turner—and my own, too, my mommy. I closed my eyes and her image stayed as if projected on the lids. Suddenly, *wham,* I reeled around a corner and went swallowing down a yawn. All those nips of champagne.

"I forgot to tell you," she said, touching my arm. "I rented a house, a nice big one on Bedford Drive."

"Beverly Hills?"

"Yes, 730 Bedford, corner of Lomitas. Less than three minutes' drive from Gran, and about the same from your father's restaurant. Sweetheart, your bedroom has a fireplace, a den, your own telephone. I think you're going to love it."

She had saved this for last, I saw, setting me up for a pitch because she realized I was unsure about ever wanting to live with her again. I had run away from her the year before, and, ever since, she had consulted me more on decisions that affected my life. But live with her? Well, on the one hand I craved release from my banishment to boarding school. But on the other, I hated to give up the freedoms I enjoyed by staying sometimes on weekends at Gran's apartment. Living with Mother might mean heavy-handed supervision again, maybe even another governess, while still not guaranteeing that I would enjoy any closer contact with her than I'd had before.

Besides, after clawing my way through the horror of these last four years, did I still yearn for her love as I used to? I suppose I did, yes, but somehow in a different way. The old past was past. I was growing up and so was she. Look how open and friendly she had been tonight, treating me almost as she would an adult. And she did say that I would have my own fireplace in the new house.

"When do you move in?" I asked.

"April first—one week away," she replied, draining her drink and rising. "I'll tell John to come over to Gran's and move all your stuff. Now, bedtime, Baby. It's three A.M., and we have to be up by eight."

I hated that our magical evening was ending. Gran had made me take a two-hour nap that afternoon, but since I never closed my eyes, I was tired. We unzipped each oth-

er's dresses, pecked our good-nights, and headed for bedrooms at opposite ends of the bungalow.

"Oh . . . uh," said Mother, pausing inside her door.
"You know to take your makeup off now, don't you,
Cherie?" It was a confiding, we-girls tone, and I smiled
sleepily. "I always scrub the makeup off when I get
home," she stressed, "no matter how smashed I am. If I
can hardly stand up—if I have to hang on to the sink with
one hand to see the mirror—I still wash off every speck.
Love you. Sweet dreams."

More M-G-M training, but I liked the way she told me
about it, one woman to another. How I dreaded creaming
off my lovely green-shadow doe eyes and donning a
schoolgirl nightie. I slid into bed and stared for a while at
shadows of banana leaves on the ceiling. Maybe everything is going to work out now and get better—please God,
better. Time for prayers. I always kept them short: Now I
lay me down to sleep, I pray the Lord my soul to keep,
God bless Gran, Daddy, Mother, Helen, Johnny, Gypsy,
Tinkette—"

"You bitch!" shouted a man's voice from Mother's
bedroom. "How *dare* you tell me to leave? You think
you're such a big *star!*"

Bam! *Smash!* Something heavy against a wall, glass
shattering across a floor. I sat up and pulled the covers to
my chin. A long silence. They must have been listening
to see if the noise had awakened me.

"I want you *out* of here," she said. "How *dare* you
ruin my night!"

He growled darkly: "You no good lousy—Taking your
kid and old lady to that thing tonight instead of *me!*"

It was John, Mother's boyfriend. I thought they were
still lovebirds. I knew that he had wanted to go to the
Oscars and she had said no, but this voice in the night
didn't sound like his. Johnny Stompanato spoke quietly
and carefully, like, well, John Garfield. This John was
crude, with a cold, ragged edge to his voice.

The fight continued, swelling in waves, rising and falling, some of it muffled by the living room space between
us, but the tone was unmistakable. He was hurt and furious. She was indignant and, when that failed, beseeching.

"If you don't leave here this very minute, I will call the manager."

"La-na," he leveled hoarsely, "you . . . will . . . *never* . . . get rid of me. I'm stickin' around. Don't even touch that goddamn phone."

"Ohh, dear God, what am I going to—" She began to cry. I looked at the telephone on my nightstand. Should I? Johnny had always been polite and helpful to me, even at times when Mother treated him like a servant. He gave me my horse, Rowena, and I had worked for him last summer in the back of his shop.

Familiar little waves of sensation began to move along my back. Yup, Cheryl, we've been through this before, haven't we? With those other men in her life—Papa, Uncle Fernando, Po? One day it's loud voices and slamming doors, the next day he's gone and no good-byes. Her men will come and go, and one should not get attached to them. She'll never change. Now it's so-long Johnny, and I'll have to give back the horse. I pounded my head against the pillow, pulled another on top and burrowed like a mole under the covers. No air to breathe, but it shut out the noise.

"Arwwh. *Don't!*" she screamed. "John, *please!*" The sound pierced me. Another long agonizing silence before I could make out that Mother had crept into my room and now stood watching from the foot of my bed. "Cheryl-l," she ventured softly. "Cherry Blossom, are you awake?"

I was holding my breath. What she could see in the banana leaf shadows was a fetal lump that lay still as death. After an eternity of waiting I felt her go through the door and softly pull it shut. Their noisy love rites revved up again, but it became a white sound to my ears. I knew then what I had to do: Go-to-sleep, go-to-sleep, go-to-sleep.

Mother's door was shut when I arose the next morning. Not a sound. She was supposed to drop me off at my father's house so that his chauffeur could drive me back to boarding school. But when Mother didn't have to work, she seldom rose before noon. I have hardly a memory from those days of her face by morning light. Did she oversleep? Was she all right in there? Was John gone? I wondered whether last night had even happened. Out of concern, some other daughter might have called or peeked in to check, but I could not. I was taught never to touch Mother's bedroom door—not even to knock.

Dressed and packed, I went in to wait on the living room sofa, where I nibbled absently on stale canapés. Suddenly her door swung wide and, without pause or greeting, she crossed to the door. "Gonna be late, Baby," she said cheerily, her hands busy with keys. She wore sunglasses and a white silk scarf that deep-framed her face. It was her standard incognito. She drove us in her white convertible to my father's. Nothing was said about the strange event of the previous night, but I could see something was up. Her hands were trembling again and she wore orange Technicolor makeup that looked eerie in the light.

"How did you sleep last night?" she asked.

"Oh, fine, Mom."

As I finished out the week before Easter vacation, she phoned me at school on Friday to talk about moving arrangements. Her good nature was meant to convey that there was nothing amiss, but she was overacting. Since *Peyton Place*, I could almost always tell when she was pretending with me, and she often was. I could picture her sitting there talking to me in the Bel Air bungalow on her bedroom phone, legs crossed and smoking, inhaling in nervous gasps. I decided to risk a question.

". . . and John?" I said in a tiny voice.

"Fine," she said. Puff-*puff*. She was thinking. "Have you heard from him or anything?"

"No. Um . . . I was wondering when he's coming to get my stuff?"

"You've got the dentist on Monday, Baby, which shoots Monday. I'll tell him Tuesday. Early, around eleven."

Mother was going to pretend the other night hadn't happened, which was fine with me. I was beginning to think that, in the last analysis, it was only a champagne fantasy. That next day in school I had had my first dog's-tongue hangover, and, sitting in science class, my mind had begun to doubt the whole thing.

On Monday, the first day of April, I had oral surgery, for which the dentist gave me sodium pentothal and painkiller pills. Since my grandmother was working and we no longer had chauffeurs, Mother drove me to the dentist herself. When we got back to Gran's apartment on Charleville Boulevard, a quiet, tree-lined side street in Beverly Hills, I was still dazed by the drugs, so Mother tucked me into bed. I don't know how long I was suspended in half sleep before the shouting began. This time it came from the living room, and it was meaner.

"You got that, bitch?" he was saying. "You will *never* pull that on me again! You will *never* leave me out of anything. If you go someplace, I go there too. This time I let you get away with it, but next—"

"Take your hands *off!*" she demanded. "You get *out* of here."

"M-Mother," I cried. "What's going on? Is that John out there?" Maybe the drugs were giving me courage. My door flew open, and she walked in, barking at him over her shoulder, "Goddammit, you woke up the baby!"

"I h-heard yelling, what's wrong?"

"Nothing, everything's fine. John came by to say hello, *but he's leaving.*" This last was said loud enough for him to hear. One cheek of her face looked puffy red and there were those trembling hands again.

"Darling, go to sleep," she whispered with finality and closed the door. I slipped back into my Demerol twilight, but not for long.

"You motherfucker," he yelled, "you'll do what I say or I'll cut up your face. Maybe I'll have it done for me. No one will ev-er want to look at that pretty face again!"

"Mom, what are you fighting about?" I was struggling to stand.

"Everything's all right," she called back. "John is just leaving." In another wave of curses and mutterings he threw out some challenge to her. "No, just go," she repeated. "The baby can hear you. Just *GO!*"

The front door slammed hard enough to stir my Elvis

poster on the wall and excite the goldfish. Mother peered
uncertainly through my doorway and I beckoned her in.
Her eyes were hurt and questioning. This was no fantasy—
champagne, drug-induced, or otherwise. "Please, tell me
what it's all about," I pleaded. I had to have some explanation.

"I can't. I can't tell you."

"Oh *Muth*-err."

"No, I just can't."

"All that swearing and hollering. Did he slap you?"

For a moment she searched my face. Her lips pouted
skeptically and her eyes began to moisten. Finally, in a
jerking movement, she plucked a hanky from the waist of
her slacks and swung smartly round on the bed to put her
face at close range. I could see all the way into her eyes.

"Baby, things aren't . . . good . . . between John and
me," she said. "I don't know what to do."

"Leave him, Mother," I said. "Make him vanish."

"I can't, Baby. You see, the truth is I'm afraid of him.
He threatened to hurt me if I try to leave him. He knows
people he can hire to harm my face or even kill me." She
let out a tiny shudder, then, hugging her bosom, she rolled
her eyes so that they rested on my left shoulder. "Baby,
what am I going to *do?*" she said plaintively. "You've
got to help me. Please . . . will you?"

She had played the lingering close-up well—now cut,
that's a print. I swallowed hard because I believed she was
in danger, but something inside me said that eighty percent
of what she was doing at this moment was playacting.
Screen art blurred into life. She was in a jam, it was clear
to see, but at some level in her mind, she was already
beginning to self-dramatize in order to manipulate an escape. She was—incredibly—reaching out for help from me,
a fourteen-year-old.

I had seen her do things like this before, unloading her
personal problems onto others for them to straighten out.
Until her M-G-M contract was dropped two years before,
an army of service departments had made all her great and
small worries go away. In addition, there were always her
lawyers, agents, managers, maids, hairdressers, boyfriends, and Gran to turn to before economies had to be

made and the soldiers cut back. Now, raw recruit that I was, it was my turn.

"Mother, why don't you call the police?"

She cringed. "The pub-*liss*-ity," she said. "The press would have a field day."

"But you could call Chief Anderson," I said brightly. "He'd understand." Clinton P. Anderson, head of the Beverly Hills Police Department, was a family friend and often a guest at my father's Rodeo Drive restaurant. When he dined with Dad and me on Sundays, I would egg him on to order grogs, a flaming coffee drink that made the chief adorably tipsy.

"No, no, the papers would still get ahold of it," she said. "I couldn't live with the scandal. No one must know about this, Baby, especially your father."

I felt as though I were talking to somebody with no brain.

The afternoon sun was slanting across her face through venetian blinds as the story of her romance with Johnny Stompanato began to tumble out. Her voice grew trance-like as she dragged furiously on cigarettes and twisted a hanky.

They had met the year before, she remembered, but she didn't know until three months afterward that he had "friends I'm frightened of." (She meant, I later learned, gangster Mickey Cohen, for whom Johnny had served as a bodyguard.)

He pretended to be a respectable businessman who ran a gift shop, and when she confronted him with the truth, which was whispered by friends, he was penitent. "You'd never have given me a chance if you knew," he said, adding with emphasis that his gangland past was behind him. "I don't see those guys no more—promise." Mother doesn't stay mad for long and she believed him. She was in love.

Soon he felt sure enough of himself to brag to her about his bodyguard days when he "roughed people up." He bled her for money as his gambling losses mounted, and within six months she had become his woman, his woman alone. Neurotically possessive, he grew jealous while visiting her in England, where she was making a picture, provoking—and losing—a fast punch-up with Sean Connery.

When Mother refused to back him as executive producer of her next picture, he attacked her in an empty country house, smothering her senseless with a pillow. Learning of the assault, her makeup man called Scotland Yard, and John was quietly bounced out of England within twenty-four hours. But Mother grew lonely again, and when she finished the picture, he put himself adoringly at her side as they headed for six weeks in Acapulco.

There, in their sprawling Villa Vera suite, he battered her bloody and held a gun to her head. He was growing ever more frustrated by her flat refusal to involve him in her career, a policy Mother had never swerved from with the men in her life. Though she felt squeamish about being seen with him because of his reputation, he insisted they hit all the Mexican nightspots.

When her agent phoned to say she had been nominated for *Peyton Place,* it set off a blazing row. John realized that escorting her to the Oscars would provide him with a supreme leap to respectability. He leaned on her with threats, oaths, pleadings, but she stood firm, always putting career first, determined to attend the awards with her mother and daughter.

In the Bel Air bungalow that Oscar night when she and I retired, he was there in her bedroom, waiting in the dark. When she snapped on the light, she found him stretched out on her bed, a cigarette in his mouth, arms crossed, eyes filled with hate. This was the dreaded showdown, the prospect of which had made her tremble in the limousine.

"He beat me up," she said hoarsely. "He slapped me so hard that the earrings scratched my cheeks. He punched me and threw me around. Baby, he held a razor to my face. I tried not to scream because I was afraid you would wake up and then the hotel would—"

She broke down, and I threw my arms around her. Poor Mother dear, I was crying too. I felt scared and confused and overwhelmingly guilty. To think that the very first time she needed me, I hid under the covers. Now here we were a second time and my advice about calling the police was deemed unthinkable. How could any of this be real?

In a teenager's room filled with pom-poms and goldfish sat a mother and daughter weeping over a problem about a boyfriend. The *mother's* boyfriend. Who was the parent here and who the child?

"Baby, what am I going to do?" she said, looking imploringly into my eyes.

Three

Johnny Stompanato's white Thunderbird convertible drew up to my grandmother's place in Beverly Hills the next morning. He grinned and waved to me as I stood peeking through the curtains. Having worried all morning about how to behave under the circumstances, I waved back and gave a wan smile. An instinct suddenly told me to act unconcerned and play the chatterbox.

"Hi Johnny, have you seen it?" I trilled gaily, running to the car. "Oh, tell me—tell me, is it wonderful? I can't wait. Have you seen my room and everything?"

"See for yourself," he said mildly. "We can be there in three minutes. Where's your stuff?"

We packed the T-bird to overflowing and sped northeast along palmy vistas toward North Bedford Drive. It was a crisp sunny morning and, with a glance my way, John floored the accelerator. He knew I loved speed as much as he and Mother did. I had since I was eight years old. With the radio playing full blast, my father would let me steer his big Cadillac and bounce on his lap shouting, "Faster, Daddy, faster!" There were times last summer when John and I had bounced along, racing the horse trails above Culver City, and I had hollered, "Faster, Johnny, faster."

Through my dark glasses I stole looks at this man who sat behind the wheel. I had never really studied him. He was handsome in an oily kind of way. He had the B-picture good looks that were not unremarkable in a town where almost every waiter had a star's profile. Thick-set, powerfully built, and softspoken, he talked in short sentences to cover a poor grasp of grammar. He seldom smiled or laughed out loud but seemed always coiled, holding himself in. His watchful hooded eyes took in more than he wanted anyone to notice, I think, and he had that heavy quiet about him that made you wonder what he was thinking. I seldom wondered, however. He was just Mother's new one. I called him Johnny, not Uncle John, refusing for the first time Mother's wish that I give her suitors loving nicknames. If John was kind and helpful, even generous to me, and he was, I had stopped investing myself in her husbands and lovers because they always wound up vanishing in the night. Besides, he was obviously trying to ingratiate himself with the daughter only because he hoped to marry the mother.

I thought it fun that he was a jazzy dresser. He wore roomy, draped slacks, a silk shirt, a skinny belt with a real silver buckle, and lizard shoes. There was a heavy gold-link ID bracelet dangling from his wrist that glittered expensively in the sun, a gift from Mother with a private message inside signed "Lanita."

Could this be the guy I had heard raging at her? Could he really slash a woman? I had never seen anyone treat Mother badly. Everyone deferred to her, feared her, treated her as a star. She made things happen to people—*not* the other way around. And especially with Johnny here, a nice guy who was forever running errands, holding her coat, and ferrying the daughter around. It was all so confounding that I wanted to pound my head.

I loved the new house at first sight. It was a big side-gabled colonial with black shutters and a curved brick driveway. It had been built by actress Laura Hope Crews with what she had earned playing Aunt Pittypat in *Gone With The Wind*. While Johnny hauled things up to my second floor bedroom, Mother gave me a tour of the house and back garden, which had a tennis court squeezed into it.

The second floor was reached by climbing a center hall staircase, off which lay two big bedroom suites connected by a passageway. The passageway opened onto the entrance hall on one side and a French-doored balcony that ran along the front of the house on the other. Any passerby at night could look up and see someone crossing between the bedrooms.

As we completed the tour, Mother and I stood with arms folded looking doubtfully at a blue floral living room. I touched her arm. "You okay?"

"Fine," she said, looking away, avoiding my eyes. What was happening was not happening. Subject closed.

Those next two days were a blur of moving, shopping, and seeing my father, who owned a famous Beverly Hills Polynesian restaurant named the Luau. I spent a lot of time with his fiancée, Helen, after whom I had decided to pattern myself. Helen was the last word in style. Twenty-four to my fourteen, she related to me as a big sister. Mother soon came to resent her for giving me style pointers. "I suppose you picked that up from Helen," she sniffed, catching sight of my new poodle skirt.

When I sometimes bumped into Mother and John at the house, I sensed an unspoken truce between them, one intended to last until she was at least settled in the house. While he kept his own apartment, he had put a few of his things in her new bedroom. I was beginning to imagine that she thought my living in the house with her would hold John at bay. It seemed to have worked Monday during their fight at Gran's.

Wednesday evening the three of us dined with my grandmother at Mario's, a spaghetti house in Westwood. Prickly tension hung over the back booth where we always sat. On some recent occasions we had made a jolly foursome here, but that night Mother spoke listlessly to Gran and me about nothing, while John stared off into space. I learned later that after the Monday afternoon fight, Mother had poured her heart out to Gran, who then telephoned Chief Anderson to describe her daughter's predicament. The chief was sympathetic, but he pointed out that a complaint to the police must come from the person in danger. "Mildred," he said, "please have Lana call me about this, will you?" Mother never did.

I stared out my bedroom window at the rain-slicked driveway curving into Bedford. Today was Good Friday. I threw a longing glance at my new fireplace. The night before I had lit an inaugural blaze and dreamed the evening away. But now the ashes were cold. Mother came in once to caution me about switching off the gas starter. She was edgy and distant.

Alas, tempting as the prospect was, for me there could be no morning by a cozy hearth. I was facing a busy day, much of it to be spent with a school chum at the public library and maybe lunch with Dad.

That afternoon John drove Mother around town buying incidentals for the kitchen, everyday china, pots, knives, and the like. A fastidious nature compelled her to personalize the food equipment in houses she rented, so this had become a moving-in ritual.

They returned home around 4:30, an hour late for a drinks appointment Mother had made with two friends. One was Del Armstrong, her makeup man for fifteen years. (It was Del who, four months earlier, had come to Mother's rescue and gotten John bounced out of England, though John never knew it.)

The other was Bill Brooks, a businessman from Hawaii with whom Mother had once had a little flirtation. Brooks was a well-off bachelor, darkly good-looking in the way of Tyrone Power. Both men, drinks in hand, sat lounging in a glassed-in bar area off the living room when Mother and John bustled in. Before she could make introductions, John abruptly greeted Bill Brooks, saying, "Hello, Pineapple."

"Yeah, I remember you," laughed Bill. "Stompanato, right?" He turned to Mother. "John and I went to Kemper Military Academy in Missouri way back when," he explained. "I was the only cadet from Hawaii, so, of course, they dubbed me Pineapple."

The remarks that followed between the pair showed that they had known each other in school, had even by chance double-dated coeds who were roommates at a nearby college. John's grin began to sag when he noticed that Mother and Del were watching them in fascination. He brightened and laughed uncomfortably, then, drawing Brooks aside, found a spot by the windows where they could look at the rain and speak quietly.

Mother stepped behind the bar and poured tonic into a

glass of vodka. Then, her elbows on the counter and eyes narrowing, she studied these erstwhile schoolmates across the rim of her glass. "Well-ll, wadda y'know about that," she muttered to Del.

John suddenly turned to go. "Say, I'm just going to get rid of this stuff," he announced, swinging over his shoulder a few items of dry cleaning that were on hangers. His exit seemed abrupt, and after the tap-tap of his tread died away up the stairs, silence filled the room as rain sighed against the glass.

Brooks spoke first. "Lana," he said dryly, "how did you get stuck with a guy like that?"

"Do you mind if I ask your age?" she said, ignoring his remark. "How old are you, Bill?"

"Thirty-five next week."

"Then how could you be in school with John? He's so much older."

"Older?" Brooks chuckled. "I was two years ahead of him. He couldn't be more than thirty-three. And let me tell you, Lana, that guy's a snake. In school he was mean and cocky and deceptive. He started trouble and everyone avoided him—including me—but he always pushed his way in."

"Thirty-three," Mother repeated, looking bleakly at Del. "That's funny. John swore to me he was *forty*-three."

When I returned a while later, the rain had let up and the house felt gloomy. John had gone somewhere. Mother and guests sat slumped in the barroom facing the garden's twilight. Telephone men had been swarming around the house all week, but they had departed now, leaving me my own Princess phone. I greeted everyone, chatted a moment with Uncle Del, then headed upstairs to test my phone.

After calling some girlfriends, I faced the fact that my physiology term paper was due on Monday and I hadn't even started writing it. Science was my favorite subject and I had chosen as my topic the human circulatory system. Mother called from downstairs. She said her guests had gone, and she wanted me to come down and talk. She was pacing the living room as I entered, smoking furiously.

"It's just too much," she said, her eyes chasing patterns in the carpet. "I just learned that John has been lying to me about something else. His age! He's not forty-three, he's thirty-three! Which makes me five years *older* than he is! Oh, shit. I'm such a fool."

Uh-oh. I tried to look unimpressed.

"He's making me seem like one of those old has-beens you see around who pay for young men. It's too much. I can't take one more of his lies. This is absolutely the last. The *end*. It's over." She slumped dramatically on the sofa and covered her face.

"Don't cry, Mother." I wrapped her in my arms and began to rock.

"I'm going to get rid of him," she said with sudden clarity. "Tonight. I don't know how. Baby, this is not going to be easy, you know. He's not going to want to leave. It won't be pleasant."

I could not think what to say: "Maybe it won't be as bad as you think."

"I don't want to be alone with him in this *house.*"

"I'm here, Mother; nothing's going to happen."

"Baby, I don't want you to be part of this. When he comes back, I wish you didn't have to hear this, because he could get—"

A silent figure was standing in the doorway, and Mother drew back with a start. It was Armenda, her personal maid, wearing an Easter hat and one of Mother's hand-me-down coats. She had come to say good-bye for the holiday weekend and get instructions. Mother dabbed at her mascara with her wrists, and when it looked like Armenda would take time, I went upstairs.

A long shower helped to cleanse my sense of dread. I knew John would arrive any minute. Slipping into my fuzzy pink mules and an old nylon peignoir, I dropped into a chair and pulled the term paper research onto my lap. Homework was easier with the television playing in the background, of course, so I clicked on the set.

Phil Silvers was one of Mother's longtime friends, and his series *Sergeant Bilko* was coming up on Channel Two. Good old Bilko, it seems, was about to face temptation. His blustery boss, Colonel Hall, has a rich nephew who has died leaving him $5,000 in cash. Picking up the smell of money, Bilko's nose begins to twitch. At the same time I learned that *the vertebrate circulatory system consists of a muscular heart and a set of vessels, which carry the blood through—*

I heard the front door slam. John had arrived, but it was her voice that followed in an odd tone, first teasing, then angry and defiant. I couldn't make out the words, but muffled yelling seeped under the door and I turned up the television.

Colonel Hall has given orders to deposit his inheritance in the bank, but Bilko gets an idea. He has his M.P.s "borrow" the suitcase full of money so that he can flash it around and impress his creditors. *The vessels that carry the blood away from the heart are called arteries. The vessels that bring blood back—*

"So WHAT, goddammit?!" John boomed.

"That's just one lie too many," she wailed. "I've had it." They were both furious but she seemed to be holding her own. I had to know. I tiptoed out to the hall railing. Coming from the living room, his voice was ragged again, and they were both yelling at once.

"Mother-r-r," I called, letting him know I was there. "What's going on? Is that John?"

"Go back to your schoolwork, Baby," she said. "John's just leaving."

"Hi, Johnny," I sang out in an offhand way and returned, as ordered, to my room. I was used to obeying and I really didn't want to get too involved anyway, but this could make a person nervous.

Bilko is in a jam. Believing an insider tip, he risks all the money on a fast-rising stock, which suddenly collapses. Now he must get $5,000 in the bank by 3:00 P.M. or face jail. *The vessels that bring blood back to the heart are called veins.*

"You damn BITCH!!" he screamed. "You're not getting rid of me that easy. I'll cut you up first!"

I flew back to the hall and looked below. Mother strode angrily into view and was starting up the stairs with Stompanato trailing in her wake waving a fist. As they stormed into my room, I was doing homework.

"John's going to leave now," she announced ridiculously, as he crossed his arms and planted his bulk behind her.

"Not so fast, lady," he said, his mouth twisting into a snarl. I stared at him, and in one chilling moment I saw for the first time what he looked like when he was angry. He seethed. He clearly hated her. It was controlled anger, but his neck veins stood out and he breathed from one side of his mouth. He hunched his shoulders as though he were going to pull out a pair of six-shooters, while the hands at his sides clenched and writhed like a snake's tail in death. He never once looked at me, but burned his glare into Mother, who stood in profile between us.

"You're not getting rid of me so easy, Miss Moviestar."

"Now, look," she said in a patient voice. "I told you and I *told* you. I don't want to argue in front of the baby."

"Why the hell not," he snapped. "She should hear the truth about you—everything."

"Well, we're not going to," she said with unsure finality. She noticed Phil Silvers' face and, changing the subject, turned to scold me. "How can you do homework with the TV on?" Then obsequiously to John: "I've been out of the country so long, you know, and I haven't seen American TV. I'd like to be able to watch this show for a moment."

His look said, *Forget it.* She bustled on. "Sweetheart, John's going to go now. I'm going downstairs for a drink, and I'm coming right back up, and then I'm going right into my room . . ."

"Yes," I said, terribly confused. There he stood, about to explode. *Please, John, go.*

"You watch me leave," she added inanely. I nodded.

Ostentatiously arching her back and puffing her chest, she proceeded out the door as he followed at her heels. By bluffing, she had won the round. "You said you would go to the movies tonight," he whined at her back as they went down the stairs. "Then you change your mind. You break promises too, and now you're going to get drunk. You drink too goddamned much! . . ."

I tried to follow the yelling as it trailed off, wondering

if it leaked out to ruffle the Easter weekend quiet that had settled on Bedford Drive. Returning to her bedroom, Mother darted in and locked the door. "Open up this motherfucker or I'll break it down!" he hollered, ramming against it and repeating the threat. In a moment, there came the submissive sound of a click as she undid the lock and he slammed recklessly inside.

My heart sank. I padded in my mules along the passageway and knocked. "Please, Mother," I said, "can I see you for a second? Please?" She told me to enter. John would still not look at me. "Shit," he snorted, retreating to a far corner where he stretched his back and rested his palms on the wall above her fireplace.

Mother stood by her bed. It was in wrinkled disarray, which was not like her. Promptly on rising she always made her own bed. It was the only housework she knew—maids were never to touch the intimate place where she slept. The owner of the house had done the room entirely in pink, not baby pink but a faint blush of arousal pink on all the walls, carpeting, bed, chairs, fireplace, and fixtures. I took her hand, which was icy, and led us out of the room. Locked safely inside my bathroom, we embraced. "Oh Baby, we're in for a terrible night," she moaned.

"Why don't you just tell him to go?" I said. "You're a coward, Mother."

"You don't understand. I'm deathly afraid of him—I'm *terrified.*" She examined her face in the mirror, exploring little puffs under her eyes with jittery fingers. Maybe he had been roughing her up on the bed. Turning suddenly, she took hold of my shoulders. "I'm going to go in and do it now," she said. "Baby, this could get ugly. Are you prepared for it?"

"Yes, don't worry," I said. "I won't leave you—I won't be far away."

What unseen night traveler on Bedford could have glanced up at the house and guessed the tragedy that was unfolding as Mother passed the French doors? Though I stood like a prompter in the wings, my face frozen in a rictus of dread, I could not even begin to imagine what was coming. Mother paused in shadow beside her door,

gathering strength, squaring back and lifting her chin. I
was struck by the idiotic thought that for this, perhaps the
biggest moment in her off-screen life, Mother's designer
Helen Rose would never have costumed her this way,
barefoot in pedal pushers.

Stompanato still posed before the fireplace, but now his
eyes tried to seize hers. She reached for the drink she had
left on a counter beside the door and said with measured
calm, "I really can't go on like this. There is no use discussing it any further. This is a brand new house, a brand
new start for me, and I want you to leave. Just leave.
Please. Good-bye."

"YOU'LL FUCKIN' DO AS I SAY!" he exploded.
"You think you can order people around? From now on
I'll be doing the ordering! When I say 'hop,' you'll hop!
When I say 'jump,' you'll jump!" He grabbed her arms
roughly and shook her. "Baby, you'll do what I tell you!"

I dashed along the shadows to crouch beside the door.
"Leave me alone," she cried. "Don't ever touch me
again." She pulled away with a violent yank and spun
around to discover me. I felt sick.

"Please, Cherie, *please* don't listen to this. Go back to
your room."

I looked at her questioningly.

"It'll be all right—yes, go back to your room." She
watched as I started away and then quickly closed the door.
"That's just *great,*" she said. "The baby had to see that."
In the hall I could still make out their muffled voices.
"Don't ever touch me again. It's over. I want you out
of—*ohhh!*" She screamed. My knees were starting to
buckle. "You're horrible. No, *no,* I can't do a thing, truly,
not anything more."

"You will or I'll carve you up!"

Sudden silence. "Cherie, is that you?" she called. I
froze. "You're still out there, I can hear you." I was
wearing a bracelet that bore tinkling gold charms, and I
unhooked the catch, letting it slip to the floor.

"You'll never get away from me," he said, his voice
becoming a snarl. "Wherever you go, I'll find you. Or I
have people who can. Like I say, if someone makes a
living with his hands, break his hands. If someone makes

a living with her face, destroy her face. I'll cut you good, Baby. You'll never work again. And don't think I won't also get your mother and your kid. I don't even have to be there. I have people to do the job *for* me—and I'll *watch.*" He let out a rich laugh.

I raced down the stairs in panic. I have to do something. Phone the police. God, no—who can I phone? Suppose something happens while I'm down here. I'm trapped— how can I stop this? I ran through the kitchen door. On the sink lay a gleaming butcher knife. Scare him, that's it. I grabbed the knife, ran upstairs, and laid it beside the door.

"*Get out, get out, get out!*" she sobbed.

"This time you'll get it," he said, his voice cruel and twisting. "No one will ev-er look at that pret-ty face again."

"Mother," I cried. "Don't keep arguing. Let me talk to you both." I banged on the door, but even now I still could not violate the sanctity of her boudoir.

"Don't think this is the end," he snarled. "You won't even *live* to see the end!"

"This *is* the end—oh yes!"

"Please!" I pounded. "Johnny, don't talk to Mother like that."

"I've just had *enough,*" she shrieked.

"Cunt, you're dead."

I pounded again. "Mother, please!"

"Out! Get Out!"

I picked the knife up off the floor. The door flew open. Mother stood there, her hand on the knob. He was coming at her from behind, his arm raised to strike. I took a step forward and lifted the weapon. He ran on the blade. It went in. *In!* For three ghastly heartbeats, our bodies fused. He looked straight at me, unblinking. "My God, Cheryl, what have you done?" In slow motion he pulled off and jerked in backward steps toward the bed, every second his unbelieving eyes fixed on mine. But why? they asked. Then they fluttered toward the ceiling, and when he looked back at me his face hardened. He knew that his life was ending, and he hadn't seen it coming.

My hand held a shaft of gleaming red steel and I

screamed. I dropped it and raced to my room where I clawed my way under the bedpillows. I realized he might come roaring through that door like a wounded tiger. I must hide! I listened for footsteps. On the window sill . . . raindrops. The inane drone of Edward R. Murrow on TV talking to Anna Maria Alberghetti. But nothing otherwise. No tiger. Nothing. Nobody's coming. Just emptiness. This is really happening—it's not television. Dry racking sobs began to burn their way up my throat.

"Cheryl!" It was Mother from across the darkness. "Come quickly! You've got to help! I need you! *Cheryl!*"

Uh-uh. No ma'am. I smeared the tears around my cheeks and shook my head. *I'm not going back in there.*

"Cherie, I *need* you!" She was desperate. Was he there? Trembling and sniffling, I crept doubtfully past the French doors.

Mother was bent over the body holding a bloody towel. She dabbed at a cut that oozed below his right nipple. I tried not to look. The skin was gray. His pupils had rolled back to show glazed half-moon eyes staring out of slits. All of a sudden a terrible phlegmy sound bubbled up through his lips. He fell quiet again.

"John, speak to me!" She was slapping his cheeks. "JOHN!" The bubbling started again and stopped, leaving his jaw slacked downward.

"Oh Mommy, I'm so sorry!"

She threw me a sharp look and waved at the bathroom. "Get something—a wet cloth. JOHN!" The knife lay draining in the sink where she had flung it, and blood ran down the bowl. I backed away in horror and went to the second sink. Returning to the bedroom, I could not bear to get near John. "I'm so *sorry*, Mother," I pleaded, handing her the cloth at arm's length and turning my clenched face. "I didn't *mean* to do it, I really didn't, I'm so *sorry.*"

"Speak to me, John," she cried, mopping his forehead. "Baby, help me here." She bent forward, adjusted the jaw and breathed into his open mouth.

My brain careened into shock. I spun around and ran back to my room where I picked up the phone and dialed my father.

"Good evening, the Luau . . ." came his pleasant baritone.

"Daddy, come *quickly!*"

"What's wrong, Baby? What happened?"

"Something terrible. It's John. Come *quickly.*"

I put down the receiver and saw that my hands trembled. Hugging them under my arms, I lay on the bed and curled into a ball. What was happening was not happening, I told myself. Suddenly I sat up with a jolt and pulled my knees to my chin, letting out little sobs and sniffles and hiccups. I began to moan and rock myself. This is n-n-not happening.

My hands, in their feverish movement, caught on a hole that had been cut in my housecoat. What's this? Underneath there was a fresh cut on my leg. Then I realized. When Johnny and I collided, the knife must have accidentally—*no, this is not happening.*

Indeed, by next morning, it had not. An asbestos curtain had descended. The scab on my leg actually puzzled me, as did the jail cell. Overnight, in a sweeping act of nihilistic self-will, my sense of guilt and shame, my feeling of unworthiness and need for punishment, became so deeply buried that my mind blocked out the why of it.

Even to this day when Mother and I refer to the tragedy in conversation, we euphemize it as "the paragraph," because no press mention of us seems to be complete unless it includes a paragraph about what happened that Good Friday in 1958. Though I was destined to travel an odyssey through the depths of the juvenile justice system, lurching crazily through jails and reformatory, through a mental hospital and flights from the law, my mind consistently refused to go back and relive that monstrous night.

Twenty-seven years would pass before I would feel able to dig out those memories, and, with the gentling of time, come to understand why my young life of promise and privilege made a detour through hell.

II

JUDY AND JOE

Four

"Hollywood princess" may be a timeworn phrase, but I guess it describes the life that I lived well into my teens. Famous at birth and pampered silly, I was born in 1943 to Lana Turner, one of the most celebrated screen beauties of the time. My father was Steve Crane, a dashing but impoverished businessman whose restaurants finally made millions. Both of my parents were driven personalities—vain, gifted, selfish, and wild. I was enthralled by them, but I lived at a distance, their princess in a tower.

During World War II and throughout the forties, Mother was queen of the M-G-M lot, and even into the 1960s she retained enough box office potency to be top billed in big hit movies. In a career that spanned an impressive thirty-three years and forty-seven pictures, she came to epitomize a kind of wanton allure and peerless glamour. She was a star whose turbulent personal life rivaled—and even mirrored—the sort of melodramatic movies that were her trademark.

She came along as the Golden Era of film was declining during the war years, and it could be said that she filled the sex goddess job left vacant by Jean Harlow's death in 1936, and then passed it on to Marilyn Monroe at the start of the fifties. Of course there were other great beauties around (such as Ava Gardner), other sirens (Rita Hayworth), better actresses (Katharine Hepburn), and bigger box office draws (Betty Grable). But Mother flourished and endured for nearly a decade as Hollywood's most-headlined blond Venus.

The way she got her start in pictures gave rise, I think, to what is the all-time best known story of "discovery." Though it happened more than a half-century ago, the tale of her overnight stardom probably still fires the dreams of hopeful actors as they get off the downtown Hollywood bus. According to legend, she was spotted by a talent scout while sitting at a drugstore fountain sipping a soda, and when asked if she'd like to be in the movies, she replied, "I'll have to ask my mother." Then, with her hair changed from brown to yellow, her name changed from Julia Jean ("Judy") to Lana, she squeezed into a sweater and caused a sensation in her very first role. The next day she was a star.

With certain refinements, those are the facts. Unfortunately, since movie studios no longer develop actors under long-term contracts, it could never happen Mother's way again.

The story put out by press agents at the time had her being discovered in Schwab's drugstore at Sunset and Laurel. Actually, it took place a mile away at the Top Hat Soda Shop across from Hollywood High School, where in October 1935 she was a fifteen-year-old junior cutting typing class. She and my grandmother had moved from San Francisco six weeks earlier to board with a friend named Gladys Heath in a two-bedroom apartment. Gran, humbly born, unschooled, and wed to a drifter at sixteen, found herself at thirty-one starting all over again as a widow and working mother. The Depression spawned a migration of pretty shop girls and handsome farm boys who swarmed west to break into pictures, and while Gran was not a would-be starlet, she did share many of their aspirations. So did a whole underclass of Americans in the thirties who dreamed of bettering themselves and felt the lure of Southern California. (Whether she hoped her daughter would land in the movies is open to question, despite Mother's disavowal.)

Gran's pursuit of respectability manifested itself in two ways. Though she was poor, she saw to it that she and her daughter were always very well dressed and that they conducted themselves with finishing-school manners. In those days of breadlines, appearances were everything.

Years later I asked Gran how she and Mother managed to dress so well and to acquire their sure way of knowing which fork to use. She said they doggedly read aloud to each other from *Etiquette: The Blue Book of Social Usage* by Emily Post. As for the stylish clothes, they poured over *Vogue* and memorized outfits they saw in movies. Gran splurged on Mother's wardrobe, and for herself she cleverly rotated, mended, and accessorized just three good dresses. She was always fully turned out, no matter what the setting.

A beautician by trade, she found work that December in a salon near M-G-M paying twelve dollars a week, which required a long bus ride to work. When other passengers glanced at her, they must have thought she was a woman of wealth and breeding, so smart was her bearing. Gran's sense of theater did not stop when she got to work either. She stood all day on high spiked heels giving permanent waves. This obsession with appearance may well have repeated itself in Mother's lifelong absorption with pretty clothes and an outwardly ladylike demeanor.

Happily for Mother, the pencil-mustached "talent scout" who approached her on that balmy day at the malt shop was legitimate. His name was Billy Wilkerson, and he was the publisher of *The Hollywood Reporter*. He soon launched her on the routine of making the rounds at RKO, Paramount, and Twentieth Century-Fox, accompanied usually by a changing roster of agents, and sometimes amid a whole group of hopeful starlets.

After nine months of this grind, she had landed only one job—doing extra work on the 1937 version of *A Star Is Born*. (Mother denies this—she insists she was *never* an extra.) The title proved prophetic, for she was then selected by Warner Brothers producer Mervyn Le Roy for a small part in his film *They Won't Forget*. A tiny, eighteen-line role that ends twelve minutes after the credits, it nonetheless packed enough wallop to launch her.

Her figure was 35"—24½"—34½" and Director Le Roy made the most of it. To suggest the budding sexuality of a high school virgin, he costumed her in a clingy sweater and tight skirt. She opens the movie sitting at a soda fountain, then leaves and heads up the street, hurrying to catch a parade that's passing. Two cameras follow her, fore and aft, dwelling on her curves. Moments later, in an incident that takes place off screen, she is raped and murdered.

During the long-running shot, a spirited brass band version of "Dixie" plays on the sound track. It was an intentional touch. "I scored the music," said Le Roy, "to match the up and down of that sweater." It was standard movie practice in those days to wear bras that were padded, but Mother's was made of unlined silk and offered little more than uplift.

Le Roy could see how the male audience especially would react to Mother's bit-part appearance, and he boosted her billing. If the scene sounds exploitative, the film *They Won't Forget* was in fact an early denunciation of racism and went on to become a respected success, landing on some critics' ten-best lists. Though she still had a long way to go, Mother was on her way.

Warner Brothers trumpeted her as the "Sweater Girl," coining a phrase that has sinced become part of American slang. Mervyn Le Roy, to whom she was under personal contract at seventy-five dollars per week, mounted a major personal publicity build-up.

Both he and she claim credit for coming up with the name "Lana." According to Mother, the moment of inspiration struck her "as clearly as though God had decided to speak to me." She explains that *lana* means "wool" in Spanish, "the warm and comforting material of that fateful tight sweater." Le Roy, on the other hand, insists he once dated a chorus girl named Donna who looked like Mother, and he just rhymed his way down the alphabet. (Early in her career, Mother would facetiously instruct the press on the correct pronunciation of her name, saying, "That's Lana as in la-dee-da, not lady.")

To the industry, Mother was now "that new girl of Le Roy's," and producers were avidly bidding for her services. Samuel Goldwyn, Hollywood's Mr. Malaprop, approached Le Roy to say he was interested in hiring "Lily, Lani, Looni—what's her name?" (No doubt the foxy Goldwyn was only pretending not to know a name that was on nearly everyone's lips, in order to help him negotiate a cheaper loan-out fee.)

Mother did do Goldwyn's film, a Gary Cooper swash-
buckler entitled *The Adventures of Marco Polo*. She played
a Eurasian handmaiden who spoke just four lines in love
scenes with a stout Mongolian warlord. The makeup department shaved her eyebrows in order to paint on those
of an Oriental, and they never grew back. Afterward the
dyspeptic Goldwyn was not very complementary about
Mother, saying in characteristically mixed-up fashion,
"Take away the sweater and what have you got?"

The following year, 1938, when Le Roy moved from
Warners to Metro-Goldwyn-Mayer (at $6,000 per week),
he brought along his protégée, who had now gone from
red hair to light golden brown. When Mother signed her
contract that February, M-G-M was flush with the previous year's record profit of $14 million. Known for a de-
cade as "the Tiffany of studios," Metro was the biggest
and the best, home to Greta Garbo, Clark Gable, Joan
Crawford, Spencer Tracy, the Barrymores, the Marx
Brothers, and more than 300 contract players. There was
not much danger of Mother's getting lost in the starry shuf-
fle, however, because she had Le Roy's strong backing.
And behind Le Roy loomed the studio's legendary boss,
Louis B. Mayer.

Just seventeen, Mother looked a lot older than two
classmates nearly her age with whom she attended the famous Little Red School House on the studio lot. One was
Mickey Rooney, at sixteen a veteran star with two dozen
movies under his belt. The other was Judy Garland, fifteen, who in the next year would make *The Wizard of Oz*.
On Mother's arrival, Mayer cast her, over some 200 contenders, in *Love Finds Andy Hardy* opposite Rooney and
Garland. Mother played the role of Carvel High's bubble-
headed flirt. This was the fourth (and some say the best)
of the twelve Andy Hardy pictures, whose sentimental
family-based formula had tapped a box-office bonanza and
bore Mayer's personal stamp.

The M-G-M head had a good handle on America's love
of wholesome values. Unfortunately, in *Love Finds Andy
Hardy* Mother photographed too old when she stood next
to baby-faced Rooney. It was to be the first of her many
miscastings at Metro. She didn't fit into the studio's

family-oriented formula, and with the exception of a few pictures like *The Postman Always Rings Twice,* her modern sultriness would often be wasted in florid costume dramas. Critics have wondered if she might have been better used in grittier films at smaller, more experimental studios like Warner Brothers.

When Mayer approved Mother for a juvenile role in the Hardy picture, he knew that she was already starting to live in nightclubs. He gave orders to have her cocktails and cigarettes airbrushed out of photos. Mayer was used to worrying about his teenage stars. Judy Garland was already fighting fat with too many pep pills, and Mickey Rooney, when he was not making passes at Mother, was on the phone betting horses or lining up women.

Le Roy saw to it that Mother was carefully groomed and tutored. During the next three years she acted in eight pictures, mostly B's. The roles got larger and more interesting as she went blond. The studio was surprised to see her growth. More than beauty, she had that indefinable "it." In a group of starlets on the screen, she was the one you watched.

As a result, Metro decided to shape her future as a straight dramatic actress who projected glamour and sexuality. Though she was a terrific dancer, she couldn't sing and she lacked the comic flair of Carole Lombard or Jean Harlow, who had died suddenly eight months before Mother signed with Metro. Twentieth Century-Fox could boast warmhearted Alice Faye and Betty Grable, but, funnily enough, the blondes who were really selling movie tickets then were Sonja Henie and Shirley Temple. The bombshell job was open and Mayer had his eye on Mother.

Her starting salary at M-G-M was $100 a week (America's average at the time was twenty dollars), and Gran gladly quit the beauty shop. "Mom, you'll never work again," Mother promised, "not as long as you live." She bought a red roadster and rented an all-white, three-bedroom house in Laurel Canyon for herself and Gran, who now settled down to full-time housekeeping.

For discreet comings and goings, Mother had her own private entrance. She had displayed a certain maidenly shyness until now, but signing with M-G-M released something inside. "Once I came out of my shell," she said, "I wanted to live it up." Her social set included Mickey Rooney, Judy Garland, Linda Darnell, Robert Stack, Ann Rutherford, and countless handsome young men.

By 1940, Hollywood nightlife was getting an infusion of new energy. With war raging in Europe, Southern California aircraft and munitions manufacturers were booming, and the town was awash in fast money. The Sunset Strip was jumping. Every night at Ciro's, Trocadero, and the Cocoanut Grove, revelers tried to shake off the late Depression blues. The liquor curfew was midnight, the earliest of any major American city, but guests could nurse doubles into the wee hours. Mother was often among the last to leave when the doors finally closed at 2:00 A.M. She still faced a heavy work schedule with 6:00 A.M. wake-up calls, and she was underage besides, but she became such a hot-spot regular that columnists dubbed her the "Nightclub Queen."

Gran complained, but Mother had by now shrugged off any authority except that of Louis B. Mayer. The mogul became so lathered by her behavior that he summoned her and Gran to his cream-colored office one day for a tongue-lashing. He spoke about her brilliant star potential until his eyes filled with tears and so did hers. Suddenly he leapt from behind his horseshoe desk to shout, "The only thing you're interested in is. . . ." He was pointing at his crotch.

Because Mayer and publisher William Randolph Hearst were entwined professionally, gossip columnist Louella Parsons was enlisted to scold Mother in the Hearst syndicate of nearly 200 newspapers. "If Lana Turner will behave herself and not go completely berserk," wrote Louella, "she is headed to a top spot in motion pictures."

She thought that Mother was "an ingratiating little soul" and "the most glamorous actress since Jean Harlow," but one who has "the nightclub spirit." Louella feared that Mother might be too much like the ill-fated "It" girl of the 1920s, Clara Bow: "Both of them, trusting and loveable, use their hearts instead of their heads. Lana, of course, has never been in any scandal, but she has always acted hastily and been guided more by her own ideas than

by any advice the studio gave her.'' She hoped that Mother
would discover good books, paintings, and culture before
it was too late.

But nothing could stop Mother from having her fun, not
Gran, Mayer, Le Roy, Louella, or anyone else. She just
didn't care. Young and beautiful, she was on her way to
becoming rich and famous, driven by a restless spirit. She
was doing everything else by the book. She cooperated
totally with the demands of Metro's publicity department.
Her work was improving in successful pictures, and fan
clubs were beginning to form.

She correctly sensed that her reputation as a romantic
cutup who rebelled against rules and bosses amused
younger ticket buyers. It also caught the tenor of the times.
The Depression was over and America was on the eve of
war. A jitterbug generation that would soon face war's
tragic dislocations could identify with her sense of aban-
don. Her image as a party girl, swathed in an aura of
glamour and beauty, seemed to capture the attitude of the
moment.

Although the press often feigned disapproval, it covered
her antics eagerly, for she tossed off quotable quotes as
readily as she discarded boyfriends. Her love life never
stopped churning and sometimes she was seen out with a
different man every week for months at a stretch. Usually
she chose famous actors, but always good-looking ones.
''Let's face it,'' she explained, ''it's the physical that at-
tracts me first. If you get to know a man's heart and soul,
that's icing on the cake.''

Souls aside, Mother was attracted, however briefly, to
George Raft, Victor Mature, Robert Hutton, and many
others. ''I liked the boys and the boys liked me,'' she told
a reporter. ''The gal who denies that men are exciting is
either a lady with no corpuscles or a statue.''

The first man to keep her interest was Greg Bautzer, a
square-jawed bachelor of about thirty who was one of Hollywood's fastest-rising lawyers. He was also a famed escort, most recently Joan Crawford's. Mother says Bautzer
was the first man she slept with, and she did so because
she was daffy in love. She wore his engagement ring ''un-

til the skin grew over it." When she finally gave up hope, she labeled him a matrimonial "escape artist."

For her nineteenth birthday on February 8, 1940, Bautzer planned to take her and Gran to dinner, but he phoned at the last minute to beg off because of some stomach upset. Mother sulked. A moment later the phone rang again. It was Artie Shaw, the clarinetist and "King of Swing" bandleader who had appeared as himself in her recent movie *Dancing Co-ed,* the first in which she was top billed. They detested each other while on the set, but months later, meeting again by chance, Mother flirted. The twice-divorced Shaw was now phoning to invite her out.

That night, cruising along the moonlit Pacific Coast Highway with the top down, they poured their hearts out to each other. Shaw was fed up with jitterbugs and the music business. Mother hated 6:00 A.M. wake-ups and studio bosses. What both really wanted, they agreed, was hearth, home, and babies. Mother admitted to herself that she was in the mood "to get even with Greg," so when Shaw suggested they marry, Mother actually said, "Let's go."

They eloped that night to Las Vegas, and next day Greg Bautzer told the press that he was heartbroken. Betty Grable and Judy Garland quietly felt the same way about Shaw. (It was Shaw's ankle bracelet Betty was wearing in her famous wartime pinup photo.)

Ten weeks later, after making thirteen pictures, Mother's star was born at last. The release of *Ziegfeld Girl,* for which she had gone quite blond to play a Brooklyn-born showgirl whose rise and fall from stardom climaxes in one of the screen's most memorable fadeouts as Mother tumbles down a staircase, made her an "overnight" success.

At the very same time, Mother filed for divorce from Shaw (using Greg Bautzer as her lawyer) on the grounds that the marriage was based on no relationship, just the heat of the moonlight. Shaw proclaimed that there were two kinds of women, some you talked to, the others you slept with, and he complained that when he got Mother to read Nietzsche and Freud, nothing stuck.

Mother claims that Shaw hoped she would become his

little hausfrau. With their hectic work schedules and a combined income of some $4,000 a week, however, she was not about to cook and clean. To this day the only housework I've ever seen Mother do is make her bed and empty an ashtray.

On a cruise to Hawaii to forget it all, Mother discovered she was pregnant. Mayer had personally pleaded with Shaw to use contraceptives for her career's sake, and Shaw had laughed in his face. Shaw disowned the expected child, and Mother sought a secret abortion in downtown Los Angeles. (Betty Grable had aborted a child of Shaw's only a month before.)

Never one to mope for long, she flung herself back into dating: Victor Mature, Robert Stack, Howard Hughes, Greg Bautzer, drummers Gene Krupa and Buddy Rich, Frank Sinatra, and Tommy Dorsey. A romance bloomed with singer Tony Martin.

On the impressive success of *Ziegfeld Girl,* Metro boosted her new contract to $1,500 a week and slated her to costar with two of the studio's longtime biggest names: Spencer Tracy in *Dr. Jekyll and Mr. Hyde,* followed by Clark Gable in *Honky Tonk.*

With money to spend, Mother bought a bigger house in Brentwood and began to throw parties. Some were well planned, but often, when the spirit grabbed her, she would round up friends and musicians for impromptu gatherings at home around her big white grand piano. Ciro's closed at 2:00 A.M., and she often rented its piano player or invited back enough musician friends to make a combo. She was partial to jazz musicians, and their sessions could go all night.

It was to just such a round-up party one Saturday that her friends Tommy and Jimmy Dorsey brought back most of their band and played from the early morning into Sunday afternoon. Mother had been dating Tommy Dorsey, but other men she was seeing, like Sinatra and Buddy Rich, also attended. She has always had that nice talent of staying on good terms with old boyfriends.

Everyone was having fun when Gran suddenly walked in with a suitcase in her hand and irritation in her eye. Returning from a weekend trip, she brought news of the world. "Haven't you *heard?*" she asked. "The Japanese bombed Pearl Harbor."

From that day everything changed. Hollywood swung solidly behind the wartime effort. Stars like Jimmy Stewart and Clark Gable enlisted, and the studios cranked up movies that were either escapist or a call-to-arms. For her part, Mother appeared widely at bond drives and sold $50,000 worth of kisses for the war effort. Still, the partying didn't stop, and her restless nights continued with the usual round of clubs or jam sessions back home.

Then one night it happened. She was dining in a new club named Mocambo, and somehow she met a handsome stranger. The man she met would become my father.

Five

While there's no question that Mom and Dad met in 1942, the exact time and circumstances are a little hard to nail down. The month was February or May or June—depending upon whose account you go by. But everyone agrees that the setting was Mocambo, the swankiest night spot west of Manhattan's El Morocco.

Mocambo had opened on Sunset Boulevard the year before. It was the last hurrah of Hollywood's glittering nightlife, which had been in decline since the end of the Golden Era of the thirties. During Prohibition, nightlife in Los Angeles had offered a choice of funky roadhouses, speakeasies, offshore casinos, and starchy ballrooms like the Cocoanut Grove spread all around the metropolitan area. Repeal ushered in a dozen years of serious glamour, which saw the opening of a series of sophisticated clubs and eateries in the heart of town. Having inherited my parents' love of nightlife, I still daydream about that fabled period. The top hangouts included The Colony, the Clover Club, Versailles, Don the Beachcomber, the Brown Derby (for hamburgers), the Palladium Ballroom (for big band swing), and Earl Carroll's (for the ultimate floorshow). By the time the era reached full flower, just before World War II, Ciro's and Trocadero were the most famous of them all.

Ciro's and the "Troc" were both opened by Billy Wilkerson, the man who had discovered Mother in the malt shop. I don't know whether or not there was any connection, but his clubs became her favorite haunts. Indeed, her visits were so well covered by the paparazzi that by the time Mocambo finally opened in January 1941, she had long since been dubbed by the press Hollywood's queen of the night.

Mocambo was the perfect setting for new romance. Its unrivaled luxury and flamboyance earned it praise as "the nightclubber's nightclub." It boasted Brazilian decor and harlequin flourishes that mixed oversized tin flowers and surreal paintings with ball-fringed awnings and cages of jungle birds, all daubed in a bizarre palette of red, sky blue, terra cotta, and silver.

Dad loved the place, finding it the ideal setting for a young man on the make. He had come to Los Angeles in 1940, joining the legion of actors and self-styled playboys who leaned on its no-cover bar each night, looking to line up contacts of either a business or romantic nature. He soon worked his way into the pricey tables section as a guest of various friends.

Mother dined and danced at Mocambo almost every week, usually sweeping in on the arm of some well-known actor. Her entrances were so charged with glamour that they turned heads and brought a hush to the room. Looking neither left nor right, she floated straight to her table, and, once enthroned on the banquette, glanced around to acknowledge friends with little nods and big-eyed smiles. Her dresses were exotic, even eccentric, usually in white or black, but sometimes red or silver when she was feeling especially gay. On those occasional nights when there was no man around and the going-out mood set upon her soul, she was not too proud to dine with someone like Gran or a publicist (and years later, even with me).

One night, during a period when Tony Martin's interest in her had cooled in favor of glamour girl Carole Landis, Mother agreed to join a small party at Mocambo put together by agent Johnny Hyde. She had no particular escort—she simply hated staying home nights, especially during those lulls in which there was no romantic interest.

Midway through the evening, a tall, slender man appeared at the table and spoke to her. His opening remark was drowned out by the orchestra, but she knew he was asking if she cared to dance. Johnny Hyde introduced the man as Steve Crane. Mother felt an immediate rush of romantic interest. A moment later she was in his arms dancing, politely calling him "Stephen," and when the club closed, she permitted him to see her home. She recalls that she fell "heels-over-chin, pinwheels-on-fire in love" that night.

According to Mother, the wedding followed their first meeting by three weeks. Dad claims it took more than three months. Others say just one week. But whether it took days or months, the pace of their trip from Mocambo to the justice of the peace seems downright sluggish compared to what she and Artie Shaw had accomplished in five hours.

Still, even people bored with tales of Hollywood's marriage-go-round blinked at the news of Mother's second snap wedding in two years—especially since this time it was to a nobody. Stephen *Who?*

In response to a wave of movie-fan curiosity, the press put out a number of articles based mainly on guesswork and studio handouts. Dad's personal interviews did not go into much detail, and the story changed with every telling. He said that he and Mother had been casually introduced at the Palladium, the West Side Tennis Club, "and around" before they got acquainted at Mocambo. It was a "funny thing," he told a reporter. "We never met formally. I don't remember that anyone ever said, 'Miss Turner, this is Mr. Crane.' " In another version, he said he prevailed on a mutual friend for her number and phoned for a date. They then romanced out of the public eye for three months.

Another widely printed story of unknown source had Father standing at the Mocambo bar with a pal one night, both men ogling Mother, when the pal bet that Dad could not get Lana Turner up to dance with him. Accepting the two-to-one five-dollar dare, Dad pretended to stumble against her chair, blurted out some opening line, and charmed her onto the floor.

Before they divorced, Dad told intimates a story that made *him* the love object. He claimed they were dining in Mocambo at nearby tables and began to observe each other. It was instant animal attraction. Finally a waiter slipped him a note reading, "I'd like to meet you. Will you call me? Lana Turner." It bore her phone number.

Well, it's possible. He was handsome and magnetic. She was always ready for new romance. But whether the truth was closer to his version or hers, his went along with the sexy jokes about Mother then going around America's locker rooms and beauty parlors. There were many such stories, however apocryphal, and they helped to sell her as the new Harlow, adding to the Metro-crafted image of Mother as an angel-faced mankiller.

Mother certainly was something. Just twenty-two, having already played out a number of romances in the glare of flashbulbs, she had eloped for the second time. Moviegoers saw her as love's plaything onscreen *and* off, and they were eating it up.

Columnist Dorothy Kilgallen wrote that Mother was a major star "chiefly because she is the same off screen as she is on. Some of the great stars are magnetic dazzlers on celluloid [but they are] ordinary, practical, polo-coated little things in private life. Not so Lana. No one who adored her in movies would be disappointed to meet her in the flesh. . . . The clothes she wears are just like the clothes you pay to see her in on Saturday night at the Bijou. The physical allure is just as heavy when she looks at a headwaiter as when she looks at the hero."

L. B. Mayer, fearing audience backlash, was appalled by the sexy stories. The angel-faced side of Mother's image was more his style. After all, most of Metro's fifty pictures a year glorified goodness.

No matter. Mother continued to run her love life exactly as she pleased. When her elopement with Dad made headlines, she made light of it. Only later, after the marriage fell apart with messy finality, did she offer any explanation. "There is nobody so charming as Steve Crane when he wants to be charming," she said. "I am lonely unless I have someone to love—and there was Steve. I married him."

It tells something about the make-believe world into which I was born that not until recently was I able to dig out the facts of my father's background. It was reported after the

wedding that he was a little-known man-about-town named
J. Stephen Crane III, heir to big Indiana tobacco money,
a Phi Beta Kappa graduate of Butler University, who had
worked as a broker in New York and Chicago and who
shared a Malibu beach house with department-store heir
Alfred Bloomingdale. Most of this was marmalade. The
truth is more fun.

Born in 1917, he was actually a middle-class Hoosier
boy, a city-slicker type buried alive in Crawfordsville, Indiana, a town of 12,000 souls. His father owned a double-
front poolhall off the courthouse square that purveyed
cigars and ice cream sundaes in front and sponsored a bit
of illegal penny-ante gambling in back. On weekend
nights, seventy-five factory workers and hog farmers
crowded around the poolhall's six green felt tables, their
laughs and curses accented by amber jets aimed at brass
spittoons.

No one under eighteen was admitted, and if a woman
ventured into its smoky din in search of her husband, a
ship's bell would ring out to call silence. Once her task
was completed, the woman would flee, the bell would be
rung again, and the manly talk would resume more noisily
than ever, as if the second bell had opened some clogged
drain.

Grandfather's cigar counter did a brisk business in five-
cent Philly Panatellas, and that was as close as Dad came
to being a tobacco heir. That is not to say that the Stephenson & Crane Cigar Store on State Street was not a
moneymaker. Every payday from the 1920s through the
late 1940s, customers stood four deep in the rear gambling
area, where punch boards, baseball tickets, and other
nickel-and-dime games of chance pulled in good profits.
It wasn't exactly a stable business. The local Crawford
County grand jury staged periodic cleanups, and as a result, Grandfather had to shut down about twice a year.

Dad was not J. Stephen Crane III. He was Josef Stephenson Crane, the first and only, plain Joe to his friends.
Back in Ireland in the mid-nineteenth century, the family
name had been O'Cryan. His maternal grandfather was
Black Irish, a pro-English Protestant who wore the color
orange, not green. Even a century later, Dad still swore

Black Irish allegiance, and I recall one St. Patrick's Day when he appeared on my doorstep sporting an orange carnation in his lapel. I, eight years old, was dressed head-to-toe in green. He looked me up and down, smiled, then frowned a little. "I had better change color," he said good-naturedly, "or, honey, you won't lunch with Daddy today."

Dad's grandfather fled Ireland's first potato famine in the 1850s, sailing steerage for America, where he found work on the Philadelphia docks and saved enough money to bring over his Catholic sweetheart from southern Ireland. To become his bride, Henrietta Eldridge had to steal away in the night from her disapproving parents. They took the English-sounding name of Crane and settled in Indiana's Montgomery county where they prospered modestly in farming and land.

The youngest of their four sons was Dad's father, William Eldridge Crane. He grew up to become the genial proprietor of the town's leading poolhall. (There was another one across the tracks, but not as nice.) He gave up selling home-brew beer out of his basement by the time he was elected city councilman.

I never met Dad's parents, but my grandfather is remembered as a rough diamond who joked easily and seldom smiled because nicotine had turned his teeth brown. A two-fisted drinker and outdoorsman, he kept five English setters for quail hunting.

Dad adored his mother, Kathryn Stephenson Crane, a retiring woman of folksy Hoosier charm with a weakness for contract bridge. Her people were homesteaders who had emigrated from England to settle in Hamilton county, where they did well as horse traders. She bore three children, a daughter whose death in infancy was always kept secret, then Father, and a second son four years later. She doted on her irrepressible older son who, in a tiny town, certainly must have stood out.

An A-minus student with a photographic memory, Dad made weekly raids on Crawfordsville's public library for books on science and the classics, often reading all night. He decided that two things really counted in life—women and money. The girls he dated were seldom local, living instead within a fifty-mile radius of Crawfordsville in towns like Lebanon and Frankfort, so that neighbors would not talk about his prodigious skirt chasing. Girls fell into his arms, often in the back seat of his red Plymouth. His long suit was charm, a sweetly disarming will that he applied with a feather stroke, and that few women could resist.

By the age of fifteen, he was 6′2″ and as gangly as Jimmy Stewart, even to the loping walk. He affected the preppy look of baggy flannels and rep ties. Photographs never captured the appeal of his brown eyes and slender face, his earnest smile and thick dark hair. Fistfights had twice resulted in a broken nose, the slight crook and bump of which gave just the right amount of coarsening to his almost too boyish features. It was his fastidious grooming and ardent good manners that made women think he was handsome.

Dad seemed to be one of those restless fixtures in small-town life, a disconnected person who longed to escape beyond the horizon. "Too damn small here," he grumbled to his kid brother. His dream to get away was fueled in part by a desire to one-up the neighbors. A big antebellum mansion stood in the middle of Crawfordsville, built by proud native son Lew Wallace, the Civil War general who wrote *Ben-Hur*. "You watch," Dad boasted. "We'll come back some day and buy that place. Then every Sunday afternoon, we'll plant our feet up on the front porch and drink beer."

Dad's plan to go away to a university was dashed when his father died. Instead, he enrolled at local Wabash College, where he earned a B.A. in business (but no Phi Beta Kappa). To support his mother, grandmother, and brother, he also took charge of the poolroom, running it with the help of a manager.

After graduating college in 1937, he decided to let off steam by driving to Mexico City with his kid brother, Bill (who was nicknamed "Beezer" because he caught bees with bare hands and pulled the wings off). Reaching Oklahoma City on the return leg of their trip, Dad sprang an idea as if he had just thought of it—"Hey," he said, "let's go see Hollywood"—and they made a fortuitous detour.

Joe and Beezer—two Hoosiers adrift in Movieland. The visit would prove a watershed. Dad rented an apartment with a Spanish courtyard above Hollywood Boulevard and promptly sent his brother to the movies so that he could head out alone for adult excitement. Driving a new red Ford Phaeton roadster (for which he had paid $637), spiffed up in a Chicago-bought suit, he cruised top down along the Sunset Strip to check out the clubs. He quickly found The Troc, Don the Beachcomber, and the Florentine Gardens, a slightly down-market tourist magnet.

Dad's dedicated nightcrawling puzzled his brother. "He was very secretive," remembers Uncle Bill. "I would suggest we take a bus tour or visit a movie studio, but he always had other plans. 'Oh, I gotta meet this gal,' he'd say. 'Oh, I'm busy with these people.' What people? He didn't know a soul in California, but then he worked fast."

Los Angeles has never had much street life, but in those days young Turks on the make hung out in front of the Plaza Hotel on Vine Street. There Dad met others like himself—beginner agents, actors, writers, and publicists— and he could see how he measured up. He was reassured by what he saw, and made friendships on that sidewalk that would last the rest of his life.

Impressed by Hollywood's possibilities, Dad might never have left but for the fact that he was registered to start law courses that fall at Butler University in Indianapolis. Once back home, Hollywood must have seemed to him a remote Shangri-la, for he immersed himself in school, new business ventures, and a marriage.

At a Sigma Chi fraternity party one night, he met Carol Ann Kurtz, a brown-eyed coed with masses of blue-black curls who attended Indiana University in nearby Bloomington. An Alpha Chi Omega sorority girl, she was vivacious and, like him, loved dancing, dressing up, and going out. (Dad would later describe Carol Kurtz to the press as an "Indianapolis socialite"; in fact, she was the daughter of a pharmaceuticals salesman.) They eloped on New Year's Eve in a blinding snowstorm.

Dad dropped out of law school that spring and moved back to Crawfordsville, where he and Carol took an upstairs apartment near the poolroom.

They moved three times in the next two years as his business ventures shifted focus. To begin with, he saw that while gambling profits at the poolroom were a sometime thing, cigar profits were steady. As a result, he had a manufacturer make a five-cent stogie bearing his name. Though the factory was in Chicago and it rolled an Indiana blend, he called the cigars "Crane's Imported." His father-in-law, Frank Kurtz, came aboard as sales manager.

In the end, none of his schemes worked out. After a year of operations in a lingering Depression, thousands of Crane's Imported still waited dejectedly in warehouses, unsmoked. Expensive poker tables he'd bought to install above the poolroom were also gathering dust because the county grand jury had gotten wind of the illegal plan. A theatrical venture of some sort that he tried in Chicago in 1939 also failed.

Frustrated in the pursuit of his first love, money, he turned to another pursuit. Before long it was obvious to Carol that he was seeing other women. That summer they agreed to a trial separation. He went to New York briefly, later telling reporters that he "worked in the stockmarket." Actually, he speculated in the market with poolhall profits while driving a cab.

As a result of some sudden and unknown change in luck, he found himself holding a $10,000 bankroll. Whether it came from trading, gin rummy, or a pyramiding of punchboard profits, no one can say, and he never did. The money might have been the last of his father's inheritance, even something shady. Obviously, Dad was a fast-scrambling rogue.

In all the close years we spent together as adults, he never spoke of those early days, and it was clear that I should not press the subject. Much of what I've learned about him comes from scouring his papers and the public record, quizzing pals, partners, and family. Father was so very private, I think, because he had things to hide. In his drive for success, he did what was expedient, and if the law got bent a little in the process, well, that's how a man moved up in the world.

He may have covered those Indiana tracks for another reason, too. He hadn't forgotten that on the 1937 trip with

Beezer he had scored in Hollywood. That was where the action was, where celluloid dreams came true, where a guy with a little dough could begin again. Everyone knew that Cary Grant had started out as Archibald Leach. Spangler Arlington Breugh had become Robert Taylor. Maybe Joe Crane at twenty-three could reinvent himself as, say . . . J. Stephen Crane III, tobacco heir and all around *bon vivant*.

Six

Late in the summer of 1939 Dad headed west in a yellow Buick convertible, determined to try out his new personality.

He rented a third-floor apartment on Doheney Drive just below Sunset, a well-heeled area of small houses a few minutes' drive from the clubs. Assuming that he would soon be drafted into the army, he did not look for a job. Instead, he got busy reheating the social contacts he had made on his visit two years before. Nights, he began to chase showgirls, in particular a tall leggy brunette named Levonne, a dancer in the line at Earl Carroll's Vanities. He soon was a familiar figure waiting around each night backstage, joking with the other boyfriends until the second show broke.

As a result of his polite manner, he was never labeled a "wolf" or "stage-door Johnny." A Vanities producer summed it up by saying, "Steve had class. He was an operator—always operating—but not like some of those guys who could be crude. He had a good line of talk, a car, a few bucks, nice clothes. He was careful what he said and who he associated with because he was going places."

In the process of inventing a new self, Joe Crane realized that Steve Crane would not drive a Buick, so he bought himself a new Lincoln Continental. Then he took an even bolder step—cosmetic surgery. He thought his chin receded a little and his twice-flattened nose looked like it belonged on a mug. Plastic surgery was hardly a routine practice at the time, having been developed only after

World War I. People were aware of miraculous face and hand restorations done on disfigured soldiers, and they had heard rumors of voodoo surgery that explained the enduring youth of stars like Marlene Dietrich. But surgery to enhance *male* good looks was unknown.

Dad made it his job to find the right surgeon and get the money together for an elective operation that involved real risk. He confided to friends that the surgery was for a "deviated septum," soon to become the hoariest of covers for a nose job. But he said nothing about how his lower jaw was lengthened by grafting bone from his thigh.

After the operation, he went back to Crawfordsville to hide the swelling. It was Christmas, the time he and Carol had previously agreed they would try a reconciliation. Though they spent a cheerless holiday together, he, Carol, and his mother (acting in the role of peacemaker) all returned to Hollywood in January, staying at his apartment on Doheney. Carol soon answered enough phone calls from women asking for "Stevie" to realize that reconciliation was futile.

They separated again but did not sign a separate maintenance allowance agreement until a year later, on January 17, 1941. This was an important date because it officially set the clock ticking on the one-year residency period Carol needed before she could apply for a California divorce. In those days the state required proof of a one-year residency before it would process a divorce application. Even after the divorce was granted, there was another one-year waiting period before the "interlocutory decree" could become absolutely final.

After they parted, Carol found jobs designing sportswear and did extra work at Monogram Pictures. Eventually, she opened her own dress shop on Sunset right across from the Trocadero. Kathryn Crane stayed on for another year in her own apartment but wasn't happy in California, and returned to Indiana.

Dad's profile was only marginally improved by cosmetic surgery. Nonetheless, he now felt he looked something like a movie star, a notion that was beginning to grow on him. In any case, he had become a new man. For the next two years he maneuvered a kind of rake's progress, befriending the right people and traveling in fast company. He was free of ties to Indiana, marriage, and any real need to work. With the climate for gambling generally warming at the poolhall, he had been able to get himself on a new financial footing. As long as Dad kept an eye on the books, his manager could be trusted to run things and deliver Dad's share of profits from the newly renamed Stephen Crane Cigar Store.

Since the money's source was illegal, it went unrecorded and remained in the form of cash. With the heat off, he was occasionally receiving as much as $1,000 a week in small bills, and the transfer of this bulk to California presented a funny challenge. Sometimes Dad concealed it under his clothes, taping wads of cash to his body.

It did not take long for him to discover the role the press played in helping a go-getter in the movie capital. He developed a bantering relationship with most of the columnists, particularly Harrison Carroll, whose flattering celebrity chitchat appeared daily in the *Los Angeles Examiner*. Carroll took a liking to Dad and began to give him one-line mentions, partly in exchange for items Dad passed back to him. On Friday nights, Carroll wrote his column from Table Seven at the newly opened Ciro's, and Father was usually at his elbow. It was an enviable vantage point that provided him with introductions to important people, inside information, and free liquor. "But he didn't take advantage," says a Ciro's manager. "He ordered one drink all night. A nice young man, Steve. I liked him."

Club owners did not hesitate to extend him credit for dinner tabs, too, which he used and always finally paid back. With his good looks and suave manner, he was just the kind of customer that gave a joint class. It also didn't hurt that he was beginning to turn up with celebrities on his arm. For a while he dated French film star Simone Simon, whose feline beauty would make audiences shiver the next year, 1942, in *The Cat People*, a classic horror movie in which she turns into a panther.

Among the celebrities he squired around was Sonja Henie, the Norwegian Olympic gold-medal skater. Just as he did with club owners and columnists, he sought to make friends with famous party givers, and Miss Henie was one of the best. The surprising popularity of her ice-skating movies earned her huge picture fees at Twentieth Century-Fox, and she laid on lavish affairs to which Dad was invited.

Though he was now toying with the idea of acting in pictures, Dad was also practical. He saw the need to learn some kind of safe, profitable trade to fall back on. The business of entertaining—of playing host—had stirred him since childhood, when he daydreamed of owning a restaurant. So from his start in Hollywood, he cultivated friendships with club owners, restaurateurs and famous hosts and hostesses like Miss Henie.

He took his first concrete step in that direction when he began to host regular Sunday afternoon card parties at his apartment. Gin rummy, the ten-card rummy game invented in 1907, was coming back as a national rage, and Dad's photographic memory made him a winning player. His charm also made him a winning host, and his two-table parties became a popular ritual with a growing social circle, a way to develop and reward friends that continued for years. Cronies played for a penny a point while "the girls" made the sandwiches and drinks.

Seldom were the women wives. They tended to be a fun-loving bunch of girlfriends, starlets, and off-duty hookers. The men included actors, realtors, directors, sportsmen, playboys, businessmen, and assorted union officials.

There were even gangsters, the kind that had polish. In those days in the movie colony, powerful underworld figures mingled with polite company. There was no shame attached to socializing with gangsters as long as the public didn't notice. Indeed, there was something exciting and darkly glamorous about getting close without getting singed. Most of the major studio heads dropped mobster names and kept phone numbers. Even Walt Disney, that symbol of goodness, was amused by the fact that he knew mugs in the mob.

Dad kept a friendly arm's-length relationship with a number of mobsters, in particular Bugsy Siegel, kingpin of the West Coast crime syndicate. Siegel, suave and handsome, was chin deep in everything from heroin to Murder Incorporated. He would later be credited with turning a sleepy Nevada ghost town into Las Vegas by building the $6 million Flamingo Hotel. Although he was a product of Hell's Kitchen, Siegel posed as a well-bred man-about-town, and he got respect. It was said at the time that the best table in any restaurant would be given to "The King," Clark Gable—unless, that is, Bugsy came in first.

Siegel had a famous mistress named Virginia Hill. She showed up on some union official's arm at a Sunday afternoon rummy party and soon became Dad's friend. A red-headed ex-carnival girl from Alabama who had no shoes until she was fourteen, she had set out to act in pictures (Ball of Fire) and wound up the moll supreme. Her sad tale eventually became a TV movie.

As "Queen of the Mafia," she lived innocently inside a kind of honey trap, basking in costly jewels, cars, and houses, knowing everyone and going everywhere first class. Supported by syndicate money, she played hostess for some of the most glittering parties in town, where the guest list might include godfathers Frank Costello and Lucky Luciano. One such party at Mocambo cost $7,500. Of course, it couldn't last, and it didn't. Siegel was shot-gunned to death by an unknown assailant one night in 1947 while he was reading the papers on her living room sofa.

Dad was fond of "Sugar" Hill. She loved to laugh and hated to miss anything. When Siegel was out of town, Dad would escort her to The Colony and the Clover Club, both of which had underworld ties. The columnists would report their being seen together, but everyone knew that the date was strictly platonic, his favor to Siegel. She was Bugsy's girl, and any guy fool enough to cut in on him risked winding up in cement. (Bugsy got his nickname because of the way he went berserk when angry.)

Respectable people like Father played footsie with underworld biggies for many reasons, including the option to exchange innocent favors. Indeed, it was Sugar who lent Dad the money for his cosmetic surgery.

After they were married, Mother enjoyed going with Dad to Virginia Hill's parties. On a guest list divided between the bad and the beautiful, celebrities well outnumbered the guys with short necks, and Mother felt right at home. Bugsy was "a great dancer," she remembers. She found Virginia "a fun gal" and didn't flinch when photographers snapped them together laughing and gabbing at mob-backed clubs.

M-G-M wasn't so tolerant. The studio tongue-lashed her about the dangers of getting involved with underworld figures who, of course, were always eager to develop ties with legitimate people, especially rich and famous ones. Mother, incautious as always, did exactly what she pleased, and L. B. Mayer, who discreetly kept his own mob phone numbers, could finally only fume.

The studio had a lot more to protect and hold on to in Mother since she had lit up *Ziegfeld Girl* in 1941. Going into 1942, she and Rita Hayworth at Columbia seemed the most likely contenders for Betty Grable's crown as number one pinup. A dark horse named Ava Gardner was three or four years away from hitting her stride, Harlow was gone, and Alice Faye had retired from active duty. All eyes were on everything Mother did now.

Though it's uncertain exactly how and when they met, it is an indisputable fact that Mother and Dad eloped to Las Vegas on July 17, 1942.

The engagement ring was a three-carat diamond that belonged to his mother. He had worn it himself as a pinky ring and had it cut down to fit Mother's finger. No one seemed to notice it on her hand when they dined at Andre's restaurant that fateful Thursday in July. They were joined by actress Linda Darnell and publicist Alan Gordon. Mother introduced him as "Stevie," and he called her "Lanabelle." Darnell remembered that Dad seemed "quiet, sweet, considerate."

It was Mother who announced that, while on the dance floor a moment before, they had agreed to move up their secretly planned marriage ceremony to the very next day. "Why wait for Sunday?" she asked. Their friends agreed to act as bridesmaid and best man.

After catching the late show at Mocambo, they all regrouped at the airport for a 6:00 A.M. flight to Las Vegas. The wedding was one of those quickie turnstile ceremonies presided over by a justice of the peace. It was followed by bacon and eggs at a coffee shop named the Apache. They hired the same shirt-sleeved judge who had tied the knot for Mother and Artie Shaw two years before. She denies that she quipped, "Tie it tighter this time, Judge."

The following night a small reception was thrown together by Gran with help from Judy Garland and Judy's new husband, conductor David Rose, which took place at Mother's house on MacCulloch Drive in Brentwood.

The next day she moved into Dad's apartment, but it proved too small in every way. Her hundreds of dresses and shoes required a room-sized closet, so they moved back to MacCulloch. It seemed to go without saying that household expenses would be shared, but Dad's up-and-down income, even though it was now often supplemented by gambling wins (at gin rummy, the Santa Anita racetrack, and prizefights), proved to be no match for her salary and her unbridled spending.

Instead of asking why Dad couldn't pay his share, Mother did slow burns. All her life it has been her way to pay for almost everything. She is proud of the fact that through seven marriages, it was mainly her money that bought the jewels and furs and gowns—her money alone that paid for cars and houses. It is one of her ways of controlling people and staying unbeholden.

Since Dad had wooed her with no care for cost, Mother was certainly surprised to discover his small resources and essential meanness with a buck. Dad rarely reached for a check, and he appears to have scorned her extravagance with a fine detachment. "Lana spends every dime she makes," he told a friend at the time. "She'll be broke all her life."

In September 1942 Mother went to work on a light comedy called *Nothing Ventured* that would be the next rung in her career. After having made three films in a row with major costars—Spencer Tracy, Clark Gable, and Robert Taylor—this would be the first A picture that was centered on her alone. With Robert Young supporting, she would "carry" the picture, and she'd have to give it her all.

As she got up for work at 6:00 A.M., Dad would often be returning from a night on the town. When he stayed home, she often worked late and retired early. When they did go out, people noticed they looked bored with each other—except when photographers came near. She denied persistent rumors that there were problems. Everything was "blissful," she told the press, and for a time it probably was. They were young and in love.

It's hard for me to imagine how their marriage could have lasted, hewn as it was out of lust and opportunism. They faced an impossible clash of values. Mother expected to get her way 100 percent of the time; Dad held hidebound views on what a woman's place should be. She put her career before everything; he was jobless and didn't care. She had a millionaire's income; he scrambled. She was famous; he was Stephen Who?

Dad was thrilled, of course, with his overnight celebrity. Ciro's even named a tongue sandwich after him. Soon, however, he came to have second thoughts. To describe living with Mother, he used a dull cliché. "Life in a goldfish bowl," he groused to the press, and maybe he meant it.

There's no mistaking what their marriage was. Mother projected her needs onto a charming opportunist, while Dad hitched himself to a famous romantic. Over the years, when I saw them in the same room together, which was not very often, Mother held herself at a tight and distant remove, while Dad seemed to needle her in that mocking tone people take when they have grudgingly accepted someone's rejection. I could always sense malice on simmer, waiting to boil.

Whatever its chances, the marriage ended after five months, on December 8, 1942, with an announcement that set off a rush of events and was followed by headlines, tears, and, finally, little me. Through Metro's publicity department, Mother announced she was pregnant. Louella Parsons reported that Mother wanted to have a son, but at home she referred to the fetal me as "her," which made

Dad see red. "Don't say *her*—it's a *he!*" he snapped. She just shrugged.

One day in November 1942 Dad walked into her dressing room at home and sat down. "Lana," he said softly, "I don't know how to tell you this. . . ." He explained that Carol Kurtz Crane had telephoned to say that there was a little problem. Though he had exchanged vows with Mother four months earlier, the one-year waiting period before his interlocutory divorce decree would be final was still two months away. By this technicality—this unwitting act of bigamy—he and Carol were still married. He and Mother were not.

She nearly fainted. Was this why he had been so eager to marry while she was having a weak moment? Two headlines flashed across her mind: LANA UNWED MOTHER and MAYER COLLAPSES.

There was an angry get-together next morning in Carol's apartment. Mother accused her of lying in wait until the pregnancy was announced, a most vulnerable time, before pouncing with her bigamy bombshell. What was Kurtz after? Hush money? Dad looked on, hangdog with chagrin. He pleaded that the mistake was his, that he had misunderstood the legalities, and that the thing to do was for him and Mother to remarry as soon as legally possible. The same day Mother ordered him out of the house, changed the locks, and filed suit for annulment.

Her lawyer described the petition as "not a friendly one," and it was granted in just twenty-eight days. Little me was there in utero, as the judge ruled on what was to be the first of many custody battles over me. He awarded the unborn child to its mother and proclaimed that the annulment would protect my "legitimacy." I don't see how, incidentally. Legally, the annulment meant that her marriage to Dad had never happened in the first place. Nor did it seem likely that it would ever happen again. Strong-willed spirit that she was, Mother was squarely opposed to pressures from Dad, fans, columnists, and Metro-Goldwyn-Mayer to marry again "for the sake of the child." She had been unhappy with my father. She was free of him on a fluke, and she intended to stay that way.

Ten days went by, and her resolve wavered. On the

night of Valentine's Day, she and he were back at Mocambo flashing their double wedding rings and getting coy with reporters. "I haven't much to say now," Dad allowed carefully, "but time may bring a happy ending for us both."

Whether he still loved her, he stood to lose more than an object of affection. He stood to lose his access to her elite circle in the movie colony. If Mother were to persist in her head-down rejection of him, doors would slam all over town. He would still be a celebrity, but for decidedly the wrong reasons. If Mother preferred unwed motherhood to remarriage, people were certain to think, What kind of louse must this guy be?

After their evening together at Mocambo, Mother did not stay softened up for long. The following night she reportedly told him, "Sorry, darling, I can't do it now." Dad gobbled a handful of barbiturates and stormed out the door. Then he raced his Lincoln coupe up the canyon road and ran it off the cliff. Or tried to, at least. His car became tangled in rocks and dense underbrush, and stalled just above Mother's house.

Uninjured, there he sat in the dark, zonked, coughing dust, his message of love being conveyed by headlights that beamed toward her bedroom windows. Mother was not impressed. (Nor were many other people. When columnist Hedda Hopper scurried to the scene, she proclaimed it "all a sham.")

Still, when Dad was taken in critical condition to Cedars of Lebanon Hospital, Mother rushed to his side, where she collapsed and remained to keep vigil until his stomach was pumped and he was out of danger. In remarks to the press, Dad called it a nervous breakdown. Mother remained noncommittal. "It's all so terrible and everybody is so unhappy," she said with a sigh.

Her resistance broke down one day in March when he was about to be drafted and she was six months pregnant. In secrecy they drove down to Tijuana and got married again. It was a squalid ceremony in the midday Mexican heat. An ironic sign over the magistrate's office said "Legal Matters Adjusted," and their witness was an innocent passerby pulled off the street with pesos.

Why did Mother give in? She later admitted to feeling lonely and wrung out by what turned out to be a difficult pregnancy, which called for endless blood transfusions. It mattered, too, that Dad was going off to the army. For Mother, life was a movie. Patriotic war fever was sweeping America, and the father of her baby could conceivably die on some godforsaken battlefield. The idea was: anything for the boys. And from a practical standpoint, her downright refusal to let a departing soldier confer legitimacy on his newborn baby would not have played very well with the fans.

As it happened, Dad never went overseas. He had foot and back trouble that consigned him to limited service at nearby Fort MacArthur, and he was given an honorable discharge after six months.

Mother paid Carol Kurtz $5,000 not to sue for bigamy. But the bribe did not buy her silence, and Kurtz's side of the story began to appear in articles and column items. Carol said that Dad had come to her in May of the year before (around the time he first met Mother), claiming that he was flat broke and headed for the army. Could she let him off the hook? Touched by his appeal, she said, she signed a legal document that waived the monthly allowance she received from him. Two months later she read of his marriage to a movie star. "Steve isn't just one man," she observed. "He's a thousand different men."

Of course, she had a point. Her Joe Crane, the poolroom guy, wasn't Steve Crane the *bon vivant*. In any case, Carol also told reporters that she herself was planning on a movie career.

In the midst of all this, Mother's first top-billed picture was about to be released after having gone through two title changes. It was first called *Nothing Ventured*, but that didn't seem right for a Lana Turner picture so they spiced it up as *Lawless*. Then as her maternal-marital problems began to turn on legalities, *Lawless* began to seem tasteless. They finally settled on *Slightly Dangerous*, even though the movie was a fairly daffy comedy.

Metro knew what it was doing. A curious thing was starting to happen to the public's perception of Mother. As if by pentimento, the ironic figure of a second woman was forming beside her celluloid image, that of her real-life self. What the public saw was a shadow based on what they read about her smash-up personal life—the romances, partings, and nightlife, the heavy glamour and those mankiller jokes. Metro knew that fans saw her as really being *Slightly Dangerous*. In years to come, many of her pictures would borrow shamelessly from her private life, especially the melodrama of our anguished years together.

It was eerie how her real life was played out on the silver screen and vice versa. Soda fountain scenes were worked into six of her pictures. She played mankillers as sexy as the censors allowed. She also played more than her share of weepy courtroom scenes, and ultimately she made millions at the box office portraying valiant mothers with troubled daughters.

This was the chaotic Hollywood of my birth, of self-invention and glittering high-life, of illusion merging with reality, and always a sugarcoating of the truth.

They were both miserable when they remarried in Tijuana, signing the marriage registry Judy Turner and Joe Crane. They later said they used the misleading names to shake off the press. One wonders.

III

THE BABY

Seven

I didn't just slip into this world like most babies, sweetly red-faced and mewling. Nothing as simple as that. My birth was a life and death struggle that swayed in the balance for nearly two months. That was me all over.

I arrived in the muggy dawn of July 25, 1943, at Hollywood Hospital, the palest baby the nurses had seen in quite a while. Actually, I was half-dead and dying, because Mother's blood and mine were incompatible. Her RH negative blood was producing antibodies to destroy my RH positive, and after eighteen hours of labor, the contest ended in a draw. As an "RH factor baby," my entire blood system had to be flushed out with transfusions every four hours for weeks. The veins on a seven-pound fourteen-ounce infant are so small and collapsible that dozens of tiny needles were inserted from my toes to the top of my head. Weak from her own ordeal, Mother was shielded from any knowledge of this necessary torture. But in my ninth day of life, she happened to catch sight of the process and collapsed in shock. She saw me just after the needles had been removed, and, looking like a doughy pincushion, I oozed from a dozen openings. If it is true that traumas we suffer at birth can affect our adult personality, it would explain why even today I have a perfectly unnatural dread of needles.

Father wasn't around at the delivery. He had grown bored in the waiting room and ducked out to see a boxing match. Convinced and determined that I would be born a boy he could name Stephen IV, he returned with presents that included a football, a catcher's mitt, and a baseball

75

bat. In later retellings he was always quick to stress that he'd brought me a giant (unisex) teddy bear, too, but he admitted that when told of my gender, he scowled.

Earlier he and Mother had agreed on a girl's name of Stephanie, the female of Stephen; however, Mother's friends, actress Joan Bennett and producer Walter Wanger had just given the name to their daughter, born a month before. There's a certain need for exclusivity in the names of Hollywood princesses, so Stephanie was out. Mother loved Christina, but as every movie fan in America knew, that was the name Joan Crawford had given to her first adopted child two years earlier. What the heck, my parents decided, Christina could be my middle name.

If the inspiration for "Lana" came to Mother from God's lips, "Cheryl" came to her in a dream, she said. It was not an especially sweet dream as far as I'm concerned, and I'm still not crazy about the name. Later on, when I became so notorious that headline writers could, for the sake of brevity, omit the family name ("CHERYL FREE AGAIN"), I rejected a judge's suggestion to change it and take up a new identity. I will always be Cheryl Christina Crane.

Two years after my well-publicized birth, a fan of Mother's named Georgia Holt put a spin on Cheryl and baptized her daughter as Cherlyn. Before little Cherlyn grew old enough to see her name in lights, she had the good sense to trim it to Cher (otherwise, there would have been a duo known as Sonny and Cherlyn).

Bundled home to MacCulloch Drive after two months in the hospital, I lay in my crib just a fortnight before Mother booked some radio appearances in New York. Dad maneuvered time off from Fort MacArthur to go with her. What he had in mind was a detour through Crawfordsville so that he could put in a local-boy-makes-good visit. He must have realized that the days of his and Mother's second marriage were numbered, that there would be little to lose now if Mother clapped eyes on the modesty of his Hoosier home.

Her own youth spent drifting through mining towns was far less stable than Dad's, but at least she was honest enough to say that she had lived a hard-knocks childhood.

It was known that the Turners had been poor, that her father had been murdered, and that she had often been boarded in foster homes where she was abused. Dad, on the other hand, told whoppers, and the good people of Crawfordsville simply smiled and shrugged when they read in the papers that he was a big tobacco heir.

On their way back from New York in mid-October, Mother and Dad got off the Super Chief in Chicago and drove down to Crawfordsville for a planned five-night stay in the Crane family house on Pike Street. Expecting an old ancestral place along the lines of the General Wallace mansion, which was how Dad had described his home, Mother swallowed hard when she saw its prairie-style plainness and the rockers on its weather-beaten front porch.

Back home in Indiana with a movie-star wife on his arm, Dad was too puffed with pride to notice her deflation. Their visit was an event to rival the publication of *Ben-Hur*. The front page of the Crawfordsville daily *Journal & Review* proclaimed that everyone was "thrilled," while the social column exulted in Katherine Crane's planned dinner party.

Dad paraded her around town like a homecoming queen, taking her first to see the family business ("BEER TOBACCO POOL," said the sign in the window). They toured past his schools and paid a call at the Sigma Chi house. Though her health was still not strong, Mother smiled gamely when neighbors poured into the Crane place that first day to gawk. Inside she was angry. She saw that his homespun roots were perfectly respectable, but in trying to marry up, he had lied about them. First the deception about his first marriage, now this!

Mother's heart closed. On retiring to their bedroom that night, she looked around at the situation and laughed at how simple it would be to get out of this mess. "Just think," she told herself, "tomorrow I'm off to *Hollywood*."

Early the next morning, claiming Mother was ill and exhausted, the Cranes left Crawfordsville. Their departure was so sudden that the *Journal & Review* did not have time to kill a prewritten item about Mother's planned visit to the county orphanage where she "gave out sweets."

Back home in California, she went to work on a romantic comedy that Metro drolly titled *Marriage Is a Private Affair*. Over Thanksgiving she insisted on a divorce, and she and Dad agreed to a quiet separation.

Dad set about making the most of his last days as a pinup's husband. Nearly all the top young actors had gone into the service, and, with wartime film production soaring, the studios were rooting around for good-looking guys who weren't subject to the draft. It hardly mattered if they could act or had experience. Dad had only acted twice. The first time was at age four, when he appeared in a *tableau vivant,* which he spoiled by scratching his nose. Years later he played the pirate king in a Crawfordsville production of *The Pirates of Penzance,* ever after to howl at himself as the world's worst actor. Still, he had a deferment, he looked like an actor, and he had the most important qualification of all—connections.

Without Mother's help, he promoted a screen test at M-G-M, which he either flunked or failed to show up for. Soon items about his quest for a movie contract began to appear in the columns, and his newly hired agent managed to gain the interest of the talent head at Columbia Pictures. In February 1944 he tested with Janet Blair in a scene from *Tonight and Every Night.* They did well enough to be cast, with Dad signing a standard seven-year player's contract starting at $250 a week. It was only a bit part, with Dad playing a G.I. and listed ninth in the billing (over Shelley Winters). Nonetheless the casting was noteworthy, for *Tonight* starred Rita Hayworth, at the time his wife's chief rival in the pinup department. Mother wasn't thrilled.

Once again she was being used. Though everyone had wondered when they married if he saw her as a wedge into movies, he had assured her that he had absolutely no interest in being an actor. For a while, even though they were no longer living together, they continued to go out nightclubbing. But after a few weeks her hurt and anger hardened, and she went public with the divorce.

Ironically, this only added more flavor to Columbia's planned buildup of Dad. The studio shamelessly exploited his connection to Mother by stressing the point that Steve Crane gave them flat orders not to do so. When asked in interviews about the reasons behind the pending divorce, he magnanimously admitted, "It was just one of those situations. And I am a stubborn guy. I guess it was just as much my fault as anybody's."

Marriage to a movie star, he said, interfered with those wonderful evenings he cherished by the fireside. "I thought we'd live quietly at home like my mother and dad used to in Indiana." As for his ten-month-old daughter, Cheryl, she was "at the moment, the biggest thing in my life."

With these last remarks Dad was laying the groundwork for two legal actions of his own. One was a fight for custody of me and the other was a cross suit to her divorce petition in which he claimed mental cruelty as well. "How can any woman be a good mother when she is working all day in pictures?" he asked a group of reporters, adding that after the second marriage, they had quarreled again. "I can't go into detail on the reason for that—it wouldn't be cricket. Perhaps you know what happened. I'll just say that the present fight is entirely over my baby daughter, Cheryl Christina Crane. If I get her—and I think I shall— my mother will come out here and care for her. At present Lana's mother is caring for the child. . . . And I reckon that if it has to be a grandmother, mine is as good as any I know."

Production on *Tonight and Every Night* was delayed while Rita Hayworth finished the big musical *Cover Girl.* In the meantime Dad was assigned as leading man in one of the quickies ground out by Columbia's B-picture unit, a horror movie entitled *Cry of the Werewolf.* Shooting began May 8, and from my crib I sent him a wire reading, "DEAREST DADDY, MAMA TOLD ME ABOUT TODAY. CALLED A MEETING OF THE ANGELS. THEY PROMISED TO TAKE EXTRA-SPECIAL CARE. ALL MY LOVE—CHERYL."

It was Gran who sent the wire. Always trying to play peacemaker, my grandmother had grown fretfully supportive of her son-in-law. She found his courtly manners irresistible, and she believed he still offered some hope for stability in her daughter's madcap life. Gran was appalled that before Mother's second marriage had been dissolved, she was already late-nighting with other men. But Gran knew it did no good to scold. In all matters professional, financial, and romantic, Mother now kept her own counsel.

Gran still waited up nights for her daughter to come home, and as a result she had been banished after a certain hour to her part of the house. Still, Mother's escorts were sometimes startled when the lights were turned on to find Gran sitting in a chair, her arms crossed defiantly.

The divorce proceeding that August took a reported five minutes. Mother testified that Dad made unreasonable demands on her time while she was working, that he yelled at, berated, and quarreled with her so much that she caught colds. He became, both in front of friends and alone with her, "quite sullen."

She won. There was no money or property settlement, and she retained custody of me for the second time. Dad had decided at the last minute not to fight for me, accepting, instead, visitation rights at convenient times as well as custody on weekends and holidays as I grew older. He withdrew his dark hints about Mother's being an "unfit custodian." He was confident that "the child will get wonderful care. It won't go hungry."

What finally can be said about this crazy marriage that gave me life? Maybe it was little more than a sign of the times, an impetuous act taken amidst war fever and the dying days of Hollywood's Golden Era. The breakup, I believe, had a lot to do with the way Dad treated women. Women (except perhaps for me) were meant to serve, to fix the drinks and pass the sandwiches at gin rummy games. Back then, he felt it was Mother's duty to pave the way for his career, to let him show her off to the folks back home, and to buy him custom-tailored army uniforms.

In five years, Hedda Hopper—who was no friend of Mother's—would be citing Dad as a "brash and tragic example of the sexy promoters Lana is so susceptible to."

On the other hand, Mother's aggressiveness, her self-reliance and confident sexuality were evidence of a surprising, vaguely feminist side of her. Even if their motivations hadn't been mismatched, divorce may have been inevitable between a chauvinist and a queen bee.

Oddly enough, Dad claimed never to have understood

why the marriage failed. "Why did she do it?" he lamented to friends. "Why did she walk away like that?"

Mother seemed to sum up the folly of their marriage when she asked, "How does it happen that something that makes so much sense in the moonlight doesn't make any sense in the sunlight?"

Before the divorce papers were signed, Mother was dating a Turkish screen actor named Turhan Bey. One night my father and Bey got into a public fistfight over her, although the ostensible issue was a piece of jewelry.

It happened during a party for 200 guests at the Beverly Hills house of Tom and Anita May. Mother and the handsome Turk were dancing when Dad cut in and drew her aside. He pointed out that she was wearing his mother's diamond, which he had given her as an engagement ring. Since it was a Crane family heirloom, he wanted it back. Bey invited Father to step outside to the terrace.

Dressed in patent leather slippers and dinner jackets, the two men started swinging. Bey blackened Dad's eye and suffered some facial scratches, while Mother, who was looking on in dismay, slipped off the ring and threw it into the bushes. The next day the tabloids reported the incident as front-page news. They pointed out that the ex-husband of America's number one dream girl could be seen the morning after in the garden searching through the Mays' shrubbery on his hands and knees.

Not incidentally, ten days later Columbia planted items in the press saying that he was taking boxing lessons. Not true, of course (that new nose and chin of his), but he really did love the sport and in six years he would own half the contract of an Italian heavyweight.

If Mother now claimed bungalow A on the Metro lot (together with a new weekly $4,000 salary), it was Rita Hayworth who was riding high at Columbia. Dad set out to charm her, but having played no scenes together, they did not meet while making *Tonight and Every Night*. True to his nature, he had developed friendships with powerful executives close to Columbia's boss Harry Cohn, one of whom phoned Dad one day with a romantic idea. Cohn was sending Rita to make a *Cover Girl* promotion appearance in New York, the executive said, and Rita would be traveling on the Super Chief by herself. Why couldn't Steve just happen to be on the same train, traveling in a nearby drawing room? Since they had appeared in the same movie, he could introduce himself, and one thing might lead to another.

That's just what happened, with the "chance" meeting, heating up into an ardent affair that lasted all the way to New York and back. Actually, Dad didn't know that Rita had been in on the ruse. She admired him, knew his reputation as a Romeo, and approved his coming aboard.

After his fling with Rita, Dad threw himself into romancing celebrated women with such dedication that it sometimes seemed as if he hoped Mother was watching. He and Mother themselves still had an occasional night out together—when he was not with Deanna Durbin, Olga San Juan, Nina Foch, Sonja Henie, and countless others. One of Ciro's owners remembers three consecutive nights during which Father turned up with Mother, Ava Gardner, and Rita Hayworth. "This town's three top queens," he exulted. "I never saw *anybody* do that."

As fast as Dad's star was rising on the Hollywood nightlife scene, it was falling at Columbia. Mother privately screened *Cry of the Werewolf* for him at the house to save embarrassment, but Dad just roared with laughter. When she gently suggested that he might do better in some other line of work, he gave his typical noncommittal reply. ". . . Eh," he said with an easy shrug.

The New York Times found the movie "utterly suspenseless," but it expressed profound admiration for a line of dialogue in which someone asks Dad, "What's new at the mortuary?" *Werewolf* pops up on the Late Late Show every once in a while, and it always makes me laugh (but, then, I loved the leading man).

Dad's third picture was a dismal whodunit called *Crime Doctor's Revenge*. The *Times* judged him "a nice enough looking chap who is suspected of being a maniac or something" before he gets bumped off in his study. It may have been an omen.

One night Dad went to a surprise birthday party attended by a flock of *Cover Girl* fashion models who had been brought from New York. He was attracted to one of the guests, a stunning Polish ballerina, and he brought her back to his all-white high-rise apartment overlooking the lights of Hollywood.

The next morning he was summoned to Harry Cohn's office. The mogul stood with clenched fists, eyes glaring, his rubber lips rolling a cigar from one side of his mouth to the other. "Out!" he shouted, pointing at the door. "OUT!"

The Polish ballerina, it seemed, was Harry Cohn's new girlfriend, and when the option on Dad's contract came up for review, he was dropped.

Eight

Throughout the melodrama of Mother and Dad's nominal try at remarriage, I was sleeping blissfully in my crib. People say I was a sunny baby whose face—whether as the result of a sweet disposition or simple gas—often lit up with a smile.

By 1945, a year after my parents parted, I had been fattened into good health and was living with Mother in a house she bought overlooking the ninth hole at the Bel Air Country Club. The fattening up was begun by a wet nurse and completed by a nanny. Mother was not one to get herself involved in diapers and feedings. After she and Dad settled the dire matter of who would have custody of me, they hurried back to their moviemaking and night-clubbing with hardly a backward glance at the nursery.

That was standard operating procedure in Hollywood. There was nothing unusual about a star mother being uninvolved with her children. Until the 1950s, when television changed everything and the old studio system collapsed, cinema goddesses kept murderous work schedules, often making as many as three pictures a year. Most stars had little time and less inclination to take on the extra job of raising children. The task was usually turned over to hired help—nurses, nannies, governesses, and, later on, boarding schools. This age-old rich man's practice tends to rupture child-parent bonding, and it resulted in any number of movie-star offspring with childhoods like mine, distorted by too much privilege and too little attention.

English nannies and governesses were the bedrock of this system of absentee parenting. Anglophilia had swept

Hollywood years before talkies came in. If you were any-one *at all*, or pretended to be, you hired an English nanny. It was simply a matter of snob appeal. Most stars and movie executives came from humble backgrounds, as Mother had, and they believed that giving one's child the best rearing that money could buy—strict, protected, and classy English—was a bountiful gift of love, something most of them never had. The sting of its cost helped atone for any guilt they may have felt about having chosen to withhold their own loving hands-on care. The bottom line, of course, was that nannies freed one from the dreary chores of child raising.

Mother subscribed to every one of these reasons—es-pecially the last, and so it was that my launch in life was charted. With my ancestry in Ireland, Scotland, France, and Holland, lately by way of Idaho, Indiana, and Hol-lywood Hospital, I was to be raised as a perfect English princess.

Actually, my first nanny was Scottish, not English, a slight breach of custom that was typical of Mother, who was destined never to be completely accepted by Holly-wood's prewar establishment. (They considered her flashy, unschooled, her style a bit "off.")

Mary Margaret MacMurry, my dear Nana, was a widow from Edinburgh in her seventies. A sturdy reed of a woman, she had steady blue eyes and a lilting burr that, for all its oddness, reassured me inside even more. Child-less herself, she had in one lifetime probably raised a dozen other people's kids, but her expression of love for me felt as if it came from a tender heart, not professionalism.

I am naturally affectionate, and I looked forward to the moments at nap time and bedtime when she dispensed a light diet of love pats. "Sweet dreams then, Petty," she'd say, brushing her lips to my forehead and tapping my shoulder. She called me Pet or Petty. "Mmm, what a luvly goot girl."

Her long-sleeved white uniform had a bib that was starched as stiffly as a nun's wimple, so that when she pressed me to her bosom, she crackled. I longed to smother her in hugs and kisses, but she was an elderly woman of

British reserve who discouraged any such show. The only one who hugged me was Gran, usually on Thursdays.

Nana saw eye to eye with Mother and was determined that I be raised properly upper-upper, no slouching toward the loose gentilities she had observed in her own service class.

Cleanliness was the first thing. She carried everywhere a bottle of soapy water in a satchel, so that in the park, when I smudged an elbow or scuffed my white ankle-strap Mary Janes, they could be scrubbed clean *then and there*. (The bag also held white shoe polish for really stubborn scuffs.) When I slid down a jungle gym in our garden, Nana stood poised to catch me midway. I never reached the bottom. She feared that the Mary Pickford starch and lace pinafores I wore to play in would brush the dirty grass ("Ooof!"), grass that was manicured, I might add, as smoothly as the ninth green and swept free of leaves each and every day by groundskeepers with a vacuum cleaner.

Despite this obsession with hygiene, it was Nana's practice to wash my hair only once a week, no more, something she learned about catching colds in the English damp. It mattered not that we were living in a palmy oasis along the Mojave. My foot-long sausage curls were given 100 strokes every morning and again at bedtime with a brush wrapped in silk. The swatch of fabric served to clean, but the root-pulling was terrible. This was followed by finger rolling of the curls and tying on of ribbons. In all, the process took thirty minutes. Before I knew the word for them, I knew that curls hurt, took forever, and I hated them. One day I would find a way to fix that.

On Mother's strict orders, I was never *ever* to be left alone, not even in my room. Nana tended me twenty-four hours a day, except for Thursdays and every other Sunday, when Gran came in. Devoted as an abbess to her calling, Nana lived a life of watchfulness at the far end of my bedroom. During the night's vigil she read pulp novels by the rosy light of a scarf-veiled lamp while a radio softly played the "Jack Benny Show" or "Amos 'n' Andy." I drifted off to sleep beneath a big headboard stuffed to resemble a valentine in pink shirred silk (usually shrouded in a dust cover), while she slept on a hard hospital single.

So intent was she that I never be out of her sight that until I was nine years old I was not allowed to close the bathroom door. (This open-door policy was revived for a brief period when I was fifteen.) No matter what, someone always kept an eye on the baby. I was "the baby," and, by the way, that's what I would remain. Although I tower over mother by nearly half a foot these days, she called me "Baby" or "the baby" until I was nearly forty years old.

It is impossible, I know, but I carry a dim memory of my second birthday: the merry-go-round cake is brought in, I reach for its pretty roses, and plunge my hand right down the middle. "No no, Petty-Petty, no," Nana says firmly but gently, getting out the soapy water.

I remember the delight of seeing pigeons on the roof flapping away to the freedom of sky, of riding on the back of Billy, our snow-white Great Dane. I remember scratching the sheets of my crib, which signaled Nana to tickle my back.

Much like Mad King Ludwig of Bavaria, I had phosphorescent stars on my bedroom ceiling and a slice-of-lemon moon that glowed in the dark. There were hand-painted cherubs swinging on clouds doing happy little things waving and winking at me. If this early memory actually comes from the later viewing of photos, they must have been in color, because I can close my eyes and see salmon pink, custard creams, and the palest Tiepolo blue.

There were events I dearly wish I could remember. Rain or shine, Nana took me for airings in a big-wheeled perambulator, and our neighbor Greta Garbo often lifted me from the carriage to stroll by the park and hold me close to her lips cooing endearments. What-oh-what was that like?

Mother says her one-time fiancé Tyrone Power and I were the best of friends, that we roughhoused and played horsey, but I just can't remember him, even though their stormy affair went on until I was nearly four. But most lamentably, what I cannot bring back from the mist of those first postwar years is a memory of Mother herself.

I have seen all the posed press photos from that era. They show her gazing adoringly at the baby bundle in her arms or leading me somewhere by the mittens, but they inspire in me no sense memory whatsoever, no recollection of the warmth of a cuddle or the softness of a kiss. Most of the time Mother was off somewhere making movies or on holiday. Metro was using her in two pictures a year, for which she was paid $226,000, making her one of the country's ten highest paid women. When she wasn't getting ready for or shooting or promoting a movie, she was having fun in New York or resting at some pleasure spa such as Rio or Palm Springs. I was trundled along on a couple of New York trips in Nana's arms, but only as a "beard" to disguise the true nature of some romantic pilgrimage. As for when she was at home, until my sixth year I rarely saw her.

When she was filming, she left for the studio by 6:30 A.M. while I slept, and she seldom returned before Nana tucked me in twelve hours later. When she was not filming, her nightclubbing put our schedules in reverse, because she seldom stirred before noon. Sleeping late may seem an unremarkable practice for a movie queen, but it was still viewed as too Marie Antoinettish by the go-getting movie community. One fan magazine summed it up by proclaiming her to be a "monument to inertia." She was "such a late sleeper," noted *Modern Screen*, that she gave "cause to wonder how she ever got anything accomplished."

When Mother's door was closed, I stood gazing as if across a moat. I was forbidden to knock or listen or make sounds that might wake her. When I sometimes managed to steal away from Nana, I lingered outside and pondered for long solemn moments, yearning for the castle keep to yield my fairy princess. To my child's mind, she was the perfect dream of golden beauty, unattainable, beyond reach, everything delicate and soft and feminine that one day I wanted to . . . *what?* To be? To possess?

The rare moments when she sat by my valentine bed, just the two of us, always wrenched my heart because they were too brief. They lingered in the air like the perfume she wore, a sweet floral scent named Tuberose that defined her aura and filled my mind after she was gone, leaving me to stare for sleepless hours at my lemon moon.

Though Mother's all-white boudoir was off-limits, the rules didn't always apply when she was away, especially on Thursdays when lenient Gran was in charge. Then I would creep into Mother's room-size closet and, eyes closed, swirl around in the gossamer cloud of dresses and furs to inhale her essence.

I tried this one time when I was brought to her on a movie set. As she smiled hello and beckoned eagerly, I wrapped my one-yard height in the folds of her skirt where I peered out at the world through black chiffon. For one transcendent moment I was Mommy, or a part of her anyway, I belonged to her, I was inside of her—until the world yanked me back.

"No, Pet, you'll muss Mummy."

"Mommy's dress, Baby."

That she was in every way a seductive but untouchable mother was hardly what Metro had in mind to tell the fans. This was especially true after her glamour image had been tarnished by the dubious circumstances of my birth. Originally, the studio had feared that motherhood itself might render its reigning sex symbol unsexy, but it turned out that her fan mail jumped surprisingly when I came along. M-G-M's mail count for a nine-month period in 1944 showed Mother and Judy Garland running neck and neck at 191,000 letters each. (Greer Garson ran a distant third.)

When "for the sake of the child" she remarried a G.I. going off to war, the press coverage gave moviegoers the vague impression that it was an act of patriotism. As a result, her sexy arc light took on a bit of a Madonna glow. Soon even lonesome Yanks in the South Pacific were knitting booties for Baby Cheryl. The studio was swamped with presents—dresses, dolls, toys, needlepoint, rattles, rings, bibs, jewelry—everything imaginable. All the stuff was sent to orphanages. I saw none of it except for one extraordinary gift that a fan sent me through Mother. It was a stunningly lifelike, handmade model of her that stood three feet tall, like me. The blond hair was real. The seed pearl buttons that ran down the long sleeves and back of a silvery dress were real. The doll had high-heel shoes that I could remove, and a ring and earrings made of real diamond chips, but when I checked, she was wearing no panties. She was my beautiful Mommy doll, and because she was so fragile and precious, I was forbidden to play with her. Until years later when she vanished in the chaos, my Mommy doll stood atop a bookcase shelf beside my bed where I could gaze at the eternal smile painted on her lips.

M-G-M got the message from all the letters and baby presents that flooded in. The publicity department went to work and wove tales that would color in the new picture of her as a model mother, one who was "proud as a peacock of her little girl." A national woman's organization voted her America's "most glamorous mother" (along with Marlene Dietrich). Magazines dutifully reported things like "the minute she gets home, Lana always scrubs her face and removes all lipstick so she can kiss the bambino all she wants."

In truth, by age four, when I sometimes began to be presented to her on sets or at home in the barroom, I knew the rules. I had been warned. As I was handed up for a careful hug and peck, lips never touched lips, skin hardly touched skin. It was for show, a "cocktail kiss" like a half-slide down the jungle gym. I knew never to touch pretty Mommy, her hair, her makeup, her dress. In her commitment to seamless glamour, she kept herself in a perpetual state of camera-readiness, even at home. "The hair," she would say flatly if it seemed I was about to forget. "Sweetheart, the lipstick."

Maybe she was indeed kissing "the bambino" all she wanted. But my child's mind could not make any sense out of her ineffable specialness. Silken hair and radiant skin you could kinda see through were meant to be touched, weren't they?

Mother's heart was in the right place about mothering, I suppose. Life had miscast her in the role, but she still made the occasional stab at it. She decided one Sunday afternoon, Nana's day off, to give me a bath. It was around the time of my first birthday and the very first time the two of us had ever been alone together. Nana had given her pointers, but the task both terrified and exasperated Mother. She remembers losing her temper in the struggle with a soapy squirming baby, when her hands slipped and all of a sudden she realized she was clutching me by the throat.

"I gasped," Mother recalled in her autobiography, *Lana.* "I dropped [Cheryl] on a side table and, though she was sopping wet, pulled her up close to me, saying, 'Cherry, Cherry, I didn't mean it.' Almost like a grownup, [Cheryl] pulled away from me, then looked me straight in the face and laughed." The incident ended happily in hugs, but afterward Mother couldn't help feeling "as though I had been through a contest of some kind."

A similar thing happened one day when I was four. Mother took me shopping as a treat at Saks Fifth Avenue, her favorite store in Beverly Hills. She knew many of the clerks by name, even last names and nicknames, and this was the first chance she had to show off the famous Baby Cheryl. As we passed through the millinery department, I saw a hat, a big self-confident one with flowers all over it, and I stopped dead in my Mary Janes.

"Can I have that, Mommy?"

"No, that's a lady's hat, too old for you. C'mon."

"I want it."

"No, I said."

I was used to being denied the pleasure of touch and feelings, but never *things.* I knew she lacked the easy command of Nana or Gran, and something perverse in me needed to test her. Another contest. I grabbed for the hat and tried to pull away from her grasp, but I couldn't reach far enough and landed on the floor where I flailed about like an upended turtle. As shoppers circled the commotion and Mother's smile turned grim, I threw a heels-kicking, breath-holding tantrum, the kind that makes parents want to kill. Embarrassed and angry, Mother grabbed me up and flew out of the store. It had been our very first mother-daughter outing. It would be a long time before the next.

Oddly enough, the tantrum represented my first act of rebellion. Up to then I obeyed authority so readily that I seemed downright meek. To Mother's friends, I was an automaton child, shy, polite, and solemn. "Too grown-up," they said. Photos of me after the age of two show an unsure little person who *never* smiled. Everyone knew how to fix that. "Smile, Baby, why don't you smile?" still echoes in my head.

I was taught to curtsey and shake grown-up hands. My own were wearing gloves so tiny that they had to be custom-made. (Whether cotton or French kid, they were always snow white, and Nana's bag held clean second pairs.)

"How do you do, ma'am?" I'd always say when introduced. "Very well, thank you, ma'am."

"Good day, sir. My name is Cheryl."

The studio's portrayal of our supposedly ideal family life sometimes borrowed a bit of fact to make the fiction sound more plausible. Noting correctly that Nana had Thursdays off, one fan magazine reported that on that particular day Metro bosses knew it was no use scheduling Mother to do any work that was not absolutely necessary: "That's the day Lana takes over the complete care of Cheryl, a job she wouldn't miss for all the bonuses M-G-M could vote her," the magazine gushed.

In fact, the opposite was true. When she was at home, Mother hardly looked into my room. I was brought to her, but rarely in her boudoir. It was usually in the barroom, and always freshly starched and sausage-curled. Like many women, she had no natural instinct for mothering.

The source of that mistaken fan magazine item was probably the self-effacing, self-denying woman who actually cared for me on Thursdays—my beloved Gran. Gran gave me the only warm nurturing I knew. Her life was loveless too, but we had each other.

Nine

My grandmother belonged to that informal sister-hood tolerantly but snidely referred to around Hollywood as ''the star mothers.'' There was—and still is—an actual club by that name of which she was an eager member. As Lana Turner's mother, her life was one of reflected glamour and relative ease, but the price was a growing sense of futility, of lost identity and loneliness. At age thirty-one, when she arrived in Los Angeles with her daughter, she simply gave up trying to make a life of her own.

As her parental influence on Mother continued to wane during my childhood, she clung more tightly to me, I believe, partly as a way of holding on. I became something of a link between them, yet before long Gran and I would both come to feel spurned by the same woman.

Gran was the one who most shaped me from birth through adolescence, and I feel blessed to have inherited some of her qualities. Her forebears came to America in the great immigration wave of the mid-nineteenth century, unskilled workers from Ireland and Scotland, but there was some vague French connection too. Her angular bone structure had a Gallic severity which I share, but unfortunately the records that might explain the connection are lost. I think genetics offers clues to one's nature and destiny. Is my stubbornness somehow Irish? My sense of thrift, Scottish? Is my absorption today with beautiful clothes, food, and decor slightly French?

As Gran's social status rose with Mother's success, she rubbed elbows with millionaires and, as a result, her family tree sprouted fancier roots. Improving on the truth, the dubious French connection took on a whiff of aristocracy. Friends of her humble family became "doctors," her father (who drove a train) was "in engineering." The truth was no doubt more interesting and I begged her to tell me everything, but when she came to gaps of several years in the narrative, her eyes took on a faraway look. "Then there were many stops along the way," she would say in a merry singsong, and so much for that. Maybe those periods held too much pain to describe.

When she made her way to Hollywood in the thirties, that too was part of a wider migration. She had been raised dirt poor, partly in Oklahoma, but she was not one of the "Okies" described in John Steinbeck's *The Grapes of Wrath,* the hapless farmers who headed west to flee the Dust Bowl. Instead, her odyssey seems more of a piece with Nathanael West's *The Day of the Locust,* in which people who simply did not fit in anywhere else came to California in search of magic. West saw them forming a subculture of misfits that swarmed like metaphoric locusts around America's fantasy capital.

Gran would have been too proud to allow any comparison with locusts. She and Mother were nothing as mundane as movie hopefuls. She claimed that they wound up in Los Angeles simply because she had respiratory problems and a doctor had ordered her to a warmer climate. I somehow doubt that.

It was typical of the Turner girls and M-G-M to gloss over the plain truth—which was, I believe, that they were a little star-struck, like everybody else. The movies were America's escape, especially for poor people. Gran had been influenced by the style of Warner Brothers heroine Kay Francis, whom she resembled and whose hairstyle she copied, while my teenage mother swooned over the celestial Norma Shearer. They adored the clothes they saw in movies, and Gran spent her paycheck to copy certain outfits. Surely, while down on their luck, they must have heard of striking it rich in the land of limousines and lime trees.

Mother insists she had wanted to be a dress designer, not an actress. "In no sense at all was I star-struck," she bristles. But isn't there a certain cachet when one succeeds in movies without seeming to try, when stardom just sort of falls on one?

What is certain is that in August 1937, after drifting through sixteen years of rented rooms and whistlestop towns, Mother and Gran arrived in Los Angeles broke, driving along Sunset Boulevard like the Beverly Hillbillies in a mud-caked jalopy with straw suitcases on top. Within six months, an American dream had come true. Mother had a movie contract and Gran wasn't giving perms on spiked heels anymore. Though still more extraordinary times lay ahead, they'd already come a long way.

Gran started life in 1904 as Mildred Frances Cowan in the chicken-farming town of Lamar, Arkansas. Life was a hard scrabble. Her mother died giving birth, and she was raised by "Mama," an older great aunt. Her father, Henry Cowan, remarried three times, and his resulting twelve children had to be fed on the salary of a railroad man.

As a child she was sickly and was made to wear a bag of foul-smelling herbs and mustard plasters around her neck—a doubtful cure for her respiratory problems. Gran's childhood, consisting of poverty, sickness, a faraway father, and an elderly mother figure, must have been drab. She never once mentioned love.

After "many stops along the way," it was in the tank town of Picher, Oklahoma, that she met John Virgil Madison Turner, who, at twenty-four, was nine years her senior. Short and husky but blondly handsome, "Mr. Turner," as she always called him, was of Dutch descent and hailed from Alabama. Fresh out of the infantry as a decorated platoon sergeant, he asked her to dance one night at Picher's only rooftop beer garden, to which she had been escorted by her father.

Later Gran told a more colorful version—one that Mother insists is fanciful. Virgil was just starting out as a vaudeville hoofer, Gran said, and was appearing on the beer garden stage the night her father brought her. He specialized in cakewalks, hoedowns, jigs, and a Southern Black specialty called the "eepher." Gran was sitting down front, and as he danced their eyes locked. They met backstage and became inseparable for the run of his engagement. Her father forbade marriage because of the age difference, but Gran was feeling the crush of first love. "I couldn't resist Mr. Turner," she told me, with an untypical blush. Two days before her sixteenth birthday, she and Mr. Turner eloped to Wallace, Idaho, a town in the state's northwest tip. The wedding night was a disaster: she had received no sex education whatever and his rough-handed lovemaking literally put her off sex for the rest of her life.

My mother, Julia Jean Turner—called Judy—was born the first year. Virgil gave up hoofing for steadier work in the mines, but the Turners were not very happy. Gran was still an unschooled child bride, tall and gawky, who found herself unprepared for the roles of wife, mother, and homemaker all at once. Virgil's persistent ardor resulted in a second pregnancy which did not go full term.

During the twenties, they moved through a number of northwest mining towns as he tried to master other work, such as selling insurance. But he always wound up returning to the mines, finally perhaps as a foreman. The Turners traveled light, sometimes living under an assumed name because of irredeemable gambling losses and his mishaps in bootlegging. (He would sell home-brew corn liquor until the police caught on and once again they would have to skip town.)

Virgil was an inveterate gambler who often made or lost the rent money on dice and cards. He taught his young "Jujean" (Julia Jean) how to play poker, and to this day Mother manages a very mean game. He loved drinking and dancing and partying, and his large personality swept the family along on a near decade of small misadventures. One of Mother's happiest memories is of watching her parents gaily fox-trot around a kitchen to the tune of "You're the Cream in My Coffee," played on a wind-up Victrola. Then it came Jujean's turn to dance, and he'd make her laugh doing deep dips and spins. Finally exhausted, he went to a straight chair and tap-danced sitting down.

Gran's prayer that real happiness was waiting for them in the next town may have somehow prompted a strange incident that traumatized young Judy. During a time when their backyard faced railroad tracks, Gran liked to gather up her three-year-old and step outside to wave at passing trains. One day she pointed to a particular passenger in a window, a woman wearing long white gloves, and she said suddenly, "Wave to that lady." Judy objected, but she insisted. "Wave to her."

Judy did so and the mystery woman waved back. The child pleaded for an explanation, and Gran finally announced that the woman in the window "is your real mother—I'm just taking care of you." Judy burst into tears. Though Gran then admitted it wasn't true, and petted and reassured her, Judy eyed her mother with suspicion for a long time and could never quite sweep that tiny insecurity from the attic of her mind.

Gran herself was baffled by and ashamed of the cruel act she had committed. The incident said something about her yearnings for escape, of course, feelings that soon led her into a quirky practice that went on for years—running away from Mr. Turner. Using saved-up household money, she would go on department-store shopping sprees, buying frilly outfits for herself and her daughter. Then, all done up and suitcases bulging, she and Judy would hop the next train to anywhere. "We would ride and ride," said Gran, "until the rest of the money ran out, and then we'd have to call home. I would say, 'Here we are in Yuma, Mr. Turner, y'better come get us.' He would arrive and scold me, but I could never explain why I ran away. I didn't know why. Bored, I guess. Poor man, I was so mean to him."

By the time Judy was seven and they had migrated to San Francisco, Virgil and Millie agreed to separate. Still gambling heavily, he found work as a stevedore at the Pacific Coast Steamship Co., while Gran became a beauty operator. Judy was boarded out in a series of unhappy foster homes.

One foster home was run by a married couple in Modesto who were friends of Gran. The arrangement was that Mother would be treated as well as their own adolescent daughter, Valentine, in return for doing light chores and paying the couple a weekly fee. The plan soured as Judy became saddled with the hard labor of a scullery maid,

cooking meals, doing the family wash on Saturdays, and
ironing on Sundays. With Gran able to make the ninety-
mile bus trip from San Francisco only infrequently, and
Virgil hardly ever, Judy sank into a despairing loneliness.
The memory of desertion haunted her as an adult and
doubtless fed into her obsession that I never be left alone
(even if she had to hire a nanny to ensure it).

On one of Gran's Sunday afternoon visits to Modesto,
she discovered bruises and cuts on her daughter's body
where she had been beaten with a stick. They both returned to San Francisco that day, ending two terrible years
that Mother had endured in silence because she had been
threatened with more beatings if she complained. "Your
Mother's coming," she remembers her foster parents saying. "Keep your mouth shut."

When Gran could be coaxed to speak of the incident,
she would wrinkle her nose and look away as though she
doubted its truth—as if she felt that Judy, like some willful
child who was unhappy at summer camp, would have done
anything to escape the foster home, even have made cuts
on her body. Gran may have been masking the guilt she
felt for parking her child in an unkind foster home, but
there was no doubt about Mother's budding flair for self-
dramatization.

In the struggle to hold on to her child, Gran took other
measures that failed, including brief reconciliations with
Virgil and, at one point, the cramped sharing of a San
Francisco apartment with two female roommates. The
apartment didn't work out because on nights when the
roommates entertained men friends, Mother had to bed
down in a closet.

They once had nothing to eat for three days, and Mother
took to begging at grocery stores for crackers and milk
dressed pitiably as the poor little match girl in the snow.
Somehow they survived.

The worst jolt of Judy's young life came in 1930, when
she was nine. Virgil Turner was found slumped on a sidewalk one morning, half sitting up against a building wall.
His skull had been bashed in, his overcoat yanked over
his head, and he was dead. What had happened was that
the night before, calling himself Tex Johnson, he had won

handsomely at a traveling crap game in the basement of the *San Francisco Chronicle* building. It was known among the players that he had a habit of stuffing big winnings inside his left sock. When he was found the next morning, in a slum district called Butchertown, his left shoe had been removed and the sock was missing. It was ten days before Christmas, and he had told the boys around the table that he had promised to buy his little girl a bicycle. No arrest was ever made.

Mother says that word of his death came to her in a dream. God's face appeared on a gold medallion and spoke to her, at which point she felt awe and a strange sense of peace. Then, she remembers, "I closed my eyes and went back to sleep."

At the funeral home Mother was jolted by fright when she saw Virgil in the casket. Gran asked, "Do you want to kiss your father good-bye?" Never having seen a dead person, she reached out fearfully. His hand felt hard, cold, *terrifying*. She pulled back and clung to her mother.

Her feelings about men had to be shaped in part by the odd example of her father, a fun-loving bounder whose dreams and schemes never did pan out, a Wilkins Micawber really, and the only tap dancer in her unmusical life. On the one hand, he was utterly magnetic. If she sensed Gran's growing coldness to him, it was nothing like the warmth that she felt every time he swept her up and spun her around to the music on the wind-up Victrola. But on the other hand, he rejected her and her mother, leaving them in great hardship.

To further confuse young Judy's already contradictory sense of men, Sergeant Turner was buried with full honors at the Presidio, a military cemetery that sprawls beside the Golden Gate Bridge. After his misspent life and shabby death, Virgil was given a hero's funeral, complete with a gun salute that boomed across the sky.

His loss produced in her a confused sorrow that went unaired for twenty years. The murder was disguised in studio publicity as death "by accident." It wasn't until 1951 that she felt free enough to go public with the truth. "I was nine years old . . ." she wrote in the *Woman's Home Companion*. "The shock I suffered then may be a valid excuse for me now. It may explain things I do not myself understand. I know that my father's sweetness and gaiety, his warmth and his tragedy have never been far from me—that, and a sense of loss and of growing up too fast.''

Having turned thirty that year, Mother admitted in the article that her life to that point had been "wayward and impulsive, always a search for something that is not there and then disillusionment.'' She added, tellingly, ''I need all the excuses I can make.''

Virgil's death did not change the material side of their drab lives one way or the other. Though America was heading into the depths of the Depression, Gran could usually find beautician's work to scratch out a living. After a few other ill-fated attempts to board Mother in foster homes, the two began sharing an apartment in the Richmond district of San Francisco with a woman named Chila Meadows, who owned the beauty shop where Gran worked.

In her early teens, Mother was beginning to think about growing up, and it was clear that a conventional life would not do. After attending three Catholic schools in a row, she decided to become a nun. Reportedly, she badgered the teachers about her plan until she learned that nuns of that time kept their heads shaved.

It was already very important to Mother how she looked, and she was developing early. With her thick reddish hair, gray eyes, pouty lips, fair skin, and perfectly proportioned figure, she was the prettiest girl in the class. Boys were beginning to ogle her, and she loved it.

For a time she hoped to be a bandstand pop singer. Those hopes were dashed when she flunked an audition for the Major Bowes Amateur Hour, belting out ''The Basin Street Blues'' in a light, virginal soprano.

Despite the daydreams about life in a cloister or on a bandstand, Mother always came back to a continuing obsession with clothes. When they weren't reading aloud to each other from etiquette books, she and Gran were poring over fashion magazines or trying to remember what styles they had seen on the screen. ''I loved the costumes in the movies," Mother recalled of her youth, and, indeed, by some now-clouded alchemy of luck and ambition, she went on to become one of the most *costumed* women of her time.

Ten

The postwar year of 1946 brought changes in my family's circumstances that only increased my isolation in the nursery. We were still living in the path of golf balls hooked off the country club's ninth green when Gran was exiled from our house and made to live elsewhere.

It was inevitable, I suppose. The Turner girls had not been getting along all that well since Mother signed her first movie contract. Gran's prim attitude toward men, her handwringing about respectability and appearances, clashed with Mother's freewheeling pursuit of fun.

At the time, the roll call of men Mother was being seen with included Dad, Greg Bautzer, Tony Martin, Peter Lawford, Frank Sinatra, Rex Harrison, Howard Hughes, and Huntington Hartford. (According to one cruel—no doubt apocryphal—story, in her eagerness to marry Hughes, Mother had towels made up that were monogrammed "H.H." When they abruptly split up, Hughes supposedly advised her, "Go marry Huntington Hartford.")

For her part, Gran continued to wait up nights for her child, although she was by now a twenty-five-year-old, twice divorced woman of the world. Even more maddening to Mother was the fact that Gran stayed close with Dad, for my sake, and encouraged our father-daughter outings. Gran was finally ousted in the first of what would become Mother's occasional sneak attacks from the rear.

Just before leaving on a six-week pleasure and promotion tour of Latin America, she instructed Greg Bautzer to

sell the Bel Air house and find another that was too small
to accommodate Gran. Bautzer handled everything, even
breaking the news to Gran himself, and lined up a new
place on Crown Drive in Brentwood Heights.

Gran was packed off to a two-bedroom second-floor
apartment in Beverly Hills for which Mother paid the rent.
While my grandmother was hurt and dismayed, there was
little she could do about it—not as long as she accepted
her daughter's weekly stipend. Having grown used to the
living standards of a star mother, she could never go back
to doing manicures and fingerwaves, work that would be
thought too low-paying and too public. (She often still did
Mother's hair in her boudoir, but that was private.)

Mother would certainly never permit Gran to do service
work again. She had seen how other star mothers, after
being cut off from their famous child's help, wound up in
reduced circumstances—and how that invariably resulted
in bad publicity.

Though Nana ruled the roost at our Bel Air house, Gran
could always visit my bedroom to nourish me with hugs
and kisses. But at the new house on Crown Drive, her
contact with me was more confined to Nana's days off.
("Granny, pleeease don't go home.")

Meanwhile, the lifestyle of my Sunday father was also
changing drastically. That spring he dived into a business
venture, and his dutiful Sunday outings with me slowed to
a trickle. He had bought Lucy's, a trendy restaurant and
star hangout on Melrose Avenue that wedged nicely on
the southeast corner opposite Paramount Studio's front
gate. It was a big vine-covered steakhouse, medieval in
design, already well established when Dad took it over.
Since Universal and RKO Studios were nearby, Lucy's
drew a colorful crowd of performers, sometimes still in
working costume and makeup, whose regulars included
Humphrey Bogart, John Garfield, Ava Gardner, and Robert Mitchum.

After Dad was dropped by Columbia, it took him a year
to pull together the financing for Lucy's—mainly through
the successful leveraging of gambling wins and a fifty-fifty
partnership with one of his gin rummy pals. This partner
(and soon-to-be roommate) was Al Mathes, a former boxer

and noted gambler from L.A.'s rough Boyle Heights section, a man whose parents had done well in the garment business. Invariably described as tough, quiet, and shy, "Uncle Al" (as I called him) would become Dad's life-long partner.

After four years of dubious celebrity, Dad was finally coming into his own. As the host at Lucy's, he could unfurl his fatal charm. Moreover, he could use what he learned from his friendships with club owners and party givers, while calling in favors from columnists and famous friends. It didn't hurt, either, that he was widely known as Lana's ex, though he made light of it.

At Lucy's, Dad starred in the role of a traffic cop at a celebrity crossroads. Friends observed that his already admirable savoir faire seemed to billow exponentially. Gossip columns had him dating the likes of French sex kitten Corinne Calvet, *Werewolf* costar Nina Foch, and a new "Latin spitfire" at Columbia named Olga San Juan.

He would soon begin to date seriously a new actress under contract at Metro whom he met when she sold him cigarettes from her tray at Ciro's. This starlet, when decked out in blond hair, white shorts, and ankle-strap heels, was an unmistakable Lana Turner look-alike. Her name was Lila Leeds.

I have a happy memory of standing up at Lucy's in a front booth at the age of three, wearing a white lace dress. People are calling me Cherry and I'm enjoying my first chocolate sundae. At home I was forbidden to have sweets; I only knew the taste of sugar as a result of pinching Juicy Fruit gum from a drawer in our barroom.

The notion of "Daddy" was an abstract concept to me. Since I was not allowed to play with other children, I had little idea of what other families were like. Indeed, the children I saw at the star-baby birthday parties I was allowed to attend seemed to be a strange species, almost fearsome. Nana literally had to push me at them. ("Pet, go over there and *play*. Go on . . . I mean it.")

The nice man called my "Daddy" was tall and kind, a person who made me laugh and feel *protected*. Nobody else ever tossed me in the air or handled me roughly and made me squeal with delight. He knew the adult trick that wins over any child—when he spoke to me, it was in the same tone of voice he used with grown-ups. It was a deep, resonant bass, the kind men try for in the shower.

A visit with Daddy meant giggles and fun, giant pandas waiting in his arms, happy times in a happy place with noisy people who fussed over me and gave me sweets. I could say I almost looked forward to these outings with him, but they occurred infrequently enough for each occasion to retain the wonder of surprise.

As Dad was opening Lucy's that spring of 1946, Mother's career entered a new phase, too, with release of *The Postman Always Rings Twice*. A sexy but censor-resistant adaptation of James M. Cain's 1934 best-seller, the movie represented a peak in her campaign to be taken seriously as an actress, a peak that would not be rivaled again until she was perfectly cast as a movie star in *The Bad and the Beautiful* seven years later. *Postman,* probably the movie for which she will be best remembered, secured her position in the front rank of household names—and threw her life into a frenzy.

In contrast to the light romantic roles she had made her name on, in *Postman* she played a villainess who was all the more deadly for her devouring sexuality. Metro was worried about censorship, and one offsetting device that director Tay Garnett and producer Carey Wilson came up with was to costume her throughout in stark virginal white. Metro was worried too about whether the public would accept their top female star in an image-shattering role, one that showed her as a roadside hash house waitress with a decidedly amoral disposition. Enter Baby Cheryl.

As part of a prerelease campaign that would show her in a warm, maternal light, we were photographed together one day when I visited the film set in Laguna Beach. Too young to understand the PR task in which we were engaged, I impishly snubbed Mother and her costar, John Garfield, to race for the water. I had never seen waves and I was thrilled. Dull as the photos of that visit turned out, they were made available to the press together with stories about Lana, the model mother.

As *Postman* was about to open that spring, Lana and

Baby Cheryl walked up Fifth Avenue in the Easter Parade to be photographed in blue forget-me-not bonnets, standing on the steps of St. Patrick's Cathedral. That fall she smiled and I frowned my way through Hollywood's Santa Claus Parade down Hollywood Boulevard in the featured spot atop Santa's float.

Mother's generosity was emphasized by releasing her Christmas gift list, a staggering testament to good business practice that showed some 500 purchases, including an ermine coat for me and a diamond-and-sapphire clip for Gran. "There were two dozen cashmere sweaters (at $35 apiece) for her young men friends," observed *Time,* "and wallets with engraved gold plates ('Eddie from Lana') for her older men friends."

These and other steps were calculated to soothe censors and blunt a potential blue-nose backlash against Mother by presenting her in a tableau of mother-daughter domesticity. Left unmentioned was the fact that after the parades I was immediately handed over to Nana.

The post-*Postman* frenzy began for me with a trauma. Our prerelease trip to New York had gone off without a hitch. Fans gathered happily around us on Fifth Avenue, but they were respectful. We rated good media coverage but we didn't stop traffic, and that was that.

On our next New York trip together after *Postman* had become a smash, a trip to promote her stupendous new costume drama *Green Dolphin Street,* Mother took me along (but not Gran), partly because I was good for the image and partly as a beard to disguise a rendezvous she had arranged.

From the moment we checked into the Sherry Netherland Hotel on Central Park, crowds of fans and the curious began gathering on the sidewalk around its front and side doors. Since my face was not famous, Nana could sneak me out for daily airings in the park, where I eagerly greeted my new friends, the mounted police. I loved to pat the sweet noses of their horses and feed them sugar from Nana's bag.

One day a half-dozen fans spotted us, and with kind intent, delighted me by tying helium balloons to my wrists. I weighed about forty pounds, and as the balloons in-

creased in number, one after another, I began to feel as if
I were being lifted off the pavement. The fans wouldn't
stop. Hopelessly snarled in strings, I both feared and hoped
I would fly. My near lift-off was scary, but these friendly
strangers—I didn't know why they knew my name—did
little to prepare me for the assault that was coming.

The next day Mother, Nana, and I were packed up and
ready to embark on a visit to some place called Connecticut. Mother had met, she told me that morning, a "very
nice gentleman." His name was Mr. Topping, and he had
invited us to visit his house in Connecticut where there
was a farm and I could play with the ducks and chickens.

The doorbell rang and Nana ushered someone into the
suite. It was the hotel manager and he was nervous. "Miss
Turner," he said calmly, "we'd better get you out the
back way." Mother smiled and, with that, he lifted me in
his arms and led us down the elevator into a confusing
maze of double doorways that opened like valves through
halls and kitchens and dropped us suddenly on a delivery
dock. The screams exploded, deafening, keening, screeching.

"There she is!"

"Here she comes!"

"LAA-NA!"

"Watch out!"

"Move back."

"This way! This way!"

"The kid! Hey, the kid!"

"Over here! This way, Lana. Look this way, Lana!"

"LANA! LANA!"

"Cher-ULL!"

All the while, the cameras were going pop-pop-pop-
pop-pop-pop.

A score of police, some of them my friends on horseback, strained to hold back the mob. It had engulfed our
two limos and was swarming toward us with tidal force.
No one smiled or waved. Autograph books and sharp pencils stabbed the air. Faces looked anguished, surly, surprised. Gathering strength we dived toward the cars only
to be swallowed up, struggling like prey in their mouths.

"Get back—get back—*get back!*"

Police beat the mob back with sticks. Hands reached up
to claw at my coat, my *hair.* "Mommy," I screamed.
"Mommy! Mommy! Mommy!" But Mommy was peeling
off in the direction of her own limo, and as I reached mine,
I was thrown through the air, landing on the back-seat
cushions as Nana swung in beside me. The door sliced
shut, and the reaching hands recoiled to avoid being cut
off, only to reassert their blood lust by pounding on the
roof. Faces pressed against the windows, squashed into
twisted mouths and wild eyes.

The limo broke away through the entrance to Central
Park and sped uptown to freedom, at which point I let out
a little choke. "Now, now, darling," said Nana. "It's all
right. You're safe."

The skirt of my coat was shredded in places and flapped
free along one side where it had been ripped from the
waist. I touched a tenderness on my scalp where someone
had yanked at my hair. I had no left glove. Oh my goodness, what was *that* about?

"Look! Look!" said Nana brightly. "We're going by
the zoo. You love the zoo. Wave to the animals."

I waved. I never asked questions.

IV

PAPA TOPPING

Eleven

Mr. Topping's house in Connecticut was more beautiful than any Christmas card, but that's what it made me think of. The setting in swank suburban Greenwich was a wonderland of red oak leaves trembling as they struggled to cling through the frost. When I sniffed the air, it had that crackle which comes just before snow.

The house was called Round Hill, a red brick Tudor fantasy that crowned a gentle rise and surveyed 500 wooded acres on which a pool, garden, stables, private lake, and working farm were enclosed behind ancient-looking walls. The building itself was a blend of several sixteenth-century manor houses that had been brought from England, brick by brick, to be recombined into a vast structure. The servants' wing alone had twenty-two rooms.

We glided through Round Hill's iron gates that afternoon along a crunchy driveway to the most massive double doors anyone has ever seen. As wonder piled on wonder, I found myself holding on to Nana, herself brusquely unimpressed, as we stood in a three-story entrance hall the size of a tennis court. A double staircase faced us, and at either side stood carved marble fireplaces high enough for a grown-up to stand inside.

"Cherry, darling," Mother said demurely, "I would like you to meet my friend, Mr. Henry J. Topping. He is our host. You may call him Uncle Bob."

As I curtsied, I already knew that I liked him. He was pink and round, and his smile said: I think we're going to be friends. I had met so many gentlemen lately that I never dreamed Uncle Bob was going to be my new father. He hadn't proposed yet, but Mother was in a vulnerable state, both romantically and financially (a result of IRS troubles).

Only three months before, when Tyrone Power went off on a two-month world tour, she had given a $10,000 farewell party at Mocambo complete with Jimmy Dorsey's band and orchids flown in from Hawaii. But weeks later in London, Power met actress Linda Christian, whom he later married. At the same time, Mother's avowed friendship with Frank Sinatra was making his wife nervous enough to give out unhappy remarks about it to the newspapers.

Bob Topping was still married, but during all of Mother's romantic turmoil, he had conducted a quiet, year-long campaign for her attention, lavishing her with flowers and candy. By the second week in December, she permitted herself to accept both a gift of diamond earrings and his invitation for her and her family to spend Christmas in Connecticut.

After New Year's, when she also accepted a fifteen-carat diamond engagement ring that he had dropped into her martini, the press would say she was marrying a millionaire on the rebound from Ty Power. But I could see why she liked him. He was a good-time guy, playful and hard drinking. He had a take-charge way about him, the money to make things happen, and was obviously awed by her—the way she liked men to be. It was she, however, who invited him out for their first evening on the town. She needed an escort for a New York film premiere, and when her phone call came, he was in a poker game. After accepting, he reportedly turned to his pals and bragged, "You didn't think I could make it with the little lady, did you, you bums?"

Bob Topping's grandfather, Daniel G. Reid, had founded the family fortune back in the nineteenth century by manufacturing tinplate, an economical sheeting material, and then went on to amass $140 million in steel, railroads, and also (ironically) tobacco. Dan Topping, one of Bob's two brothers, owned the New York Yankees and had recently gone through an expensive divorce from Sonja

Henie. Bob himself was still married to retired movie actress Arline Judge (who starred in *Pigskin Parade*), but they were not speaking.

Coming right after the terrifying fan riot in New York, those halcyon days at Round Hill were the happiest two weeks I had ever had. Though I took meals and tea with Nana, during lazy afternoons there was unaccustomed access to Mother, and we enjoyed walks together, fed the squirrels, even toasted marshmallows.

It was the first time I had ever seen radiators or bath tubs with feet. The working farm offered irresistible ponies and lambs and baby ducks I could touch and play with. I found a nice friend in the butler, a grown-up even taller than the fireplace, who one day led me up four flights of stairs for an expedition through the attic. Nana and I found wondrous things like Uncle Bob's toys, feathered hats and ball gowns and a funny old sleigh with curlicue runners like in the Santa Claus parade.

Christmas day was celebrated around a thirty-foot tree that had been chopped down on the estate and set up in the entrance hall. The ornaments at the very top were hung by parlor maids standing on ladders and using library tongs. The house was magically transformed. Even the antique eight-room doll house gracing my bedroom had its own miniature Christmas tree.

It snowed the day after Christmas, with the East Coast getting socked by one of the heaviest storms on record. New York City was buried for six days under twenty-six inches of snow, and roads were blocked everywhere. People endured a kind of festive chaos, but up in Greenwich, we didn't mind. We were enjoying a storybook holiday cut off from the world for two weeks without heat, electricity, or fresh food. We lit the house with candles and warmed it with great blazes in all the fireplaces. The chef used the fireplaces to cook the bounteous fare that he already had on hand for the giant New Year's party, which had to be canceled. When the storage freezers shut down, I watched with incredulous eyes as servants saved slabs of meat by tossing them into the snow. It was a happy time.

When we returned to California, I lost the grasp I thought I had managed to get on Mother's attention. She went back to work on an elaborate costume drama, *The Three Musketeers*, unhappy about playing second fiddle to Gene Kelly. One day in her pink and white boudoir, she announced she was going to marry Uncle Bob. I took this to mean that I would have to be sharing her with yet another person.

"What's marriage?" I asked.

"Well," she said, gently tugging me closer. "We will all live *together*—you, Nana, me, and Uncle Bob. Except now Uncle Bob will be your daddy. You know what a daddy is."

"Yes, I have a daddy."

"Well now you'll have *two* daddies, and one will live with you all of the time."

I couldn't quite grasp this. While I thought Uncle Bob was fine, I already had a wonderful father. It's true that he was working too hard at Lucy's and hadn't shown up much lately, but I felt a fierce loyalty to him. (Eventually, I agreed, at Mother's suggestion, to call Uncle Bob "Papa.")

When it seemed that I would be losing Mother again, this time to "marriage," I embarked on a series of high jinks intended, I suppose, to recapture her attention. First came the hat tantrum in Saks Fifth Avenue, and, when that didn't work, I cooked up some mischief in our backyard. I was forbidden to go unescorted beyond the high fence that surrounded every house of ours. Also, because I could fall and hurt myself, I was never to run or climb trees. But an overriding rule, one that was unspoken, mandated that I was never to make friends with children who were, well, "unsuitable"—that is, children who were not the offspring of important members of the movie colony.

At Crown Drive, however, there was a way to break that cardinal rule. I found that I could duck from Gran's notice and slip away to the leafy quiet of our isolated woods along the back property line. Sometimes I just sat and thought, but before long I discovered that we shared a fence with middle-class neighbors who had noisy sons and a little girl my age. I never even knew her name, but we met through the fence and could inspect each other by peering through the cracks. Our little ten-minute chats would be cut short each Thursday as Gran hollered for me to come back to the house.

One day I saw that the little girl was wearing high-top sneakers, corduroy pants, her brother's baseball cap, and a T-shirt. It was the neatest outfit I had ever seen. She thought that my starched pinafore, hair ribbons, and long white stockings held up by a garter belt were neat, too, so we swapped. When I turned up at our back door dressed like Buckwheat, Gran did not explode (I was *never* spanked), but she gave me a lecture and put me to bed. One of our maids washed, ironed, and returned the little girl's clothing; she was allowed to keep my clothes and I never saw her again.

Mother was slightly irked. "I heard what you did the other day," she said, arranging a stern face. "I don't want to hear that."

I made a stronger bid for her notice as her wedding to Uncle Bob approached in late April. Without giving the deed much thought, I pinched two packs of Juicy Fruit from the barroom and stored them under my mattress. Then, at my first unattended nap one afternoon, I got out the gum and chewed it into a terrific wad that braided nicely through my curls. On seeing what I'd done, Gran nearly fainted. As if I had suffered a coronary arrest, I was rushed by limousine to M-G-M, where the head hairdresser tried soap, alcohol, chemicals, anything to dissolve the snarled globs, especially at the forehead where a nice big hunk had stuck to my scalp. In the end the only solution was to trim three years of hair down to a short pageboy and just leave the bald spot in front. I adored it.

"How *could* you have *done* this to your beautiful *hair?*" pleaded Mother in a hurt voice.

"I don't know, Mommy," I said, and I didn't.

Maybe I sensed that the big upcoming wedding would put me in a spotlight again surrounded by clamoring, grasping people. In any case, I didn't want to have waist-length curls when I wore what Mother kept calling my "1835 dress," meaning empire style with a high waist and puff sleeves.

As it happened, their wedding on April 26, 1948, turned into a fiasco that, to Mother's mortification, was gleefully reported as such by most of the world press. Her luck was changing with the times. The new medium of television was posing a threat to movie production and profits. A dispiriting cloud from the House Un-American Activities Committee hung over movieland, and old L. B. Mayer's reign at M-G·M would soon fall to a challenger who was unfriendly to Mother. Hollywood's Golden Era was now long gone with the wind, and the few remaining glamour gals from that era were beginning to look passé.

After Mother's ubiquitous (some said scandalous) public romancing of the prior year, it didn't help that the wedding was overdone and that Mother, at twenty-seven, was beginning to look a little too well-fed. The press was just waiting to give her a kick in the pants. Maybe she sensed how badly the event was going in that respect, because after the ceremony she retired upstairs early to lie down and later denied that she had fainted from nerves.

It was all so well intended. Since the Crown Drive house was too small for a splashy wedding, Billy Wilkerson loaned his vast place on Sunset Boulevard, which was then stripped and redecorated by M-G-M. Florists followed like crop dusters with 6,000 gardenias and gladioli. The nuptials began on a cloudless day with a private ceremony in the living room before twelve witnesses, then opened up to a garden party for an all-star guest list of sixty-four. Later, seventy-four members of the press were admitted, and, savoring disaster, they were the last to go.

Having zipped through three elopements (two with my father), Mother wanted her fourth big day to be lovely and dignified. Since the press had done so much to build her up, Mother paid careful attention to their needs. They were given both fact-sheets and entrée to the champagne party. To accommodate their deadlines, the ceremony was moved from 4:00 P.M. to 2:00. The matron of honor was a magazine writer, while the host was a publisher, and the bridal couple cooperated with photographers until Mother's knees gave out.

Nonetheless, starting with the early editions, the coverage was scathing. Reporters noted that "filmland's number one cinema cutie" had gotten through a ceremony of "six drama-packed minutes" after which, when photog-

raphers swarmed through the garden door, she seemed as
nervous as a "high school bride." She wept, shook,
gasped, breathed, whispered, and collapsed. The *Los Angeles Times* wondered about a case of nerves in "the
blonde star who has coolly torn out men's hearts on the
screen."

I was identified as the "shaking" flower girl who looked
bewildered. After the I-do's, I kissed Mother's wrist, and
she bent to kiss my forehead, patted me kindly, and said,
"Now you run off to Granny."

My new papa (who had, for a $500,000 settlement, shed
his fourth wife just three days before) then told Mother,
"This is forever," to which she replied, "Yes, darling."
Life reported this last exchange in a story headlined "LANA
TURNER'S FOURTH AND POSITIVELY LAST TIME," noting
dryly that "Nobody with a spark of romance could help
being touched." Mother was so upset with *Life,* especially
by a photo they chose that made her look dazed and bovine
(Bob looked chinless, I looked intense), that for years she
refused to have any further contact with the magazine.

The press had a field day reporting every hilarious detail: the heaving buffet table that displayed a ham em-
bossed with "I love you" (as well as a roast beef which
seemed to reply, "She loves him"); a precious little European country scene that had been fashioned out of food
using figures carved from potatoes; and a wishing well
woven from carrots (live goldfish swam in its streams, and
the hills were made of caviar); the ice-sculpted figures of
the bride and groom locked in an embrace that stood melting on a pedestal; and the two lobsters frozen in blocks
that were said to represent the newlyweds in the act of
taking their pleasure.

And then there was Baby Cheryl. Decked out in a lace-
over-turquoise satin gown, my face wan and sad, I was
the subject of rather cruel interest by the cameramen, especially after they lost the bridal couple, who ducked upstairs early, a maneuver that enraged the press. By now, I
was frightened of crowds. I was having persistent nightmares of the fan riot in New York—claws reaching at me,
the sky red and black. In addition, my life had been rigidly

scheduled to the quarter hour, and a mid-afternoon dress-up affair like this played havoc with my internal clock.

While Gran and Nana merrily drank champagne, I was able to slip away to stare goggle-eyed at the festivities. Moving around under a warm April sun, I squirmed uncomfortably in scratchy leather gloves that were too tight. I think I curtsied to Joan Crawford and Louella Parsons, but the only guest I talked with was the Presbyterian minister, who later crowed to the press that "the little girl told me it was her ambition to be a missionary when she grows up." I said this to please Nana, who was standing within earshot, resplendent in slightly moth-eaten foxes and mauve silver satin. Nana always plied me with tales about her donations to African missions for starving children. Of course, I had fibbed to the reverend. I was really going to be Billy the Kid.

All of a sudden I spied the six-layer wedding cake. It was a photo opportunity that set off the lensmen like a blood trail before sharks. As the cameras snapped, Gran snatched me away (a fact widely reported) and steered me to a corner. There stood Nana, chatting with Gladys "Gladdy" Heath, Gran's old friend and former boss at the beauty shop.

"This child is ready for her nap," huffed Gran to Nana, handing me over.

"Aw, c'mon, Millie," said Gladdy. "Let the kid stay."

"No—nap time."

"Letturr-r stay," insisted Gladdy, who wasn't a regular imbiber of champagne. As Nana watched in alarm and I burst into tears, the two former beauty shop colleagues grabbed my wrists in a tug-of-war.

"To *bed.*"

"*Why?*"

"I said so."

"Millie, it's early."

"No!"

Gladdy at last gave in, and I was marched upstairs to a borrowed bed where I lay for what seemed like endless hours, listening to a twelve-piece string orchestra that wouldn't stop. Mother had unwisely assumed the press would leave when the guests wandered off, allowing her and her bridegroom to slip away to their honeymoon bungalow just down the road at the Beverly Hills Hotel. But the nondeadline press staged a sit-in waiting for her exit, all the while scooping up caviar hills and souvenirs from the house. To call in their stories, they tied up the phone lines, leaving Mother to fume in a bedroom upstairs.

When the bridal couple did finally manage to escape in their limo, they discovered that someone had filled the hubcaps with industrial nuts and bolts.

Twelve

The autumn after the wedding, I was reduced to having one daddy again when my natural father ran into troubles and went out of my life completely.

The trouble began in the early morning hours of September 1, 1948, when Beverly Hills narcotics agents broke into a Coldwater Canyon bungalow and arrested four people for possession of a dangerous substance called marijuana. One was movie star Robert Mitchum. Another was Dad's fiancée, Lila Leeds.

Screaming front-page headlines told the story, educating Mr. and Mrs. America about usage in certain select circles of an illegal weed grown in Mexico. It was a drug, they said, that when smoked was as powerful and addictive as heroin. Readers scratched their heads. Probably not one citizen in a hundred had heard of marijuana.

Ever since the disclosure of silent star Wallace Reid's death as a result of morphine addiction in 1923, Hollywood's never-ending dalliance with drugs had been soft-pedaled by the papers. Churchgoing America had been outraged over the Reid shocker, and thereafter the movie industry quietly closed ranks with press and law enforcement officials to keep Hollywood drug abuse out of the public glare. The Coldwater Canyon arrests, coming as they did right out of the blue, rocked America. Clearly, the careers of Mitchum, a major star at RKO, and Leeds, a Warner Brothers starlet, were in ruins.

Mitchum had gotten to know Lila at Dad's restaurant two years earlier, and on that late summer night, apparently on the spur of the moment, he and a pal dropped by to visit Lila and a girlfriend at Lila's small hillside house (called by reporters a "marijuana shack"). As Mitchum walked through the door, he threw a pack of joints on the table. "Let's get high," he said. "Help yourselves." Drug agents who had surrounded the house suddenly burst through the door. (As it happened, Mitchum had been scheduled the next morning to make a speech on the City Hall steps in honor of National Youth Week.)

My father was stunned by the news because he loved Lila. The scandal also came at a time when he was battling his own difficulties. His mother had died and there were the problems of selling the family house in Crawfordsville and possibly losing the poolroom as a result of an expired lease. Worst of all, Lucy's was going under. While still one of the trendiest and friendliest spots in town, it ran a monthly deficit that continued to mount. He would have to cut his losses.

Dad knew that Lila had smoked pot ever since she tried it at a St. Louis party three years before with members of the Stan Kenton orchestra, and sometimes she overdid it. A late party one night made her oversleep and miss a work call, which resulted in her being suspended from Warner Brothers. She was often stoned, and his friends cautioned Dad that she had a problem, but he knew pot was no enslaving "devil's weed," as it had been painted in the unintentionally hilarious 1936 cautionary film *Reefer Madness*. He liked alcohol himself, and what others did to feel good didn't concern him. But he and Lila were a well-known couple, and a scandal involving her could by association tar him with the same brush.

They had been seeing each other since soon after Dad's divorce from Mother, and it escaped no one's notice that Lila resembled Mother in appearance and in background. Born in Kansas of Irish-Swedish descent, she was brought to Hollywood by her mother at fifteen. Within a month, she found herself buttonholed on the street by former child star Jackie Cooper, who asked, "Why aren't you in the movies?"

As a start, Cooper got her one of the coveted, high-visibility hat-check jobs at Ciro's, which was where she met Dad. She was soon signed by M-G-M, and, like Mother, her third acting assignment was that of a Eurasian girl. The picture was Mother's own *Green Dolphin Street,* in which a bit role called for her to drug the leading man and roll him.

Lila and Dad soon became a celebrated battling twosome. They were involved in scuffles on the front steps of Ciro's and Mocambo. Dad punched some man who had insulted her at the Chanteclair restaurant, and Lila tried suicide that March. Yet they spoke of marriage, and Dad gave her a three-carat diamond engagement ring, the same ring that he was forced to retrieve on hands and knees in the Mays' garden.

But if Lila were convicted for possession of drugs, she would almost surely face a stretch in prison. It was an impossible situation, and Dad moved fast. He and partner Al Mathes leased Lucy's to new operators for a percentage of the profits, and he arranged to go abroad, thinking to stay indefinitely.

It was sad for Lila how things turned out. She and Mitchum both drew sixty days in the county jail. She claimed that, while serving her time, she was introduced by inmates to heroin, and it grew into an addiction.

Two weeks after her release, she was speeding along the Sunset Strip at 3:00 A.M. when she smashed into a car waiting at a red light. She sustained a broken arm and other injuries. Climbing from the wreck, she said, "Why did this have to happen to me? I've been in enough trouble."

When police arrived, Lila was gone. Three hours later, they learned that a passerby had picked her up and rushed her to his own doctor. The passerby was Al Mathes. One version has it that Father, on a brief return visit from Europe, was spending the evening with Lila, who sped off in her car to keep a 3:00 A.M. date with her drug connection, and that's when the smashup occurred.

Dad received a call about it, but not wanting to risk the publicity, he turned to his partner and said, "Al, will you do me a favor?" Mathes explained to patrol officers that he just happened to be driving by and saw Lila standing near the wreck.

The macho sleepy-eyed Robert Mitchum, after serving his time, was embraced again by the public, continuing on to this day as one of film's most durable leading men. Lila appeared that fall in *Wild Weed* ("See and Learn the Truth about those Wild Hollywood parties," said the ad), and much later in something called *She Shoulda Said No*.

During the hard times that followed, Lila hocked the fabled Crane diamond for $750. The press stumbled across her again in the seventies living in Los Angeles, where she worked as a faith healer of addicts.

I get sentimental over memories of that last visit with Dad before he sailed away to France. He and Al Mathes were sharing columnist Jimmy Fidler's big house in Sherman Oaks. He was out of Lucy's by then, so we had the whole sun-filled day together. He had invited friends for a buffet brunch by the pool, but I felt his full loving attention on me.

We romped in the pool with Margo and Flynn, his gentle boxers. We showed off by jumping from the diving board as I rode horsey on Dad's neck. Encouraged by applause, we did it over and over again. I ate with the grown-ups, enjoying everything I wanted, including a strawberry ice cream bombe that was inscribed "Hooray for Cheryl."

When it came time for my afternoon nap, Daddy bore me on his shoulders to his bedroom, a big wood-paneled space upstairs with louvered windows through which sunlight bounced off the pool to form lacy patterns on the ceiling. With infinite tenderness, he undressed me and wrapped me in one of his monogrammed pajama tops which dragged on the floor and was slippery on my skin.

"This feels so good, Daddy. What is it?"

"Silk, honey."

He gave me a big kiss on my lips (the first I can remember from anyone), and tucked me into an enormous bed with cool silk sheets that were the same yummy peach color as his pajamas. After drawing the curtains he said, "I love you, Baby," and softly closed the door. I sighed. I wished I lived with my daddy.

But though I was only five, I knew the significance of that day. That was good-bye. He was sailing for Europe, leaving for good, going to Paris, from where I had just returned myself only weeks before.

Earlier that summer Gran and I had joined the Topping honeymoon in Cannes, while Nana took her summer off in

Scotland. Gran and I set up house at the Miramar Hotel, paying visits, when we were allowed, to Mother and Papa, who had taken a high oceanfront suite. It comes back as a pleasant blur, that summer, spent among French waiters and baby-sitters. It was a time of such exotica as mosquito netting around my bed, the fascinating sight of hair under women's arms, and, for my birthday, a rum-soaked cake that tasted like gasoline. I even learned to speak some French.

I didn't see all that much of my parents, and unfortunately Gran hated the sand, so our seashore visits were brief. The newlyweds rented an eighty-foot yacht, off whose fantail I learned to dive with an aqualung. Mother tried it once, but when her hair crept in view around the goggle-eye mask it looked to her like tentacles, and I watched with fright as her screams and thrashings produced an explosion of bubbles. She refused ever to go down again.

During our return trip on the *Ile De Grasse,* I seized my first chance at total freedom. Violent storms rocked the boat, adding two days to the crossing and making everyone seasick—everyone but *me.* Like Eloise at the Plaza, I exulted in the free run of the boat, exploring without an escort every gunwale and gangway. At one point Gran caught me playing on a high perch where there were no railings. As virtually the only child in first class, I was everybody's pet, and the crewmen gave me candy.

One day I managed to slip into the ship's screening room and watch my first movie. It was called *That Lady in Ermine.* I was less impressed by the image projection process than by the pretty costumes. It starred Betty Grable, and, since no one explained these things to me, I did not understand that Miss Grable and my mother did the same kind of work. Who knew? It would be nine years before I was allowed to see Mother on the screen.

Dad sailed for Europe via New York that autumn. In Paris he first tried his hand at writing a gossip column called ''Champagne and Vinegar,'' which he hoped to sell as a correspondent feature in the *Los Angeles Herald.* In his debut column one prominent item noted that Robert Mitchum was then awaiting trial on drug charges. ''Yet,'' said Dad, "if Mitchum should come to Paris he could attend a small private jive club on the Left Bank where waiters come around to the tables and roll the marijuana cigarettes for you." No less than three Hollywood stars, he noted, were "seen entering" the place the previous week. The column might have helped open doors for him among café society, but it did not attract much interest and he moved on to other things.

Mother and my stepfather returned from their honeymoon that September to join the high-life of Manhattan and retreat for long stays at Round Hill. She liked being Mrs. Henry J. Topping, Jr., and soon announced that she was retiring from the screen. She was pregnant again, expecting in April or May, and putting on pounds, thanks to the French chef's food at Round Hill.

Nana had taught me how to print, and I realized that this could open a tunnel to Mother. Using gray airplane stationery on which Nana drew lines, I spent hours each week block-printing notes that went, "Dear Mommy, I was vaccinated. When are you coming home? I miss you. Love, Cheryl." I don't remember any replies, but then Mother would never have stopped to wonder if she were feeding my emotional needs.

Round Hill kept her madly on the run. The Topping brothers gave parties for as many as 200 people, and its twelve bedrooms were packed on weekends. "Some of the couples who slept there were married," Mother recalled in her book, "and some were not—it didn't seem to matter. Couples who were together in the evening would have changed partners by the next morning when the ritual Bloody Marys were delivered to their rooms."

All I knew was that everyone had gone. Mother was off again with my new daddy. My real daddy had left for good. Gran lived elsewhere. I lived alone with an elderly nanny in the back of a house. I saw only servants whom I was not permitted to speak to, and I never left the grounds.

I accepted isolation as being part of every little girl's life. I had no way to make a comparison. Gran, thinking to assuage my loneliness, brought me a calico kitten, but it gave both Gran and me ringworm and the next day kitty was gone.

A note finally came saying that Gran, Nana, and I were to come spend another Christmas in Connecticut.

This trip was even nicer than the first, six weeks in length and not quite as snowy. As a Christmas present to me, my stepfather had the grounds keepers clear a line of trees through the woods for a toboggan slide. It ran a steep, straight half mile down to the frozen lake, and we got off to a 25-mph start by trailing behind a jeep and cutting the rope. We shot down the run in howling winds, Mother, Papa, and I, screaming and laughing with delight as if each time were the first.

Once Mother, Papa, and a friend of theirs skidded off the track and hit a rock which flipped them into a snowbank. The laughter stopped. Everyone was badly shaken; in the crush, my stepfather's chin had slammed into the back of Mother's neck, compressing vertebrae and giving her a back injury that sent her into seclusion for a week.

One afternoon, as I was playing under Nana's supervision at Round Hill's farm, I tried to sprout fairy wings in the hay loft. I lost my footing, fell back on concrete, and snapped my wrist. The local hospital put on a cast, and that night I was groggy from ether when Papa brought me home. As he stood in the entrance hall clasping me in his arms, my eyes followed his upward gaze. Mother stood poised where the double staircase crossed, looking plaintive in a Lady Macbeth peignoir.

"Baby," she sighed, beckoning with wiggly fingers, "I was worried to *pieces.*"

Papa bounded up the stairs like Rhett Butler and deposited me in her arms. It was the kind of nice cinematic moment that often happened around Mother. But I must have still smelled of ether. "Oh *take* her," she said, passing me back. "I'm going to faint."

A while later in her bedroom, she spied me through the mirror and waved me inside. "Next week," she said, "Bob and I are leaving to spend spring in Florida. Baby, there's just no reason to go back to California."

Thirteen

Mother had suffered a miscarriage during those six weeks at Round Hill. She was physically drained, and since M-G-M had placed her on contract suspension for refusing to make another costume drama, she and Papa headed off for nearly five months of deep-sea fishing in the Caribbean aboard Papa's yacht, the *Snuffy*.

I returned to the empty house on Crown Drive, and that spring I might have sunk into despair were it not for the fact that I suddenly acquired a lovely new friend. One day she simply appeared, sitting on my bed, smiling. Her name was Elizabeth, and she existed only in my mind. She was my age and my size. She was very confident, very smart, and very pretty. Not blond like Mother, my imaginary playmate had naturally curly, short black hair and blue eyes. In fact, Elizabeth was perfect. She never cried, and she'd tell me not to be afraid of other kids at birthday parties. She was vividly real and got me through a lot of hard moments. I made space for her in the bed, at the table, and in the car. She lived with me in my room, where we played house and spoke out loud to each other.

Though it hurt me, Nana gently scoffed at my friend's existence, but wise old Gran spoke to her through me. "Elizabeth drank all her milk," she'd say. "Tell her she's a good girl. And what about you?"

With Mother's absences now lasting for up to six months at a stretch, during which time she would hardly phone or write me, Gran began to spend more time again at Crown Drive. Asserting an authority over Nana that was clearly not granted by Mother, Gran sought to soften my melancholy by arranging for me to play with Vana, the daughter of actor Van Heflin, and with Joan Bennett's daughter, Stephanie Wanger. One on one, I was not so afraid of other children, but even at those times, Elizabeth hovered at my shoulder.

Since I was being raised as a princess, my daily calendar read like a court diary of appointments. Bathed at 7:00 A.M., I was dressed and curled for breakfast by 8:15, when I sat down to eggs or oatmeal on a tray in my room. "Good morning, Cook," I would say while being served, and no more. I was not allowed to chat with the help or go into their area. There was the difference of class, and also, maybe I would slow them down or touch a hot pot.

School began at 9:00 sharp, a rotating sequence of reading, drawing, spelling, knitting, and sums. Even before age four I could write such doggerel as "the cat jumped into the hat."

Lunch was served on a tray at 11:30. Nana called it having our "elevenses." Next came a one-hour nap followed by a long walk up a Crown Drive so empty of autos as to be simply perfect for hopscotch (which, unfortunately, was deemed to be too rough for me to play). Except for occasional visits to Vana Heflin's or Stephanie Wanger's house, four o'clock brought English teatime and an hour of unstructured play. Free as meadowlarks, Elizabeth and I cuddled our dollies and made small talk that was frightfully adult: "This child won't eat her oatmeal, Elizabeth. What does one do?"

A tray brought dinner at 5:00 P.M., then another bath, another hundred strokes with a swatch of silk, and bed before 6:30. Having been awake for barely eleven hours, I usually tossed for a long while, listening to the sound of dogs barking from across the valley and to Nana's radio across the room. Often I stared at my Mommy doll and at a new addition Gran had bought for me to perch atop the bookcase. It was a nightlight clock, inside of which lived a little two-inch girl dressed in blue with hair like mine who swung back and forth on a pendulum to the rhythm of the tick-tock. The glow from the clock's internal light spilled onto the Mommy doll, and as I gazed at these two prized objects, I could see myself as the tiny little girl herself, swinging beneath the baleful stare of a blond colossus.

During these wide-awake hours before Elizabeth came into my life, my mind sailed into such transports of longing for Mother that I came to dread twilight. Twilight meant moist eyes and a gnawing in my tummy. (For years, even as an adult, I tried to avoid twilight by turning lights on early and drawing the shades.)

Things finally began to pick up in June when Mother and Papa returned to Los Angeles from Florida. Mother described that homecoming in a bylined article for *Modern Screen*. She wrote:

> [Cheryl] was sleeping when I tiptoed in, and for a long moment I stood by her bed and looked at her. Her hair was tousled on the pillow. On her face was that lovely pure expression of a sleeping child.
>
> [After Cheryl awoke] she cried "Oh Mommy, I went for a walk yesterday and saw the prettiest horse." And then, as sleep rolled away, she hugged me to her and said, "Mommy is it really you? Oh you're really home. You won't go away anymore, will you?"
>
> I won't ever again. I don't think I'll ever separate from my little girl until the day she wants to go herself.

I remember Mother telling me that night of her return that she was now determined to make "a real home for us," but that Crown Drive was too small. She and Papa would not be moving in. They had moved instead to a bungalow at the Bel Air Hotel and would soon be looking for a new house.

I asked Mother one day why she always went away.

"Because I work," she replied.

"Why do you?"

"Well, Baby, just who do you think pays for all those dresses and toys and riding lessons you love so much? Mother's got to work and make money." I wanted to tell

her that I'd give up all that stuff if she'd just stay at home,
but I didn't.

I was given permission to watch a television set (newly
installed in the barroom) during my free-time hour at four
o'clock. I was devoted to the Hopalong Cassidy Western
series, mainly because I loved the star's handsome sidekick, a cowboy named Lucky. Lucky got the girl while
Hoppy kissed his horse, and I nursed a mad crush on him.
One day as I sat watching the show, Mother passed through
the room and I grabbed the chance to engage her.

"Look, Mommy, there's Lucky!"

She peered at the screen.

"I know him," she said absently. "That's Russell Hay-
den."

"You do?!" I gasped. I felt both awe and doubt.

"Of course," she said, adding that because of her work
she knew lots of actors. But my five-year-old mind could
not put Mother's "work at the studio" together with what
Betty Grable did in *That Lady in Ermine* and I was unable
to comprehend that she might really associate with Lucky.
I decided she was just showing off—she couldn't know
Lucky.

To make up for the disappointment of my last birthday
with its gasoline-flavored cake, Mother promised something special for my sixth birthday that July. On the day
before the event, she came into my room. "Darling," she
said, her face looking solemn, "I'm so sorry to have to
tell you this but I forgot to mail the invitations to your
birthday. We won't have a party this year." She studied
my face. "Oh, but we'll have fun anyway, you and I.
After your nap tomorrow, I'll take you horseback riding."

I had not blinked. No party, but at least I'd have
Mommy. I could also look forward that next morning to
receiving a roomful of presents, a hundred or more, from
Mommy's friends and associates. Routinely, Gran and I
would pick through them to decide which we'd send to an
orphanage. I had no regrets passing most of the stuff on
to other children because the largess was overwhelming
and the duplication often comic. (Perhaps as a result of
those days, I have an underdeveloped instinct to possess

things. I've given away a treasury of clothes, jewelry, and furniture.)

The afternoon of my birthday, dressed in matching cow-girl outfits, Mother and I drove out to the Riviera Country Club in Brentwood where I had been taking riding lessons. Waiting for us in the driveway was Papa, standing with a big smile on his face and a boxer puppy nestled in one arm. "Happy Birthday," he sang out and held up the puppy to lick my ear.

We headed for the stables, and as we turned the ranch house corner, I saw my regular gang of star babies, dressed up like cowpokes, singing happy birthday.

The best was yet to come. Galloping toward us from the corral's far end was a cowboy on a palomino horse, leading a black pony with ribbons streaming from its mane. The cowboy was my idol, Lucky. Mother swears that I fainted. Christmas in Connecticut—now this!

"Happy birthday, Cheryl," drawled Lucky, dismount-ing and planting a kiss on my cheek. Mother joined on the other cheek to pose for press photographers. Pop-pop-pop-pop. The black pony that Lucky led by the reins was Prince Valiant, and he was mine—Mother's present.

She must have spent long afternoons on the *Snuffy* plan-ning the party. Instead of using the usual clowns and ma-gicians, she hired a whole rodeo show to entertain me and my twenty-six guests. There were trick riders and steer-roping contests and a tribe of Ute Indians who danced and crowned me princess of the tribe. (Their chief was Iron Eyes Cody, best known today as the "weeping Indian" in the famous antipollution commercial.) The star babies wore denims, and, instead of dining on the usual fare of creamed chicken in patty shells, they chomped down miniature hot dogs and burgers to their tummies' delight.

From that day onward I looked at Mother a little differ-ently. I saw that she did love me. She did think about me. And if she could produce Lucky, she had real power. I learned years later that Gran and Mother had quarreled just before the birthday party. Mother accused Gran of alien-ating my affections, of turning daughter against mother. "Are you out of your mind, Lana?" Gran said. "Do you know that when you're away she sneaks into your closet and smells your clothes? Cheryl *worships* you.'' Whereupon Mother burst into tears and drove away.

The new house Mother found that September stood on four acres in the exclusive Holmby Hills district of Bel Air. A staff of ten was needed to maintain its twenty-four rooms, terraced garden, pool, tennis court, kennels, and greenhouse. Facing Mapleton Drive at the corner of Sunset, the white two-story Georgian was neighbor to Humphrey Bogart and Lauren Bacall. Beyond them up the drive lived Bing Crosby, and across Sunset were Alan Ladd and our old friend Sonja Henie. We were moving up.

Though she had not made a film in more than a year, Mother had been voted in a national poll as the nation's Number One Box Office Attraction. Three of her leading men of the prior year who had also landed on the top-ten list, Clark Gable, Spencer Tracy, and Van Heflin, ran an ad in the trade papers saying, ''Lana, Thanks a million, Love, Clark, Spence and Van.''

Though Betty Grable still sold more tickets, Mother's every move and utterance were now lightning rods for publicity. She was top-of-the-heap, and Metro was paying her $5,000 a week when she was not on suspension. But she was indeed refusing all scripts. She had decided to live a little.

Having grown fond of the finer things she saw at Round Hill, she was determined that our proper movie-star mansion at 120 South Mapleton Drive would be filled with a meticulous selection of Limoges, cut crystal, and monogrammed silver. Though Mother paid for the house and fancy furnishings (Papa had just lost a lot of money), it was named Mapletop.

Even after Round Hill, I was impressed with Mapletop. Its entrance featured a wedding-cake staircase that curved wider at the bottom. Above a black-and-white marble floor hung a crystal chandelier the size of a Christmas tree. The pine-paneled library featured books bought by the yard (which no one but me would touch), and the dining-room table sat thirty-two.

I had my own big bedroom and Nana had hers, connected through a pair of bath-dressing rooms. All airy, new, and light, my bedroom had a white carpet and half-canopy bed with tied-back curtains made of pink-and-blue plaid organdy. My bathroom dropped off into a sunken tub with gold dolphin fixtures. The only reminders of Crown Drive rested atop the bookcase—my Mommy doll and the little clock girl on a swing.

Mother had planned for me to attend Marymount that autumn. Marymount was a top Catholic grammar school for girls in Beverly Hills, and to ensure my acceptance she had for years been contributing to its fund drives. When she applied for my admission to first grade, however, she was politely told that it was their policy not to take children of divorced parents. She exploded, then went elsewhere. In the end, I was admitted to the more congenial St. Paul the Apostle, a small parish school in Westwood. Its students were the children of local working people—clerks, carpenters, shopkeepers, and the like. Neither the children nor their parents had ever clapped eyes on a Hollywood princess. Then again, neither had I, at least not that I was aware of. As far as I knew, all I was was a *Ute* princess.

As most every child does, I dreaded the first day of school. I can't imagine how my white-gloved arrival went over with those regular apple-cheeked kids. I arrived in a chauffeur-driven limousine accompanied by a uniformed nanny. While I wore the school's regulation blue jumper, the standard beanie with a pompom on top accentuated that I was already three inches taller than everyone. I was also the only one crying. All the other kids had spent their kindergarten year together, and I was the stranger. They saw my shame about the tears, my anguished shyness, and my waist-length curls with big pink bows above both ears.

The teacher placed me in a front-row seat, and the stares from behind made my back burn. I wanted to be dead. Since most of the children read my fear as standoffishness, it took weeks before anyone spoke to me. One day at recess, as I shrank back against a wall, a huddle of girls began to eye me. Finally, they approached.

"Who's that lady in the uniform?" one girl asked.

"M-my Nana," I explained.

"Why doesn't your mother come to pick you up?" said another.

"I don't know . . . My mother works, she works."

"Why don't you ever stay after school and play?" demanded a third.

"Because they want me at home," I said lamely. I didn't know why myself.

Exchanging shrugs, they turned and walked away.

That night I told Gran that everyone hated me, and she gathered me into her arms to explain that these things take time. Indeed, I did adjust after a while to being the conspicuous outsider. Though I liked to study, I learned how to conceal the fact that I could already read, write, and add long columns. I learned to hide what our French chef put in my lunchbox—the carrot curls, linen napkins, and fancy sandwiches with the crusts trimmed off.

I finally persuaded Gran to drive me to school, instead of the chauffeur. Still, she used her powder-blue Cadillac convertible with red leather seats, or worse, one of the house's station wagons with Mapletop printed in inch-high gold letters on its wooden sides. ("What's a Mapletop?" they taunted.) I even learned how to cope with having my hair yanked, muttering my pain to Elizabeth.

One day in the second month a little girl walked up to me at recess. "Hello, I'm Edwina," she said sweetly, and I felt a gush of warmth. She was a plump child, and the only other girl with huge hair ribbons like mine. She had the black-curled, pale-eyed beauty of Elizabeth Taylor, whom I was starting to see as a guest in our house. Edwina's father was a butcher, and it was her aunt's shop that stitched all of my handmade underthings. We became supportive friends, and I began to see a little less of Elizabeth.

Before long I developed a terrible crush on an older girl at school. Her name was Charlene, and she seemed as pretty as Mother, with green eyes, a cute figure, and long blond hair. She let me hold her hand or a fold in her skirt as I followed her around, yearning and moon-eyed. I was dubbed "Charlene's Little Shadow" and always flushed with embarrassment while standing my ground by her side.

Seven years my senior, she just laughed sweetly and went on her way.

I was almost starting to feel like a member of the human race when, one day in that first semester, my chance to belong was dashed. Once again a group of girls circled me in the schoolyard, but now their tone was accusing.

"We know who your mother is—"

"She's Lana Turner, *isn't* she?"

"No, she's not," I said feebly. "She's my mommy."

"She is so—*we* know."

They chimed together and sneered, "She's *La*-na *Tur*-ner, na-*na*-na-na-*na!*"

The way they said it, it sounded like a very bad thing to be. I felt so dumb. I didn't know.

Later that afternoon I sat thinking in the glassed-in loggia that overlooked our tennis court at home. Mother hurried in from shopping with her arms full of parcels, and I decided to be daring.

"Hello, Lana Turner," I said.

Her mouth dropped. "What did you say?"

I said it again in a tiny fearful voice.

"Where did you hear that?" she said, her eyes glaring.

I burst into tears. Putting her packages on the floor, she drew me to a sofa and lifted me onto her lap. It took time for me to explain my bewilderment, and she seemed to understand. Yes, she was Lana Turner and she was my mommy too. She told me about actresses who became something called stars and how people became interested in what stars did. "We're not any different from those schoolmates of yours," she said, "but this is the way I earn money to pay for your toys and your pretty clothes."

"Why aren't I named Turner too?" I asked.

"Crane was your father's name," she said with a dismissive shrug.

I was not very reassured. The kids at school didn't use that tone in talking about anybody else's mother. It conveyed a mixture, I sensed, of resentment and envy and something else I couldn't really understand, but I think it was blame. What did they know about my mommy? Who told them things? In any case, the work that she did made me different from the others, and I didn't want to be singled out. I wanted to belong. Better still, to be invisible.

After months of brooding, I hit on an idea. Maybe I could win the approval of some of the girls if Gran let me give a party. Valentine's Day was coming. She said yes, and we set about making preparations. Nana and I spent afternoons cutting out red felt hearts edged in doilies to decorate the breakfast room where the luncheon would be held. We put up streamers and balloons. The cook made heart-shaped sandwiches, and I wore hearts stuck all over my dress. (Please love me.) I invited seven girls who seemed less hostile than the others, though I didn't know them very well. The only one who had ever visited Mapletop before was Edwina.

Everything was perfect and I was so excited. Mother was not there, but Gran and Nana would come in later to help with our games like pin-the-tail-on-the-donkey, while I played capable hostess, age six.

From the moment the doorbell rang, disaster began to unreel. Ushered into the hallway, the little girls gazed with wondering eyes at the butler, the chandelier, the staircase—and me. They were awed. I stiffened. If they had not been full of questions, we would have dined in silence.

"Who's that?" asked one, as a serving maid stepped away.

"The maid," I replied.

"You have a maid?"

When the woman came back to pass a platter, someone asked if she were the person who had prepared it.

"No," I interjected, "the cook made them."

"You have a *cook?*"

"Doesn't your mother cook?" accused a second girl.

"Gee, how big is this place?" frowned a third. And so it went, until one finally asked, "Where's Lana Turner?"

"Yeah, where's Lana Turner?" they all chimed in.

My heart sank as I realized that their mothers had told them to remember everything they saw and did—especially if they met Lana Turner—so they could retell it when they got home. Wide awake that evening at twilight, I vowed never again to have a party.

Fourteen

One day I looked out the window to see a surprising sight on Mapleton Drive. Policemen were stepping from squad cars and fanning out around the grounds as our butler opened the gates. In a short time they were joined by security guards in tan uniforms who had guns on their hips and guard dogs on leashes.

They lingered all day, and the next morning brought more mysterious doings. Floodlights were constructed on poles at points along the fence that edged our property. As I looked on with a wrinkled brow, workmen noticed me and elbowed each other, but no one volunteered to tell me what it was all about, and I didn't ask.

I learned later. One of Gran's half brothers, a son of Grandpa Henry Cowan by a later marriage, had been doing time in jail, where he bragged to a cellmate that he was Lana Turner's uncle. That triggered a plot to snatch Baby Cheryl for ransom. Someone tipped off the authorities, and the FBI contacted Mother. Nothing ever came of it except that for months afterward Mapletop's grounds were patrolled by attack dogs and guards disguised as gardeners, and at night the whole four acres were flooded with light.

I decided later that the kidnap idea was a little farfetched. A great-uncle would know little more about Baby Cheryl than what was printed in magazine articles and those "Homes of the Stars" maps in which our address was plainly listed. Still, Mother was linked to her big clan of Cowan kinfolk through Gran. Gran paid visits to Arkansas and made a practice of sending money home even though she could hardly afford it. Catching her in the act, Mother closed Gran's checking account and paid her bills directly, allowing her only pocket money after that.

Still, since I was born, Mother's rationale for keeping me isolated had been the fear of kidnapping, and after this incident she could feel that her high wall around me was more justified than ever. For the next six years, until the start of my teens, I would not be allowed to go alone beyond the eight-foot chain-link fence that surrounded Mapletop. I came to think of the world outside as "off property," the term my guardians used for it.

I faced any number of other boundaries. In those days Beverly Hills—and especially Mapleton Drive—was as sleepy as Dry Gulch. Still, I could not walk the three blocks to Stephanie's house. Selling Girl Scout cookies door-to-door, I was tailed by the butler. The only hard surface on which I could ride my bike was the tennis court, so, like a convict pacing his cell, I pedaled round and round in circles. Even when I began to be allowed to see children's movies like *Dumbo* and *Bambi,* they were run for me specially in an empty screening room at Metro.

There was a bright side to all this, I told myself, because after a while life at Mapletop brought me into more contact with Mother. News photos began to show me with a smile on my face. If she were there and the door to her gray and lavender bedroom was open, I could knock and go in. Saying little so as not to be dismissed as a nuisance, I simply sat and basked in her presence. Sometimes she said, "You know, Baby, you can talk about anything you want to with me," but I couldn't. These times were too precious to bring up anything disagreeable like loneliness. *She* was the problem, and I had a feeling that if I didn't please her, I wouldn't see her. Maybe I was afraid that she'd send me away like Gran.

In the evening when she and Papa went out, she allowed me to watch her be made up. She knew I adored to see her dressed up, and on special occasions, she would sometimes dart into my bedroom to give a twirl of her dress and a good-night embrace ("the lipstick," she'd say, if I went for a kiss).

In a whoosh of silk and chiffon she was off, leaving a

mist of perfume to curl round my pillow. I stared at my
Mommy doll and the girl on the swing, feeling protected
and contented for the moment, thanking my good fortune
that I had been able to stay awake until her visit. If I had
nodded off in the twilight, she would have looked in and
closed the door. I would have *missed* her.

Oftentimes at Mapletop I saw Mother during daylight
hours and, for the first time, actually eating breakfast. Returning each day from St. Paul's just after two o'clock, I
scampered up the back stairs (front stairs were verboten)
and pulled off my scratchy uniform. After Nana had
scrubbed, curled, and dressed me, she used the house in-
tercom to phone Mother, who, with Papa, hung out afternoons in Mapletop's barroom, a homey cocktail lounge of
fifties Moderne design.

"Mrs. Topping, your daughter is home," Nana would
say, as I held my breath. If there were business guests or
Mother wasn't in the mood, Nana tried to let me down
easily. "Pet, Mother's got company."

Otherwise, her crinkly smile signaled a go-ahead, and I
tore down the stairs. Usually there was Papa or Gran and
a guest or two. After introductions and curtsies, I took up
my regular place just beside Mother in a white leather club
chair. She always sat alongside a felt-top card table on
which rested a drink. I stood there, fascinated by her, my
feet glued to the floor, and as the grown-ups talked, I
never looked away from her. She hardly noticed as I fid-
dled with her bracelet or stroked the fabric of her blouse.
During lulls in their conversation, I sometimes found
voice. "Oh Mommy, you're so pretty," I'd say. "I love
your hair, your beautiful hair." Her smile looked blasé,
but I knew she was pleased.

She and Papa were not working, and they often spent
evenings on the town. The great nightclub era was about
over, but Mocambo was still riding high, rivaled now by
LaRue's across the street (another Billy Wilkerson venture). They loved to throw parties with hired orchestras in
Mapletop's interconnecting rooms for as many as 150
guests.

Since Nana slept in a separate bedroom, I was able to
creep into the hallway and observe the parties through the

stair railings. I remember gazing with sleepy eyes at performers such as Johnny Ray, Sammy Davis, Frank Sinatra, and Judy Garland. Singer Billy Daniels ("That Old
Black Magic") was a particular favorite of Mother's until
Papa apparently got jealous and the whole thing blew up
in *Confidential* magazine.

Mother never knew of my stealthy party-gazing because
hardly anyone caught me at it. One night actor Robert
Wagner was prowling around in search of a bathroom and
nearly fell over me on the stairs. He laughed and agreed
when I begged him not to tell Mother.

Papa and I were friendly but never found ourselves alone
together. It still bothered him that I resisted calling him
Daddy. I often asked to meet his children by his previous
marriages ("Oh yes, certainly, some time"), but I never
did. He assured me that I would realize my cherished wish
of returning to Round Hill, but, in fact, it had already been
sold. The cost of maintaining it had become staggering.
The Topping millions were largely tied up in trusts, and
Papa's share had been dissipated by years of high living
and losses in such ventures as midget racing cars and plastic boats. Once again Mother was covering the household
expenses as well as some of her husband's.

As I was passing the pool one morning, Papa called me
over to a breakfast table where he sat dining by himself.
He was holding a Sunday newspaper.

"Now I don't want you to be upset," he said, "but I
have to tell you something. Your Daddy's been in a terrible accident." He held up the paper to show an article
bannered, "LANA'S EX IN PARIS CRASH." The photo
showed an auto that looked like crumpled tin foil.

"He was killed, sweetheart, I'm sorry," he said. "I
want you to be a brave little girl and not cry. He wouldn't
want you to. And, you know, this makes me your only
father now, so I guess you can finally call me Daddy."

My heart ached to think that my father was gone, that
I would never see him again. But why Papa felt it was his
job to break the news I never knew. It's true that, in speaking with me of my father, Mother barely disguised her
contempt for him. Six months earlier, as we were moving
into Mapletop, she had announced that Dad had married a

blond French movie star, adding: "And you are *never* going to meet her."

My thoughts slipped back to the happy times at Lucy's, the full mouth kisses, and the yummy silk sheets, but two years had gone by now since I had last seen him. He had become a remote, abstract figure, and, anyway, there was little time to mourn.

Loss piled on loss that spring of 1950. One late afternoon Nana instructed me not to come into her room because she was "having company," something she had seldom done, and when her door remained shut for hours, I peeked inside. Nana was sitting on her bed, facing two lady friends on chairs, and the room was filled with open luggage. I burst in. "Nana, Nana, where are you going?" It was time to retire to Scotland, she explained. She did what she could to comfort me, but in my shifting world, she had been my one anchor, and I sobbed myself to sleep that night.

In the morning I locked my arms around her waist and clung to her, refusing to go to school until Gran promised that Nana would still be there when I returned. She was not. Standing where Nana had stood the night before was my new governess, a tall, tailored woman named Miss Hulley. I was inconsolable, and for days could not push from my mind that Gran had lied to me and Nana didn't even say good-bye.

That spring Mother went back to work, starting a movie that took her out of town, and then, to add to the losses, I had to say farewell to my birthday pony. Prince Valiant had been mistreated by former owners, and while he was gentle with me, he had bitten stable hands and had to be destroyed.

Though I hated to see Nana go, the fact is she was overdue for retirement. She was eighty years old and still suffering from an arm injury incurred months before in a fall. In addition, I had reached the age when child care passed from a nanny, who could handle simple toilet training and the ABC's, to a governess, who could teach language and shape behavior.

A childless widow from Arizona in her early forties, Irene Hulley was well suited to the task. Slender, brown-eyed, and honey-haired, she wore a pageboy and tailored suits that gave her the trim look of a stewardess. She could never replace Nana, but her relative youth provided a vitality and modern outlook to which I soon warmed. She began by asking to meet my dollies, then gently coaxed from me an introduction to Elizabeth. She was good at her work.

Her last job had been as governess to Gary Cooper's daughter, Maria, and she was plugged into the younger set of Hollywood nannies and governesses who spent both their strolls through Beverly Glen Park and their days off together exchanging gossip. They called it the "nanny network," and, when Miss Hulley took me out for afternoon airings, I couldn't help but overhear the tittle-tattle that passed between them on the benches. (My life as a virtual shut-in was turning me into a little snoop.)

The network knew all about Joan Crawford's troubled relationship with Christina and Christopher. I heard the bed harness story and I shuddered. ("Well, it's going to be interesting to see how *those* two turn out," said Miss Hulley with satisfaction.) My big little ears scooped up tales about Bing Crosby's cruel treatment of his kids and the painful chaos in a lot of other Hollywood homes that was never to become public knowledge. A good nanny, of course, passed along tidbits from the network to her employer, so that in the end everyone in the movie colony knew how and why everyone else was handling—or mishandling—their kids. "Of course we all knew about Joan," Mother told me years later, "but nobody talked—the industry closed ranks." It never occurred to me that anyone would be curious as to what was going on at Mapleton.

Miss Hulley's best friend was governess to Fred MacMurray's children, Susan and Fred, Jr., and as a kind of counterbalance to the generally nasty gossip I was hearing on the nanny network, our occasional visits to the MacMurray place offered a sunny example of a real-life father who really did know best. Fred MacMurray seemed to me the most wonderful man. He set aside inviolable time to play with his children, and, on returning from a long day at the studio, was genial and unhurried. In his earnest way, he sat down and *listened* to his children, challenged them with meaty questions, and rough-housed until they were overheated with joy. If he spotted me watching from the sidelines with a lump in my throat, he would pull me into the fun. Years later, when I saw his TV series *My Three Sons*, it struck me that he was simply playing himself, and something stirred inside me as I wondered how I might have grown up had I enjoyed such a good start in life.

One morning I awakened to find Gran sitting on my bed, smiling devilishly. "Sweet Baby," she said. "I have the most wonderful news."

I sat up and rubbed my eyes.

"Your father," she said, "he's coming to see you today."

Fifteen

Gran didn't understand why the news of Dad's imminent return made me hysterical, why I kept screaming over and over again, "He can't! He can't!" When she finally managed to calm me down, I haltingly explained that Dad couldn't be coming home because he was dead.

"Where did you hear that?" Gran asked me.

"Papa told me. He said Daddy was in a car crash in Paris and he died."

Gran put her arms around me. I must have misunderstood Papa, she assured me. Dad had been hurt in a car crash, but he hadn't been killed. He was all right and he was coming to see me in a few hours.

I fretted the rest of the day. I desperately wanted to believe Gran, but I was so afraid of being hurt again. I had been lied to so many times. Of one thing I was certain: I hadn't misunderstood Papa. He had definitely told me that Daddy had been killed in the crash.

To this day, I'm still not sure why Bob Topping lied to me about my father. He was a jealous man, and I know it was important to him that I think of him as "Daddy," that he come first in my affections. As far as I was concerned, it was just another indication that grown-ups were not to be trusted.

I waited atop Mother's staircase that afternoon, pink-ribboned and lacy-frocked, until the bell rang and a maid opened the door. There he stood, grinning, with an armful of packages. Slowly, hesitantly, I started down the stairs,

144

holding onto the banister as I studied him. Halfway down
I paused. Then, snap, it was DADDY! I ran the rest of
the way down, throwing myself at him.

We sped off in his new limousine ("Faster, Daddy, faster!") to a restaurant where we sat down to lunch and
talked. He explained that he was returning to live in Los
Angeles and that, under the terms of the visitation agreement he had worked out with Mother, we would thereafter
be able to spend Sunday afternoons together.

He looked distinguished in his ascot, silk shirt, and ma-
roon blazer with gold buttons. At thirty-three, he had acquired a dusting of gray at the temples, and I could see
that when he walked he slightly favored one leg. Wrap-
ping the sports car around a light pole had nearly killed
him, but not quite, and after a steel plate was implanted
in his skull, he dangled for weeks on the critical list. I
was intensely curious about his new movie-star wife, but
he did not speak of her, and it was only later that I pieced
together the rough details of his two-year absence.

On what was his first time in Europe, he had cut a
dashing figure. As the well-known Hollywood restaurateur
and rich ex-husband of Lana Turner, he enjoyed easy entrée to Europe's postwar fast set. Paris became the base
from which he conducted the life of a playboy expatriate
along the French Riviera and North African coast. He
spread his charm in a triangle from Paris to Cairo to Tangier. Among his friends were Prince Aly Khan, Prince
Rainier of Monaco, Aristotle Onassis, King Farouk, and
Barbara Hutton, the dime-store heiress. Miss Hutton
played hostess to the rich and naughty at her famous house
in Tangier, then the sin capital of the world.

To help support himself and his love of baccarat and
chemin de fer at the casino in Monte Carlo, Dad took up
smuggling. There were shortages of liquor, luxury items,
and other contraband to be exploited in those years. Dad
was the idea man while his gofer, Little Joe Green, was
the operations man. Compared to other illicit traffickers in
the Mediterranean, Dad was small potatoes, and he kept
himself at a safe remove so that he never ran afoul of the
law.

When Dad met Martine Carol in Paris, she was already

a big star in Europe and something of a sex kitten. (Years later she starred in *Lola Montes*.) A beautiful twenty-seven-year-old blonde who was being touted as the French Lana Turner, she made headlines in the tabloids because of her reckless love affairs and endless nightclubbing. When one of her amours went sour, she tried to end it all one midnight by tearing off her dress and jumping into the Seine. That was not long before she and Dad married in Monte Carlo, where he was living in a villa close to that of Aly Khan and Rita Hayworth.

When he and my new stepmother sailed for America in October of 1950, he traveled with a well-lined wallet as well as plans for his new wife's career in Hollywood. They also carried some heavy jewelry in their luggage, which they neglected to declare. The stash was discovered by customs agents and both of them were detained. The whole matter was hushed up.

With my father back home, I concentrated on the idea that I was a pretty lucky girl. Among the presents he brought was a heart-shaped ruby locket that I treasured and a little French beret that I flaunted before Mother until she finally snapped, "If you don't stop wearing that goddamn thing—"

Although Dad drew me out on every detail of Mother's life, she seemed blithely unconcerned about his and never once showed her face when he turned up at Mapletop on Sundays to collect me. Dad looked expectantly over my shoulder every time.

At first I could hardly bear waiting for our every-other-Sunday together. We dined at all the smart restaurants: LaRue's, Chasen's, Romanoff's, the Polo Lounge, and often at a small Polynesian restaurant on Rodeo Drive named Sugie's Tropics. As a result of these six or eight hours a month together, I was seeing more of Dad than of Mother. I could pour my heart out to him, and he would listen with sad eyes, but it seemed there was little he could do to help.

"Daddy, can I come live with you?"

"Aw, honey, wouldn't that be nice? I wish it were possible."

"Please, let me."

"Well, hon, I have a small apartment and I'm always away. Who would take care of you?"

"Miss Hulley."

He'd smile and change the subject. I never told him that loneliness could sometimes make my stomach hurt. I didn't voice those hurts, not even to him. I didn't know how.

He picked me up one Sunday to announce in the car that there would be a special treat. He was going to show me his new apartment, which was in a gray stucco building in West Hollywood. He occupied two of the building's four units and was negotiating to spread into the others. As we walked in, there was a smoky party in progress, a revival of his old Sunday afternoon gin rummy club.

"Stevie, darleeng," swooned actress Corinne Calvet.

"Hey, buddy boy," yelled a man I didn't know. "What took so long?"

"And who do we have here?" said a woman with a cloud of red hair. She meant me.

I made my curtsies to everyone and shook hands around both tables. Miss Calvet supplied me with a sandwich and Coke, and when all eyes returned to the game, I drifted off into a bedroom where I spent the afternoon reading magazines. For some time this was how we spent our Sundays together.

No doubt Mother had been getting routine reports of my outings with Dad from Miss Hulley, but one day, looking suspicious, she sat down and grilled me. When she finally dragged out the truth about the gin rummy parties, steam came out of her ears. Through her lawyer she threatened to sue Dad for discontinuance of visitation rights. He had to swear never again to bring me to his house or into contact with gambling, drinking, or any of his friends.

Reluctant to fight a third battle for custody of me, Dad acquiesced, and we began dining again in restaurants, if less often. After a while the heat from Mother abated. Embroiled in a series of crises, she was too distracted to notice when Dad and I rejoined his pals and their girlfriends at prizefights and football games—about which I kept mum.

One of Dad's closest friends was a real estate man who gave Sunday afternoon pool parties, and at one of them I recall being introduced to a shy movie starlet with no spark. We exchanged perhaps six words, then I sat in a corner studying her. Something of her remains indelible in my mind to this day. She was Marilyn Monroe, then getting started at Twentieth Century-Fox.

One evening at twilight Mother walked in and sat on my bed. "Cherry Blossom . . ." she began. She used that name when she had bad news. "Sweetheart—" She couldn't get it out. "Baby, I have to tell you something. Papa has moved out. We weren't getting along." She went on to explain about the things that happen between adults, and I felt frightened because someone else was gone. She seemed to have the power to make people appear and disappear.

I should have seen it coming because there were several incidents. Papa had a low boiling point, and once I watched, aghast, as he beat with a cane the boxer dog he had given me. Another time he threw my poodle, Tinkette, against a wall. He and Mother had grown chilly with each other at cocktail hour, and recently I had been startled by the sound of a crash from downstairs. He had hurled a Baccarat decanter at Kathryn Grayson's head. Fortunately, he missed, shattering the bar mirror. The sound of fighting and slamming doors was increasingly common in their wing of the house. But this day, as I returned from school and passed the dog run, everything was oddly quiet. The boxer did not bark and wag his happy hello. He was gone, along with every other sign of Papa in the house.

On September 11, 1951, after three and a half years of what the public imagined was a storybook marriage, Metro announced Mother's intention to divorce Bob Topping. Late that night Miss Hulley awakened me. "Your mother's not well," she whispered. "You're spending tonight at your grandmother's." With that, I was led off in robe and slippers.

In the morning she told me that Mother had suffered a slight accident, that she had become dizzy in the shower and fallen against the glass door, cutting her wrist. When I got back to the house, I went right to her bath and looked around. The door was not shattered. I shook my head in puzzlement.

For Mother's release from the hospital, Gran had pulled together for her an all-white outfit that included slacks, a babushka, and an ankle-length coat. Mother scoffed at reporters' questions of suicide. "I'm not the type," she said. The press noted that the third letter from the "LTT" monogram on her car door had been removed, leaving a ghostly "T" beside the "LT".

It turned out that Mother had swallowed sleeping pills and slashed two tendons in her wrist with a razor in a feeble attempt to kill herself. The first person on the scene after Gran was her business manager, Benton Cole, who happened to be Gran's best friend. When their efforts failed to staunch the bleeding, they called in our longtime family physician, Dr. John McDonald. Dear "Doctor Mac," with his silver hair and kindly manner, had no idea what he was in for with Mother and me in the years to come.

It is true that Mother is not the suicide type, but her life had never fallen before to such a low. Her third husband had walked out on her for a figure skater in Sun Valley. Her last two movies had bombed and, now, about to turn thirty, she faced the drama of contract negotiations at an M-G-M ruled by a new chief, Dore Schary, who was promoting younger femmes fatales such as Liz Taylor.

There were increasing signs around the house that money was getting tight. First to go was Chef Henri. In fact, his absence had little impact on me, since I ate children's food from a lunchbox or on a tray in my room. I recall sampling the best of his culinary art just once. The Toppings were away and, for the first and only time, Miss Hulley and I ate like swells at the big dining room table. Henri's first course was a clear soup in the middle of which floated a chicken foot, claws and all. Miss Hulley assured me it was a rare and delicious delicacy, but I had no interest in finding out.

When the chauffeur was fired along with some housemaids, my isolation got worse. I was kept busy with lessons—ballet, tennis, swimming—but with no one to drive me around, instructors had to come to the house. Visits with Vana and Stephanie became fewer. Learning to live with internal exile, I came to discover the contents of almost every drawer in the house and every yard of the property—Little Miss Snoop.

Miss Hulley did allow me to play in the rear of the garden without eyes-on supervision. Our three gardeners had become my friends, and their kindly hearts prompted them to build for me a one-room house in the woods where Elizabeth and I gave tea parties. In the sun-dappled area around the little house, they created an enchanted garden of boxwood inhabited by lawn statues of gremlins and imps. I gave the statues names like Oscar, Pookey, and Annie, and periodically I was delighted to discover that with new plantings they had been magically moved about like chess pieces. But after two of the gardeners were let go, the imps turned mossy green from lack of exercise.

One day I made a wonderful discovery. Down at the corner where Mapleton met Sunset, a three-foot hole big enough to poke a head through had been torn in our chain fence. Sticking my head through the hole, I spied a little old lady on the far corner in front of Alan Ladd's hedges. Sitting on a camp stool, she wore orthopedic shoes on swollen feet and a shapeless house dress. A baseball cap crowned a mass of unruly white hair and a sandwich board stood beside her proclaiming, "MOVIE STAR MAPS 25¢."

I waved at her. She waved back, and I retreated to the thicket. But when I later returned to wave again, she eagerly gathered up her things and hurried across to visit.

"Hi ya," she called.

I curtsied and smiled. "How do you do, Ma'am," I said. "May I ask what those maps are that you're selling?" I wished I'd had twenty-five cents, but I hadn't seen my first nickel yet.

"Tourist maps," she said, letting out a funny cackle. "What a pretty dress you have on, Cheryl."

Uh-oh, another one of Mother's fans. She was a nice one, though, I decided—a gnarled old dear—and I felt sorry for her. For a while she became my secret friend, an adult I had met on my own. In our quick visits through the fence, I talked about dogs and horses; she gave me candy and asked about Mother. I told her what little I knew, even though I had been sternly lectured never to tell anyone about "how we live." Mother said, "They could be jealous—especially the press." I looked forward to our visits until one day my little map lady was gone.

At the start of 1952 Judy Garland and her husband Sid Luft moved into the big Norman chateau next door to us. It was a happy development. Mother and Judy grew close as friends again, giving each other some needed feminine support. While Mother was a man's woman (her preferred party mix was eighty percent male), she was able to commit herself to a couple of close friendships with women. They were usually not movie stars, but, rather, women with whom she worked, such as her hairdresser Helen Young and supporting actress Virginia Grey.

Though a star, Judy was different. She liked to kick off her shoes and party just like Mother did. They had a lot in common: schooldays at Metro, roles in the same movies, shared boyfriends, equal star status, and now equal career slumps. Both were on their third marriage, had recently tried suicide, and were coping with pre-adolescent daughters.

Judy's daughter, Liza Minnelli, was seven (two years younger than me) when I first heard her Judy-like voice coming over the eight-foot cinder-block wall that separated our properties. Liza and I hollered hello to each other, and I climbed up a woodpile to go over the wall. In my life so far, this was the very first unchaperoned moment I had ever spent outside our fence.

Liza was an adorable little person who was more mature than I. Over the next four years, we would become back-fence pals. We were both well-known star babies with Sunday fathers and outrageous mothers, so we understood each other and could share problems. For the first time, I was able to speak of my loneliness and Mother's remoteness. Liza hated to look after her baby sister, Lorna, and I was impressed by how much she knew about her mother's career and personal problems. She had seen every one of Judy's movies.

We soon built steps of firewood alongside the wall, and after school we avoided grown-up eyes by playing on the asphalt roof of her garage. Liza knew all her mother's stage routines and in full voice belted out numbers like

"Button Up Your Overcoat" using a pinecone for a microphone. Deeply impressed, I sat cross-legged and applauded till my hands hurt. She begged me to get up and dance or sing something, but I smiled and shook my head. I had never really heard many popular songs, and even if I knew one, I'd rather die than show off.

I was utterly drawn to Liza's mother and she to mine. I could kiss and cuddle Judy and not worry about messing her up since she never wore makeup or fancy clothes. She was always in flats, black toreador pants, and a short ponytail. She and my mother would chitchat the afternoon away in Mother's pink-and-gold Louis XIV dressing room. Judy was always full of laughter, and I would plant myself adoringly at her feet to stare at her. She seemed wonderful in every way. She even permitted Liza to ride her bike on Mapleton wearing sneakers, blue jeans, and T-shirts, while I was stuck behind the fence in my hairshirt pinafore.

For her part, as Judy had done a decade before, Liza admired Mother's beauty and glamour. As a result, we decided to swap.

"You're doing *what?*" said Mother.

"Liza and I are trading," I said. "She's going to take you as a mommy and I'm going to have Judy."

After putting their heads together and working out some ground rules, both mothers decided to humor us. The plan soon fizzled, however. For my part, it got off to a bad start when I came to my new mother with a first request. "Mommy," I said eagerly, "can I ride my bike on Mapleton?"

"No," said Judy, smiling sadly.

V

KING OF THE JUNGLE

Sixteen

We all breathed more easily when Mother was in love, and, happily, it soon became obvious that she had a new boyfriend. I could tell by the way she threw her head back and laughed, the way she slimmed down and was more patient with everyone. The boyfriend came not a minute too soon, because a cloud of gloom had settled over the house after Papa's walkout and Mother's flirtation with suicide.

His name was Fernando Lamas, and he was her leading man in a Technicolor remake of *The Merry Widow*.

Mother was glad to be back at work, and she was rather lucky to have been able to do so on such favorable terms. Even though her last two pictures had flopped, Metro offered her a new seven-year contract with more perks and a handsome increase in salary. Since the war, the coming of television had darkened more than twenty percent of America's movie houses, and, to economize, studios were dropping stars' contracts left and right. But Mother, they reasoned, still had a big following; she needed no buildup, was only thirty-one, and could carry the type of movie with which black-and-white television couldn't compete—namely, adult dramas and color spectacles. For the next five years Metro would toast her beauty in one overdressed star vehicle after another, and as these met with a declining box office, Mother's self-confidence would begin to erode, prompting her to inflate her behavior with a certain grandness.

Fernando Lamas, her new "gentleman friend," as she spoke of boyfriends in front of me, was tall, droll, and handsome. He had been a film star in South America, and it was a career break for him to be billed alongside Mother. I was instructed to call him Uncle Fernando after we were introduced on the set. One day I came to watch them shoot the big waltz scene (set visits were carefully scheduled to avoid my seeing clinches or violence), and his debonair manner made me think of Daddy. Though he was separated from his Uruguayan wife, and Mother was separated from Topping, the complicated rules of divorce in those days forced the two of them to date on the sly.

That June, she, Miss Hulley, and I moved to Lake Tahoe for a summer holiday and Lamas paid furtive visits to our big waterside cabin. Mother needed to establish a six-week Nevada residency to qualify for a Reno divorce, and I was told to be quiet about Uncle Fernando's comings and goings for fear that the press would find out.

It was a difficult time for Mother. She grew restless between Lamas's visits, and was tied down to lazy days with me. Miss Hulley cooked and read; I swam and fished and boated.

There were no other children around for me to play with except for an eleven-year-old boy named Bobby Westbrook, the orphaned heir to an oil fortune who owned his own sleek ''cigarette'' speedboat. No minimum age or driver's license was required to operate the high-powered craft, so Bobby and I became a familiar sight together, a pair of chubby, topless pre-adolescents with zinc oxide noses knifing across Tahoe's bottomless crater lake (''Faster, Bobby, faster!''). Mother and Miss Hulley did not realize that soon after we had cruised far enough from our dock at low speed, Bobby would gun the motor to 45 mph while I steered. Mother's friend Frank Sinatra was appearing at a nearby lodge, and when we gave him a top-speed spin in the boat, he turned white and couldn't get back to shore fast enough.

Despite Mother's enforced presence that summer, I still felt unable to grab her attention, and I began to try mischief again. I preferred being scolded to being ignored. One night I put Junior, my pet four-foot-long king snake, in her bed, and she bawled me out as I covered my giggles and pretended to be asleep. Junior was gone in the morning.

Sworn off romance for a while, Mother told Louella Parsons that her immediate objective was "dignity and peace and a home where I can bring up Cheryl right." Louella approved, observing that "in the back of Lana's mind has always been that yearning to be a dignified matron."

At the same time, Lamas was being quoted on the matter of how Latins make love. "We grab a girl around the neck," he said, "grasp her arms until they are black and blue, and shred her clothing."

Mother started another picture, *The Bad and the Beautiful,* and I began to see more of Uncle Fernando—in every way. He had a key to Mapletop (now just called Mapleton) and would let himself in to relax and take afternoon swims. One day after school I was playing alone by the pool when I looked up to see him descending the stone steps wearing a terry bathrobe.

"I don't suppose you've ever seen a naked man before," he said, dropping the robe.

I shook my curls no. All I knew was that boys had short hair and statues had fig leaves. He examined my face with a widening grin and seemed to invite me to stare a while. He was lean and classically muscled, having been a competitive swimmer in Argentina, and I noticed that boys had a *what's-it* there. (I realize now that I should have said, "You look *mah*-velous.")

I liked Uncle Fernando, so I didn't feel uneasy or anything, especially when he suavely declared that "nudity is perfectly natural" and dived into the pool. From then on his skinny dips became our secret. Of course, I wouldn't tell anyone; Mother would have exploded, and he knew it.

I sensed from the beginning that Fernando wouldn't last, so I held back my feelings. He wasn't all that impressed with Mother, and soon enough his machismo and feistiness clashed with Mother's complex needs. The affair ended with a public incident that has since passed into Hollywood legend. It happened one night when they were attending a party at Marion Davies's gigantic Malibu beach

house. A handsome blond actor caught Mother's eye. He
was Lex Barker, who starred in Tarzan movies and was
then separated from actress Arlene Dahl. M-G-M swimming star Esther Williams, who was seated at Mother's
table, invited Barker to join them.

He sat beside Mother, and it led to fireworks. Lamas
seethed as Barker proceeded to monopolize Mother on the
dance floor. To make matters worse, she flirted openly
with Barker to make Lamas jealous. Finally, he lunged at
Barker, shouting, "Why don't you just take her out in the
bushes and fuck her?"

Later that night at Mapleton, Mother and Uncle Fernando quarreled. The next day he was gone, soon to be
replaced also in *Latin Lovers,* their next planned picture
together. In a kind of double switcheroo on the marriage-
go-round, Lamas went on to wed Barker's friend Esther
Williams, while Barker wed Lamas's friend, my mother.

Lex Barker, it turned out, was a strange man whose
affability concealed cruel self-interest. His success in pictures was based on an ability to look good in a loincloth,
deliver earnest grunts, and swing through the trees in a
way that appealingly updated Tarzan. Johnny Weissmuller
had grown paunchy in the role after ten outings, and Barker
promptly reshaped the ape man as his own, becoming in
the process type-cast as a handsome hunk of few words.

The only son of a socially prominent family in Rye,
New York, Lex was a graduate of Phillips Exeter Academy and Princeton. To please his father, who was in civil
engineering, he spent a year working as an electrician,
pipe fitter, and bricklayer, but after a fling in summer
stock, he decided it was Hollywood or bust. Bit roles led
to six Tarzan movies, and by the time he met Mother he
was ready to hang up his loincloth and break through the
image.

He had two children from an eight-year marriage to a
former New York debutante: a daughter, Lynne, and a
namesake son, Alexander Crichlow Barker III. He infor-
mally shared custody with his ex-wife, but she seemed
about to remarry and he was eager to have his children
return to live with him. To have them live with *us,* I soon
realized. It was on this question of living arrangements

that I drew a doubtful first impression of my new "Uncle Lex."

"You're going to love my kids," he said the day we met in the barroom. I sensed Mother watching my reaction. "I've got a girl just your age and you can play together," he said eagerly. He seemed so anxious to please everyone, holding me by the waist and patting my bottom. Perhaps not so incidentally, his romance with Mother was putting him on Hollywood's A list. It was easy to read the infatuation in Mother's eyes, but I was feeling hustled.

Despite her new, higher-salaried contract, Mother's finances continued to worsen. There was some problem about back taxes her accounting people hadn't filed, and that spring new economies around Mapleton were leading to cobwebs and dust covers. So far only such basic necessities of life as the "sewing room" and the "sub-pantry" had been closed; now the living room, dining room, library, and servants' quarters were also sealed off as Mother converted to the use of day help and an Irish cook. As ever, she doggedly retained Jeanne, her personal French maid who still wore a frilly cap and starched apron (white by day, black after 5:00 P.M.). The shrinking living space at Mapleton didn't affect me much because I seldom walked about downstairs, and, when I did, I always felt rather like a visitor.

Handmade clothes were a thing of the past. Everything was now off the rack from Saks Fifth Avenue—until suddenly one day they refused a charge. "The idea!" Mother shouted. "We will never walk into that goddamn store again!" Feast or famine, Mother never stinted on our clothes, and she indeed went elsewhere to maintain her shopping with a vengeance.

Our new economies showed in even the small things. Previously, I was never allowed to answer the phone except to say, "Please hold on and I'll have an adult pick up." Now, with the reduced household staff, I was instructed to get the caller's name and press the hold button. If Mother wrinkled her nose, I would get back on the line and say she wasn't there.

To ease the money problem, Mother considered taking advantage of a new tax loophole that movie people were

using, one that offered Americans who worked abroad for
more than eighteen months an exemption from U.S. taxes
on their overseas earnings. She was thinking of marrying
Lex and moving their base to London so that each could
make movies with European locales. As for Baby Cheryl,
she could be put in a French finishing school, possibly in
Switzerland. No one said anything about this to me, but I
caught the hint of "our possible trip to Europe with Lex
this summer" and began to feel apprehensive.

Daddy, at one of our Sunday dinners, was reassuring.
A stay in Europe could do me good, he said. It had given
him a new start in life. And it's true, he was on the move
again. After his marriage to Martine Carol ended in divorce, he began dating starlets such as Mamie Van Doren.
He had expanded his bachelor's haven in Hollywood to
all four apartments, and the gin rummy gang had become
a very "in" circle of power people. By means of gambling
wins and other profitable ventures he had leveraged out of
the proceeds from his rum-running days, Dad had enough
capital to start over. He and Al Mathes, his old partner at
Lucy's, were planning a new restaurant that would make
Hollywood sit up and take notice.

Dad always enjoyed goading Mother about his and my
happy relationship, and that Easter of 1953 he sent me a
live angora bunny, knowing full well it would cause pan-
demonium at the house. I jumped up and down with delight
and threw myself into a faithful regimen of brushing,
grooming and walking the rabbit on a leash. Despite the
joy she could see it gave me, our Irish cook threatened to
stew it. "You're eating bunny tonight," she'd say dead-
pan. Terrified, I begged to run outside and check if the
rabbit were still safely in its hutch, but Miss Hulley
stopped me every time. She brooked no nonsense.

That spring Mother caused a fuss in the press by appearing on the arm of Lex Barker at the Cannes Film Fes-
tival. In those days, unmarried couples did not share hotel
rooms openly. Barker had found some spaghetti westerns
to make in Italy, so they decided to go ahead and become
tax exiles from America. Mother signed to do a couple of
movies in Rome and Holland, and Gran and I were sent
for. Miss Hulley was given the summer off.

I would soon be ten years old, and at a time when most girls that age looked like Annette Funicello, my waist-length sausage curls were laughable. I begged Gran to cut them, and, before we flew to England to join Mother, she caved in and got the studio to bob my hair shoulder length in casual permed curls. When we arrived at Mother's suite at the Dorchester in London, she looked at my hair and flushed with anger. "How could you have done that to the baby?" she said, glaring at Gran.

There was nothing Mother could do about twenty inches of lost curls (I took delight in flushing them down the toilet), but she could take out her anger on the new suit that Gran had bought for me to travel in on the plane. It consisted of a modest red jacket and matching A-line skirt, sweetly junior miss, but Mother thought it was too grown-up, and, besides, I was not allowed to wear primary colors. The next day it was gone from my closet.

I could sense the age-old strain between Mother and Gran beginning to boil on the issue of how fast I would be permitted to grow up. I was now about as tall as Mother, yet I still had to wear doll clothes—Mary Janes, little white socks, and horrid pinafores sashed with a bow. No child wore white gloves anymore, but I was still never to go anywhere without them. And above all, no T-shirts, no sneakers, no pants.

"But all the other kids wear them—*Liza* wears them."

"You're not like other children," she would reply. "You're different, special. You're *my* child, and when you're not in pajamas I want to see *beauty*."

Maybe she thought that a Baby Cheryl growing into a tall ten would make her look older than thirty-two. When she was my age, she was burdened by labor in a foster home. Perhaps she imagined that by force of will she could make my life an endless spring. Still, she found my 5'2" height a bit daunting, which helped Gran to persuade her that there was no use trying to hold back the dawn of my puberty. "Lana, she will soon be 'a young lady,' " Gran said delicately.

One day in London Mother sat me down and delivered an explanation of the facts of life that was resolutely taste-ful. The menstruation part was easy, but her account of sex didn't go much beyond the information that it involved "making love" to a wonderful boy I would meet many years in the future. Men's bodies were different from women's, did I know that?

"Oh yes," I said, biting my lip so as not to mention Uncle Fernando's anatomy lessons.

A new governess was hired in London to look after me that summer—replacing Gran—and it was clear that Mother had instructed the woman to keep me busy and away from the corrupting influence of my grandmother. A stern English spinster, she filled the day with French lessons and long walks in Hyde Park, where, if I dallied, she would pull me along with socket-wrenching yanks. Gran was totally shut out, and whenever I asked about her, the governess would pinch me hard in the armpits where a mark would not show.

One morning I was brought up to Mother's suite and presented to her friend Ava Gardner. Ava looked breathtaking, even in a cardigan and flats. She was bound for Africa to make *Mogambo,* a picture that Mother had unwisely turned down in order to do *The Flame and the Flesh* in Rome, where she could be near Lex Barker. Lana and Ava (even their names were musical) bid me good-bye and hurried off arm in arm to the shops, looking more like sorority girls than Metro's twin champs in the love goddess sweepstakes.

I yearned to go with them, but since my tantrum at Saks five years before, Mother rarely took me places. I was impeccably well behaved in public—if a bit glum-faced—but it was the governess who showed me Harrod's and the Tower of London.

After Mother left with Miss Gardner and until the governess came back to fetch me, I was alone for a while in her suite. I plopped on a sofa and picked up from the coffee table an English magazine named *The Tatler*. Leafing through its cartoons, I came upon a sheet of paper tucked inside. It was the carbon copy of a letter Mother had sent someone a few days earlier. But to whom? "To Whom It May Concern," it began coldly. "Miss Irene Hulley has served in my employ for three years as governess to my daughter—" My heart skipped as I read on.

It was a reference letter. She was now having Miss Hulley vanish, too!

Later that week, two more people vanished. The English governess was dismissed, and Mother informed Gran that she would not be accompanying me on our planned trip to Italy. It was a pathetic scene as Mother pulled me from Gran's arms at the airport. I settled down after a while on the plane, comforted by her promise that in Italy we would have more time together than ever—I'd see. Uncle Lex and his two children were waiting there for us, and we were all heading into a perfectly blissful summer. "Almost like a family," she said earnestly.

Mother's presence on the plane caused a stir. Flight attendants hovered by her seat, soon to be edged out by the navigator and copilot, who blocked the aisle as they chatted her up. She felt gay and friendly, especially when the gray-haired pilot himself lumbered back from the cockpit to brush her cheek with kisses and play the *grand seigneur*. Everyone was having a great time when abruptly Mother's face went white. "Oh my God," she said, "who's flying this thing?"

Seventeen

Before our arrival in Italy, Lex Barker rented a cavernous hillside villa fifteen miles from Turin. Set high on the eastern slope, it was named Villa Primo Sole (First Daylight). The place commanded a staggering view of the brown-hazed industrial valley and the River Po snaking through.

Lex's ten-year-old daughter, Lynne, was standing beside him at the door as we drove up. She appeared to have his blond good looks and easy confidence, but her quick, beautiful eyes flashed with resentment. I was an interloper, and she could read victim all over my face. When I extended my hand, she studied it without expression.

Alexander, her six-year-old brother who had the nickname "Zan," stood behind her looking small and unsure of himself, but folding his hands like a perfect little gentleman. I could tell in a glance that he was no match for his big sister's dominant nature, which, though I didn't know it, was about to draw me in, too. With his matchstick limbs and big brown eyes, Zan looked adorably vulnerable, and since I identified with underdogs, I felt sorry for him already.

What would become the overall tone of the summer was established that day. Mother forgot to say good-night as she and Lex hurried off to their faraway wing, while a new Italian governess led me through a maze of clammy stone passages to another wing where I was presented with what seemed to be a dungeon of a bedroom.

Lynne, Zan, and I squirmed our way through a supper of stares in the servants' hall, and that night under the

blankets I cried myself to sleep. I felt ashamed when anyone caught me crying. I tried so hard not to cry, but sometimes I just couldn't stop the tears. Lying alone in the
dark, I would get a lump in my throat and I'd swallow
until it came back harder and hurt. Then I would try to
choke down a welling dryness, but a gasp would break
through and make a noise, a tiny *sob*—and that was it.

From her bedroom next door, Lynne heard what she
was listening for, and from then on I was "the crybaby"
who needed the kind of discipline she meted out to Zan.
Though she would lock Zan in a closet, I was only
scratched and kicked in the shins or teased about my curt-
seying and baby-doll clothes. When I finally complained
to Mother about it, she said, "Don't be a tattletale."

Sensing weakness, children can be cruel, and I guess
Lynne had good enough reason to feel threatened by me.
I was the insecure daughter of a movie queen who was
taking her father away. To her, I must have seemed a
coddled monster. Still, out of necessity, she and I made a
separate peace by summer's end. By then we had become
stepsisters.

"Cheryl, I have some exciting news," Mother said one
day, having summoned me to her medieval bedroom. She
took my hands. "Lex and I are going to get married. Now
you will have your very own brother and sister."

"When?" I asked feebly.

"In about half an hour," she said, checking her lipstick
in the mirror.

At the appointed time the bride and groom tried a deception to throw off the paparazzi who were clamoring for
them at the villa's iron gate. Lynne, Zan, and I were conspicuously driven away to a local movie house (to watch
The Greatest Show on Earth in Italian). The idea was that
if the kids were going to the movies, then the wedding
must be off. But the wily Italians were not fooled, and
when they later cornered the bridal couple inside city hall,
Mother yelled at them to "get out of here or I just won't
get married."

The world was told of another Lana Turner wedding
fiasco, but she seemed happily unconcerned that night
wearing sandals and double-strand pearls at the celebration

dinner in Primo Sole's banquet hall. I felt downcast and tried not to attract notice, to be tiny and quiet, but they caught me not eating, and all eyes turned to stare.

In his determined attempt to make us one big happy family, Lex began a campaign to woo my affections. If I won a kiss from Mother, he had to give me one, too, and a squeeze besides. He wanted to change my name legally to Cheryl Barker, but I declined. I felt desperately attached to my real father, even if I seldom saw him.

One afternoon Lynne and I were brought to visit Lex on the outdoor location of a sword-and-sandal epic he was making at Cinecittà Studios near Rome. Unlike studio visits in Hollywood, where I was on a short leash, Lynne and I could run free, and we found that there were wild rabbits about. I came upon a little motherless gray bunny, and Lex seemed fascinated watching me pet and love it, just as I had with the bunny Dad gave me at Easter.

"Cheryl," he said, squatting down and stroking the animal's ears. "I'm your father now. Why don't you call me Father . . . or okay, Daddy. I don't care—Papa? Pa? Pop?" He laughed.

"Can I call you Po?" I said, squinting into the sun. I don't know what made me think of that word, but Po was the river that wound through the Turin valley below my bedroom window.

"Po it is," he exclaimed happily, lifting the baby rabbit by the ears so that its feet thrashed the air in fright.

Before starting our journey home that autumn, Mother had important news for me. The plans were all changed, she said. She and Po had decided that I would not return to the United States. I would remain with them in her new Paris apartment and attend a Swiss boarding school. It was Lynne and Zan who would go to Mapleton and live with Gran.

"I won't," I broke in. "I'm going home with Gran!" This was the moment I knew I had to make my stand or I was lost. Mother was about to try and sell me the notion that Paris would be our first real opportunity to live together—just her, me, and Lex. But why? She would still be working all over Europe while I was stuck away in some foreign school where I didn't speak the language, away from everything familiar—my home, my school, my friends. She had fired Miss Hulley and exiled Gran. Now it was my turn to vanish.

"If Gran leaves me here, I will run away," I said with a calmness that surprised me. I meant it. Mother fixed me with a look that said this was an injury so great she might not survive it. During the resulting uproar, Gran rushed in and supported my plea. But as we retired that final night at the Paris apartment, nothing had been resolved except that Gran vowed she would stay with me no matter what.

The next morning, the day of our departure, the place stood piled with trunks bound for places unknown. Mother walked into my bedroom, a strange look in her eye. Okay, she said, Lynne and Zan would return to live with their mother in Los Angeles and I would return to live with Gran at Mapleton. "I hope you know how upset this has made me," she said with icy hauteur. "To think that you don't want to stay here with me. But that's all right. You got your wish, and I hope you're satisfied."

No one said a word in Po's Jaguar on the way to Orly airport. Po was driving. Lynne and I sat beside him. In back were Zan, Gran, and Mother, who sat dejectedly, chin in hand, staring at the French suburban landscape that slid by her window.

"Y'know, Mother," she suddenly said to Gran. "You've had it pretty soft all these years. I've looked after you, supported you—well, I've *had* it. You're not getting another dime from me. When you get back to L.A., you better get yourself a job."

I spun around.

"You just look straight ahead, young lady, and mind your own business."

Gran burst into tears and covered her face as Mother harangued her all the way to the airport. Everyone solemnly studied the road. She accused Gran of using people, of taking from them and being selfish. I was screaming inside, *You're the one that uses and you're the one that's selfish—I hate you I hate you I hate you.* That moment I vowed to myself that I would never again call her Mommy.

When we got back to Los Angeles, Gran wrote frightened letters to Mother which went mostly unanswered. In one, written in schoolgirl curlicues on yellow-lined paper, Gran described the intervening weeks as "time to try and regain part of something I lost—Faith." It closed with: "Lana—I have tried to explain—I have always to the best of my ability—done the things you have asked me to do. I have never taken a thing from you, that you haven't given me. And from my heart I thank you for the years you have taken or rather supported me—Hurry home—Me."

My notes to Mother were cold. If Gran had not insisted, I would not have written at all because I had resolved to cap my volcanic love for her. I was determined to leave her before she left me.

After weeks of thinking about it, I decided that the reason Miss Hulley had been fired was that she and Po had had a fight. It happened when a family outing he had planned was frustrated once too often because Miss Hulley had already scheduled me for a piano lesson or something. He protested, but she would not budge. "It is *ridiculous* the way that woman never gives Cheryl a moment alone," I heard him complain to Mother one day as I was passing the barroom. I paused.

"That's the way I want it," Mother said with a bored sigh.

"But Lana, she's too sheltered. She's not a baby. She's growing—"

"Cherry, is that you out there?" Mother interrupted.

Years later I learned the truth about Miss Hulley's dismissal. Word had come to Mother that Miss Hulley had been feeding the nanny network with items about our life at 120 Mapleton. Both the grandmother and mother were alcoholics, Miss Hulley contended, and the mother was a tramp who didn't give a damn about her mixed-up daughter, whom she kept locked up.

Since the target of gossip is often the last person to hear it, Gran and Mother were then learning what had already been accepted knowledge about us in the movie colony for some three years. Our family melodrama was an open secret around which the industry tactfully closed ranks, just as it had done for so many others.

This was 1953, and the press would not openly question the manufactured image of our home life as one of bliss and maternal fulfillment. Even when the newly successful scandal magazine *Confidential* exulted in some alleged sexual escapade of Mother's in its December 1952 issue, it still didn't dare to impugn her fitness as a mother—though it, too, had surely heard all the nanny network whispers.

After so many years of being gossiped about, Mother had developed a fireproof hide. What finally got her, oddly enough, was the fact that even after Gran learned of Miss Hulley's disloyalty, she still kept up their drinks-and-dinner friendship. In fact, Gran had such a forgiving nature that she was able to plead successfully with Mother to allow Miss Hulley to return to Mapleton briefly that winter in order to help us during Christmas. "Cheryl and I have been through quite emotional times," she wrote Mother. "We're in no condition to be alone."

Ironically, the movie that Mother was making in Holland at that time was titled *Betrayed,* while the next one—for which she would return home—was called *The Prodigal.*

That autumn, when I returned to St. Paul's for the start of fifth grade, classmates fussed about the change in my appearance, my shorter hair and rounder hips, but also I think they sensed a certain astringency in my manner. I had been through a lot that summer, and my successful showdown with Mother gave a slight lift to my chin. Even the way I spoke was changing. The unconscious patterning of my voice after Mother's satin purr had always resulted in a breathy kind of whisper, but now I was learning how to raise the volume without losing a certain demureness. The class underdog was discovering her growl. The kids could tell, and some of them spoke to me as if we had never met before.

I knew I was finally onto something that October when I got my first period. Gran was alarmed that I was menstruating at ten, but Dr. McDonald was not. "Most California girls start early," he laughed.

The newly wed Barkers gave up their eighteen-month tax plan and returned home two days before Christmas.

The first order of business was to repeat their vows in a small ceremony at Mapleton. The legality of the marriage in Turin was questionable because Lex had failed to wait long enough after his divorce from Arlene Dahl to satisfy Italian law. Mother's divorce from Bob Topping, however, had gone down smooth as oysters after she agreed to a larger cash settlement in return for giving back some of the Topping jewels. Topping soon wed his ice skater and Mother quipped to the press, "She must have taught him how to skate—he never skated with me."

That autumn I think I struck people as a pretty cold kid. Mother, Gran, and I were well practiced, of course, in pretending that what was happening was not happening— the elephant is not standing on my foot. But now I so feared Mother's power to control me and exploit my adoration that I just plain withdrew. It surprised me that Gran had forgiven Mother's humiliation of her. The car incident had never happened, and they were as sweet with each other as ever.

My new governess, Miss Rockenbach, was a mannish German lady whom I heard the cook call "Rocky." Heavy-set, with kinky sandy hair, she wore straight shirts and loafers, and arrived on our doorstep holding a caged blue parrot named Gwen. She was brusquely affectionate and oh so lenient with me. One day I shut the bathroom door and waited for her to pound in protest. She did not. Suddenly I had captured an oasis of privacy within the house.

We often drove down to Muscle Beach in Venice, where she would leave me to wander alone on the sand while she disappeared into a woman's bar. But Rocky was a stickler about some things. I was beginning to hate having a governess give me a bath each morning and night. It was the suds-me-all-over part I didn't like. I mean, after all, I had started having my *period*. When I appealed to Gran about my being too old for Rocky to scrub me like a baby, she smiled and sighed. "Well, we'll see," she said. "I guess you are getting pretty big." *Pretty* big? I now shared with her movie-queen daughter the same height (5'3"), weight (110 pounds), hip measurement (34½") and waist size (24").

Mapleton was often empty when I returned from school
in the afternoon. Gran had taken a sales job and Mother
was making a movie. Rocky kept to her room, and even
Dad's Sunday visits were less frequent because he was
busy opening a new restaurant. My new stepfather, however, now under contract to Universal-International, was
more in evidence that late winter. He was waiting around
for better scripts than *The Yellow Mountain*, which he had
just finished shooting. As for his doing another Tarzan, he
swore after *Tarzan and the She-Devil* that six was enough.

One March afternoon as warm Santa Ana breezes wafted
over Holmby Hills, I sat alone with my thoughts beside
the swimming pool. I thought I was alone, anyway, until
I glanced up with a start to see my stepfather poised atop
the high garden steps, his arms crossed, his gaze directed
my way. He had a towel around his waist and his stomach
muscles bulged like braided bread, especially when he
sucked in his breath. He was Tarzan, all right, except for
the sunglasses. At six feet four inches and 200 pounds, he
dwarfed Uncle Fernando. Because he shaved his body hair
for movies, his acres of skin gleamed with the smoothness
of glove leather. I suppose Coppertone helped.

"Hullo," he hollered and started down the stairs. In a
moment he had crossed to the sauna adjoining the pool
house and was standing inside the door. "C'mere," he
said, waving an arm, "I want to show you something."

I was not allowed in the sauna, had never even explored
it. He led me by the hand into its redwood recesses and
indicated that I should sit on the lowest of three stepped-
up benches along the wall. He shut the door. There were
no windows, and the only light came from a bare amber
bulb on the ceiling. He still wore dark glasses.

"Have you ever seen what a man looks like naked?"
he asked, and yanked the towel away.

"Y-yes," I replied in a very small voice. "Uncle Fernando used to swim without clothes."

"Ohh," he said, his voice rising with interest. "In front
of you, huh? And did he ever touch you?"

"No."

"Are you sure?" he said skeptically. "Are you sure he

never touched you . . . here?'' He ran the spread of his fingers across both my breasts.

"No," I said, squirming.

"Or here?" Bending down he slid a hand inside my thigh and began to knead me through the bathing suit.

"Don't, that hurts," I said.

He withdrew and stood to consider me, rubbing the stubble on his chin.

"Well, then, are you sure Uncle Fernando never did anything like this?" he said. Slowly his hand moved to his penis and he began to fondle it.

"Yes, Po, I'm sure he never did. Never."

"So you have never seen what happens to a man," he added very sadly and sat down beside me. I was cornered against the wall. He explained with a serious face that I would be a woman soon, and it was important that I learn what a man was like. Had my mother talked to me about what went on between men and women?

"I know about babies," I said hopefully.

"Well, I'm your father now, and it's up to every little girl's father to show her about men. You see here?" He slid closer and, cupping his penis, began to milk it back. "This is a man's rabbit," he said. "There's a li'l bunny rabbit hiding inside here. He's sleeping in his nest now but watch, he's gonna wake up pretty soon. See? Say hello to Mr. Rabbit."

I knew this wasn't right. It was something bad. As I turned away he grabbed my hair and jerked my head to look. "No, I want you to watch what's happening," he said firmly. "The rabbit's growing up and coming out of his little nest. See Mister Rabbit get big?"

I was growing rigid with fear, digging my nails in the bench. With his eyes fixed on my stomach, he began to pump away at himself, slowly at first, his mouth finally going twitchy and slack until, with a buck and a grimace and a moan, he ejaculated on the floor. I stared at the door, wanting to run. He cleaned himself with a towel and started to go, then stopped and turned. Using a fussy hand gesture with a bent little finger, he lowered his sunglasses and peered at me over the rim.

"Of course," he said, his eyes grabbing mine, "not

everyone would understand what we just did here. It's something people don't talk about, y'know. Remember, from now on this is going to be our secret. Y'got that?''

I nodded and looked away until he opened the door and left.

Our *secret!* Who would I tell? I felt so ashamed. I looked at his ropey globs on the floor that were melting into the redwood.

Run! I told myself. There was my own way around to the front of the house, and I tore through thickets and hollows to get there. I raced up the front stairs to my bedroom and used my back to barricade the door.

Slowly the asbestos curtain fell. I put it from my mind. What had happened had not happened.

Without thinking, I walked to the bookcase and lifted down my Mommy doll by one leg. I had sort of given up dolls since Europe, and Mommy was strictly hands-off, besides. But I didn't care now. I pulled Raggedy Ann and a Teddy bear from the toy trunk and propped them beside her at a table, then set out tiny tea cups. For a long while, as late day softened into twilight, we had a very nice tea party, chattering away all manner of tales, Mommy, me, and my friends.

Eighteen

My father's new restaurant was a stunning success from the day it opened. Determined to make no mistakes this time, he focused his boundless energy on a plan to exploit the perpetual appeal of Polynesian restaurants. He often told me that the idea rooted in his mind way back in Indiana when he dined with his mother on special occasions at a fancy Chinese place in Indianapolis. "I'm gonna have something like this, Mama," he vowed, and he often lamented that she did not live to see his million-dollar restaurant.

For three years after his return from France, he spoke endlessly of "a great big South Seas place," and our Sunday dinings-out became something of a market research expedition in which he analyzed the operational pros and cons of eateries around town. "Y'hear those dishes?" he'd say, indicating the faintest clink of china from some nearby table being served. "That," he'd grumble, "is the sign of a bad waiter."

I also sensed he was trying to whet my appetite for the restaurant business, certain in his belief that I would eventually join him one way or another (for I was obviously never going to become an actress). The unspoken message was that while, of course, I would marry one day to bear him grandsons, I should certainly make a career with him in whatever empire he built. Above all, it was vital to carry on the line. "Before you get married," he would say frankly, "we've got to get your young man to change his name to Crane." I nodded vigorously.

The Crane "empire" was launched in July 1953. Trader

Vic's and Don the Beachcomber had been popular with tourists and movie people for years, but Dad figured a way to put a spin on one or two of their successful formulas. To encourage more everyday repeat patronage, he supplemented The Luau's typical Chinese-Cantonese fare with steaks, chops, and chicken. To draw a better-heeled crowd, he charged higher prices, though the customer got his money's worth. His steak prices, for instance, compared with those of swanky Chasen's in Hollywood and Romanoff's up the street, but he used a more tender, corn-fed (not range-fed) prime beef. The meat, flown in specially from Chicago, was a delicacy available at only a handful of places on the West Coast.

He also chose the perfect location. In the 1950s Rodeo Drive was not the famed three-block stretch of international designer shops it is today. Though it could boast Romanoff's and a number of expensive, if local, retailers, as well as the posh Beverly Wilshire Hotel at its southern end, Rodeo in those days was just another shopping street that snuggled into the sun-bleached quiet of Beverly Hills.

It was not lost on Dad that as the film studios declined, elegant nightlife in Los Angeles was moving west. Dressing up to dine and dance amid big-band, big-star entertainment was giving way to dressing down at good restaurants that offered no dancing and at most a combo with one singer. The astonishing star salaries paid by Las Vegas and television had stolen from clubs the likes of Tony Bennett and Pearl Bailey, while at the same time TV had steadily been draining people's urge to go out at night.

Dad saw in all this an opportunity for himself. He and partner Al Mathes bought Sugie's Tropics, a small Hawaiian dining and dancing spot that we had often visited. It was located mid-block at 427 Rodeo, and in its sleepy setting it had prospered for nearly two decades as a celebrity hideaway and trysting place far from tourist eyes. (House policy was reflected by a menu that displayed the three monkeys that hear, see, and speak no evil.)

Though Dad spent six months rebuilding Sugie's from the ground up, he took pains to preserve and enhance the site's reputation as a rendezvous for lovers. His overriding objective was to create a movie colony hangout, and he figured that since men liked to hang out in spots that attracted women, he needed to bait the place like a honey trap. He did this in several ways.

To begin with, he decorated the restaurant as though it were a stage setting. He designed doorways that afforded sweeping entrances, cozy booths that encouraged intimacy, and shadowy hotspot lighting that cast a flattering glow (using a sexy color that lighting experts call "bastard amber").

Women who did not drink were dared to try sinful-looking but nonalcoholic concoctions with names such as "Mermaid's Revenge," "Virgin's Kiss," and "Captain Steve's Pearl." The oversized powder room was fitted with couches, mirrored walls, and sinks that boasted gold-plated fixtures. Women were also delighted by three toilet stalls painted pink, yellow, and blue with tissue in matching colors.

The men's room sported urinals that were fashioned out of giant ("man-eating!") clam shells. When movie producer Allan Carr first laid eyes on them as an eleven-year-old schoolboy on a visit from Chicago, he found the experience life-changing. "Clam shell urinals!" he laughingly recalled to me. "I knew I was really in Hollywood, and suddenly I wanted to be part of it."

At the core of Dad's honey trap was a little-known and never-voiced policy of allowing select and very expensive hookers to mingle discreetly at the bar. Often failed starlets, they were refined and beautifully dressed, their presence drawing men while not offending escorted women customers, who rarely recognized them for what they were. (I was sixteen before Dad explained to me the lively scene around the bar.)

At last able to harness his obsession with beautiful women—and in pursuit of legitimate commerce, at that—Dad launched the Luau with a splash. He hosted ten private opening nights in a row, but only after 200 of Hollywood's female elite jammed a women-*only* preview party.

The decor was South Seas schmaltz and lavishness. It was a look not unfamiliar to lovers of Polynesian eateries, but he added amusing flourishes to the usual motif of exotic plants, Tiki carvings, blowfish, and Muzak playing "Lovely Hula Hands."

The table lamps were tiny Easter Island heads (which tourists were always taking as souvenirs). You entered the Luau by crossing a bamboo bridge over a lagoon to come upon a rain forest, complete with waterfalls tumbling over volcanic rock. Meandering tributaries were stocked with fish that were eyed by hungry macaws in a bird cage. No one had seen nightclub birds since Mocambo sent theirs off to birdland.

Each evening after the 5:00 P.M. opening, Dad greeted patrons at the door with a hearty welcome. Decked out as a plantation owner, he wore white Panama suits, pastel silk shirts, two or three gardenia leis, an ascot, and a sapphire ring with matching cuff links. In all, the look would have raised a blush on his Latin-lover pal, actor Cesar Romero.

Customers loved it. They stepped in from sun-drenched Rodeo Drive to a theater of the playful. As Dad had hoped, the place immediately became a haunt of stars like Clark Gable, Jack Benny, George Raft, Lena Horne, and every columnist from Louella Parsons to Walter Winchell—as well as a steady flow of dressy tourists, who filled its 174 seats every night. Dad had done everything right.

On my first visit, he seated Gran and me in fan chairs at his personal table, which was known by the staff as "Bar One." It was the first table inside the bar, a dark room of wall aquariums and ship riggings where everyone wanted to be but only the anointed got tables. Bar One was where the *Examiner*'s Harrison Carroll would install himself every Friday night to gather column items, and it was the spot where I would spend many of my Sundays during the next years, sipping a Captain Steve's Pearl while I waited for Dad. Dressed at first in bobby sox and Peter Pan collars, I became an inveterate people watcher. I sponged up how women dressed and behaved, how sophisticates looked bored, and how grown-ups seemed to have all the fun.

Dad's success filled my heart to bursting with pride. However, if his star was on the rise, Mother's was flickering with uncertainty. The movie business was changing.

Marilyn Monroe had appeared the year before in two blockbusters, *Gentlemen Prefer Blondes* and *How to Marry a Millionaire*. Newcomers like Audrey Hepburn and Grace Kelly dawned overnight as major stars. Metro had the incomparable Liz Taylor and Columbia was getting behind an ethereal blonde named Kim Novak.

By contrast, Mother's last two films (as a brunette) had met with lukewarm reception at the box office, and M-G-M's new production chief, Dore Schary (no fan of Mother), was now insisting that she would have to carry a biblical epic called *The Prodigal*.

The casting was all wrong. Though Mother was more effective in modern dress, Schary knew that sex-soaked costume spectacles were among the last kind of movies that could still pry people from their new television sets. He also knew that Mother could hardly refuse to make the film because she was still spending her $5,000-a-week salary at a breakneck pace and was heavily in debt to the studio. Mother was then the only Hollywood star with a full fifty-two-week contract, including three months' paid vacation, but typically, when she started work on *The Prodigal* in March 1954, her income for that month was $20,319 and her expenses $34,421.

One special $4,800 item that month was part of the cost of adding a two-bedroom wing off Mapleton's garage. Lynne and Zan, Mother announced, would in several months' time be leaving their mother, who was remarrying, and coming to live with us.

That spring I tossed through countless twilights, pondering my inventory of woes. It seemed the people I needed most—Mom, Dad, and Gran—were off busily doing their work, while the expendables—like Rocky, Lex, and his children—were closing in fast. I still lived inside an eight-foot fence and was dressed as a child. Most of all, that first impression of my stepfather was proving woefully accurate. I never again called him Po after what happened that day in the sauna. When he came down to breakfast the next morning he seemed casual, regarding me with a vacant glance. He, too, it seemed, could act as if what had happened hadn't happened. If only on that

talent alone, he was going to be right at home in this
family.

What could I do about any of this? No answers came
from the girl-on-the-swing or the lips of my Mommy doll's
baked-on smile. Oh, to be free, to be grown-up and able
to run my own life!

One evening in April the clock gave its extra little tick
on the hour to announce 8:00 P.M. The house seemed filled
with emptiness. Mother was at the studio, Lex was somewhere, and Rocky had long since vanished into her faraway bedroom, which connected with mine through two
dressing rooms. In the stillness, I began to sense that my
hallway door had moved, had opened just a crack, and
that someone was looking at me. A large figure slipped
inside my room and closed the door. It was Lex in his red
Sulka dressing gown. He crossed the room, his big bare
feet padding like lion paws on the shag, and sat on the
bedside to face me. Tarzan hair fell forward to hood his
face from the lighted night clock, but I could see that his
lips were set in a grisly smile.

"Time for another lesson," he said evenly.

"W-what?" I tried to pull myself upright, but he pushed
me back and his hands came to rest along the rosebud-
stitched bodice of my nightie.

"We're not going to make a sound," he leaned close
to whisper. "Now shut *up!*" Fear stabbed at the back of
my arms and told me not to squirm. He reached inside the
nightie to fondle my breasts. My eyes slid into my head.
"Does that feel good?" he asked slyly. I held my breath.
I was afraid to look as he pulled the covers back and rested
one hand on my leg. As my mind felt the dint of recognition, he continued in a confidential voice repeating what
he'd told me in the sauna—how it was important that I
know what women were supposed to do, how it was his
duty as my father to teach me. That way, no one could
surprise or take advantage of me, he said. He went on and
on and on. "Y'know, Cheryl," he concluded, his voice
rising pleasantly, "when I was your age I was real lucky,
too. There was an older woman who showed me all about
sex, just the way I'm going to show you. I'm still very

grateful to her. And someday I'm sure you'll be grateful to me.''

My body began to tremble. He only hoped, he added, tossing back his mane of hair, that someone would take the time and trouble to give these lessons in sex to his own daughter. ''Perhaps her new stepfather will care enough,'' he sighed hopefully.

Could this be true? Could it? I was scared, but at the same time I was bewildered. Nobody had ever talked to me like this. Sex. What was sex? And I didn't like the way he was stroking my legs. Rocky does that. Somehow I knew it was wrong, but I didn't know why. Maybe stuff like this was something that just happened to people or was *supposed* to happen. I didn't know. I opened my eyes. He was fondling himself.

''Remember Mr. Rabbit?'' he asked. I squeezed my eyes shut. A hand tunneled under my nightie to wait between my legs. I stifled an urge to scream. Suddenly I felt a frightening jab. I sprang up, arms thrashing, my voice gasping to cry out, but he got his hand around my throat and threw me back. In another instant, the nightie was pulled away, my knees yanked wide, and with a bolt of pain he heaved his 200 pounds into the core of my loins.

I choked. Was he going to kill me? I couldn't breathe. The pain was more than any I had ever known. Finally he released an anguished moan in my ear and collapsed.

There came a long moment of hard breathing, finally slowing down and seeming to syncopate with the tick of the clock. My cheeks felt wet from his drool and sandpapered by his whiskers. Tears wouldn't come and my throat burned, but my body was moist and the flannel nightie lay twisted like a sweaty rag across my breasts. I looked above to see the clear blue eyes of my Mommy doll staring balefully into the distance.

He chuckled to himself, rolled off, closed the robe, and got to his feet. After studying me a moment, he came around and bent close to my ear.

''You know what they do to girls who tell, don't you?'' he said. ''Girls who tell *anyone* what we just did? They take you away and you never see your parents again. They send you to a place called Juvenile Hall.''

My mind saw a specter of hell. "Juvenile . . . Hall?"

"A prison for girls where they give you bread and water and you're alone behind bars for the rest of your life."

He started for the door and paused in a shadow. "So if you ever want to see your mother again, or your grandmother, or your father, or your dog, or your goldfish or anything else, you'd better keep your mouth shut." He let that sink in, then, glancing carefully into the hall, slipped out.

I lay as still as a run-over cat. Pain was swelling inside me and my mind tried to get up. I managed to think of proud-footed horses, of Elizabeth purring strength in my ear. Finally, I called back from age seven my fantasy in which I rode as Billy the Kid's girlfriend on a cattle rustle.

My fingers touched something cold on the sheet. It was blood. Had he broken up my insides? Then I shuddered to realize I must be going into my period.

I spent half the night staring numbly into the bathroom mirror, and the next morning I could not get out of bed. At least I told myself I couldn't. When Rocky saw the bedsheets, she scolded me for not telling her about my period but agreed I would not go to school. The following day, when I still complained of pain, Gran insisted I was babying myself, and off I was sent to St. Paul's. Classmates remarked that I seemed quiet, but if anyone noticed the tremor in my lips and hands, they didn't say.

Lex was a study in offhandedness when I came home from school that afternoon. He and Mother were sipping vodka together in the barroom, and she was in high spirits about her upcoming trip to attend the New York premiere of *The Flame and the Flesh.* She seemed not to notice that when I gave her a kiss on the cheek, Lex did not insist on his peck from me as usual. Avoiding his eyes, I shrank away to the sofa and stared into a Coke.

Mother always gave her current boyfriend or husband complete parental authority over me—superseding Gran or the current governess. If Lex had insisted then and there, I would have been obliged to kiss him or face Mother's wrath. But something told me I had given him the last dutiful kiss. By a process I didn't understand, I had been drawn into a conspiracy of silence about doing something painful and wrong with an adult I very much disliked. Still, I told myself, the humiliation and hatred he had slammed into me would never happen again. It just *couldn't*.

Mother left for New York a week later, and that night he slipped into my room again. "I know you're awake—don't pretend," he said, standing beside the bed. He parted the robe. *"Look* at me."

"Please," I murmured. "Ple-ease don't." He grunted roughly and yanked back the covers. He knew he had struck the right chord. In our unholy alliance, he held the ultimate power by threatening to inflict what I feared most—banishment from my family.

Since I could tell no one of these night attacks to which I submitted, I pushed the shame deep inside me. It didn't want to stay there. Spells of nausea came and went. My mind stormed with persistent nightmares about falling through blackness or sinking in water. When I awoke screaming, Rocky found me thrashing my limbs trying to swim or fly. My menstrual cycle became erratic, shutting down sometimes for three months at a time, then returning with excruciating discomfort. I chewed my nails so hard that there was little more left than the moons. To make my hands look even worse, when they were in repose the trembling returned, and I was embarrassed to feel people's eyes on them.

I was ten-and-a-half, going on eleven. I had never been able to make even the simplest decisions about myself, and now I realized that I had lost control of my body as well. I did not even own my insides. My stepfather did.

As weeks passed, I tried to think about good things. For one, within the confines of Mapleton's fence, I was beginning to enjoy a sort of latchkey child's freedom. After Rocky brought me home from school, she went off on errands or retreated to her room, and if I had no tennis or piano lessons, I was free to roam the grounds all afternoon. I began to understand that they could no longer watch me twenty-four hours a day.

Once, I felt bold enough to venture out the front door alone and walked three blocks up Mapleton Drive to pay

(JACK ALBIN/CRANE-LEROY COLLECTION)

Mother and Dad cut the cake at the impromptu wedding reception held the day after they eloped to Las Vegas in July 1942. That's Gran in the flowered dress next to Dad, and Judy Garland leaning over the table next to her.

Mother and Dad and I celebrate my first birthday.

(CRANE-LEROY COLLECTION)

With Mother on the
Laguna Beach set of
*The Postman Always
Rings Twice* in 1945.
I was just two,
and it was the first time
I had ever seen the ocean.

(CRANE-LEROY COLLECTION)

In Mother's lap
the morning of her
April 1948 wedding to
Bob Topping.

(CRANE-LEROY COLLECTION)

By the pool at Mapletop
with Mother and
Papa Topping.

Iron Eyes Cody and a friend crown me an Indian princess
on my sixth birthday.

At age seven with Mother in our matching director's chairs at M-G-M.

Riding with Mother on the back lot at M-G-M. I was twelve.

Visiting Mother at M-G-M on the set of *Diane*, 1955.

Mother and Lex Barker in Mexico.

A deceptively tranquil moment with Mother and Lex in Acapulco, Christmas 1956.

Mother and Dad collect me at the Los Angeles police station after my abortive attempt at running away in April 1957.

With Mother and Johnny Stompanato at the Los Angeles airport on their return from Acapulco for the 1958 Academy Award ceremonies. Good Friday was just sixteen days later.

(COURTESY OF LOU VALENTINO)

Oscar Night, 1958. Cary Grant was just one of the many stars who paid court to Mother that evening.

The house at 730 North Bedford Drive where it all happened. The arrow indicates Mother's bedroom window.

(COURTESY OF LOU VALENTINO)

Good Friday, 1958: Dad stands with me as I'm brought into the Beverly Hills police station just before 11:00 P.M.

(COURTESY OF LOU VALENTINO)

On my way to being fingerprinted.

With Mother before one of my hearings. My lawyer, noted Hollywood attorney Jerry Giesler, is the man in the light-colored suit.

(COURTESY OF LOU VALENTINO)

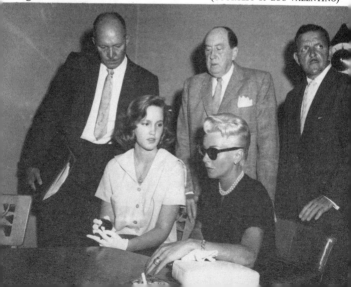

Several months after
Good Friday, the toll the
tragedy took on both
Mother and me
can be seen in our faces.

Mother and I on Rowena, early in 1959. Rowena had been
a gift from Johnny.

With Dad, Mother, and Gran at my Sweet Sixteen.

(CRANE-LEROY COLLECTION)

...ad and "Madman" Muntz outside the Luau with my ...xteenth-birthday present—a Muntz Jet.

...he gate at El Retiro. I ...ent over the wall twice.

(COURTESY OF LOU VALENTINO)

Just a few days shy of nineteen, I didn't realize I had been hired as a model by a Sunset Strip nightclub in order to exploit my notoriety.

(DON PACK/CRANE-LEROY COLLECTION)

With Dad a few years later, after I had gone to work for
im as a "seater" at the Luau.

With Josh and Mom in Hawaii in 1984.

(CRANE-LEROY COLLECTION)

Josh and I today. (MARK ALAN VIEIRA

a surprise visit on my old friend Stephanie Wanger. For no reason I knew of, we had not seen each other in four years.

"Yes?" said the butler.

"Is Stephanie in, please?" I said brightly. She popped from around the corner and gaily rushed at me laughing. She had long lashes, gray eyes, and thick raven hair like her mother, Joan Bennett, and she was growing up to be uncommonly pretty. I stayed a whole half hour and Rocky never knew.

I later understood why I had not seen Stephanie since her seventh birthday. In 1951, just before Christmas, her father, in a jealous rage, shot and wounded the theatrical agent who represented her mother. The incident generated headlines for months and sent the family into seclusion. After my surprise visit, and during our renewed friendship over that summer and fall, Stephanie never spoke of the scandal or showed signs of the hurt she must have felt, but then I never spoke of my stepfather.

I didn't know of the incident because newspapers and fan magazines (which were all well-thumbed at Mapleton) got whisked away from Baby's sight. A compulsive reader since the age of six, I was allowed to browse in Mapleton's library and devour everything from *Jane Eyre* to *Of Mice and Men*, but the reading of papers and fanzines was strictly taboo for me.

Rocky proved to be largely an absentee nanny that spring. There were afternoons when she seemed to go stir crazy, all itchy elbows and heavy sighs. With the arrival of these signs, I knew we were soon bound to hop in the car and drive down to Muscle Beach in Venice.

For the very first time in my life, I wandered freely among strangers. Digging into my fifty-cent allowance, I bought Good Humor bars and gazed in awe through my candy-striped sunglasses at bodybuilders hoisting weights. There were tumblers who built human pyramids with the prettiest girl on top, roller skaters who never fell, and beefy lifeguards stoic as statues. Children like myself played a game of tag called "You're It." I just watched and built sand castles and worked on a tan. It was great adventure.

When I returned for her, Miss Rockenbach was always

restored to good humor, which was another reason I looked forward to these outings. One day after the beach, she seemed to work extra hard at scrubbing sand from the crannies of my body as she gave me my regular evening bath. As I squirmed unhappily, because I detested the process, she turned playful. Leaning close, she nibbled my ear.

At that precise moment, my grandmother, who happened to be making one of her routine drop-ins, stood watching at the door. Gran's face turned to ice. The next day Miss Rockenbach was gone.

Nineteen

Since the start of my stepfather's attacks, new questions about Mother began to nag at the back of my mind. How could she endure the assaults he must have been inflicting on her, as well? *No* one who ever hurt my mother got away with it, so, to my distress, something told me that she liked it. Had she been given sex lessons as a little girl? And if she did find out about mine, would she send me to Juvenile Hall? Was she secretly in on all of this with him?

There was nothing in her behavior toward Lex to provide answers. As with all the men she loved, she was going through her regular pattern. This was, I saw, Stage One in their relationship. In Stage One, she gave 200 percent of herself, her money, cooperation, and emotions. She held Lex's hand, gazed adoringly at him, and openly smooched with him around the house. In the evenings, with her in lacy negligees and him nude under a robe, they seemed always to be hastily covering up some exposed body part. As they watched TV (we had six sets), she liked to plop kittenishly in his lap or snuggle beside him and trace her nails along the muscles of his arm. I assumed there was supposed to be something pleasurable about both this grown-up romancing of theirs and the hurtful things he did to me, but I couldn't see the connection.

When he noticed my stares, he returned a cold look that bristled with warning. "Juvenile Hall," it said. Sometimes it said, "Tonight we have a lesson, you and I." Two years later, I would see that "tonight" look on his face even as he was standing next to Lynne and Zan. We were circled around Mother, who lay in a hospital bed the day she had a miscarriage. On returning to Mapleton that night, he crept into my room.

Usually, however, there were no warnings, and besides, I convinced myself after each assault that that one was surely the last. There were perhaps a score in all, and I was always shocked to face another. They might have occurred more often if Mother and Lex had not traveled so much to Europe and Latin America. But when they were in Los Angeles, and even after his children had moved into the new wing, he attacked without much hesitation, often while Mother sat unawares watching TV downstairs or reading in her bedroom just fifty feet from mine. Once, in a close call, he was about to climb onto my bed when her voice from downstairs shouted his name and he hotfooted it out the door. In the morning, Mother greeted me with blood in her eye. "Lex told me," she said, "that he saw the light under your door last night and went in to find you *reading* after hours!"

I told Mother about my nightmares and my fear of prowlers, pretending I had seen shadows at the window. When I asked her if I could please lock my hall door (while still leaving the governess access through her room), Mother refused, brushing aside the fact that she herself slept behind a locked door with a .38 caliber revolver in the nightstand. "It's no because I say so," she said.

Lex owned a black German shepherd named Pulco (for Acapulco), which he beat with a bamboo cane. The dog was half timber wolf, and the beatings soon made it revert to a dangerous snarling beast—dangerous to everyone, that is, except me. Pulco and I were buddies. I could hug him, pull his tail, and yank him about, but he always wound up licking my face and rolling over for a tickle. If someone approached me in a questioning way, he bared huge yellow teeth. So I begged Mother to let him sleep at the foot of my bed. She said no—no dog, no lock. She did, however, direct the gardener to trim some tree branches that tapped at my bedroom window. The next day Mother asked cheerily, "Well now, bogeyman gone?" I shook my head and looked at the floor. Why can't she *see* what Lex is doing to me?

When she returned from New York that spring of 1955 to continue *The Prodigal*'s four-month shooting, there were no particular summer plans to keep me busy, so I grabbed every chance I was offered to visit the set. Gran had often taken me to watch Mother "work," but, to my childish eyes, her work consisted of little more than talking or dancing with strangers in front of bright lights.

I had still never, *ever* seen her face on the screen, and, at some level I imagined that getting a look at the other woman she inhabited—the Lana Turner person—could help me get closer to her. Everyone seemed to know "Lah-nna," even my classmates. Intrigued by the name's music, I savored its languorous feel on my lips.

To my surprise, Mother let me read the script for *The Prodigal*. It did little to prepare me for the first sight of her costumes—just a few beads here, a few wisps of silk there. Hanging in the closet, they looked like the last of a scarf sale. Actually, they were so brief (and she had made them even briefer with scissors) that decency groups denounced her and certain exhibitors airbrushed photos that showed her navel. (A senate committee that was examining Hollywood's morality even summoned the pictures for a closer look.)

Mother didn't fare very well in *The Prodigal*. She portrayed a love goddess who tempted the prodigal and nearly led him on to ruin. Then, before she could be stoned for wickedness, she flung herself into a pit of fire head first. I loved it.

The process of making a movie is so slow-paced that the experience of watching it compares for thrills with riding one's bike in circles around a tennis court. I often retreated in boredom to Mother's trailer dressing room to read her fan magazines. I never missed a chance, however, to watch her work with an eight-year-old actress named Sandra Descher who played what appeared to be her daughter. Actually, the character portrayed by young Miss Descher was the next in line for the high priestess job, and Mother was required to train her.

It was fascinating to watch them rehearse together. Sandra seemed a very disciplined young professional who behaved as though she were thirty. She followed directions with a precision I admired, calmly and matter-of-factly. Although we were never introduced, how I longed to be as self-willed as she seemed. Mother quite liked her.

Dressed in identical costumes, they appeared to be mother and daughter, and I was struck by the way my mother related to her. I recognized a few of her facial expressions and vocal inflections as ones she used with me. Even some of the situations were familiar, such as a schoolroom scene in which Sandra grew tired of a history lesson. "Well, then," said Mother, "let's do something else. Let me show you how to make your eyes look more mysterious."

As Mother gave her tips on applying eye shadow, my mind slid back to a happier time: for Halloween, when I was four, she had put in a rare home appearance to make me up as a gypsy, after which Gran and I went trick-or-treating.

When Sandra fretted that she could never learn to become high priestess, Mother consoled her with embraces. This reminded me of an occasion long ago when I had skinned my knee and she gathered me in her arms with Madonna-like tenderness. They filmed the scene over and over, and, every time, it tugged at my heart as I wondered a little if Mother had been putting on a show back then about my skinned knee.

At the end of each day, the film footage that had been shot the day before was run off in a screening room and I was allowed to watch from the back. Suddenly, up on the screen, there she was. *Lana Turner*—transcendent, almost naked, and two or three yards wide, with a brassiere made of snakes. I was a little disappointed. Except for the clothes, she seemed not much different from the way she always kept herself at home. Mother didn't ask my opinion of this other woman she played, and thank goodness, because I was more confused than before. Lana Turner told me hardly anything about my mother.

After Miss Rockenbach's hasty departure, my new governess was Miss Gale, a middle-aged Frenchwoman, rather like Claudette Colbert in appearance, who insisted on manners and was very much a lady. I liked her quick, birdlike movements and merry laugh. "Now dear, thees ees going to be so *amusing,*" she would say about everything, but I wasn't allowing myself to become fond of anyone anymore because no one ever stayed.

When Lynne and Zan moved in that fall, their independence proved more than Miss Gale could handle. Products of regular schools, they were not used to the owl eyes of a governess, particularly one who was acting on the kind of strict guidelines my mother laid down. Mother sniffed that her newly installed stepchildren were wild and needed "manners taught them." I was not to pick up their habits, she said. Actually, she became quite loving with Zan, who adored her and ran to her arms when he was mistreated by his macho father, his dominant sister, and (yes, I'm ashamed to admit it) even gentle me. He was a nice boy, lonely and sensitive, who turned to his older siblings for company, only to be buried by our gleeful rejection. We wanted nothing to do with a kid brother, and Lex belittled him for not standing up to us.

Living together in the same house, Lynne and I formed a tolerant friendship, though she was still boss. She arrived with a wardrobe that any normal preteen girl would have worn, and I welcomed this tacit help in softening up Mother on the matter of my superannuated little-girl look. Lynne wore saddle shoes; I still wore ankle-strap Mary Janes (but never made of patent leather, of course, since nuns said they reflected up a dress).

One afternoon with Lynne, I ventured onto the subject of sex. I had never forgotten Lex saying that he hoped his first wife's new husband might be "kind enough" to give Lynne lessons.

"What d'you mean, lessons?" she said.

"Well," I said, fumbling, "your stepfather, I mean, has he ever shown you stuff? Um, uh . . . you know. Like touched you anywhere?"

"What do you mean?" she repeated, quite unaware of my drift. I felt a tiny shiver of loneliness, and let it go.

After three months of service in Mapleton's war zone, Miss Gale resigned. The agency sent over Miss Cannon as her replacement, a tall gruff woman from Milwaukee whose method for dealing with disobedience was to lock the child in a closet. Miss Cannon stayed the course for seven weeks.

After that came a tall German woman in her thirties. She seemed off to a good start until that Christmas when Mother, Lex, Zan, and I took off for a short Acapulco holiday, leaving her lonely in Mapleton's twenty-four rooms. One day Gran paid one of her surprise visits and went upstairs to find the new nanny in Mother's bed making love with another woman.

Having been through five governesses in two years, Mother decided she had to get more involved in my upbringing. She knew there were limits to her dominion over her stepchildren, especially when Lynne and Zan's own father approved of their spirited ways, but she could still do something about me. Lex was away making a movie called *Cry Innocent*, so when Mother had an afternoon off she sometimes summoned me to her sitting room, where we sat facing each other in satin chairs by a bay window overlooking the front lawn.

Gone were the days when Mother praised my curly eyelashes and thick hair. At twelve I was going into the awkward stage, and it seemed there was nothing pleasing about me. I averaged A's in school, spoke only when spoken to, devoured uplifting books, and had just dropped ten pounds of baby fat, but all this passed without comment. We were beginning to circle in a mother-daughter face-off of authority versus will. She criticized everything from my terrible hairdos and love of too grown-up clothes to my sullen attitude and appalling posture. I was, in Mother's eyes, a mess. I became convinced that she thought I was hopelessly ugly and that she wanted to keep me a baby. I still cravenly sought her approval, but I would settle for criticism because at least it meant she was paying attention to me.

The fact is, when I was in her presence, I did indeed feel messy and awkward. She was petite, and I now stood three inches taller with very long legs and a boy's chest. I was not quite sure what to *do* with everything. Inside I was little; outside I was big. I had no fingernails, there were braces on my teeth, and my voice sounded nasal from adenoids. Yet I longed with all my heart to project a feminine grace like hers. I needed a lot of work to turn people's heads as she did, and since she was a world-class expert on beauty, I resolved to heed her criticism in order to learn to look better.

She was certainly right about my terrible posture. Increasingly self-conscious about my height, I had begun to slouch as if ducking through low doorways. I could see that Gran was resigning herself to a widow's hump, so when Mother said with meaning, "We've got to cure that before it gets worse," I agreed.

Thereafter, for more than a year I walked for thirty minutes each day balancing a book on my head, pacing a forty-foot loggia from the bar to the living room, ending with a careful walk up the stairs. When she instructed me, it was a scene right out of *Ziegfeld Girl,* one of her early movies in which the chorus girl she played was told to imagine a puppeteer's string stuck to her head pulling the backbone straight up. "And if you don't do this exercise every day," Mother warned, "I'm going to have a steel bar built up the spine in all your dresses." (I almost thought she might.) "Someday, Baby, you'll be glad you're tall—you can wear clothes." (Oh, sure, I thought.)

She shared with me the secret of her famous walk, and I was able to copy it. You step one foot just slightly in front of the other; and then, as she advised, "Pretend there's a nickel tucked between your buttocks and you have to hold it there for dear life so it won't fall out."

In her Louis XVI bathroom suite, she showed me surprising things about her beauty routine. She could afford the world's costliest creams (and had even endorsed one or two), but she herself used humble products bought in the five-and-dime. After bathing, she slathered her body with Nivea cream, and once a week, to achieve deep-down cleansing of pores, she scrubbed her face with a paste made of Twenty Mule Team Boraxo, an industrial-strength scouring powder (for which Ronald Reagan was once the television spokesman) used to clean greasy hands. Mother recalled with a laugh that back when she shared her Boraxo secret with Kathryn Grayson, at the time the leading soprano at M-G-M, Kathryn accused Mother of trying to sabotage her face.

Such moments of sharing came as happy contrast to our normally strained relations. But even then Mother did not speak in the tones of a sister or friend, as one might have hoped. She was always self-conscious as a mother, often speaking of herself in the third person: "Mother doesn't like your tone of voice, young lady."

Her publicity during this period insisted that, busy star though she was, she had embraced with vast pleasure the role of playing fulltime mother to a budding adolescent. "Cherry's twelve now," she told *Photoplay*. "She's right on the threshold of her teens—the 'perilous teens,' . . . I'm young enough to remember them well. . . . You feel you have to live life all at once before it gets away from you. . . . You're scared to death of being called a wall-flower. You desperately want to be liked by everyone. . . . How I would have appreciated it if someone had just given me a set of rules to guide me through that growing-up period. Instead, it's taken me ten years of experience and study to find out some of the important answers to life. Now if I can impart them to Cheryl while she's still young, she'll be spared many of the mistakes I made . . . because [I] had no one to understand or advise [me]."

The fact is, Mother did have someone to understand and advise her at twelve. It was then that she was living in San Francisco with Gran, who paid the rent by doing finger waves. She and Gran were friends who spent long hours together, practiced etiquette, worshiped movie stars and society ladies and pretty clothes, while Mother even belted out a song in a talent contest.

That fall of 1955, through the combined wheedling of Gran, Dad, Lex, Lynne, and me, Mother was persuaded to let me transfer from St. Paul's to begin the seventh grade at the Town and Country School in Bel Air, where Lynne studied. It was a big mistake, the first of several.

A 180-degree change from hidebound St. Paul's, Town and Country was an exclusive and sophisticated junior high that took star babies in stride. The children of Dean Martin and Johnny Weissmuller were my classmates, and one of the big wheels on its fir-treed campus was Jill Schary, daughter of Dore Schary, then Mother's boss at M-G-M, though I wasn't aware of it. A bubbly, wisecracking redhead and casual friend of mine, Jill went on to write books about Hollywood, including *Perdido*, under her married name of Jill Robinson.

Being my mother's daughter gave me a measure of status in a student body derived in large part from the movie colony. In our pecking order, children of studio executives, directors, and stars were on top. Nonetheless, for once I had the feeling that classmates sought me out for myself—they didn't just point and whisper.

Mother still did not permit me to go to friends' homes after school, since they were all "too fast." Nor did I invite them to see how I was babied at Mapleton. But school was fun, and in this freer social setting, among peers who enjoyed privileges similar to mine, my interests went out of focus. The straight A's of St. Pauls slid to C's and D's in every course except English literature, and then only because I read so voraciously on my own. I contrived with a vengeance to dress older. The school had a uniform, but my friends and I wore layers of crinolines under its full skirt—so that it billowed out—and which we also hitched up—so that it came only to our knees. Freshly sprung from a convent school, I intended to make up for lost time.

I fit into some of Mother's clothes now, and I briefly "borrowed" things from her closet for my Sunday dates with Dad. It was impossible for Mother to miss anything from her sixty-foot clothing rack. One night, when she was away and I was rummaging in her vast closet for some high heels to wear, Mother's far bedroom door flew open. There stood Lex, frightened, naked, and in a crouch, as he pointed Mother's .38 revolver at me. "No! No!" I screamed, and ran out the other door. He had been sleeping and thought the sounds in the closet were those of a burglar.

I was learning that I could defy Mother about clothes behind her back, especially on big occasions. Town and Country's fall prom was to be held that November at the Beverly Wilshire Hotel. Since it would be my first formal dance, Dad took me to Bullocks and picked out a dress. He chose a sweet, antebellum frock with a high neck and tiers of white ruffles all the way to the floor. Mother saw it hanging in my room and went tight around the mouth. I was too young to wear a long gown, she said, and what I thought of as my Scarlett O'Hara dress quickly vanished. She bought, as a replacement, something that was knee-length and lace-trimmed with baby puff sleeves. I was determined not to wear it, and since Mother was scheduled to be in Mexico the night of the dance, I pulled together something halfway grown-up.

Just like Scarlett O'Hara, who had made herself a dress out of curtains, I knew that desperate times called for desperate measures. The attic yielded a ballet costume I had worn once, not too long ago, at a dance recital. It was pink tulle and came blessedly to my ankles. Gran, joining in cahoots, bought me dyed-to-match accessories and sewed on bits of tulle around the taffeta sweetheart bodice. Dad, who was escorting Lynne and me to the 200-couple affair, rented us a pair of fur capes made of pink-dyed rabbit.

Lynne had given up the fight about clothes and wore a skirt and blouse Mother had bought her. (Life was too strict around our house, and she was chafing to return home.)

That night, though I felt really grown-up in my pink tulle and taffeta swirl, I must have looked like cotton candy on legs. Then it happened—the long arm of Mother's justice reached all the way from Mexico, and I began to unravel. The ballet costume had been made to be worn only once, and while I was whirling around on the dance floor with Dad, the stitching gave out. First, panels of tulle pulled away from the waist; then a waist seam went; and suddenly the whole bodice needed fast pinning. I spent half the night in the ladies' room. By the time we arrived at Dad's late night party at the Luau, I had quite literally gone to pieces and everyone gave me a teasing. But I didn't care. I was on a high roll of happiness.

When Mother learned of the conspiracy, she vented her spleen on Gran, bringing her to tears. Mother knew all too well, of course, that the freedom Gran had allowed her had helped to produce the "Nightclub Queen," and now she could foresee the same thing happening all over again with me.

Mother promptly yanked me out of Town and Country before the year's end and sent me off to boarding school, while Lynne and Zan went back to their mother. ("Cleaning house," Mother called it.)

During these unsettling days, something even more ominous was in the air, seeming to stir the dust covers that now rested over Mapleton's furniture like ghosts. Mother was worried about something at work, and the usual quiet that prevailed upstairs was frequently shattered by loud voices and slamming doors. The Barkers were in trouble. When not in Acapulco, where they were breaking ground for a house, or at parties and premieres, where they'd long since become one of the famed fun couples, they would stay at home and quarrel.

Lex continued to press his twilight assaults. Although in interviews Mother stressed how involved as a mother she was with me, she didn't even sense what was going on. "My last bit of advice to my daughter," she confided to *Photoplay*, "will be if you have any questions or any problems please come to me and we'll discuss them together." But the things we discussed in her sitting room fell far short of my problem. What I couldn't bring to my lips was screaming in my head: *You're my mother. Why don't you sense what's going on? Why can't you see?*

No one suspected, least of all Mother. The press even saw me as one of Lex's fans. It was reported that I had watched him on television in one of his early films, *The Farmer's Daughter,* and turned to exclaim, "Oh Mother, wasn't he positively yummy!"

Twenty

I was afraid of what Mother had in mind by sending me off to boarding school after those months of freedom at Town and Country. True, it was not the remote abbey in Switzerland with which she had once threatened me, and it was not the Mexican convent she spoke of during our Christmas in Acapulco (in order to be closer to her and Lex in their favorite sunny hideaway, she said). No, the school she chose was Flintridge Sacred Heart Academy near Pasadena, just forty-five minutes from home. It was an all-girls parochial school with a reputation for being strict. I had heard that a few of the girls were "difficult."

On that day in January 1956, Sacred Heart rose up through the windshield as a forbidding Spanish-style fortress atop a winding wooded road as I approached it in the car with Mother and Gran. A former hotel, it offered such perks as carpeting, private baths, and a plush lobby, but deluxe as it was, the school might as well have been buried in the far-off Sahara. No one was allowed to sign out of its fenced confines except on weekends, and since I couldn't travel by myself, Gran would have to collect me when and if she could. More than half the students came from well-off South American families, and, like them, I was destined seldom to go home. Mother was rejecting me once and for all, it seemed.

When they deposited me that first day, I held tight to Mother's hand and wheedled a promise that I could return home the very first weekend. She said, "Yes, yes," and, looking over my shoulder, gave a squeal of delight as she recognized a student working at the front desk. It was Joan Crawford's teenage daughter, Christina, whom I had never met. Christina took special pains to welcome me and to help reduce the hassle of my midyear arrival. Seeing how downcast I looked after Mother and Gran left, she helped settle me into a three-roommate suite in the school's junior section, then sat me down for a chat.

"I know you're frightened," she said. "It's all new and strange, but you'll get used to everything. It's really a wonderful place." She smiled but her pale blue eyes were sad, and I thought of those tales I'd overheard long ago on the nanny network. "Interesting to see how *that* kid'll turn out," Miss Hulley had chortled. Now here sat Christina, soon to be seventeen.

Although I could see that we had things in common, I sensed how very different we were deep down. While she had been knocked around by a mother who seemed obsessed with her, my own had spanked me just once and I deserved it (for accidentally locking my dog in a closed space). Mother was never *intentionally* cruel to anyone, either physically or psychologically, though sometimes it may have seemed to me that she was. The violence Christina endured—whippings, deprivation, confinements—would have sent me racing out the door.

I had heard that her younger brother had been restrained in bed at night with leather harnesses. By contrast, when I had chicken pox and a hired nurse tied me to the bed to stop my scratching, I went berserk and shredded the sheets. ("She doesn't like to be restrained," Gran remarked dryly.) And when Miss Cannon locked me in a closet, my screams could be heard on Sunset.

There was fight in my nature that Christina didn't have. Facing exile in Pasadena, I was preparing to rebel against Mother. Christina, on the other hand, had apparently backed down under the weight of her problems at home and accepted her fate. To me, she seemed a bird with a broken wing, and my chick's heart was touched by her plight.

As we sat clasping hands that day, she gave pointers on how to get along at Sacred Heart—the pitfalls, the best teachers, and so on. She was as tall as I was, but ex-

tremely thin with cropped blond curls that framed a large
handsome head. Overall, she exuded wistfulness. She
seemed to coax genial smiles from herself that lingered
uncertainly, yet her gaze into my eyes was warm with—
what? Understanding? Sympathy? Why sympathy for me?
Her gaze was comforting and puzzling at the same time.

Though she was a senior scheduled to graduate that
June, and I was only in seventh grade, she had the extraordinary kindness to sometimes drop by my room and check
on my progress. "How's it going?" she'd ask with a
jaunty tilt of her head. It wasn't long before I heard the
buzz around school about Christina—how she was not allowed to go home and couldn't leave the grounds, not
even to attend her senior class picnic. She could receive
no phone calls, mail, or visitors. Effectively she was in
prison, though she never spoke about it.

I, happily, was able to go home about once a month.
Not that first weekend, as it turned out, but soon thereafter. I lined up every Tuesday at the lobby pay phones to
call home and learn my status. My going home depended
on whether Mother would be at Mapleton, and she usually
wasn't. Lex urged me to come when he would be there by
himself, but I declined his invitations. Nevertheless, he
often forced himself on me that spring with Mother in the
house. He was growing bolder. Sometimes, with the three
of us in a room and Mother's back turned, he would snatch
at my private parts before I could pull away. He was so
confident I wouldn't tell—and I wouldn't—yet part of me
wanted Mother to spin around and catch us so I could face
the terrible consequences and Lex would finally be
stopped.

One weekend in February there was a special reason
why I couldn't go home. "Mother is leaving M-G-M,"
she announced, her voice rigid with hauteur. "I'm setting
up my own production company, and I'm going to be very,
very busy with plans and whatnot."

After eighteen years at Metro as one of its top-grossing
stars, Mother was out. She puffed with self-pride to cover
the blow, but I could see she was devastated, and I hurt
inside for her. Fear of being fired would explain her recent
shortness with us all, the curious haughtiness that was

creeping into her manner, and most of all, the penny-pinching. When Metro dropped their option on her contract's remaining two years, she was obliged to pay up the studio's loans to her, which were sizable. As never before, we were in for a spell of belt-tightening. Every single household expense was checked over now, and one day when she said, "Those are too much money," it made me blink and take notice that Mother had actually said the word "money." Until then, whenever she bought a pair of shoes, she invariably added, "I'll take them in every color they come in."

There's one nice thing about a boarding school. You can become anyone you want to be, you can invent any persona you're able to make stick. I chose to become the sophisticate. I learned to say things like "Oh, that's boring" and "Let's play canasta." I memorized snippets of verse. While other kids announced they were "hitting the sack," I'd declare my Hamlet-like desire "to sleep, perchance to dream." I might greet mates at sunrise breakfast with, "But soft! What light through yonder window breaks—hey, girls?"

The perfume of envy I felt wafting my way at Town and Country had proved seductively sweet, and now instead of withdrawing, I wanted to be noticed. Along with the regulation uniforms we all wore, I sported sneakers and bright sweaters, which the authorities frowned on. Everyone went for easy-to-keep braids or ponytails, but I affected shoulder-length hair with a lock falling over one eye, in the decade-old style of Veronica Lake. I thought it was glamorous, mysterious. I patterned my voice on Tallulah Bankhead, while achieving something closer to Alexis Smith. And to complete the grown-up effect, I arranged my lips into a pout of perpetual boredom.

I did not much like the misfit I saw in my morning mirror, and I wanted to mask her. But the wise observer saw a troubled preteen in Cheryl. My pretending made nuns nervous, but they said nothing because my grades rose to B's, I merely "bent" the regulations a little, and I was well accepted by my classmates (who somehow bought the sophisticate).

In this reinvention of myself, I wanted, above all, to seem older, and I made it a point to associate with girls two and three years my senior. To look the part, I hitched up the skirt of my uniform to a fashionable length and wore some of Mother's old clothes when the school day ended. Those rare weekends at home meant Sunday dinner with Dad. When he collected me at Mapleton in his black Lincoln Continental, I would enact a hasty ritual inside the car: I loosened my hair, slapped on lipstick, and stepped into a pair of spike heels.

My furtive changes in the car made him chuckle. Impatient for me to grow up, he was proud to squire me on his arm at LaRue's and Romanoff's or install me like a girlfriend at the Luau's Bar One. "I'd like you to meet the most beautiful woman in my life," he'd say to friends. Never blushing at the introduction, I appeared to be sixteen years old and behaved as though I were thirty. Dad was on my side. "Lana," he would say, "why don't you buy the kid some dresses? We go to dinner and you send her out wearing goddamn baby clothes!"

"You're not fooling me," she fumed later. "I know your father lets you wear makeup when you're with him. He encourages that in you behind my back, and it's *not* becoming."

My use of lipstick began innocently enough that summer when Mother, caving into pressure, gave me a child's pink lip gloss on my thirteenth birthday. I, of course, applied enough layers to make my mouth look rabid. But the lipstick taboo had been broken, and in the fall I freely used Jungle Red for evenings at school and on weekends when I was stuck there with the Latin girls, who couldn't go home either. I missed Christina, who, having been graduated, was free. I heard that she had openly broken off with her mother.

That fall semester, as a result of overcrowding, I was one of a few lower school girls chosen to live in the school's upper school quarters, where ages ranged up to eighteen. At the same time, my class elected me vice president. With this newly won status, my famous parentage, and the self-styled image of a sophisticate, I began to attract ad-

olescent admirers in the lower school who wanted to polish my saddle shoes and carry my books.

It was common for impressionable girls, many of them
far away from home, to form crushes on upper school
girls, much as I had done back at St. Paul's when I became
Charlene's "Little Shadow." It was accepted form to be
tolerant of the "babies," as we called them, to accept
them as slaves and be sweet to them—which is what I did.
But when I thought about what I was doing, it gave me
pause to realize that I was only a little older than they.
Though standing 5'8", I was just a child whose confident
air was painted on, and I was as susceptible as any of them
to a crush.

I met Maria when my room assignment was reshuffled
that fall. She lived at the end of my corridor in the serene
privacy of her own single room. She was seventeen, a
pretty brunette with flashing dark eyes and curls down her
back. Her family's ranch occupied a quarter of some Latin
American country. We glanced at each other with interest,
and, during evenings after dinner, embarked on a fortnight
of pouring out our souls to each other. Soon there was
touching, then petting, then one night a kiss.

One day Gran asked, "How's school? You look
happy."

"I'm in love," I replied.

"Oh, how sweet," said Mother. "What's his name?"

"It's not a he—it's a she."

They traded glances. Mother adjusted her pearls, her
bracelet, and her sleeves, then spoke. "Oh, darling, that
happens to everyone. You get a crush, but that's not love.
All little girls go through that stage—why, I even loved
my homeroom teacher, Miss Petch."

Gran sat silent for a moment pursing her lips. "Well,
uh," she ventured, "that's nice, dear."

"—but it certainly isn't love," Mother shot back, "and
you shouldn't go around telling people it is."

That was that. The subject never riled Mother again,
and I realized there was something more about love than
they were letting on. I knew I wasn't feeling the feelings
other girls thrilled about in the bull sessions, but I played
along and said I had a crush on some boy, too. Since I

was eight, boys had seemed to speak a different language. I dreaded dancing school because of my height, my baby clothes, and because I seemed not to be the outgoing type that they went for.

I threw my young heart at Maria, so much so that she began to ease away. She felt crowded and did not want to draw attention. "Don't hang around," she'd say when I crossed to her on the upper school playground. That hurt. Like Mother and Gran, Maria also wanted to avoid discussing these wonderful feelings I had. Why would love make people squirm?

Late that semester whispers could be heard about a new girl who had come to Sacred Heart. "She's been in Juvenile Hall," girls said, which was greeted by looks of horror. I was fascinated and wanted to know more. The opportunity arrived one day during a schoolwide outing to an amusement park. I managed to sit next to her on the bus and finally summoned the courage to strike up a chat.

"Is it true you ran away from home?" I asked.

Long pause. "Uh-huh."

"Was that why they put you in Juvenile Hall?"

"Uh-huh. Is Lana Turner really your mother?"

Bonded thus by mutual sin, we spent the whole day in a rowboat going in circles around a cement pond and trading information. She corrected my information about Juvenile Hall, explaining that you were fed more than bread and water there, and, while it was sort of a jail with wire on the windows, you did someday get out. "Shit, it wasn't that bad," she said, spitting through her teeth into the water. Tiny sensations of danger shivered up my back. How darkly alluring it seemed.

The school duly phoned Mother to report my association with a problem student who, they noted, had "a bad mouth." I was secretly pleased to have irked Mother again. After that, I took to pairing off with the runaway for walks on the playground. She was the first rebel I had met, and, being an underdog, she touched something inside me. Our odd affinity didn't last for very long, however, because she was soon expelled for kicking a nun.

During the bull sessions that sprang up during long leisure hours at school, the discussion always turned to boys and sex—what you did and didn't do with them. I learned that there was something called "statutory rape" in which, if the girl was under eighteen and the boy was not, he got into trouble. If I could believe that, it meant Lex had told me two lies about what terrible things would happen if I talked: being sent to Juvenile Hall was *not* an eternity in hell, and *he*, as well as I, would be punished for what we did. These revelations led to sleepless nights, and Maria wondered what had gotten into me. I couldn't tell her or anyone, but I had ammunition to fight him now.

Mother, Lex, and I shared our third Christmas in Acapulco together, and it was a tense time. Lacking M-G-M's help, she had spent the whole year trying to line up a decent picture and managed to land only a light domestic comedy named *The Lady Takes a Flyer,* costarring Jeff Chandler. (Ironically, her role was that of a pilot who gives up her career to raise a daughter properly.)

Meanwhile, Lex had ground out six B-movies and a TV pilot. Gossip columns pointedly noted his absences for location work, one lasting for five weeks, and they linked him with various starlets working on his movies.

Despite it all, Mother had gotten pregnant, and the Barkers had pinned some hope for revitalizing their marriage on the January arrival of "baby," as she disconcertingly called it. I wondered what was to become, after thirteen years, of the "baby" she already had. They wanted a boy, they told the press, and would call it Christopher no matter which gender it was. Their hopes were dashed, though, when Mother suffered a stillbirth in October. It was the second time she had miscarried by Lex, who had boasted earlier that he was the perfect blood type to overcome her RH problem. The loss of the baby may have signaled the point of no return in the marriage.

When Lex and I went back to Mapleton the night we saw Mother in the hospital, he raped me with what seemed like a frenzied will to hurt. He was very rough and I bled.

The next time I faced him was that Christmas, when the three of us checked into their usual glass-and-marble bungalow at the Villa Vera Hotel in Acapulco. It had long been Mother's favorite place to stay, and, without her knowledge, the staff had taken to calling it the "Lana Turner suite."

Shortly after my arrival, it became clear to me that the Barkers' marriage had reached its third, and final, stage. Mother was following her usual pattern with men. Stage One was the period of Mother's selfless devotion to her spouse; Stage Two involved a reassertion of her needs, and in Stage Three she spewed out her bitter feelings of blame and reproach for all the sacrifices she had made in Stage One. Mother always overfed on love and never learned how to deal with the dyspeptic consequences.

"After all I've done for you!" she shouted at him as I splashed in the pool outside the bungalow. "After all I've *spent* on you—you bastard!"

One twilight just after returning from Acapulco, when no one was at Mapleton except for Lex and me, Lex opened my door and peered in. I sat up and covered my chest. "I'm-not-going-to-do-this-anymore," I said in a rush. "You can't make me."

"Hah," he grunted. "What makes you think you can stop me?"

"I found out you can get in trouble for this, too."

"You haven't told anybody!" he said sharply, his face darkening as he crossed to my bed.

". . . No, but I, um, I'm sure thinking about it. I . . ."

Standing above me, he flexed his shoulders as if reaching for barbells.

"I, I . . ."

"Don't get smart with me, because you're the one that'll suffer. They'll put you away for so long that you'll never—"

"But they won't—they won't!" I cried.

His forearm came up and smashed across my face. I blacked out for an instant, waking to feel warm blood in my mouth and hands choking my throat. *"You're gonna show me, huh?"* he yelled. *"You little bitch!"* And with that he plowed into me with a punishing anger. I fought not to black out again. What was happening was happening, and I was furious. I tried to scream, but he kept a hand grabbed around my throat and I couldn't breathe,

even to gasp. *Is he killing me? Am I dying?* I wondered.
My arms were as useless as flippers, and I had no air, no
voice, not even nails to scratch him. His orgasm brought
an ecstatic hiss of rage that died off in waves. I breathed
gulps of life as he rolled back and headed toward the door.
"Remember—trap *shut*," he warned as he left.

So intense was the pain that I was unable to stand until
the next morning.

"You've got to tell someone," begged Maria. "They'll
make him stop. Or else he'll just keep doing it." Her eyes
were imploring. "Oh, and Cheryl, while this is going on,
you can't be confirmed, either."

I decided to tell Gran.

I was staying at Gran's the last weekend of February 1957.
Irene Hulley had been invited to dinner that Saturday night.
I always enjoyed Gran's occasional dinners for the three
of us, for I still felt affection for Miss Hulley. Miss Hulley, who lived just two blocks away, had left her work in
child care to become a sort of house manager. At the time,
I knew nothing of the way she had contributed items about
us to the nanny network.

After dinner, while Gran cleared the dishes, Miss Hulley and I walked Gran's poodle, Jiminy Cricket, and my
own little aging Tinkette. We strolled the dark street and
talked about Mother. My heart was bursting to confess
then and there. "Miss Hulley," I began, just the way I'd
rehearsed it for Gran, "Lex has been coming into my room
at night."

"What!?" she demanded. "Oh, my God, has he
touched you?" When I nodded and started to cry, she
grabbed my hand and marched us back to Gran's. "Millie,
Lex has been molesting her," she said triumphantly,
nudging me to stand where Gran could get a good look at
me. I poured out the general facts and Gran picked up the
phone.

"You must tell this to your mother," she said to me.
My heart sank as she dialed Mapleton. "Lana, I want you
to come down here *right away*. . . . It's about the

baby. . . . No, I *can't* tell you over the phone. . . . And don't bring Lex.''

Mother's reaction surprised me. She had just returned with Lex from a dinner party at Jack Benny's, but she told him there was some crisis involving me and tore over to Gran's, arriving in an ermine coat and red sequined dress. I sat alone on the sofa looking stricken as she sank beside me and gently squeezed my arm.

''Tell me, darling, what . . .''

''It's Lex.''

''What about Lex?''

''He's been coming into my room at night and doing things to me.''

''Oh, my God!'' she gasped, covering her mouth. Her eyes flashed, then narrowed, and peered into mine as if searching for something. Not finding it, she stiffened her back and lifted her chin as a coldness seemed to form like a film across her eyes. The air in Gran's living room crackled. Tinkette let out a mighty yip-yip-yip and hopped into my lap, where she trembled and licked my hands. Mother's face hardened now. She didn't believe me.

''I hope you're telling the truth, young lady, because I am taking you to see a doctor in the morning.''

''Doctor? Tomorrow's Sunday,'' I said lamely.

''That's okay—I'll arrange it. Now tell me when this happened, how many times.''

I faced an endless drill of questions as she aligned her memory of times and dates with facts and places. Gran rose from across the room and busied herself in the kitchen as Mother then probed for intimate details. Finally seeming to be convinced, she squared her shoulders and breathed a long, resigned sigh. For a moment she studied my face, then suddenly, in an antic change of pace, she lifted her eyebrows and screwed her mouth into the frown of an imp. The tension was broken. We embraced each other in relief as Tinkette sputtered furiously to the floor.

Mother had not rejected me after all, but the blank looks she exchanged with Gran said they didn't know what to do next. I was still frightened, and to avoid facing Lex at Mapleton, I wanted to sleep at Gran's. After I went to bed, Mother and Gran talked until three in the morning.

Gran kept waking me to say, "Don't think of it—push it out of your mind."

Mother drove back to Mapleton that windy moonless night. She eased her Caddy into the driveway and, seeing no lights, stepped into the front hall. As she listened in the dark, the only sound was that made by the chandelier tinkling in the wind.

On cat feet she climbed the staircase dragging the ermine, then looked down the north wing to see a light under her door. Gathering strength to do what she intended, she turned the knob and looked inside. Lex was sleeping naked on top of the covers with a reading light on and newspapers scattered about, as a television set hissed after-hours snow. After a moment she crossed to the nightstand, took out her revolver, and stepped back to study her mate's reclining form.

You bastard, she thought. She remembered that he had talked to her about his fantasies involving young girls.

Her gloved hand rose to point the gun close to his head. She paused, frozen in doubt. *Is this rat worth the rest of my life in prison?* she thought. *The end of my career? Everyone's life ruined? What if I turned him in? But the headlines, the police, and everyone's life still ruined anyway.*

She lowered the gun, and retreated quickly through a side door to her sitting room, where for the next two hours she sat on a sofa, facing the window, thinking and smoking and waiting. As the morning light came, she heard sounds from Lex's bath before his head appeared around the door.

"What in the hell are you doing in here?" he asked. "Why didn't you come to bed?"

Slowly turning her head, Mother fixed him with an icy stare.

"What has your daughter been telling you?" he asked.

Mother held her gaze.

"She's lying!"

"Listen, you," she said. "I want you out of here in twenty minutes, and you know why. Cheryl told me everything and we're never going to discuss it." He began to sputter a protest and she cut him off. "Twenty minutes or I'm calling the police!"

That next morning Mother drove me two blocks to the Beverly Hills Clinic. It was Sunday and Dr. McDonald was away, but Mother's name was enough for the answering service to call in another staff doctor. Dr. R. H. Fagin opened the door and led us through eerie empty halls to his office.

A stout, good-natured man, Dr. Fagin recognized my fear and tried to relax me. After a private exchange with Mother, he went to work, asking no questions and saying nothing to me. I had never before had a pelvic exam, and I didn't understand what he was looking for. I could hear Mother crying in the outer waiting room. After the exam, he called her into his office. "Lana," he said, as I bent an ear to listen, "I can't tell you who's been there, but someone definitely has. She has been injured. She should have had stitches. There are definite signs of violent entry and more than once."

Years later I retrieved from the clinic's back files the only document that recorded my fifteen-dollar gynecological exam that day. Dr. Fagin's two-page report, which noted I was thirteen and one half years old and had been "Brought in by mother," displays all his medical scribbles. They seem arcane but for one telling note. On the second page, under the category of "Pelvic," all the checklist items are marked off as normal—save one. Beside INTROITUS—an item that called for his impression of the vaginal opening—he has discreetly written "Marital."

Twenty-one

"**J**eez-uz," she said, resting her forehead on the steering wheel. "I've got to tell your father."

"But Mama, he's only just out of surgery."

"I don't care, Stephen's got to know."

For the previous five days Dad had been in St. John's Hospital recovering from brain surgery. He had been having headaches, then blackouts. The doctors had feared it was brain cancer or some complication from the steel plate that had been implanted in his skull after the car crash in Paris. Exploratory surgery revealed a benign tumor—and something else as well.

It seems that back in his leading-man days at Columbia, the studio had been worried that his hair was beginning to thin. Wizards in the makeup department suggested he try a little-known miracle method of reversing hair loss. It consisted of injecting a mystery substance, a gel, in strategic places under the scalp. Dad decided to have the shots, but now, after a dozen years, the stuff had drifted out of position and had to be removed.

He was past danger from the surgery and quietly feeling foolish about it all when I entered his hospital room that Sunday afternoon. Mother had prepared him with the bad news and he was tender with me about it. "Now, honey, don't be upset," he said. "You're okay. You're gonna be okay. Don't think about it." He turned to Mother. "Lana, I'm going to kill that son-of-a-bitch." He winced in pain because he had turned his bandaged head too quickly. Mother bent forward and patted him sympathetically.

"There, there, dear Stephen," she said. He gave a brave smile.

A few years earlier it would have made my heart skip with joy to see them share a moment like this. I had so longed for them to get back together. After their respective divorces from Bob Topping and Martine Carol, I worried them with the wedding idea like a terrier with a bone. "Oh," I'd say, "wouldn't it be nice if you two got married again?" That usually brought a weak smile and a phrase like, "Well, honey, we lead such different lives."

Now Mother's fourth marriage was collapsing and Dad was still free, but nothing was less likely than their reunion, nor would I have wanted it. Their closeness at the hospital was, however, an early hint of their growing mutual regard. I guess they were getting older and more resigned to being bonded by me.

Despite their fury about Lex's criminal behavior, my parents never gave serious thought to handing him over to the police. I suppose they were afraid of the scandal. Child molestation was probably as widespread in the fifties as it is today (according to current estimates, one out of every three girls and one out of every five boys is sexually abused in some way), but people were even less inclined to report it back then.

Nor did my parents make any special effort to get me to talk about what had happened. And they never considered sending me to a psychiatrist for professional counseling. As Mother explained to me years later, "People didn't see shrinks, *period.*" Instead, I was urged never to think of "it" again.

Mother said what she regarded as the last word on the subject right there in the hospital. "Stephen, I've taken care of it—about Lex," she said wearily. "This morning he moved out of the house and tomorrow I file for divorce." She turned to me and said with sympathy in her eyes, "Baby, you won't ever, *ever* have to see that man again."

There were still the usual signs of "that man" when we got back to Mapleton—barbells, the rowing machine, lots of clothes. The only obvious thing missing besides Lex himself was Pulco, whose dog run beside the greenhouse stood quiet and forlorn.

On Monday morning Mother drove me to Westwood for a dentist's appointment. We pulled into the parking lot, and, as she was about to turn off the ignition, an arm reached in the window and grabbed her hand on the steering wheel. It was Lex's arm.

"Lana, this child has lied to you! We have to talk!"

I froze.

"Get out of here," she said. "I'm not going to speak to you. Leave us alone!"

"Tell your mother you're lying," he yelled. I shook my head and backed toward the corner. He had tears in his eyes. *Tears.*

"Get away!" With a violent lunge Mother yanked her arm free and tried to roll up the window, but he held it down.

"They're all lies, Lana!"

She revved up the engine and shifted the car jerkily into reverse. "I'm pulling out of here, and if you don't let go, I will run you over." She waited. His eyes narrowed on me. With that, she hit the gas, dragging him along for several feet until a grab of the brakes sent him tumbling to the asphalt. We sped away and he shrank to a tiny figure dusting himself off, intently watching our flight.

On Wednesday the newspapers carried a story saying that Mother and Lex had separated due to a "misunderstanding" that started outside a dentist's office. "It doesn't matter what this particular argument was about," Mother told the press. It was "just the culmination" of many fights. "In my mind I haven't gotten to the word 'divorce' yet," she added. "It's all too fresh."

Any chance of a reconciliation? "I don't know," she sighed. "Surely there must be happiness for me someplace."

After the parking lot incident, I begged Mother not to send me back to boarding school but to keep me with her at Mapleton. She flatly refused, and in a few weeks I knew why. Mapleton was up for sale.

* * *

My father's new girlfriend proved to be a sort of answered prayer for me. During the launching of the Luau, Dad had been linked in gossip columns with every new face from Terry Moore to Mamie Van Doren, but dating celebrities can be exhausting, as well he knew. They need looking after; he couldn't just park a movie star in a corner all night while he tended to customers.

His new steady was an attractive receptionist who genuinely enjoyed playing the role of the owner's girlfriend at Bar One every night. Her name was Helen DeMaree. She was a twenty-four-year-old divorcee, a policeman's daughter whose raven beauty bespoke both Irish and American Indian ancestry. Her story was not uncommon. Drawn by the town's glamour and a vague ambition to act, she came to Hollywood from Kansas to see how far looks and smarts could take her. After a short-lived marriage, she began dating Ronnie Burns (son of George and Gracie), actor Doug McClure, and restaurateur Steve Crane.

I adored Helen. Blessed with perfect style sense, she was always impeccably turned out in the latest fashions. I was looking for a role model then, a woman who could teach me something about style, about how a woman puts herself together. Mother had straightened my posture and cleared my skin, but she didn't really share her taste in clothes with me. In any case, I thought her fashion sense was dowdy. Mother was locked in the early fifties with her mid-calf skirts, platinum hair, and severely tailored curves. She gave interviews knocking Dior. But Helen, my new pal at Bar One, delighted in giving me up-to-the-minute help as if she were a big sister, even though she was ten years older than I.

That spring I found another new friend at Sacred Heart. Maggie Douglas was an arriving seventh grader who held the dubious honor of being the school's only other star baby. Her mother was Virginia Field, a British-born star of B-pictures who was an old friend of my mother's. Her father was leading character actor Paul Douglas.

Mother and Virginia decided that we would all meet in Palm Desert, California, the last weekend in March. Virginia owned a bungalow motel there, and we could join up for some sun around the pool at the Shadow Mountain Club. At first it was supposed to be just the four of us, but soon the party swelled to five. Mother was bringing a guest, a male friend who, perhaps because of her pending divorce or his youth (he was twenty-two), was not supposed to be thought of as her "boyfriend." Their relationship was never clear, but he was at least sort of a protégé. When Mother met him he was a struggling actor named Ralph Vitti, but he renamed himself Michael Dante on her advice and soon landed work in movies. Good-looking and swarthy, he played shortstop for the Hollywood Stars baseball team. I liked him.

Meanwhile, Maria was upset that I was going off to Palm Desert with Maggie. She had no reason to be jealous, though. Maggie was, as Mother noted disapprovingly, "boy crazy."

To save on a limousine, Maggie and I rode unescorted to Palm Desert on a Greyhound bus. It was my first bus ride, and the last for years to come. *"My* daughter on a bus," Mother sniffed.

Mother took a poolside bungalow at the motel, and although she wanted me to share her twin-bedded room, I insisted on joining Maggie at the Douglas house nearby. With the Lex crisis and the sale of Mapleton fresh in my mind, I wanted to keep a little distance from Mother. Newly divorced, nearly broke, her career in a slump, she was short-tempered and proud, not much fun to be with. I spent most of my time with Maggie and some other teenagers playing around the pool and tennis courts. Maggie encouraged a boy or two who came sniffing around us, and Mother seemed to bristle. She had been suspicious all weekend, but by midday Sunday, after a few Bloody Marys on the patio, she was seething about something. She cornered me in the bungalow.

"You listen to me, young lady," she said acidly, "just because you got away with some things here this weekend, don't think I didn't see them."

"What things?"

"The way you try to flirt with Michael."

I felt kicked in the stomach. *"Michael?"*

"I have eyes. I can see what you're doing. Smiling that

way. Wiggling your bottom. Arm around his shoulder—
you and Maggie both.''

"Mother, how can you say that!''

"I *saw* you—and you've done it *before.*'' She slapped
me hard across the face.

She meant Lex. She meant that I had flirted with Lex,
that I had seduced him! Had he not battered and choked
and raped me bloody? But she did not believe me after all!
And now she thought I was vying with her for Michael
Dante!

Sinking to a sofa, I wept as she stood above me and
ranted. I was boy crazy, she screamed. I was running wild
and bound to get a reputation. My denials were futile. I
hardly had breath to speak.

Mother calmed down enough to drive us back to Los
Angeles that night, sinking into testy silence. Michael sat
beside her. Maggie was next to me in the back seat.
"What's so secret back there?'' she'd snap, noticing our
hushed exchanges. "You two up to something else?''

We headed west to Holmby Hills. The plan was to drive
through downtown Los Angeles, where Maggie and I
would be put into a taxi at Union Station for the twenty-
minute drive to Pasadena. I got an idea. Mother obviously
didn't give a damn about me, and I now faced a confrontation with Maria at school. I had never seen downtown
Los Angeles, but I knew that it was seedy and no one
would look for me there.

We arrived at Union Station, bid perfunctory farewells,
and Michael put us into a cab. After a few blocks I said
to Maggie, "I'm not going back to school, I'm getting out
here.''

"Oh, Cherry, don't do that.''

"I'll be all right—call you tomorrow. Please pull over
here, sir, I have to make a phone call.'' The driver looked
doubtful. He had been prepaid ten dollars and told to deposit us safely inside the gates of Sacred Heart. "I'll only
be a minute,'' I assured him cheerily.

I went into a Walgreens drugstore and ducked out a side
exit. Maggie made some excuse, and the cabbie, tired of
waiting, drove on.

I started walking. I had never seen beggars before, or

winos, or run-down buildings, not even in movies. I can just melt into a place like this, I thought. I had loosened my hair à la Veronica Lake and carried a honey-colored alligator case. With the twelve dollars in my purse I'd rent a hotel room, then get a job, and stay hidden until I was eighteen, legal, and free. (How I thought I could ever get away with this is beyond me now.)

I heard footsteps and picked up my pace. It was turning dark and I was walking away from—not toward—the bright lights. I glanced back to see a man with a mustache following me and behind him three teenage boys who were closing in fast.

I darted into a dim little coffee shop lit only by bare fluorescent bulbs and sat at a table. The man with the mustache came through the door and walked right up to my table.

"Are you alone?" he asked. He was a slightly built Chicano around thirty, wearing work pants and a windbreaker. His mustache was more of a shadow. I thought, Well, I have to trust *someone*.

"Yes," I said.

"My name is Manuel."

"I'm Alexis," I said in my best offhand manner.

Manuel wanted to know everything, starting with my age. I was eighteen, I told him, a graduate of George Washington Public High School, and I had just gotten off the bus from Palm Springs where my parents owned a motel, but they were splitting up. I was going to get a job in a shop and, no, I didn't have a boyfriend. I asked if he noticed those three funny-looking guys who were following us on the street and did he know of a cheap hotel where I could stay?

"Yeah, I do," he said with a gold-toothed grin. "But it's a ways from here. My car is outside."

I glanced around at the customers. There were shop girls in beehives, truckers, and tradesmen with scuffed shoes, all of whom seemed to look right through me as they wearily studied the street. I'd been taught never to get into cars with strangers, but these people didn't seem to care about anything, and those three boys might still be outside.

Manuel's blue jalopy had ripped vinyl seats, and we

drove around forever. He tried to make me laugh by telling stories that I couldn't follow but which made him laugh so hard that he pounded the dashboard. These were punctuated by sidelong glances. Finally, he slid an arm around my shoulder.

"Take me to that hotel *at once,*" I commanded, saying it as Mother would.

"Okay, okay, okay," he said, grinning and raising his hands in defeat. He turned into a parking lot behind some hotel.

"I'll go in and see if they got a room," he said, getting out of the car. "Wait right here." My shoulders gave a shiver through the thin silk blouse I was wearing. It was a chilly night. A moment later, someone tapped on the glass. The car was surrounded by police.

The "hotel" turned out to be Skid Row's Hollenbeck Police Station. The police led me inside and sat me down for a grilling. Manuel, seeing no other possibilities, had turned me in as a runaway.

A bulldog-faced detective started firing questions at me, and I decided to brazen it out. My purse contained no I.D., not even a school card, so I said I was eighteen and refused to say more. I felt sorry for Manuel, who was across the room being given the third degree.

"Well, I see you're not going to talk," growled the bulldog. "It's obvious you're underage, so we're just going to have to take you to Juvenile Hall."

"O-kay," I said quickly. "My name's Cheryl Crane."

"My God," he yelled to the troops. "We've got Lana's kid!" All heads turned. I was news.

When Maggie had arrived back at Sacred Heart, she had told the nuns, who had promptly phoned Mother. Mother wasn't home yet, so they informed Dad and then the police. By midnight, a general alarm had gone out, and the radio was broadcasting bulletins that Lana's daughter had run away. Louella Parsons reached Mother by phone around midnight and asked what she thought of my being swallowed up in Skid Row. "I almost go out of my mind," said Mother.

In her column the next day, Louella chastised me, noting that if I'd heard my mother sobbing that night, I would "think twice" before worrying her again. "I have to say for Lana," Louella wrote, "she has always been a wonderful mother and strict with her daughter."

My poor parents showed up at the station house around one in the morning trailed by a mob of reporters and cameramen. Fearing Mother's reaction, I ran to Dad. Her first words were: "Thank God you're safe." Her second, said angrily once we were beyond the press's hearing were: "How could you do this to me?"

Dad asked why I did it, and I said I didn't want to go back to school. That wasn't true, and he knew it. I was getting to like Sacred Heart. But I couldn't tell him that Mother hated me and thought I was after her men. Disliking school was the easiest explanation—one that had been planted in my mind by the police. "Don't you like your parents?" they hounded. "How about school?"

During the glum ride home, Mother's rage was on simmer. My thoughts poked at the open sore: How could I have done this to *her?*

A nonplussed Michael Dante was waiting at the front door, and he quickly poured something for Mother's nerves. "Go to your room," she snapped. "Go to bed."

At the top of the stairs, I hesitated for a moment, then headed for her bedroom. Among the debris inside the top drawer of her nightstand lay both a full bottle of Nembutal and a revolver. The choice was easy since I hated violence. I poured the sleeping pills into my hand and went to my bedroom, planning to gobble every one after Mother had fallen asleep. I hid them in a Kleenex box, then crawled under the covers to wait. While I waited, I took a final look around.

In a few days some other young girl, a child of the new owners, would be sleeping in this room. I'd like to will her my things, my morocco-bound Big Little collection and Nancy Drew treasury, my street scenes of Paris, and my little girl-on-the-swing. Not my Mommy doll, though, whose glass eyes had watched a decade's turnings in my life. No new tenant should live under that scrutiny. Those eyes should close forever with mine.

Suddenly Mother was shaking me violently. I had drifted off. "Did you take those pills?!" she shouted.

"Wake up, Cheryl!" said Michael. "How many did you take?"

Groggily, I explained my plan. Both Mother and I dissolved into tears. Michael poured the pills down the toilet.

The next morning's newspapers carried big black headlines. "LANA TURNER'S RUNAWAY DAUGHTER FOUND," screamed the *Los Angeles Examiner*'s front page. Though Dad knew that my story about disliking school wasn't true, he gave it to the press as a cover explanation. Unfortunately, something got lost in translation. I was quoted as saying, "I don't want to go back to school. I hate school! I hate it!"

Manuel was quoted describing me as "frightened of something" and "well built," but he claimed that I had approached *him* in his car. Some papers said I arrived in Los Angeles by train, some that Maggie chased me into Walgreens, and some that I had been having "difficulties with some of the other girls" at Sacred Heart.

That afternoon Mother called me into her room. "I hope you slept well—*I* didn't," she said.

"I'm so sorry I worried you like that, Mama. I'm so sorry."

"Well, we're in a fine mess now," she added, with a dismissive wave of her hand. "Sacred Heart called to say they won't let you back because you said you hated it there. Very inconsiderate. Mother really doesn't know what she's going to do with you."

Two weeks later Mother signed to appear in *Peyton Place* portraying the chic and self-denying mother of an obstinate daughter.

VI

JOHN

Twenty-two

T he day after my abortive runaway attempt, Mapleton was leased pending sale and most of its contents
were put in storage—me included. Unwelcome at
Sacred Heart, I enrolled that week at a public junior
high school in West Los Angeles and went to live in Gran's
guest room.

Mother took a penthouse near Wilshire. Though her favorite color in home decor was movie-star white, with
accents of gray, mauve, or pink, this sublet was done up
in gay reds, and she said it fit her new mood. *Peyton Place*
was about to start production, she had a second picture in
the works, and her spirits were lifting. I should have recognized the telltale signs of Stage One. She was in love.

Word of Johnny Stompanato's existence popped into my
life innocuously enough. Gran and I were paying an afternoon visit to Mother's new apartment. "Darling," she
said, reclining on a red lipstick-colored lounge. "Mother
has met a very nice gentleman . . . His name is John
Stompanato, and he's got a horse."

I liked this guy before I even met him, for I had just
entered that horse-crazy stage that many girls go through.
There is something about the challenge of mastering a
creature so much stronger and more sensitive than yourself. "Oh boy, where's the horse?" I said eagerly.

"Well," she replied, "I'm sure that one of these weekends when I'm off, we can arrange to take you to the stable
where he keeps it. It's out near the old M-G-M lot."

A few days later, Mother and I dressed in riding garb
and drove up to the virgin foothills of Culver City, two

cowgirls again, just as we were on my sixth birthday when
Prince Valiant was the prize. Stompanato was waiting for
us in the parking lot, a thick-shouldered man with a suntan
and slicked-down, wavy hair. His boots and Levi's seemed
incongruous with a diamond pinkie ring.

He and Mother greeted each other with an unaffected
kiss, his hands lightly resting on her hips. They had met
a few weeks earlier on what was technically, I suppose, a
blind date that he had arranged. He had obtained her private telephone number and began a campaign of making
calls and sending flowers to her movie set with cards signed
"John Steele." He was charming in a terse, manly way,
and as part of his gentle pressure, he dropped the names
of friends he said they had in common. Mother somehow
did not get around to checking with their supposedly mutual friends before she agreed to give him a drink one
evening at her Wilshire apartment.

In no time at all, she was in love. Friends soon tipped
her off about Stompanato's gangland pals, but it was too
late. In any case, she did not yet know the full extent of
his notoriety around Hollywood, partly for being a
"Handsome Harry" who befriended rich women and borrowed money which was seldom paid back, and partly for
the Academy-Award size of his phallus, which had earned
him the nickname "Oscar."

Mother introduced us for the first time in that Culver
City parking lot.

"Call me John," he said, not that eager to impress,
which impressed me all the more. (New boyfriends usually gushed.) He turned, clasped Mother's waist, and led
us to an enclosure of box stalls. Then he disappeared inside, and when he returned he was leading a red Arabian
mare with a flaxen mane and tail.

"She's yours to ride, Cheryl," he said. "Her name's
Rowena. She spooks easy as hell."

We agreed that I would groom her and clean out her
stall every day that he or Gran could drive me to the stable. In return, she would, for all practical purposes, be
mine. While I had a good seat after years of lessons at
riding academies, John was an expert, and he taught me
much over the next three months. We often rode together

("Faster, Johnny, faster!") in the scrubby hills that overlooked the flatlands where the chariot races in the original
Ben-Hur had been staged. These were halcyon days, and
I saw my sidekick Johnny as Mother's friend, nothing
more.

An associate of my father who kept his horse at the
same stable saw John giving me riding lessons. To him,
it looked as if John was putting "his hands all over" [me].
He told Dad, who then initiated the only conversation he
ever had with John. "My daughter's the most important
thing in the world to me," Dad thundered on the phone
to John, "and I do care what happens to her."

People would later gossip that John and I were involved
romantically, but, if anything, he bent over backward to
make sure our friendship was not misunderstood. Mother
denies she would have ever told anyone about Lex's abuse
of me, but I believe she told John as a precaution, as a
result of which he took pains to stay at arm's length. He
was ever so careful with me—careful not to touch, not to
startle, not to be too friendly. His manner was almost gruff
and tight-lipped. In any case, his goal was marriage to my
mother, and with her working again (she made three movies in 1957), there were times I'd see more of him than
she did. We had chats over ice cream, and he would say,
"I want you to know I really care for your mother."
Sometimes he'd add, "Wouldn't it be nice if she and I got
married. Then I'd always be your friend like this."

With his dark good looks, stealthy movements, watchful eyes, and deep baritone, it's not hard to see the mystery he held for restless women. But not for me. I had
discovered girls and had never known a male lover who
was tender. If I flirted with John at all, it was no different
from the way I flirted with everyone, just like my mother
did. Soon to be fourteen, I was in the full flower of pu-
bescence and my father's girlfriend Helen was tutoring me
on how to be fascinating.

Emerson Junior High in West Los Angeles was my first
venture into the public school system. With a student body
of 2,000, it was four times larger than anything I'd known.
Marilyn Monroe—or, rather, an obscure coed named

Norma Jean Baker—had once swayed her hips across its dusty campus, but Emerson's connection to Hollywood was as a back-fence, middle-class neighbor. Besides myself, the only star baby there was Frank Sinatra, Jr.

Since everyone knew who I was, I enjoyed easy entrée to both of the two main student cliques, each of which reflected its own distinct style. One was the social group known as the "soshes," a quiet majority of students who aspired to establishment values. The other was the "juvies," for juvenile delinquents, who wanted to look like—if not actually be—rebels.

The look was the thing. Soshes wore cashmere sweaters, white bucks, crew cuts, and penny loafers. In contrast, juvie girls wore tight pegged skirts and stacked curls with a tail down the back, while juvie boys copied James Dean and Elvis Presley. Somehow I was accepted by both groups and managed to pull together a double wardrobe. I dressed for school according to whether I felt sosh or juvie that day.

Identification with the soshes reflected my exposure to Dad and Helen's world of achievers. But soshes were often snooty, which I found sad. As a star baby and product of private schools, I would do anything to not be considered a snob. And like Natalie Wood in *Rebel Without a Cause*, I felt tugged toward the juvies, who seemed to have troubles I knew about.

My juvie tendencies did not go unnoticed by Mother and Dad. Having set my heart on getting a motorcycle jacket to match that of a juvie boy I had started dating, I persuaded Dad to give me the money for a "leather coat." Though he assumed I meant a designer-type blazer, what I bought was the typical fearsome black jacket, with chains and zippers and studs. On days of mixed mood I even wore it with a Peter Pan collar and fuzzy ankle socks. I happened to be wearing the jacket in question one day when I went into Bullocks-Wilshire, a very sosh department store. Everyone stared, and I flushed red. Since Mother and I were well known to the sales people, Mother quickly learned of the incident, and the jacket vanished.

Things of mine that Mother didn't like often vanished. This included some of my friends of whom she disap-

proved. In the last sad days at Mapleton I had come across
a letter written to me by a friend at Sacred Heart. "Why
haven't you answered my other letters?" she asked. *What
other letters?* It was then that I suddenly realized Mother
must have been destroying my mail all along, especially
from former classmates whom she considered fast.

I had found the purloined letter from Sacred Heart when
Gran and I returned to Mapleton the day before the movers
arrived. We were making a sentimental journey through
its rooms, filled with memories of Nana, Papa, Lex, Uncle
Fernando, and five governesses. Having never been redecorated, my bedroom was frozen in time, forever 1949. The
Priscilla curtains and the plaid taffeta ruffles that had curled
around me like friends during all those sleepless twilights
would now be swept away. My other friends—the books,
pictures, and furniture, the little clock-girl-on-a-swing and
my Mommy doll—would be stored temporarily, Mother
promised, and would be brought out when we found a new
house. I wondered if they wouldn't meet the fate of my
classmate's letters to me. Sure enough, years later when I
unpacked what was stored, my treasures had all vanished.

When school let out that June, I faced a month of in-
activity before Gran and I left for a dude ranch in Colorado. Stompanato was just going into a retail venture, and,
to help keep me busy, he offered a make-work job in his
shop. It was my first job, and I was delighted.

The store was called the Myrtlewood Gift Shop, and it
faced Glendon Avenue in a quiet section of Westwood. It
was a puzzling operation. For sale out front were some
inexpensive pieces of crude pottery and wood carvings
displayed as though they were art. The few shoppers who
did walk in off the street were either served by a sometime
clerk or ignored altogether. When he was around, John
spent all his time in a brightly lit back office and store-
room, speaking on the phone in low mumbles. Two or
three men came to see him each day, but I paid no attention, burying my nose in Miss Marple mysteries.

For twenty-five cents an hour, my job was to dust, answer the phone, and run to the post office with brown
packages eight inches square. Judging by their size and
weight, they probably weren't pottery. Just what the shop

was fronting for, we'll never know. But its dubious financing, which was revealed later, demonstrates how Stompanato's life turned into a balancing act.

Like Dad, he grew up in heartland America and was drawn to the Hollywood dream. He started out in Woodstock, Illinois, population 8,000, a prairie farming town sixty miles northwest of Chicago. Youngest of four, John ("Jackie") R. Stompanato was born on October 19, 1925, to one of the few Italian families in an Irish-American town.

His father, John, Sr., did so well as a barber and dabbler in real estate that their big clapboard house on Blakely Street had a much-envied garden with florid statuary. The family called it "the villa." John's mother died after his birth, and his father then married a woman named Verena whom neighbors admired as "very much a lady."

Accounts differ as to whether John got into trouble as a child, but in 1940, after his freshman year at Woodstock High School, he was sent to Kemper Military Academy, a strict boys' school in Missouri. He had discipline problems there, but was graduated at seventeen. In 1943 he joined the Marines. He served in the South Pacific, facing enemy fire in the Peleliu and Okinawa campaigns, then landed with the Marines in China in 1945.

John later claimed to have stayed in China when the war ended, operating nightclubs and going broke in the process. In fact, he probably worked as a minor bureaucrat at a U.S. government office in Tientsin. That's where he met and married in a Muslim ceremony a Turkish woman named Sarah Utich who was six years his senior. He converted to her faith, and they returned to Woodstock, where she bore a son whom they named John III. For a few months, John worked as a bread salesman.

Having seen some of the world and grown bored with his marriage, he soon left for Hollywood. His route to California ran through Chicago, where he gained the help of Sir Charles Hubbard, heir to an English fortune.

Hubbard was in the United States looking for investments when he took John to California as a companion in 1948. During the next two years Hubbard gave him $85,000. John told the IRS he had "borrowed" the money, but the agency suspected that he was blackmailing Hubbard. Tried for vagrancy in 1949, John testified that $7,500 of Hubbard's loans were invested in a jewelry business, which, it later developed, went broke when the manager cleaned out the store and skipped town.

After John left for Hollywood, his wife moved with their son to Hammond, Indiana, and sued him for divorce on grounds of desertion. Meanwhile, Sir Charles ran into almost immediate trouble when police raided his Hollywood apartment and found marijuana. Hubbard said he had bought the pot from Vicki Evans, a roommate of Lila Leeds, who had been arrested with her in the famous Robert Mitchum pot bust three months earlier.

Going from bread man to con man in little more than a year, Stompanato soon got noticed around Hollywood. He met mob boss Mickey Cohen while working as a greeter-bouncer in one of Cohen's clubs. Before long he was promoted to being one of the gangster's $300-a-week bodyguards (dubbed by the press Cohen's ''Seven Dwarfs'').

Despite his wholesome past as a small-town boy and decorated Marine, Stompanato embraced the excitement of low-life crime in a Hollywood that winked at classy criminals. His friend Mickey Cohen was no classy criminal like Bugsy Siegel, however. A flamboyant publicity seeker, Cohen was mocked by the press as something of a clown. While Siegel might be an honored guest, Cohen and his dwarfs would be excluded from the polite company of picture people. Cohen was decidedly not on Virginia Hill's list.

For the next few years, Stompanato ran mob errands and scrambled in the *demimonde* of petty fraud and extortion. He was suspected of being Cohen's ''bank,'' and was arrested several times while carrying sums as large as $50,000 in cash. He was also pulled in six times on charges ranging from vagrancy to suspicion of burglary, but he was never convicted.

As a cover for his shady activities, and to lure investors, he ran a variety of small business operations. At various times he sold cars, pets, flowers, maple furniture, and lovebirds, the latter bred and raised in his own home aviary.

After Sarah Utich, he married at least twice more; there is evidence of a third marriage that was covered up. In 1949 he wed actress Helen Gilbert, who was eight years his senior and had appeared as Andy's teacher in the *Andy Hardy* series. The fourth of Miss Gilbert's seven husbands, Stompanato was known as "John Valentine" when they checked into the honeymoon suite at the Flamingo in Las Vegas (the hotel Bugsy Siegel built). When they divorced three months later, Miss Gilbert testified, "Johnny had no means. I did what I could to support him."

Stompanato kept moving. In 1953 he married actress Helen Stanley, a veteran of B-pictures considerably his senior, in a ceremony kept secret "for the sake of Helen's career." The marriage lasted two years, and at divorce proceedings she charged that he had once tried to strangle her mother when she mislaid his handkerchiefs. "He used to stay out all night two or three times a week," Miss Stanley said. "Then he'd say, 'You ought to be happy that I came home at all. I don't take you any place because you bore me.'"

Stompanato used a number of aliases, including John Holliday, Jay Hubbard, John Truppa (Miss Stanley's real surname), and even John Valentine. He introduced himself to Mother as John Steele until she called his bluff. His specialty was winning the trust of lonely women, then borrowing money from them. "When the victim's money is dissipated," his police file noted, "he becomes interested in another woman. Usually he frequents expensive nightspots to meet wealthy female types."

Stompanato kept a "little black book," actually a tan leather one that locked, which contained the private phone numbers of many famous people. When police later released a sampling of its contents, they were quick to point out that doubtless many of those listed were people he had never met but who appeared in the book out of his wishful thinking. He had Mother's number, of course, and also the numbers of the likes of Anita Ekberg, Zsa Zsa Gabor, and June Allyson.

If he was not welcome among the Hollywood elite, he could mingle around its edges. He was a familiar figure at Ciro's, Trocadero, and Mocambo. He often displayed his tanned muscles and blinding smile around the Beverly Hills Hotel swimming pool and sometimes came into the Luau. Dad would not have permitted someone like him at one of his Sunday afternoon gin rummy parties, but he did wind up elsewhere playing in card games with Stompanato. Friends of Dad recall that Stompanato was a poor player who often welshed on his losses. (One bitter disagreement between him and Mother at the time of his death concerned her refusal to cover a $3,600 debt of his.)

The Myrtlewood Gift Shop was financed mostly by an $8,150 loan from an attractive, redheaded widow he had met in January 1957, just as he was starting to woo Mother with flowers and phone calls. "He was a perfect gentleman with me at all times," the widow later told newsmen. "I didn't know anything about his background. He used to call on me and talk about everyday things. He treated me almost as a sister. I guess that's why he came around. He said he needed someone to talk to. I supposedly was going to help out in the store."

That July Mother sent Gran and me off for what looked to be six weeks of perfect bliss in Estes Park, Colorado. She was busy on *Peyton Place* at Twentieth Century-Fox and reasoned that nowhere would I be safer from harm than on an isolated dude ranch. She didn't imagine that the horse they assigned me would be a huge golden palomino, seventeen hands high, named King, who spooked easily. I was not supposed to ride him outside the ranch's large enclosed area, but one afternoon I snuck off with a couple of teenage friends for an hour's ride beyond the corral. As we were walking along, King saw a snake and took off at a gallop, grabbing the bit in his teeth. To wrest the bit away from a horse, you must use both hands in a sawing motion, but I was riding bareback and couldn't regain control.

King stopped as fast as he started, pitching me over his head and into a ravine, where they found me bloody and unconscious with five cracked vertebrae and a brain concussion. A Denver hospital encased me in a body cast from chest to upper thigh as Mother and Dad flew to my side.

It had been less than four months since the Skid Row

runaway incident, and the papers covered the horse accident in a tone of here-we-go-again. One led with "trouble continues to dog the heels of Lana Turner's active daughter, Cheryl." It did not help that on the day of my accident Mother had been awarded her divorce from Lex amid claims that she was calling it quits on marriage. "Not me; no sir. I'll never get married again," she said.

As my parents swept into the hospital room wearing sunglasses big as bug shields, they were singing "Happy Birthday." I was fourteen that day, and before she returned to work the next day Mother came to say good-bye. I was feeling rather happy. She sat on the bed and stared at my traction and bandages. "Why is it," she asked sweetly, "that every time I go away, you have an emergency?"

Mother gave lots of interviews that fall. The word on *Peyton Place* was very good, and since she was defying her glamour image by portraying the mother of a teenage girl, she wanted to talk about her character. "She's not supposed to be prim or dowdy," she explained. "She's supposed to be the most attractive woman in that town— just inhibited and frustrated. The mother of a teenage daughter doesn't have to look matronly."

A reporter asked what might have happened if she had not been discovered at that soda fountain. "I don't know," she said. "I think I'd have married early, had two or three kids. But I'd have been too restless to be a housewife. . . . Left to my own devices, I'd starve to death—I can't boil water."

She had thought a lot about these things since leaving M-G-M, she said, and recalled the period of unemployment months before. "I couldn't see ahead in my life for a while. Everything was pretty dark. But I'm happy now. I can see where I'm going."

Twenty-three

"**C**heryl," said Stompanato, "how would you like to go to Woodstock and live with my mom?"

I darted a look at him. We were in his T-bird one afternoon headed for the Culver City stables. The subject of where I would go to school that fall had never before come up with him.

"Mom has a big house," he said, "and there are lots of kids like you at Woodstock High School. You could change your name and make a lot of friends." He glanced at the passing countryside and added, "Lana thinks it's a great idea."

My insides tightened. It seems that once again Mother wanted to send me away, but Woodstock was *2,000 miles* off in Illinois. She had already barred my return to Emerson Junior High, where I was happy, because, as she pointed out, she would soon be leaving for London to make a movie. My grades were also not A-level.

Mother had decided that Emerson was too fast for me. Not that she didn't approve of my sosh friends, who included Frank Sinatra, Jr., a warmhearted boy and devotee of music that went beyond his father's pop style. I hung out with Frank after school at a music store, the old-fashioned kind that let you listen to records through earphones. We would sit mutely side by side, he pantomiming jazz drums or directing an unseen symphony, me tapping my toes to Elvis. Mother hated rock 'n' roll, and she had determined that a boarding school must be found to

shield me from the influences of such bad company as
Dad, Helen, Gran, and Elvis.

"So how about that?" John asked.

My mind had wandered. "About what?"

"Woodstock High School? Living with my mother?"

"I would not like that, thank you," I said.

A week or so later John raised the idea again, adding
that his mother was enthusiastic. I stood firm. After that,
apparently at Mother's direction, he began to conduct a
search for a proper new school for me. He found the Happy
Valley School in Ojai, an hour's drive north of Los Angeles.

Co-educational and very progressive, Happy Valley
encouraged free expression, which included running barefoot, wearing Levi's, and attending classes as you pleased.
Academic standards were very high, the classes small, and
they were often given in the beautiful surrounding orchards that rolled up to the Los Padres Mountains. In this
paradisal setting, boys and girls lived in separate, distant
dorms and were closely supervised. There was absolutely
no television, and the authorities actively discouraged the
new music. You could get away with Johnny Mathis but
not Elvis Presley. I was constantly in trouble for smuggling in rock albums.

As the former sophisticate of Sacred Heart, I now
worked to regain my reputation for being worldly. Sneaking off with friends into the orchards, sometimes as ring-
leader, I learned to smoke cigarettes without inhaling and
share nips from a gin bottle without getting much pleasure.
Trying to achieve doelike eyes, I painted them with so
much liner that I began to look like a raccoon.

Though we were allowed to return home for only one
long weekend a month, Happy Valley was not cut off from
trends in the youth culture. While the prevailing atmosphere was intellectual and arty, there were soshes and
juvies here, too. I still switched, chameleonlike, between
them. Indeed, I intensified the ambiguity by falling into a
romance with a boy from each group. The first was Ziggy
Huxley, the nephew of the writer Aldous Huxley. Ziggy
affected the greaser look with a ducktail (DA) haircut,

T-shirt, and Wellington boots, but he was too young to have his own motorcycle.

My other boyfriend was Peter Duvall. An unmistakable sosh, he set off his blond square-top hair and blue eyes with ascots, Old Spice, and V-neck cashmeres. He had the white-bread appeal of Pat Boone with a hint of Dad's *savoir faire*. But I couldn't make up my mind. White bread or rye? I'd go out with Peter for two weeks, then break up and go back to Ziggy. Then Peter, then Ziggy again. And so it went into spring. The innocent kissing and petting we did drove the poor boys crazy, but, in the fifties, children didn't go any further than that. Besides, playing the flirt gave me delicious satisfaction. I had seen Mother tease, and Helen and Maria, too.

Mother flew to London that November to start work on a picture made by her new Lanturn Productions, Inc. John followed. Entitled *Another Time, Another Place,* the movie featured, as the male love interest, Sean Connery, who had already scored in British television but was still unknown in America. *Another Time* was a heavy-breathing "woman's picture" that offered plenty of clinches between Mother and her leading man. Gossip inevitably put her in bed with any man she smiled at, but people working on *Another Time* were persuaded that Mother and Sean really were having a secret fling. They had a certain familiar air with each other.

Her backstairs lover, Stompanato, was forbidden to visit the set. Instead, he was obliged to spend his time at their rented house in suburban Hampstead. Then one day he heard about Mother's interest in Connery.

Seized with anger and jealousy, John forced Mother's chauffeur to drive him to Pinewood Studios, where he stormed inside and waved a gun at Connery. Unperturbed, the soon-to-be James Bond flattened John with a right to the nose.

John had followed Mother to England by prearrangement, borrowing the cost of the plane ticket from Mickey Cohen. He had film ambitions of his own, it seemed, that would require her help. He boasted to creditors before leaving that he was going abroad to "sew up a picture deal.'' What he had in mind was producing a screenplay, which he hoped to option, with Mother starring and Lanturn financing. In addition, he thought he might even act in the movie himself.

Implacably opposed to mixing love and business, Mother killed the project. They quarreled about it in London, in Hampstead, and on a trip to Paris. After he lost the confrontation with Connery, his frustration with Mother boiled over.

It happened just before Christmas. Once more Mother insisted that while she might give him love and money, he could never be her business partner in any real sense. John exploded. He knocked her around, nearly smothering her with a pillow before she tore away and was saved by a maid who heard screams.

Mother's larynx was bruised in the struggle, and the next day on the set she could barely speak. A publicist called it laryngitis, explaining that her facial swelling had been caused by a piece of canvas flapping loose in the wind.

Mother described John's beating to her longtime makeup artist Del Armstrong, who was also the film's associate producer. By chance, Armstrong had been introduced over lunch a few days earlier to one of the top men at Scotland Yard. A phone call now set the wheels in motion for John's quiet expulsion from England that same day.

Mother and John's notes to me gave no hint of trouble, of course. Mother hated the weather—it affected her voice. John had given her a poodle puppy named Gypsy.

It had been arranged from the start that I would join them both for Christmas in London, but I was more excited about an event that would immediately precede the trip—the premiere of *Peyton Place*.

Dad rented me a pink-dyed mink stole that night to go with my all-red ensemble. Gran also wore high regalia, and, as we stepped from the limo, a rustle stirred among the fans who lined the velvet ropes. The *Hollywood Reporter*'s Army Archerd introduced us as ''Lana's whole family'' and stuck a microphone in my face.

As the lights went down and the film began, I found myself riveted. I had read the Grace Metalious novel and recalled its themes, but seeing it in Cinemascope on the Pantages Theater's sixty-foot screen was overwhelming. Two of the film's subplots might have been lifted right from my life. One concerned a man's repeated rape of his stepdaughter (who in desperation clubs him to death), while the other involved a youngish mother (Mother) and her rebellious daughter (played by Diane Varsi). After the daughter mildly misbehaves early in the picture, Mother storms into a teen party and looks at her with an expression whose familiarity gave me chills. The look said, "You're in trouble, young lady, and we'll talk about this when we get home." I was perplexed that she could use that expression on someone else.

The parallels to our relationship continued, culminating in a scene in which Mother slaps Miss Varsi—a reminder to me of that terrible instant in Palm Desert. I reached for the handkerchief in Dad's breast pocket.

The most moving moment came in the climactic courtroom scene. Mother is testifying in a murder trial. She's being crisp, gracious, elegant. Her hair never moves as she otherwise begins to wilt under the pressure of a tough district attorney. "Mrs. McKenzie," he says, "doesn't your daughter ever bring home her problems?"

"How many times do I have to answer your questions?" she asks.

"Well, until we find out the truth."

"The truth is . . ." Mother directs a long, poignant gaze at her daughter, who is seated in the courtroom. "The truth is my daughter did bring her troubles home . . . I wouldn't understand."

"Well, if she did—"

"I wouldn't understand," repeats Mother, burying her face in shame.

In the end, mother and daughter reconcile, embracing as the camera pulls back for a fade-out. "Oh sure," I thought miserably as the lights came up, "a happy ending."

Gran made me send Mother a congratulatory wire, but those next few days before Christmas in London, I couldn't get *Peyton Place* out of my mind. As I watched Mother act with Miss Varsi some tiny membrane snapped inside me. They were all too familiar, those icy, dangerous looks Mother gave, the imperial manner and tight-assed way of crossing a room, the way she would turn and punch home a line.

I had watched her act with a screen "daughter" before in *The Prodigal*. But that child was eight years old and their interplay was loving. Now, for the first time, I sat engulfed by her Cinemascopic image, watching her scold a tall teenager, one whose soft-voiced manner reminded me of me. With that snap came a moment of realization: the techniques Mother used to intimidate and control me came not from a well of feeling but from her bag of actress tricks. To her, life was a movie. She did not live in reality.

If my love for her suffered with the slapping incident in Palm Desert, I now saw she was able to control me only because I fell for the acting. I let her control me. If she said yes and I said no, what could she really do? She lectured me endlessly on showing respect and obedience to one's mother, yet look how she treated Gran.

I traveled by myself that Christmas on Pan Am's inaugural flight over the North Pole to London. After takeoff, I assumed my most bored smile and ordered a martini, which they served me without question. With my raccoon eyes and spiked heels, no one would have thought I was fourteen.

I'm a nervous flyer, and in those days planes still had sleeping berths in first class, so after the second martini I climbed up into bed and fell asleep. I awakened after a while with a shiver and tilted one ear to listen. Nothing. Pin-drop silence. Even the engines had stopped. Pulling back the curtains revealed the astonishing sight of an empty airplane, and it was freezing. I was alone in a twilight zone. Before I could panic, a stewardess bundled in fur came running up the aisle. "We forgot you," she cried. "I'm so sorry. We've had engine trouble and landed in northern Canada."

I joined the other passengers, who were huddled in the communal room of a fuel stop in Frobisher Bay. It wasn't long before the plane was fixed, but then a blizzard hit and we were socked in for thirty-six hours. There were no

beds or dining facilities, but there was plenty of gin, and
when the adults got smashed, I joined the fun.

On arrival in London, I discovered that Mother's indig-
nation over the delay had sent airline officials into a crouch,
as a result of which I was taken off first and whisked
through customs. Luckily they didn't open my luggage
and discover Mother's contraband cigarettes. When I remarked to her about Johnny's absence, she replied off-
handedly that they had had a misunderstanding. "I've just
decided I don't want to see him anymore," she said lightly.

I fumbled around in my purse for a cigarette, lit up
smartly, and took an exaggerated drag of smoke. Then,
without inhaling, I blew an explosive puff. Imitating
Mother, I crossed my arms, and, resting my elbow on my
wrist, held the cigarette away as if it were a nuisance. She
sighed wearily. "Are we having this again?" she asked.
"You're too young to smoke!"

"You smoked at fourteen," I said, holding my breath.

"But—" she began, then let out a string of sputters and
growls that finally died on her lips. Her shoulders dropped,
and she cast a resigned look out the car window.

Checkmate, I thought, and drew in another deep mouth-
ful.

The next twenty-three days in London were the happiest
time I had ever spent with Mother. Stompanato's name
never came up, and I couldn't bring myself to talk about
Peyton Place. "Oh, you were wonderful," was all I said.
"I cried all the way," I added, and let it go at that. Ex-
uding an unprecedented warmth and closeness, she shared
all her free hours with me, shopping, posing for mother-
daughter photos, and taking me to adult parties. "We've
got to think of something you can drink," she said, choos-
ing Dubonnet and soda.

She let me select my clothes and borrow her mink and
said nothing about my eye makeup. The only disappointment came when the planned presentation to Queen Elizabeth and Prince Philip did not take place, no doubt
because of the fracas with Stompanato.

The best times came on quiet weeknights at the manor
house in Hampstead, where we dined before a fire, just
the two of us. We watched television in her king-sized bed

and often slept together. One night she snored so loudly that the imp in me poured drops of water in her mouth.

"What are you doing?" she sputtered, waking with a jolt.

"Well, you were snoring and I couldn't sleep," I said, ashamed of my prank.

Mother's love was heavenly. I was getting a peek into what might have been, were it not for that other woman, Lana Turner, and I dared to hope that our problems were dropping behind us. We could be friends and enjoy each other. There was so much to be repaired after Palm Desert, and now here we were holding hands and resting our heads on each other's shoulder.

I never questioned the why of this sudden change in her feelings for me, but it surely had to do with loneliness for John and being trapped in a suburban blandness she disliked. I believe the love for me was genuinely felt, however. Mother utterly needed to love somebody.

She delayed my return to California for nearly two weeks so that we could leave England on the same day. I departed just hours before her flight left for Copenhagen, where she would join up with Stompanato before heading on to Acapulco. When I learned they were patching things up again, I thought nothing of it. What I didn't know was that, growing lonely after his expulsion from England, she had bombarded him with a number of blazing love letters and transatlantic phone calls, which led them to resolve to try again. The question of who reopened the affair is still a sticky matter with Mother. She maintains that he phoned her persistently when he returned to California and that his joining her at the Copenhagen airport was a complete surprise. Supposedly he had tracked her there. Mother did send him a letter just before she left for Copenhagen telling him not to come. "I need more time to think," she wrote. The letter arrived too late; he had already left.

What happened during their two-month stay in Acapulco is a matter of some debate. Mother says she lived in terror and just barely survived his physical brutality. Other holidaymakers at the Mexican beach resort confirmed that her behavior toward him seemed tense and frightened. But at other times she seemed adoring. Ted

Stauffer, the manager of Villa Vera, said that Stompanato "wouldn't let her alone for a minute. She had no chance to talk with anyone alone. . . . He stuck like glue." Stauffer and his wife did manage to take Mother aside. "I got the impression," he said, "that Lana was worried because she knew she had gotten herself into something, decided she didn't like it, and didn't know how to get out. . . . Johnny acted as if he knew it."

John, on the other hand, sent a breezy letter to his stepmother in Woodstock telling of an enjoyable time and hinting of marriage. "Lana's as brown as a berry," he wrote.

They sailed around for twenty days on the *Rosa Maria,* whose captain, Leonel Vargus, saw the adoring side of Mother. "No matter what he was doing on board," Vargus said later, "she was at his side. He would be sitting in a deck chair, and she would come along and all of a sudden sit right down on his lap without being asked. I couldn't understand why a movie queen would want to keep chasing after him."

Mother checked into the Villa Vera's so-called "Lana Turner bungalow" on January 21, 1958. Having booked late in high season, John was obliged to take smaller accommodations in a hotel annex across the street until Stauffer, under John's pressure, finally moved him next to Mother. "He was tough," said Stauffer. "He gave me orders I couldn't take."

Mother recalls life inside their hideaway as "a sort of armed truce, marred by a few violent arguments." He smashed a door, slapped her around, and held a gun to her head, mainly because she refused to sleep with him. Instead, she preferred to get drunk and blot everything out. She still resisted being linked with him in public. Mentions of Stompanato had started to appear in the press when she divorced Barker, and she fretted now about the kind of gossip that would bring mean smiles in the Polo Lounge.

The last straw came on February 22 when mighty Louella Parsons scolded Mother in her international column. "I sincerely hope it isn't true that Lana Turner, who is now in Acapulco, is marrying Johnny Stampanato [sic]."

Still, whether she was coerced into it or simply went along in a gay mood, Mother did go out in public with John to clubs, restaurants, and bullfights. Paparazzi usually captured her looking straight-faced as John basked in the heat of flashbulbs.

John had phoned me to say good-bye when he left for Mexico, and I made him promise to write me at Happy Valley. While Mother's few notes were brief and affectionate, Johnny's gave chatty accounts of a fish they caught or an exciting bullfight they saw. He was full of questions about Rowena, Gypsy the poodle, and my double crush then raging with Ziggy and Peter. Here's what I wrote him on February 18, 1958, misspellings and all:

Dear Johnny—
First of all please excuse this paper but its really all I have right now.

I just got your letter this morning because I was home for the weekend.

How have you been? And how is mother?

Rowenia is just fine. I'm not afraid of her anymore and she acts just like she used to last summer. Yes, I still want to take her to Estes Park this summer. I thought for awhile that I wouldn't be able to handle her but I know now that I can.

School is just fine but not getting any easier.

I went to see Johnny Mathes at the Crescendo Sunday nite he was terrific.

Have you been doing any water sking lately? Please do and think of me, I love it.

When are you all coming back? soon I hope.

Mother and I really had a wonderful time in Europe. I can't remember when we've been that close.

My hair is way past my shoulders now and I have been wearing it in a french-roll in back with pixie bangs in frount which are all the rage now.

Peter and I had a big fight over another guy and he made me so mad by being so jelious that I broke up with him. But I really regret it now. Oh well something has to happen.

I am writing this in Study Hall as I have finished

my work. I thought I better write now before I forget
and put it off.

This writing is very mesy I know, but the bell is
going to ring and I'm in a hurry.

Guess what I'm a member of the Student Council
. . . pretty good huh!!!

Well the bell just rang so I've gotta get now—

I'll write again real soon I promise but now its
your turn— Love ya & miss ya loads
CHERIE
PS—Give my love to Mother.
Write soon & be good—

A month later, the Motion Picture Academy announced
their Oscar nominations. Mother's performance in *Peyton
Place* had earned her a place on the ballot for best actress.
She was surprised. She had certainly done better work in
Postman and *The Bad and the Beautiful,* but Academy
voting sometimes tacitly honors past work as well, and
besides, *Peyton Place* was on its way to becoming the
biggest box office attraction of 1958. In all, the picture
received an unprecedented nine Oscar nominations. When
Mother wired Gran to say she would be flying back five
days before the ceremony, I took a day off from school to
meet her and Johnny at the airport.

Mother stepped from the plane looking tanned and happy
as a handful of press waited below. John's grin appeared
in back of her, and as she walked along the tarmac, he
followed two paces behind. Flashbulbs began to pop. He
grabbed her arm and stepped close. Surprised, she continued to smile but did not look his way. We had all waved
and blown kisses from afar, but now he beckoned me to
join them and step into the photo-taking. "Closer please,"
said a photographer. "This way, Cheryl," said another,
as I laughed and curled my arm around John's waist.
Mother answered questions and reporters scribbled in their
pads and it was over in a moment.

Mother and John had flashed gay smiles for the press,
but as we drove off in Gran's car the smiles collapsed.
John concentrated on driving and Mother stared out the
window as I chattered away. I had fallen in love with her

again after our cheery Christmas in London, and while I
resented that our private moments had been used in *Peyton
Place*, I was glad she had gotten a nomination for it. Anyway, I knew why her acting was so good. It wasn't acting.

"Can I go to the Oscars?" I said, spreading my elbows
on the front seat. "Please, Mama."

She gave a teasing smile. "We'll see."

"Please let me go, please, please."

"Ohhh . . . I guess sooo." She caressed my arm and
turned to look at Gran. "You too, Mom. We'll make it a
family night." She glanced at John and faced front. He
had not spoken since we left the airport.

The next day almost every newspaper in the English-
speaking world carried a photo of our smiling threesome,
headlined with some version of "LANA TURNER RETURNS
WITH MOB FIGURE."

Describing Mother as "tanned of face and bleached of
hair," the *Los Angeles Times* bannered the story that a
former Mickey Cohen associate had traveled through London, Paris, and Mexico as her escort. Mother had not denied it. "But," she insisted, "there is definitely no
romantic interest between us."

Was there any similarity between the *Peyton Place* story
and relations with her own daughter? Mother scoffed.
"Cheryl is happy at her new school," she said, noting
that to her I was "a friend as well as a daughter."

The awards were only days away, and Mother had to
press her dressmaker to complete designs she had sent
ahead for the fishtail dress and my fashion statement in
Prell green. Joining her at a fitting one morning, I asked
about John.

"Oh, he won't be coming," she said. "I told him it
was just family." Funny, I thought, Mother not making
an entrance on the arm of her next husband?

She had given up her Wilshire apartment when she went
abroad and was now staying in a favorite two-bedroom
bungalow at the Bel Air Hotel. When Gran and I got there
late in the afternoon of Oscar day, she was not ready, so
we cooled our high heels in the living room. Finally, she
swept in, trailing a cloud of experts still fussing over her
hair, dress, and makeup.

She looked so stunning that I wanted to kiss her, but an inner voice cautioned, "Mommy's hair, Mommy's lipstick." She wore a clunky diamond bracelet that had survived the Topping divorce, the one he supposedly slipped on her wrist while she was getting off a bath scale. "I jumped right back on the scale," she quipped to the press.

Finally made perfect, Mother stood poised before the fireplace, raising her tanned arm to make a toast with the last of a vodka and soda. "Mom, Cherie . . . if they don't like the dress, to hell with 'em."

Soon we were settled into our limousine, inching through the Sunset Boulevard traffic, bound for the Academy Awards. Then I noticed something odd.

I had never seen Mother actually tremble before, not until that day. Staring at her hands made me sort of edgy myself. Her fingers were twitching as if they were troubled by bad dreams, and I had no idea why.

VII

JUSTICE

Twenty-four

There I sat curled in a ball on my bed, moaning and whimpering a kind of mantra of despair. No sound came from Mother's room, but I knew she was there. Stompanato must still be on the floor or he would have jumped up and come at me with the knife by now. What was happening? Where was Daddy?

I got unsteadily to my feet and moved to the door. Mother's excited voice drifted from across the hall.

The bell rang. I tore down the stairs, swung the door wide, and flung myself into his arms. "Daddy-Daddy-Daddy! It's John! I didn't mean to do it!"

"What, honey? What?"

"He's hurt. Upstairs. He was going to harm Mommy—"

Pulling me with him, he bounded up the stairs and stopped dead at the door to Mother's bedroom.

Bent over Johnny in pedal pushers and bare feet, Mother looked at us with a start. "Stephen!" she cried. "Why are you here?" She ran forward as if to bar our view.

"Oh, my God, this is terrible," said Dad, peering over her shoulder. There were blood-spattered towels around the now silent body and a telephone near his head.

"Yes, I know," she replied, "and I don't know what more to do than I've done. The doctor should be here in a minute. Mother told him it was an emergency."

I stood staring from behind the protection of Dad's big frame, squeezing his wrist with both my hands. "Aw, honey, let's go somewhere else," he said, turning me around and urging me toward my room.

"I did it, Daddy, but I didn't *mean* to," I pleaded.

247

"John was going to hurt Mommy. I'm so sorry. Is he going to be all right?"

"Everything will be all right," he said. "Just lie down on your bed. Don't worry about a thing."

"Lana! Lana!" It was Gran's voice coming up the stairs.

"Mother, please don't look. It's John."

"What happened?"

Dad tried to distract me from Mother's explanation by talking over it. Then he paused: "I'll be right back."

A moment later Gran appeared at my bedside and took me in her arms. "There, there, there, there, there, my darling. Shhh. Shhh."

"I'm so sorry. I didn't *mean*—"

"Shh. Put it out of your mind. It's all right. It's all over."

Noises began to drift in from the hallway, sounds of people arriving, footsteps, doors slamming, gruff voices giving orders, metal sliding on metal.

Dr. McDonald came in. "I'm going to give you something to calm you down a little," he said, digging into his bag. "I don't want that," I said, seeing the needle, but to no avail, for it went right into my arm. For a moment I stared at him with hurt on my face. "Dr. Mac" had been poking and prodding my body since birth. "I'm so sorry," I said. "I didn't mean to—"

"Everything's going to be fine."

"Will John be all right?"

"John's gone. Don't worry about it—everything will be okay."

I cannot remember feeling shock at this news. I guess I knew he was dead, and a numbness was beginning to still the trembling in my extremities.

Dr. McDonald had arrived some thirty minutes after the stabbing. He immediately shot adrenaline into John's heart but could not raise a pulse. Mouth-to-mouth resuscitation by Mother and Gran just brought forth a death rattle. Mother was too panicked to deal with a telephone, so McDonald called for an ambulance, which alerted the police. Then, turning to Mother, he said, "Lana, you'd better call Jerry Giesler."

Giesler (pronounced "Geese-ler") was Hollywood's top criminal attorney, the man who got both Errol Flynn and Charlie Chaplin acquitted of statutory rape charges. Mother reached him at a dinner party, and he agreed to come at once.

The ambulance arrived, followed by a squad car that was cruising the neighborhood and had picked up the emergency call. Dad opened the door and said, "Something terrible has happened."

"Is it a suicide?" asked the officer.

"Worse than that."

The cop phoned his headquarters for assistance, then went upstairs to find Mother, McDonald, and a second doctor hovering beside two ambulance attendants whose resuscitator pumped convulsions into a lifeless form.

Some sixty minutes after the stabbing, Beverly Hills police chief Clinton B. Anderson finally walked through the door. Mother greeted him at the top of the stairs, still barefoot, her face haggard. "Chief . . . oh . . ." she called, hesitating wretchedly. "It's all my fault, Clinton."

Anderson stiffened at the familiarity, then introduced himself as chief of police and paced around the crime scene as officers gave him a briefing. Cops, medics, and attendants stood silently by, along with celebrity columnist Jim Bacon, who had slipped through the police line by saying he was from the coroner's office. Spying Bacon, Anderson asked, "What are *you* doing here?" Then he saw Giesler. "And *you!*" (The fact that Giesler preceded the cops to the scene rankled the authorities.)

Anderson drew Mother aside in a dressing area. She spoke first. "Can I take the blame for this horrible thing?" she said. "I'll say I did it?"

"No, not unless you have committed the act, Miss Turner. We will find out all of the facts, you know, so you might as well start off with that premise."

Mother buried her face. "Okay . . . It was my daughter."

After taking her brief statement, Anderson came into my room. My tranquilized brain seemed to be nuzzling the ceiling, but I knew my father's old friend. Dear Chief Anderson and the Luau's flaming grogs. But he was direct and official with me. "Hello, Cheryl. Now can you tell me a little what happened here. There was an argument?"

"I'm so sorry," I said. "Chief, I didn't *mean* to do it. Johnny said he was going to hurt Mother. . . ." The story tumbled out.

I was aware of excitement outside my window, of voices and red whirling lights. I didn't dare look. Nor could I return the looks of the uniformed men who lingered by my door. "This is the door," a man would say, pointing at my bedroom door, but staring at me. I looked away.

The next thing I can remember was Gran saying, "Come on, get up, darling, you're going to have to get dressed." She pulled from the closet some schoolgirl things that I didn't want to wear, a blouse, a wool skirt, and a camel hair coat, but I was too tired to argue. With her unerring sense of dress, she saved me from unwise choices. I wanted to wear medium heels; she insisted on flats. I wanted full makeup; she allowed me only lipstick. Though my hair was unwashed, I wanted to be bareheaded, but she framed my face in an innocent white silk scarf. Head scarves were Mother's trademark, and I hated them for that reason, but Gran ignored my objections. She knew what she was doing. When she finished dressing me, I looked the tall, gawky young girl that I was, ready to be displayed to the world press who were now clamoring on the lawn.

Dad led us down the front staircase. It was crowded with strangers, who parted to reveal Mother crying below in the hall with Giesler. We embraced and looked helplessly into each other's eyes. "C'mon, honey, we've got to go now," Dad said. "There's press outside. Don't stumble. Hang on to me. I've got you." The door opened and the pop-pop-pop of flashbulbs produced a moment of daylight. The night was filled with the crackle of police radios, reporters' shouts, sirens, and the rustling speech of onlookers. Dad slid me into a police car, and we sped off to the Beverly Hills Police Station five blocks away.

Anderson was waiting in his office as we arrived and casually waved me into a chair in front of his desk, with Mother to one side. Dad, Giesler, and a court recorder were shadows in the background. Gran had gone straight home.

Suddenly, cameramen filled the room. The chief removed his glasses and we were posed together, with my eyes abjectly focused on the floor. Finally, the press cleared out and the door smacked shut. We all sat in silence for a moment, exchanging questioning glances. Then the chief asked me to tell him what I knew. According to the transcript, I talked and answered questions for some ten minutes. It was later reported accurately that I told Anderson that I did what I did to protect Mother. However, somewhere in the retelling, damaging words were put in my mouth that had me saying at the instant of thrusting the knife, "You don't have to take that, Mama!"—a phrase that would wrongly suggest premeditation.

Calm and dry-eyed as a result of shock and tranquilizers, I finished my testimony and looked over at Mother. "Well, now, Miss Turner," said the chief, "you heard your daughter's version of this incident. Would it be better if we talked to you without her being present?"

"No. She can stay," said Mother. "Everything she said is true." And with that she began a long anguished account that for me held one new fact. I had believed that when she yanked the bedroom door open, Stompanato was advancing from behind her with his arm raised to strike. But Mother now said that his raised hand held a jacket and shirt he was carrying on hangers high behind his back. His silhouette only looked as though he were attacking.

The night was already so filled with lies and fright and violence that it is hard to say how much that mistaken impression of mine contributed to what happened. Would I have raised the knife if John's arm hadn't been raised? Or if I had caught sight of the jacket behind his shoulder? I don't know. I can't be sure. I believe that, in my fright, I jabbed at him with the knife out of a split-second impulse to scare him. There was no forethought. The fact is, having never been permitted in a kitchen, I knew little of knives. Indeed, the autopsy revealed that the blade had been inserted upside down, that is, sharp side up.

In my fog at the police station, I ended my statement to Anderson in a fluster. "I don't know what happened," I said. "I just did it." And now as I listened impassively to Mother's revelation of the jacket on a hanger, guilt clutched my heart.

Mother finished and I was excused by Anderson, who directed a blue-shirted policewoman to park me nearby in an empty office. The press were kept at a distance by the front door, but I was still being eyed. I wanted to leave, to go home, to vanish. What were they doing in that office? After an almost unendurable wait, I heard Mother's voice cry out, "Oh no! I want my baby home with me."

Looking ashen, she appeared at the doorway clinging for support to the arm of Jerry Giesler. Her new attorney was seething about something. He sucked in his jowls nervously as Mother tried to control her shaking. "Cherry Blossom," she said evenly, "you're going to have to spend the night here—but just tonight—and we'll be back for you in the morning." Dad hurried in to hug me, which set off a commotion of tears and clinging good-byes, rung down by a jail matron who walked me away by the elbow.

The jail for adults was upstairs, and we went along nightlighted corridors to a small holding cell with iron bars. It contained only a toilet and a cot that hung by chains from the wall. As instructed, I sat down to remove my shoes and belt, then pulled up my sweater to let the matron inspect me for concealed weapons. I still had my coat on, but the cell was chilly and I felt both hot and cold at once.

"How about a glass of milk?" the matron asked.

"No, Ma'am, thank you."

"A cup of tea?"

I thought of Nana and the comforting warmth of our "elevenses" at Crown Drive. "Oh yes, please."

"You should try and sleep, you know. Why don't you lie down? I'll get you a blanket." Stepping into the hall, she clanked the lock and hurried away. My mind was racing. I was frightened about what might come.

It was well past midnight, but the night's lurid trail was only starting to unwind. After my parents fought their way through the army of press camped outside the station, they went their separate, unfriendly ways. Dad avoided his West Hollywood apartment, which was well-known to the press, and retreated to the Bel Air house of his old friend Evelyn Lane. By sunrise they had phoned around to enlist the aid of friends, and Dad had hired his own high-powered attorney, Arthur J. Crowley (among whose clients was *Confidential* magazine).

Unbelievably, Mother took Giesler's limousine directly back to our newly rented house on Bedford. A handful of press were lying in wait for her—and for one other sensation as well. Giesler's limo approached the driveway just in time for Mother to see Stompanato's sheet-covered body being wheeled out the front door to a coroner's wagon.

"Oh, no," she screamed.

"Lana, stay down," said Giesler. The car backed away. He got out and told a few reporters that Mother would not be returning that night but was staying with friends.

Unconvinced, reporters found her cowering in the limo. She refused to answer questions and walked into the house, where she retreated to her boudoir and began to shake with hysterics. Dr. Mac's shots had turned me into a zombie, but whatever he gave Mother had the reverse effect on her. Reporters on the street said she could be heard sobbing and shrieking at Giesler, "Why won't they let me bring my baby home?" No one takes anything from Mother without a fight.

The charged atmosphere in the house finally proved too much for her, and after a couple of hours she fled to the house of her press agent. Bedford Drive fell silent again until crowds of the curious began to form at daybreak, some leaning against Johnny's white Thunderbird, which had been parked all night on the street.

At the police station, there had been feverish deliberations. There hadn't been a star scandal as headline-provoking as this in its jurisdiction since Stephanie's father, Walter Wanger, shot and wounded his wife's agent right across the street from the station's front door seven years before. Given Hollywood's reputation as a community of the privileged, the press had carefully scrutinized every police department action at the time, looking for any hint of favoritism being shown to a major film producer.

Though Walter Wanger finally served a four-month sentence (and then made a documentary film about prison reform), the Beverly Hills Police Department had been accused of giving him special treatment, and it remained sensitive to such charges. "Cheryl gonna get off easy?" had already been thrown at Anderson, and a policy of "no special favors" was now being shaped in the rainy predawn hours of Saturday morning.

Despite Giesler's efforts, Mother's wailings, my inarticulate testimony, and the chief's friendship with Dad—or maybe because of all these—Anderson was leaning toward a course that would be toughest on me and safest for the department. He favored my indictment for murder. The fact that Mother had offered to take the blame for me (which would have amounted to a criminal cover-up) or that in my shocked state I seemed without remorse only made things worse.

So too did the many misquotes of my testimony, issued by various police and other unnamed sources, that found their way into the morning editions. In addition to the damaging, "You don't have to take that, Mama," I was reported to have told Anderson, "I opened the door and went in . . . neither of them said anything. I didn't say anything. I just walked between them and . . . did it." Another misquote: "I pushed the knife into his stomach with all my might." The reading public might have imagined me to be a young Lizzie Borden.

While my fate was being weighed in Anderson's office and I was drinking tea in an upstairs cell, a commotion broke out at the station's entrance. The pudgy figure of Mickey Cohen tore up the stairs, taking the steps two at a time, yelling, "Who done it? Who done it?" Told that I had admitted responsibility, he rubbed his unshaven chin. "I can't understand it," he said excitedly. "I thought she liked him very much. We were happy—[Cheryl] and Johnny and me. We used to go horseback riding together."

Cohen had rushed to Bedford Drive demanding to view the body after hearing a radio bulletin about the killing. When he was told by Giesler that it had just been taken away by the county coroner's office, he headed for the police station. Cohen wanted to "pick up the body" for the family, he said, and was referred to the Hall of Justice in downtown Los Angeles. "Where's the Hall of Justice?" he deadpanned. Cohen, of course, had spent many months defending himself in a number of trials at the Hall of Justice, including one still in progress.

Cohen raced to the morgue. "That's him," he said simply when he was shown the body. Later he paused on the street to indulge one of his favorite pastimes, schmoozing with reporters. He said he had figured it was just a matter of time before John and Mother "would slip away and get married. I've been with Johnny when [Lana] would call him as many as five times in a half hour."

"I don't like the whole thing," he added gruffly. "There's a lot of unanswered questions . . . I'm going to find some of those answers no matter what happens.

"When I heard how Johnny was killed, cold chills ran through me. It's a fantastic way for a man like Stompanato to die. Johnny's been around a long time, but if what they tell me is true, he made no effort to dodge the knife. It just doesn't jell with me."

Sometime before dawn the next morning, Stompanato's apartment at the Del Capri Motel in Westwood was broken into. The burglar, who got in by jimmying a bathroom window and cutting a screen, didn't take any valuables. Indeed, it was unclear what, if anything, was missing.

By morning my immediate future was sealed. The State of California would book me on suspicion of murder. If convicted as a juvenile, I could face life in prison. If convicted as an adult, a question yet to be adjudicated, I could be sentenced to the gas chamber. On a question of even more excruciating import to me, the district attorney opposed bail. I was headed, at long last, for Juvenile Hall.

Twenty-five

Although the papers reported that I slept for five hours and spent a "remarkably restful night," I was afraid to let myself go that far. Each time I started to drop off, I jerked myself upright to keep control. I had to be cautious. I had to monitor footsteps in the hall and every pair of eyes that inspected me.

When the blue-shirted matron returned with my tea, she sat on the cot and spoke about her children. She seemed concerned about me, and I began to let down my guard. "I wish I were like Mother," I told her. "At least she is able to cry. I can't."

"Then you must sleep."

"I can't, I just can't."

Cruel ceiling lights burned all through the night, and since there were no windows to proclaim a new day, morning arrived when breakfast came in on a tray. Dad had arranged for an elaborate meal of scones and an omelet to be sent in, but the sight of it turned my stomach. I sipped coffee and waited until Dr. McDonald arrived, full of smiles and reassurance. He had no information, but gave me another shot. Finally, the door was unlocked and a policewoman stepped in.

"Good morning, Cheryl," she said. "I'm Officer Wiseberg. Would you like to stand up? You're coming with me."

"Where?"

"Downtown."

"Where?"

"To Juvenile Hall."

If Dr. Mac's shot hadn't already kicked in, my knees might have buckled. I will finally find out about Juvenile Hall, I thought calmly.

She led me downstairs to the noisy station house, where the reporters and photographers, who were being held at the room's far end, unleashed a volley of questions and flashbulbs. Mother and Dad were nowhere to be seen. In my haze, I obeyed orders to go this way and that, sign here, look in the camera, turn face left, turn face right, gimme your thumb. They had trouble taking fingerprints because my hands were shaking. As I was being pointed toward a rear door, Dad, trailed by his PR man, suddenly broke through the crowd. We clung together desperately.

"Daddy, why can't I go home?"

He held me and kept whispering, "It'll be all right, honey, you'll see," until they pried me away.

The drive downtown to Juvenile Hall reminded me of my Skid Row misadventure one year before. Here I was in police custody again, shoulder to shoulder with them in the back seat of a squad car, bound for a place that frightened me.

Juvenile Hall looked just like the hell of my imagining. It was gray and monolithic, with grime-streaked pillars and heavy-meshed windows. I was quickly taken through a back entrance into the institution's infirmary. Dad's friend Sybil Brand, who was an important figure at the County Welfare Commission (but always "Aunt Sybil" to me), had quietly arranged for me to be isolated in the jail's hospital. The press was told that I was suffering from shock and a mild temperature. In fact, Dr. McDonald gave me another checkup, an injection, and pronounced me fit.

I was prisoner in an all-white room that had a shower, a toilet, and a doorless closet. "Remove all your clothes and take a shower," said a nurse, handing me a bad-smelling soap that must have been for lice. "Be sure to wash your hair."

Afterward she brought me a scratchy muslin nightgown. With my hair still wet, I climbed into bed, pulled the covers up to my nose, and listened. There was a window high on the wall, impossible to see through unless I stood on the bed, which I didn't dare try. The only sign of life was visible through a small window in the door. I could see faces of girls through the chicken-wire glass as they jumped high to get a glimpse of me. I felt like an animal in the zoo.

Mother was something of a prisoner as well. Having just missed my arraignment at the police station, she returned to the house on Bedford to find it surrounded by a crowd of gawkers with binoculars and children on shoulders. From now on, she would have to live behind drawn shades.

There was also reason to fear for her safety. Stompanato had warned that if anything happened to him, his friends would "get even." As a result, Chief Anderson ordered several squad cars to cruise around the house and keep an eye on things.

Whether or not there was anything to Stompanato's threat, Mickey Cohen played on it to get himself space in the morning editions. The press had always mocked Cohen as a publicity hound, but, knowing he made good copy, they gave him good coverage. In this case, Cohen was able to jump into the drama as a principal player, taking the role of the grieving friend who was suspicious of police investigation methods. Cohen had good reason to want to embarrass the Beverly Hills police, with whom he had had any number of run-ins.

Before sunrise that Saturday morning, Cohen phoned John's older brother, Carmine Stompanato, in Woodstock with the news of the death. Brother Carmine, forty-five, a barber and Presbyterian church elder, authorized Cohen ("my representative") to take care of the funeral arrangements in Los Angeles until he arrived the next day for a face-to-face meeting with Chief Anderson.

Easter morning dawned wind-tossed and stormy. Though visiting hours at Juvenile Hall normally began at 1:00 P.M., the institution's electric gates opened two hours earlier to let a pair of Cadillac limousines glide into its empty courtyard. Dad stepped out of one of the cars along with his attorney and two public-relations men, while the other disgorged Mother, clutching Giesler's arm. Aunt Sybil had arranged a private visit for them, warning authorities that if my parents came at the normal time, "you'd have a mess on your hands." The press was quick to take note of this special arrangement, observing that my parents passed into Juvenile Hall under the glowering gaze of other parents who waited under the edge of a roof to avoid the rain.

On rising that morning, I was given a loose cotton dress and tie-string panties as big as a flour sack. I felt naked and drafty as the matrons delivered me to a meeting room where my parents waited. Dad stood smiling, Mother sat weeping. I ran to Dad, still fearful of what Mother might do. Would she say, "How could you do this to me?" As it turned out, no confrontations marred the strained half hour we spent together. Between silences we talked of trifles—the food at Juvenile Hall, my comfort. I didn't tell them how awful the place was because that would have put a burden on them they couldn't lift.

Mother looked so pitiable and years older. I finally held her in my arms as though she were a fragile little sister. She wasn't as physically strong as I, and I wondered if she would be able to get through this. But I didn't even know what "this" was. They told me nothing of what lay ahead. They said I'd be going home soon, "maybe even tomorrow." Yet everyone had said I was going home today. I didn't even know where home was, just that I was going there.

The main point was that everyone talked as though Good Friday had never happened. After the visit, Dad told the press, "When the matter comes up, we change the subject." Mother brushed by the reporters and hurried back to Bedford Drive, where that night she returned to sleeping in her bed. I was led back to my cell more bewildered than ever.

Later that afternoon, Carmine Stompanato, with friends of Cohen at both his elbows, came out of a two-hour meeting with Chief Anderson and District Attorney William B. McKesson to face a wall of press. He announced that he had demanded and received a promise from McKesson to conduct a "complete investigation."

"I am not satisfied with the current version of the

story," he said. The explanation of events was "too pat."
He was "not bitter at Miss Turner or the girl," he added,
but "they let my brother be there for more than an hour.
If they'd got him to the hospital, he might have been saved.
They called Giesler. They called the girl's father. They
called a doctor and only then they called Chief Anderson
. . . There was a whole hour they were there by them-
selves.

"It doesn't seem possible," he continued, "that [John]
would just stand there and let somebody put a knife into
him. He was in the Marine Corps and had lots of training.
He was very quick."

The elder Stompanato brother then leveled a charge that
made Anderson's eyes flash. The police chief, he said,
was "biased—favoring Miss Turner."

Anderson was quick to respond. Going on the offensive,
he hinted that Carmine's call for a complete investigation
had "originated with Cohen." He estimated that no more
than thirty minutes had passed before police were alerted,
a delay caused by confusion and the attempts to resuscitate
Stompanato. He denied flatly the accusation that I was
being given any special treatment, a denial later echoed
by the district attorney, a Juvenile Hall official, and press
agents for both Mother and Dad.

The question about my parents' special early visit was
fielded by Dad's man. "Cheryl's predetention hearing was
imminent," he said, "and there was a great deal of talking
to do with her in order to prepare the case."

I was becoming a hot potato.

At 9:00 A.M. Monday morning, Mother, Gran, Dad, and
their attorneys (now numbering four) filed into a Juvenile
Hall courtroom. Having been brought from a locked cell
upstairs, I was puzzled by the fact that this was called my
predetention hearing. It was presided over by Judge Don-
ald Odell.

Giesler stood up and said that he would prove that John's
death had been an act of "justifiable homicide," and that
for now I should be released in the custody of my grandmother. It took just fifteen minutes for Odell to make two

rulings. First, he ordered, there would be a coroner's inquest; second, I would meantime be held in Juvenile Hall.

District Attorney McKesson had recommended to the judge that I *not* be released on bail, and he and the judge agreed that in light of all the publicity, it was better that I remain in the "safety" of Juvenile Hall. Since I lacked a stable family, they felt that the hall would protect me from "possible pressures brought to bear on the outside." That seemed to mean the mob, the press, my parents, and their lawyers.

Chief Anderson was unhappy, insisting that an inquest was a waste of the taxpayers' money. "Let's go to trial," he said. "I am satisfied that Stompanato was killed with a knife and we have the party who did it."

After the hearing, I was moved to another, more austere room, one with no toilet and in a more open section of the infirmary. A steel cot took up nearly the whole cell, and I was warned never to sit on it during daytime hours. I suppose it was their way of discouraging sloth. The only thing to sit on was a swing-out metal seat beneath the wall-mounted desk. I was perched on it, thinking, when a matron unlocked the door. "You're going to the dayroom, Cheryl," she said. "Follow me."

The dayroom was a bright space painted institutional green and filled with chairs and tables—and girls. As I approached the door, a hush descended. Card games stopped eyes looked up, and sentences froze midair.

There was no exit. I sat in a chair near the door and stared at my hands trembling in my lap. Three girls walked over to stand before me.

"You Cheryl Crane?"

"You really kill that guy?"

I could only stare at their shoes, and they walked away. When the room noise started up again, a new sound seemed to carbonate the air, the plosive "ch" sound in Cheryl. ("That's Cheryl Crane." "Isn't that Cheryl Crane?" "Look, Cheryl Crane!") In years to come, that sound would chirp along at my heels like a sorrowful katydid.

A bell rang and we filed into the lunchroom. It had eight tables, each seating four. Placed at what would be my regular seat, I couldn't eat.

"You Cheryl Crane?" asked the freckled girl on my right. She looked fourteen, very pregnant, and was buttering a whole slice of bread at once, then cutting it into quarters. Nana would never have permitted such a thing, but I sort of wanted to try it. I couldn't bring myself to speak with anyone or join in their play that day or the next. The girls left me alone with a kind of watchful understanding punctuated by shrugs. Most of them were in Juvenile Hall because they had run away from home or were driven away by their parents for being incorrigible or unwed and pregnant. Others had simply fallen through the cracks of a broken home. I was the only *murderess*.

On Wednesday afternoon I sat slumped in the chair by the dayroom door, having still not broken my silence. From across the room I felt the stare of a girl whose movements were oddly like those of a boy. She strode over and planted her feet before mine. "I bet you didn't do it," she said loudly. "I bet your mother really did it." The room fell silent.

I glared at her and screamed, *"I did it! I did it! I did it!"*

She smirked. A second girl appeared from behind. "Oh, leave her alone," she said to my tormentor and turned to me with a smile. "Why don't you come over here. We're playing cards." She extended a hand and led me across the room to her group. "Don't you pay any attention to those kids," she laughed. "We're having fun over here. Do you play poker?"

Her name was Joanne and, deep down, I felt grateful to her. She was a slight Latino girl, a thirteen-year-old runaway from East Los Angeles who could take care of herself. I guess Joanne felt sorry for me, and with her help I stopped resisting Juvenile Hall.

Stompanato's funeral was scheduled for 2:00 P.M. Wednesday in Woodstock. His body had lain in repose at a funeral home on Judd Street, and some 500 people filed past the open bronze coffin. Mickey Cohen paid for everything, bragging that his friend would go out "the way he went in life—nothing but the best." The body was dressed in a tuxedo and lace-tufted shirt with a black initialed handkerchief in the pocket. The Presbyterian pastor said in the eulogy, "Our purpose here is not to praise John Stompanato, but to give comfort and consolation to those who remain."

Thirteen cars made up the funeral cortege, a few of them limousines from Chicago bearing friends of Mickey Cohen. Ten-year-old John Stompanato, Jr., was not brought to his father's funeral. His remarried mother in Indiana described her ex-husband to reporters: "He had a good heart, you know, but he never grew up."

As an ex-Marine, Stompanato was buried with full military honors accorded by an American Legion Post, including a gun salute that ripped through the cloud-swept skies above the Oakland Cemetery two miles from town. He was laid to rest beside the pink granite headstones of his parents.

His stepmother, Verena Stompanato, told the press that she did not hate anyone. "We're not vindictive," she said. "We're not seeking revenge. We know that nothing we can do will bring Johnny back." But she supported Carmine's call for a vigorous investigation. "My son should have a defense. Any cold-blooded murder should be investigated. I don't believe there is such a thing as 'justifiable homicide.' "

Two years had passed since John's last visit to Woodstock, but he and Verena had kept up a correspondence, and some of his letters mentioned me. "They wanted Cheryl to come to Woodstock and go to school under an assumed name," she said, adding that she had refused to accept the responsibility. "I destroyed most of the letters from Johnny," she said. "I didn't want anyone to see them. They were very damaging."

"To whom?" asked a reporter.

"Lana Turner," she replied.

She did show one letter, dated London, November 5, 1957, which was filled with the "Dear Mom" chattiness of a dutiful son. It read in part:

Received your birthday card. . . . We arrived in London October 8. Lana had a beautiful birthday party for me here. Lana has been ill for two weeks with overseas flu. . . . This is the worst country I've ever been in yet. You can't understand one word the people say. They are still a thousand years behind the times.

Carmine Stompanato, meanwhile, took advantage of an eager press to improve upon his earlier charges. He insisted that "Lana is lying to save herself, her career, and her daughter," and he demanded that she take a lie detector test.

While Stompanato's relatives tried to stir public sympathy, Mother's lawyer, Jerry Giesler, was preparing for the all-important coroner's inquest set for Friday, two days away. He had managed to have me excused from testifying, on the grounds that I was a juvenile who had already given a full statement to the police. As Giesler put it, I had "gone through enough."

Mother would be his star witness, and that worried him. Cloistered at Bedford Drive, she had taken to spells of weeping. Sedated round the clock, she couldn't eat or sleep or concentrate. Giesler knew that her testimony would make or break his case, that her failure to move the jury could, in the most extreme of scenarios, pave my way to a gas chamber.

To make matters worse, the day before Stompanato's funeral, the *Los Angeles Herald Examiner* revealed just what the mysterious burglars were after when they broke into Stompanato's apartment hours after his death—Mother's love letters. They now appeared on the front page of the *Herald Examiner*, the full panting text of twelve letters, a telegram, and several gift cards. Spread across 450 column inches that day and the next, they detailed what Mother summed up as "our love, our hopes, our dreams, our sex and longings."

Stompanato had saved all the pale blue letters she had sent him before his trip to England and after, keeping them in a toilet kit which had vanished. "I miss you, want you, and ache for you," she wrote before his London arrival. "I'm your woman and I need you MY MAN!"

Posted variously from London, Hampstead, an airport,

and a train station, the letters were sweetened with pet names such as Daddy and Honey-Pot, and a number of Spanish and Italian diminutives, including Papi, Papito, Gitano, and Juanito.

Reprinted worldwide, the letters altered overnight the public perception of what Mother had been claiming. She had described Stompanato to police as a man who had forced himself on her, who was, as she and Chief Anderson put it, "unwelcome company." But the unblushing desire for him in her early letters showed that the feelings of love were mutual.

By the same token, her later letters showed that she was cooling toward him as they prepared to rendezvous in Copenhagen and head off to Mexico. After she'd already sent him the plane ticket, she wrote:

> Please after our call, I've been thinking and thinking—yes, what a shocking thrill it would be to see you on the plane, or wherever—but this is not *right*. You must let me alone in my "own world" for a while, to rest, think, rest, think.

Mickey Cohen admitted he was the source of the letters, which he claimed to have received from "people who had a right to have them." He denied responsibility for the break-in at the Del Capri Motel, saying coyly that having once been a resident there himself, he was too recognizable to risk an illegal entry. "I guarantee the cops done it," he said. "That's a fine place for me to burglarize. I'm better known there than the owner of the joint."

Why did Cohen expose the letters? "I thought it was fair," he said, "to show that Johnny wasn't exactly 'unwelcome company' like Lana said."

As the inquest approached, it was hard for Giesler to assess how the politically charged atmosphere would affect the case. The movie colony seemed guardedly behind Mother and me, although her old friend the *Hollywood Reporter* said pointedly that the "town's sympathy is with Steve Crane and his daughter."

At the time, I knew nothing of any of this. Hard news was unwelcome at Juvenile Hall. Newspapers were forbidden, and when the news came on the dayroom's TV set, matrons hurried to snap it off. Somehow I took that personally, but it was just as well. On the eve of the inquest, two items surfaced that would have greatly upset me.

Newsmen tracked down my poor darling Nana, who was then living quietly back in Edinburgh. They described her as grief-stricken, praying for me night and day. "I cannot believe my little darling would be capable of such a terrible thing," she said. "I read Cheryl a Bible lesson every night and morning. She could quote from the scriptures when she was little more than a baby.

"After she became a Roman Catholic," Nana continued, "she went to a convent school. If she thought she had done any wrong during the day, she would run to me at night, throw her little arms around me, and sob, 'Hold me tight, Nana. I want to confess.' " Nana's voice cracked and her eyes welled with tears. "I feel so helpless," she said. "Here I am 6,000 miles away. . . ."

In another interview, given shortly before the inquest, Lex Barker spoke to a tabloid in Rome. He described me as "not a bad girl but certainly very strange . . . two-faced."

He went on to claim, "My divorce depended on Cheryl. [On February 26, 1957] the girl returned to the house and told a story to her mother. I denied that it was true, but Lana always had one great fault—to believe her daughter first, though knowing she was a girl of complexes and accustomed to lie.

"For a few weeks, naturally, I tried a reconciliation, but without success. In one of the last phone calls, I said, 'Watch out for Cheryl. That girl will end up involved in great trouble.' Time has proved me right."

Twenty-six

T hings were heating up. ABC and CBS announced that they would be working together inside the courtroom on a network pool basis to film the inquest for television and would broadcast it live on radio. Location reporting like this was expensive, but in response to the unprecedented public interest in the case, the media were determined to go all out.

Newspapers reported surges in circulation that week, as each day brought another sensation. *Peyton Place,* then in its fourth month of release, rang up a thirty-two percent jump at the box office. Exhibitors reported that friendly audiences cheered during the big courtroom scene when Mother looked at Diane Varsi and said, "My daughter did bring her troubles home . . . I wouldn't understand." People shouted, "Atta girl, Lana!"

Even the house in Hampstead where Mother and John had quarreled was besieged by photographers wanting to take pictures inside the bedroom.

The coroner's inquest was scheduled for 9:00 A.M. Friday, April 11, in the Hall of Records' largest courtroom, a somber Beaux Arts space on the eighth floor. Though the temperature soared to eighty-six degrees that day, sending hordes to the beaches, a spectators' line had already begun to form outside the courtroom in the cool 6:00 A.M. dawn.

Most of those in line were Mother's fans—fortyish housewives and shop women, pensioners and young men in dungarees. They lined the roped-off corridor three abreast in a queue that was a hundred feet long by admis-

267

sion time. Only forty of them actually got in, the court-room's other 120 seats having been reserved for press.

Mother arrived in a severely tailored Italian gray silk suit and white gloves, her duck-tailed silver hair and makeup groomed to camera readiness by artists who had appeared at Bedford Drive long before the fan line had started to form downtown. This was to be the most important performance of her life. She had not slept all night, she told press, and then, displaying delicate poise, delivered a few prepared remarks. She was grateful that the authorities saw fit to "protect Cheryl" by not having the child in court, she said, and she was happy the inquest would give them a chance to straighten everything out. "But," she added, "I'm not pretending it's easy to be here."

Mickey Cohen, who was scheduled to be the first witness, bustled in five minutes late, sending an electric reaction through the jammed and sweltering courtroom. Intending to shock, he wore a cartoon gangster gray suit and gray felt hat, and he chewed gum. Asked if he had been able to identify his former bodyguard, he replied, "I refuse to identify the body on the grounds I may be accused of this murder." The deputy coroner gulped, then repeated his question, to which Cohen gave the same answer. He was dismissed. Picking up his hat from where it rested on the rail, Cohen jammed it on his head and stormed out. Total elapsed time: two minutes.

After this odd beginning, Dr. McDonald took the stand to reaffirm his own identification of the body.

Next came the autopsy report, which showed that death had resulted from a puncture of the abdomen, kidney, and aorta. The eight-inch blade had hit the backbone and taken a freak, curving path to the heart, resulting in death in a few minutes. A "whole team of doctors on the scene" could not have saved him, said the autopsy surgeon, who then mentioned an incidental fact he had learned in the course of the autopsy. Stompanato suffered from an incurable disease of the liver, congenital in nature, and would not have lived ten more years.

Finally, it was time for Mother to take the stand. Never glancing at the microphones before her but gazing into

space, she removed one glove and rested her elbows on
the chair. Then, filling her lungs as if to say, "steady,
now," she looked at her questioner and gave the palest
suggestion of a smile. A fascinated hush filled the room
as she testified for the next sixty-two minutes, the only
other sound being that of clicking cameras and scratching
pencils.

Mother underplayed. She spoke slowly, often using the
arcane syntax that she had learned from testifying at divorce hearings, and she showed schoolgirl good manners
with the three men who questioned her. Gently chastised
for saying "we" instead of "John and I," she put a hand
to her throat and said contritely, "Oh, I'm so sorry."

Her description of her quarrel with Stompanato in the
bedroom that night as I listened outside had everyone in
the courtroom on the edge of his seat. "And he kept
swearing and threatening me," she said, her voice just
barely under control. She paused and waited two beats, a
pause that would reappear in almost every sentence to follow, as though she were bringing up from the rear some
reluctant part of herself.

"He had a jacket and shirt hanging in the closet. I forget
exactly why it was there, or if he had brought it as a
change from his apartment. Anyway, it was hanging there,
and he walked away from me and went to the closet and
it was on the . . . a hanger. And he walked back to me
and was holding the jacket on the hanger as though he was
going to strike me with it, and I said, 'Don't ever touch
me again. I'm . . . I'm *absolutely* finished. This *is* the end
. . . I want you to get out.' And after I said that, I was
walking towards the bedroom door and he was right behind me and I opened it and my daughter came in.

"I thought it was so fast . . . I truthfully thought she
had hit him in the stomach, but, the best I can remember,
they came together and . . . they parted. I still never saw
a blade. Mr. Stompanato grabbed himself here, he—"

"Above the abdomen?"

"Yes, sir. And he started to move forward and he made
almost a half a turn and then dropped on his back."

She went on to say that I ran screaming from the room
and she bent to look at the body. "I still did not see that

there was blood . . . I saw his sweater was cut, and I lifted the sweater up and saw this wound.''

She began the sentence, ''Johnny was lying there making the most horrible noises in his throat and gasping—'' then she had to stop. The audience waited in suspense as she took a sip of water, another deep breath, and finally resumed describing her mouth-to-mouth breathing efforts. She noted that, after Dr. McDonald arrived, he worked frantically for several minutes before saying, ''Lana, I can't get a heartbeat,'' and she knew that he was dead.

At the conclusion of her testimony, a fifteen-minute recess was declared and reporters crowded around. She tried to answer their questions, but feeling faint from heat and stress, turned to Giesler and said, ''Jerry, could we go somewhere for a few minutes?'' While assisting her, he stumbled, and Mother said dryly, ''Who's helping who?'' Reporters noted that from the rear of the courtroom a spectator remarked in a loud voice, ''What an act she's putting on.''

After the recess came a stream of witnesses. Dad testified that when he arrived in Mother's boudoir that night, ''I kept telling [Cheryl], 'Everything will be all right, Baby' . . . And I looked at Miss Turner and I was pretty sure it wasn't all right.''

Gran took the stand, looking shaky, and gave impatient endings to her answers. ''Well, what else do you want to know?'' she'd say testily, and finally, when despair came into her voice, she was excused.

A verbatim transcript of the testimony I had given Chief Anderson in his office that night was read into the record. It was noted that although Mother had sat four feet away, I spoke with eyes downcast, with no prompting from anyone, and the account I gave in Anderson's office did not vary from the one given earlier to Anderson in my bedroom.

The parade of witnesses continued, some providing puzzling forensic details that would raise questions for years to come. I cringe a little when I recall them.

For one thing, there were no fingerprints found on the knife when it was examined the next day, except for a bloody smudge on the handle too smeared to analyze. For another, the blood on the blade contained "several light and dark fibers or hairs." What's more, although the knife was shiny new, the handle bore light scratches. (Apparently it had been bought by Mother and John that afternoon, and the price tag from a nearby hardware store was still glued to the handle.) To top things off, the first officer to arrive on the scene testified that Mother's bedroom showed no disarray or speck of blood.

Mother looked away and Gran buried her face while a grisly reenactment of the stabbing was staged. Police deputies demonstrated the path the knife took while being held in a right hand, upside down. Unable to stand it, Mother slipped out of the courtroom.

Shortly before noon, the jury of ten men and two women stood up to retire for deliberations. The inquest was adjourning when suddenly a spectator in dark glasses leapt from his seat and shouted, "Oh, no! This can't end here. I want to testify." When denied the chance, the man went on shouting, "Lies, lies, all lies! This mother and daughter were both in love with Stompanato. He was better than any of them. All you people in Hollywood are no good!' Storming out, he kept shouting, "Johnny Stompanato was a gentleman!''

While all this was going on, I was watching television in the dayroom at Juvenile Hall, largely unaware of the fact that my fate was being weighed just a few blocks away. I had only the sketchiest idea of what an inquest was, and everyone had downplayed its importance. On the TV screen was *Seven Brides for Seven Brothers*, which featured actor-dancer Russ Tamblyn. Russ had gotten an Oscar nomination for his portrayal of Diane Varsi's boyfriend in *Peyton Place*. He had been seated at Mother's table at the Oscar dinner only eighteen days earlier, and we had danced several times. Now here I sat, slumped in a formless dress, staring at a jailhouse television set, watching the joyous image of Russ flying through the air. As the noon news came on, matrons turned off the set and I missed seeing the report of my fate.

At ten minutes after twelve, the coroner's jury announced its verdict: justifiable homicide. The vote was ten to two.

* * *

I was not yet out of jeopardy. District Attorney Mc-Kesson, who sat in on the inquest as an observer, was still to be heard from. The inquest verdict was not binding on him; he could still indict me if he wanted to. Moreover, even if he decided not to make me stand trial for murder as an adult, I faced a Juvenile Court hearing on April 24. That hearing would decide where I would live in the future—with my mother, with my father, in a foster home, or in a state institution. In the meantime, it had been decided that I would remain in Juvenile Hall for two more weeks at least.

That night Dr. McDonald paid his usual 10:00 P.M. visit to Bedford Drive to check up on Mother and give her a sedative. The inquest verdict that morning had done little to lift her depression and insomnia. She was as wrung out as I was. I'd lost four pounds that week.

Dr. Mac sat at Mother's bedside and tried to comfort her. "How we doing, Little Chick?" he asked, using his pet name for her. She shrugged and focused her eyes on a point above his head. McDonald looked around the room. Just a week earlier, this pink boudoir had been visited by death. Stompanato's body had been sprawled on this floor, its feet touching the very bed in which Mother now lay.

"Oh, my God," he suddenly said. "And I let you come back to stay here! No wonder you can't sleep. You're moving out of here." With that, he lifted her in his arms and swept her out the door.

The next day, sight unseen, Mother rented a furnished house on Canon Drive, six blocks away. Later that day she was granted a special visit with me. "Well, Baby, we got through that," she said. "That's behind us. Now all we have to face is the court hearing."

That was enough explanation for me. After a week in prison I was beginning to show the pallor of complacency, and we whiled away the visit with chitchat. All I wanted to know was "when am I getting out?"

Mother told reporters that there had been no tears during our visit, that she and I were "too happy to see each other," that I was looking fine. "They are treating her wonderfully here," she said. "I'm going to visit my baby every chance I get. We have so many things to say—so many things."

McKesson's announcement came the next morning. He would not prosecute. At the very least that meant there was no longer any chance of my going to the gas chamber. Then he added something ominous. "Cheryl never has had a real home," he said, "either with her mother or her father. I think it's about time a proper home was found for her." Translated, that meant a foster home or a reformatory.

Mother's fitness as a parent was now being placed in the public forum for debate. Her anguished performance in court had touched hearts, but it also revealed that her behavior as a mother strayed far from a healthy norm. The *Los Angeles Times* fired an opening salvo that morning in its lead editorial, concluding:

> In the turnover of husbands and wives, lovers and mistresses, the Cheryls are the misplaced baggage, lost and found and lost again, always tagging along on the next train or plane or boat. Sometimes in their loneliness they set up images of one parent or the other and worship them passionately, even savagely. In an unreal world unreality is the only substance.
>
> Miss Turner told the Coroner and his jury that Cheryl was never left alone. . . . that remark evokes a picture of the most terrible loneliness, that of the child alone in a well-meaning crowd, seeking the mother of her imagination.
>
> The real mother in this case is a simple woman, a hedonist without subtlety, who was so preoccupied with her design for living that she long ago lost the reference marks. . . . The hurts done to children of casual divorce, the later witnesses of other marriages and less formal matings don't necessarily make juvenile delinquents but they make a multitude of psychological cripples. In the Turner case Cheryl isn't the juvenile delinquent; Lana is.

When I read this editorial several weeks after it appeared, it was the first time I'd ever seen harsh words printed about Mother. I hadn't read the snide items that had been written about her for years, and was surprised to discover that others besides me thought she had faults. I learned later that the media generally took a cynical view of her performance on the witness stand, seeing it as just that—an actress's performance, and her best to date. Her old nemesis, *Life* magazine, triumphantly ran photos of the now famous *Peyton Place* courtroom scene, as well as stills from other courtroom scenes she'd played in three earlier movies.

Speaking in Woodstock, Carmine Stompanato denounced the inquest. "We were dead before we started," he said. "They've got the best lawyer in California, all of Lana Turner's money, and the chief of police is working for her."

Mickey Cohen added, "It's the first time in my life I've ever seen a dead man convicted of his own murder. So far as that jury was concerned, Johnny just walked too close to the knife."

That Sunday night, Cohen was interviewed by syndicated columnist Walter Winchell at Mocambo, where he unburdened himself of all his hard feelings toward Mother. "I love the kid and I like Steve but I hate Lana Turner," he said, citing a past grievance. Winchell pointed out that such talk added fuel to fears of the mob vengeance on her. "Respectable people in all 48 states are on Lana's and Cheryl's side," warned Winchell. "You'd have nothing but trouble."

Cohen scoffed at the idea of mob reprisal. "That's just newspaper talk," he said.

The next morning, Winchell confirmed a rumor that Carmine Stompanato had met with his lawyer in Woodstock and was about to sue Mother, Dad, and me for damages of "more than $1,000,000." The claim would be unlawful death and defamation of character. "Johnny Stompanato never was defamed while he was alive," said the Woodstock attorney, "only after he was dead. Police record? He hasn't any such reputation here. He enjoyed a fine reputation in his home town."

An ironic discovery was made that same morning, when

police found four cardboard boxes Stompanato had stored in a warehouse the previous November. Along with clothes, kitchenware, and the cowboy boots he wore on our Culver City rides, the boxes contained papers and personal items that revealed the unsavory side of his business affairs. A number of unpaid promissory notes to women showed a paper trail into heavy debt.

In addition, there were three mysterious bank books recording accounts held jointly with the wife of a Los Angeles attorney. There was also wedding jewelry inscribed to the attorney's wife, suggesting that she had been married to Stompanato. (The woman told reporters she was bewildered by it all. "We used to play cards together," she said. "I've been married to my husband for fifteen years.")

Police found several wedding rings, an unregistered .32 caliber revolver with ammunition, and a number of gifts from Mother. She had given him jewelry, a mahogany desk set, and several large silver-framed photos of herself, one of which bore her handwritten dedication in Spanish, "For my Gypsy and sugar lips with all my love and soul— Always—Zincarella."

Finally, there was one item the police chose not to reveal to the public: rolls of negative film in a little wooden box. Developed and blown up, the pictures showed nude women in sexual situations. Their faces could be recognized, but in some shots the women seemed unaware that they were being photographed by what may have been a hidden camera. Although Chief Anderson had already passed along to the district attorney word of Stompanato's involvement in a blackmail operation, McKesson viewed the photos as immaterial. Mother was a perfect target for blackmail, of course, but her face was not in any of the photographs.

As it was, Mother had already spent many thousands of dollars on Stompanato in the form of loans, gifts, and travel. Reports were now coming in from Europe that he had taken Mother for a "sucker," that he had run up huge food and hotel bills in London, Paris, and Copenhagen, all the while promising "Lana will pay."

As more and more was revealed about Stompanato's

past and Mother's foolishness in the game of love, sympathy began swinging in her favor. Of course, she was being denounced from pulpits, and lawmen took a dim view. But Mother's fans stayed loyal, while the general public seemed to be fascinated by the delicious luridness of the melodrama. We received a staggering amount of sympathy mail. Even Chief Anderson counted 200 letters written to him in our defense.

Walter Winchell helped Mother's apotheosis along with a column that began, "She is made of blue-eyed sunshine, taffy tresses and swaying charms. She is Lana Turner, a movie goddess." It ended one thousand words later with, "In brief, have a heart for a lady with a broken heart."

As Mother restored herself behind the drawn shades of her newly rented house on Canon Drive, I tried as best I could to make time pass. *Two* more weeks of this. Neither her attorneys nor Dad's had fought the ruling that I remain in custody. "We simply wish to cooperate in every possible way," said my father's man, Arthur Crowley.

My parents and their lawyers had been meeting together all week in order to present a united front at the hearing at which they hoped to win my release from custody. Dad denied rumors that he had planned to fight Mother for me. "We have one concern—the child's welfare," he said. "Throughout all this trouble, I've backed Lana one hundred percent, and we both refrained from any derogatory comments about each other."

In truth, Dad *was* about to make a bid for custody of me. He would promise to get a new house and housekeeper, provide approved schooling, and change his work hours in order to have plenty of time to be with me at home.

Mother, meanwhile, planned on my coming to live with her ("Wouldn't any mother?" said Giesler), and she was preparing the strongest possible petition of her own. To that end, Giesler was going to call a parade of witnesses who would testify that I was healthy and normal, that Good Friday was a tragic accident.

Mother and Dad both submitted to lengthy at-home interviews given by probation officers, and, horror of horrors, Mother even complied with the probation department's request that she consult with a psychiatrist. After three or four sessions at the UCLA Medical Center, the psychiatrist, having listened to Mother's account of her life, finally raised a finger and asked, "Miss Turner, when did you first realize you hated your mother?" She blinked, snapped her purse shut, rose to her feet, and strode regally out the door.

Everyone seemed to have an opinion as to what should become of me. The judge who would preside at the hearing told newsmen that he had received hundreds of letters advising him how to rule, but, under the law, he was forbidden to read them. Fortunately, it was not improper for him to take a phone call from my "Aunt Sybil," whose advice may well have weighed in the decision.

I was told that the Juvenile Court judge would probably ask if I had a preference as to which parent I lived with. The question made a deep impression, and I turned it over in my mind for days. I paced the length of my cell endlessly, varying the routine by walking heel-to-toe, then taking giant steps, then walking backward.

Here, at last, was my chance to live with Dad. But I simply could not stand up in court and say so, because it would hurt Mother terribly. Still, I knew I didn't want to live with her. The dilemma was driving me mad. Finally the answer came, and I gave a little hop. "Your honor," I rehearsed, "I want to live with my grandmother."

What was worst about those final two weeks in Juvenile Hall was that in this hardened environment I had to go along to get along. In order to fit in, I learned to butter my bread and slice it in fours. More important, I was also learning to talk street talk, to distrust authority, and to doubt my worth.

Two days before the hearing in Juvenile Court, Carmine Stompanato filed his damage suit. He was seeking $752,250, and the major assertion was that his brother had been stabbed while lying down.

Twenty-seven

I was as jumpy as a box of birds the morning of the hearing, and the silliest things got to me. By special permission, I was allowed to take a sit-down bath (instead of a shower), my first since Good Friday. But I still didn't feel really clean. One reason was that I had an embarrassing three weeks' worth of hair on my legs. The other girls managed to keep their legs smooth in a razor-free society by plucking with a fingernail and using an emery board, but I had been unable to master the technique, though I had tried.

While I was still wearing the same tired pair of shoes I had come in with on Good Friday, Gran sent me a fresh cotton shirtwaist dress in virginal pale blue. I didn't like it. There would be a circus of newsmen to greet me, and I felt as though my uncleanness were being presented to them in sheep's clothing.

While the hearing wasn't scheduled to start until 2:00 P.M., I was told to be ready in the morning in order to evade the press. By 10:00 A.M. I was sitting in a reception room, dressed and packed, my sole possessions a brush, comb, and lipstick clutched in a plastic bag. I waited an hour for the arrival of my probation officers, who would escort me to the hearing. In our two-week acquaintance, both of them had persuaded me that they cared.

My caseworker, Jeanette Muhlbach, was a divorcee in her thirties with two sons. Her calm maternal manner was belied by the smart outfits she sewed for herself. Jeanette reported to Jim Discoe, a slender, easygoing man nearing forty who suffered from emphysema as a result of his service as a navy diver in World War II. Jim became my staunchest pal. His only daughter was exactly my age, and he had learned the art of giving gentle guidance without the slightest sting of reproval.

Jim, Jeanette, and I got into a station wagon and headed for Santa Monica. Two jail counselors I had befriended waved farewell at the door. (I had been a "model inmate," one Juvenile Hall official said. "Only eleven percent of our girls achieve that.") After a stop for drive-in hamburgers on Pico Boulevard, we reached the courthouse and slipped in a back door, successfully eluding reporters.

Mother, Dad, Gran, and the lawyers were waiting for us in a second-floor chamber. After we all exchanged greetings and reassurances, an acrid silence settled smoglike on the room.

I drifted to a window and peeked at the hundreds of newsmen and spectators massed at the building's front steps. Someone saw me and a staccato of camera clicks shot my way before I jumped back.

Mother sat laconic beside Giesler, taking deep drags on her Benson & Hedges in an ivory holder. I asked her for a cigarette. "I don't know if I should," she said, wrinkling her brow.

"Oh, for God's sake," snapped Gran, "give the kid a cigarette." Having learned to inhale now, I took a long drag and sat back to smile at my grandmother. I noticed that she had lost a little weight and the chords in her neck stood out.

The hearing took ninety minutes behind closed doors in a giant courtroom that held less than twenty people, fourteen of whom were witnesses. The presiding judge bore what struck me as the ominous name of Allen T. Lynch. Fortunately, he seemed a kindly man who happened to have a spirited teenage daughter himself. Judge Lynch promptly ruled that, based on his reading of the inquest transcript, he would drop any accusation of murder. From that point on, he wanted to deal only with the case report that charged a "lack of proper parental control and supervision."

Jerry Giesler and Arthur Crowley sprang into action against each other like pit bulls in a fight for custody of me. Lynch had to gavel them to order, pointing out that, in this particular kind of court proceeding, attorneys were not necessary. Since they were present, he added, he had a question. "Who exactly is representing the child?" he asked. "I am!" both lawyers shouted, whereupon Lynch promptly told them to sit down.

Things turned nasty during the court's examination of Mother's and Dad's custody qualifications. Dad insisted he had contributed $2,000 to my education the previous year, waving checks to prove it. Mother denied receiving a cent. "For instance," she said, "last summer when Cheryl was injured in Colorado, Mr. Crane and I flew to her, and Mr. Crane had to leave that same night. And, in the hurry of his leaving, he, Mr. Crane, had said that he wanted to take care of the doctors' bills. I still have received nothing on those bills. I have paid them all."

The judge questioned Mother's ability to support me. Did she hope to continue in her present work? "A great part of me would like very much not to continue," she replied, "only because of the . . . spotlight, the glare." She said that acting was the only work she knew, however, and was the sole support of herself, her mother, and me. "I wish I could say that I had enough put away—that I wouldn't have to work. I don't."

In fact, Mother was deeply in debt. Still repaying loans to M-G-M, she faced a long wait for any producer's profits from *Another Time*, which was set to open in ten days. The role of a murderess recently offered her in a picture called *Up at the Villa* had been suddenly withdrawn. She had no job prospects, while her lawyers' bills were devouring $1,000 a day and climbing. Whether she had any career left was a topic of lively debate around Hollywood night spots and commissaries. "I need to continue working," she said with finality.

When I was finally ushered into the proceedings, Lynch showed vast sympathy in his questions to me. Asked which parent I preferred to live with if I had the choice, I looked straight into his eyes, and said, "My grandmother." Mother caught her breath and Dad shuffled his feet. I tried not to look at them. Though I was making the best of a bad situation, that didn't make it good.

After a while Lynch said, "I am interested very much in this girl's future, and she's got to be placed some place, in my opinion, where all this publicity isn't going to just be heaped on her head every time she walks out the door. I have in mind that probably some school could be worked out where she could be placed under another name." He paused to study my face. "What would you think about that, Cheryl?"

"No."

"You don't want that?"

"No."

"You'd rather stay here?"

"Yes, definitely."

"And fight it out?"

"Yes."

"That's courage," said the judge.

I could not think why. I'd been struggling for years to keep my own name and a place at home. Why would I want to run away now? And I had no idea what he meant by something being "heaped on my head every time I walked out the door."

"Cheryl," he said, "you've had a tragic experience, you know, and I hope you'll learn to forget as much as you can. You've a wonderful future ahead of you." He continued in this vein and said again that I should forget all this bother and publicity.

"Do you think you can do that?"

"I'll try," I promised.

It was not long before Lynch delivered his decision. I was to become a ward of the court until age eighteen, while my physical custody would be taken over by Gran. Mother and Dad could each see me no more than once a week, subject to review in sixty days. While they could have unlimited access by telephone, they were prohibited from taking me across the state line.

Mother gasped and Dad lowered his head. The next moments were caught up in a tide of onrushing press and police. Doors flew open as Jim and Jeanette hustled me away. Outside, we faced the familiar scene of frenzy. My eye caught on two smiling ladies in flowered hats who broke through the police and suddenly pressed blue envelopes into my hand. They were legal papers. "Don't read them! Don't read them!" Gran said in the car, but I could not resist. I was holding subpoenas to appear in the civil court matter of John Stompanato's "wrongful death."

My parents fled by other routes, but they had been handed summonses, too. Mother was trapped with reporters while waiting for Giesler's chauffeur to fix a flat tire, and she decided to brazen out what was for her embarrassing news. "It was what I was praying for," she said, "but I hope to be in full control of my daughter later."

Dad, looking glum, eluded the press, later commenting by phone, "I've always said I would be happy to see her in her grandmother's care."

Concluded Judge Lynch, "She's going to live with this thing the rest of her life, regardless of what I do."

Jim Discoe drove us speedily to the new home that I would share with Gran. It was the place at 619 North Canon Drive that Mother had just rented. She moved out and went to Gran's apartment. The house was a four-bedroom colonial of clapboard and fieldstone design, sitting close to its neighbors and the street. As we drove up, I saw that all its shades were drawn. I was told to sit still in the car until the garage door closed safely behind us.

Glancing around, I noticed that the house's backyard was surrounded by an eight-foot fence. On the plus side, there was a swimming pool. I headed straight upstairs and vanished into the cloud of a bubblebath. After three weeks in jail, I had almost forgotten what fragrant creams and fluffy towels were like.

When I came back downstairs, Gran pointed to a large wrapped carton that had just been delivered. I tore it open to find a brown leather three-speed Zenith record player and dozens of albums. The card read, "To Cheryl, To fill up your days with music. Hope you enjoy this, Love, Frank." It was from Mother's friend of fifteen years, Frank Sinatra—"Uncle Frank" since my adolescence. He enclosed a dozen of his records as well as those by artists he admired, such as Sammy Davis and Tony Bennett.

Frank often phoned to cheer me up. But the flood of other messages being sent to me then was intercepted. That was too bad, because I was in desperate need of some positive feedback. What was in store for me was just the reverse.

That night Gran sat me down and laid out the rules. Windows facing the street must always have their shades drawn, and I must never even peek out lest my face be seen. I was never to answer the phone or unbolt the front door, never to lock myself in a room or enter the car except inside the closed garage. I could go out in the backyard by myself, but never anywhere else.

That night we retired to the master bedroom, where we had pushed the twin beds together so we could sleep side by side. When I lingered in the bathroom, Gran appeared at the door. "What are you doing, dear?" she twinkled. I felt more in prison here than when I was in prison. I popped another one of the Libriums Dr. Mac had prescribed.

The next morning I dared to peek out a window and saw a squad car parked at the curb. It reminded me of the kidnap scare at Mapletop eight years earlier. What happened this time was that Giesler and a Los Angeles newspaper had received a number of telephone calls that week threatening all our lives. "Lana and Cheryl are going to be taken care of," said one gruff-voiced caller. "They let that girl go free this afternoon, but she won't get off. We'll see to that."

In another call, a tearful woman warned that Stompanato had a lot of friends, and one was "coming out from the East to get you." Earlier someone had tried to extort $10,000 from Dad for Stompanato's $2,300 funeral. Even Chief Anderson was a target. He received two threatening letters, one because he had done too much to help me, the other because he hadn't done enough.

Giesler dismissed the calls as a "bunch of baloney," and Mickey Cohen was conspicuously unavailable for comment. Still, the police couldn't be sure they were cranks and the patrol remained at our curb.

Judge Lynch had ruled that I could not go back to school in Ojai, that instead I would have to finish the spring semester with some kind of private tutoring. So it was good-bye to Happy Valley, Ziggy, Peter, and Rowena.

I don't know who found the Dubanoff School on Hollywood Boulevard, a private, one-room tutorial class for fifteen handicapped children. Most of the kids were retarded or disabled in some way, drooling, screaming, and unable to feed themselves or go to the toilet. None was more than nine years old, and I sometimes had to sit on tiny tot chairs with my knees flying high in the air.

Another of Judge Lynch's decrees was that I see a psychiatrist each week. "Nobody thinks you're incompetent in any way," he said, explaining that I needed psychiatric care "in order that you may be helped in certain emotional problems that you have."

The directive so shamed us that Mother always forgot the psychiatrist's name and referred to "your doctor's appointment," while I called him "the dentist." I found it insulting to have to talk to a head doctor. I knew that what I needed most was simply to be treated like all the other kids, and I resented anything that set me apart.

Dr. Charles Wahl was head psychiatrist at one of California's biggest medical centers. I went to see him every Thursday at four. He was a round little man in his forties with cold eyes and a brusque Germanic manner. His cupid's-bow lips often sucked on a pipe. They seldom smiled.

He and I did not make a good doctor-patient team. Everything I had been taught about internalizing feelings went smack against psychiatry's idea of talking things over. For long minutes in his book-lined office, I would sit smoking, saying nothing, while he drew on his pipe. When I did break the silence, usually to offer something mundane about the events of the week, he would respond with a question. "How do you feel about that?" he'd ask, taking a slow puff. Dr. Wahl was all import, no export.

I suppose I was waiting to hear what *he* felt about things. I needed guidance, but he seemed to want only to study me. As a result, our time together was wasted. He never even came close to bringing up Good Friday. But then, if anyone dared to mention the tragedy, I would stiffen and fall silent, a silence that unmistakably meant, "Don't ever ask me about that."

* * *

Rummaging around the house one day soon after we
moved into Canon Drive, I discovered a back staircase that
ascended to a long, narrow bowling alley of an attic that
was lit by a window at each end. Dusty sunshine beamed
through one of the windows, casting a glow onto something that caught my eye. I went closer. It was a sixteen-
inch stack of newspapers, the top one of which showed a
large photo of Dad and me looking sad.

Squatting down, I began to pick at the pile, my heart
thumping as I realized that someone had saved all the
newspapers from April and hidden them here. Was it
Mother, who insisted she couldn't bear to see the news all
month? Or Gran, the family scrapbook keeper, who was
now downstairs starting lunch and must not discover me
here? I glanced uncertainly over my shoulder. But I was
tired of being wrapped in cotton wool, I told myself. I
have a right to see what they wrote.

I began to paw through the stack, when suddenly my
hand froze on a photo of John lying dead on the floor. I
closed my eyes. But it was no good. The image of his
body seemed to be etched into the inside of my eyelids. I
had to force them open.

I began slowly at the top of the pile and, almost in an
act of atonement, made myself read every line and study
every photo. It was as though garbage were raining on my
head: "STABBING-STABBING-STABBING—LANA'S DAUGH-
TER SLAYS HOODLUM"; " 'ALL MY FAULT,' SOBS LANA";
"CHERYL'S OWN STORY"; "CHERYL TO STAY IN
CUSTODY"; "JOHNNY PREYED ON RICH WOMEN"; "LANA'S
LOVE LETTERS FOUND"—

Love letters. Mother's? With a kind of savoring dread,
I spread out the paper and read every word of them, and
then again, a second time. How very difficult it was to
think of one's mother having sex, but there it was, and
her uninhibited outpourings made me swallow and pause
and wonder.

It seemed so *wrong* that her intimate thoughts could be
splashed across the papers that way without permission.
But it was legal. No one had actually proved that the letters were stolen.

I was bewildered by the tale her letters told. To think Mother could ache with love again and let Stompanato return after he had tried to kill her!

It certainly wasn't the way she had told it to me that afternoon at Gran's when she first let down her hair. Much as he had done in the beginning, she said, John had again forced his way into her life.

Several of the attic papers included short biographies of Mother, recounting her storm-tossed marriages and affairs, gossipy tales of public quarrels and slappings and tumbles downstairs. My eyes went big when I read about them. I didn't know any of it. Mother had rarely fought with her partners in front of the baby. Gentlemen came and then simply left one day to the sound of slamming doors and no good-byes.

Normal children, who see their parents fight and reconcile their differences, come to understand that discord is a part of marital life. The sun comes up again. But I had no such background that would put Mother's fiery love-hate relationship with Stompanato into any kind of context. To me, those bitter fights of theirs that I overheard were terrifying. I found it impossible to accept that Mother would take physical mistreatment from a man—that she was not some goddess whom the rest of the world always treated like royalty, as she so utterly demanded.

I could hear Gran downstairs. She might be starting to look for me. I got to my feet and pushed the papers back to their hiding place. Having made myself digest every word, I thought the episode was closed. I left the attic and never went back.

Twenty-eight

A frost had developed between Mother and Dad since their flare-up at Juvenile Court. The following week, Dad filed suit to reverse the ruling that had made me a ward of the court—a first step toward challenging Mother for my custody. In contrast to her remarks to the press stressing our closeness and her maternal worries, Dad went on the offensive, even admitting irresponsibility as a parent. "I may not have been the best of fathers," he told newsmen, "but I'm going to do everything I can to make it up to her now."

"Maybe I shouldn't say this," he added, "but I'm proud of my Cherie. She only did what I, you, or most anyone would have done. She was frozen with fear, but she stepped in to protect her mother." Unfortunately, Dad said this to a newspaper reporter, not to me. I never knew he felt that way about what I had done.

To help his custody petition, Dad was planning to buy a big house and marry Helen DeMaree, who would be an ideal stepmother for me. For nearly two years Helen had been wearing his engagement ring (but not the famed Crane diamond—Lila Leeds had that). What Dad didn't publicize was the fact that he was about to expand the Luau into a national restaurant chain, a step that would give him even less time for his daughter.

He denied that his custody suit represented a move against his ex-wife. "I have to think first of my daughter," he said, "and I simply believe I am the better qualified at the moment to control her future and care for her."

Mother replied through Giesler that his action would be resisted "to our last breath."

My mother had her full share of miseries to deal with now. That May, just when Hollywood had decided that her film career was about to scale new heights, *Another Time, Another Place* came out to terrible reviews and bored audiences. People were starting to compare her to Joan Bennett, whose career went into decline after her husband was convicted of manslaughter. There would be no producer's profits from *Another Time* to help pay lawyers' fees, which continued to mount as a result of Dad's custody maneuvers and the Carmine Stompanato suit.

Mother's new residence, Gran's second-floor apartment, quickly proved too small and too accessible to the street. Its address had been printed in the papers (as had ours on Canon Drive), so Mother moved quietly to another house on nearby Roxbury Drive. Since she couldn't go out in public, see friends, or freely visit with her family, she embraced seclusion for perhaps the first time in her life.

The newspapers in the attic turned out to have been saved for her, and she now sent for them. When she read about how Stompanato had blackmailed rich women, she could well believe it. Days before, her second attorney, Louis Blau, had come to her house with a roll of exposed film showing Mother sleeping naked on a bed. John had taken the photos and, before traveling to England, had left them with someone for safekeeping. Blau had acquired the pictures privately without payment, and he and Mother burned them.

Things were difficult for us at Canon Drive as well. Gran, nearly overwhelmed by the weight of her responsibility, was looking frail and frightened, and her long fingers often clutched the stem of a martini glass. While the whole world knew that she had physical custody of me, few were aware that, in fact, she exercised very little control over my behavior. She shared authority with Jim Discoe, Jeanette Muhlbach, Mother, Dad, and—ultimately—Judge Lynch. This six-way division of authority was tantamount to almost no authority at all. I learned to slip through the cracks.

Perhaps to compensate, poor Gran played it very safe.

If I lazed reading in the backyard on a sunny morning, it was certain she would call, "Why don't you come in now, dear?"

Pondering my loneliness, I remembered that the court had encouraged me to make contact with wholesome new friends. Of course, I could call no one from Juvenile Hall. The girls there were forbidden to strike up friendships that might continue after release. ("Don't even tell 'em your real name," said Aunt Sybil.) But while I had received no mail from Happy Valley, I felt I still had friends there, and I hit on the jolly idea of attending June graduation exercises. Gran passed my request to Mother, who said no. I went over her head to Jim Discoe. "Gee," he said, "I don't see why not."

I spent hours with Helen planning what I'd wear, and I longed for the big day to come. Then Jim called. "Look, I hate to disappoint you," he said as I held my breath, "but I think it's best if you don't go."

"You've been talking to my mother!" I shouted. He had been, but it wasn't Mother who vetoed the trip. It seems that school authorities had learned of my intended visit and phoned Mother to say they did not want me anywhere *near* Happy Valley. They had been mortified when Happy Valley was named in the press as the exclusive boarding school I attended. My appearance at graduation, they felt, would cause an embarrassing uproar.

I was partly consoled when some former schoolmates, five girls I'd known as chums, phoned to say they'd like to visit me at Canon Drive. Their visit reminded me of the disastrous Valentine's Day party I had given at Mapleton when I was six. The Happy Valley girls were nervous, even a little frightened, and no one knew what to say. They averted their eyes when I glanced at them, but stared at me intently when I looked away. I felt they had come to see what a murderess looked like.

Mercifully, an old friend reappeared in my life around that time, Bobby Westbrook, the pudgy boy of my ninth summer who had the race boat on Lake Tahoe. Recently turned eighteen and headed for the army, Bobby phoned one day and Gran let me take the call. He wanted to visit.

He drove up in a shiny black Thunderbird and lithely sprang up the front steps like a cat. I was impressed.

Now a handsome 6′3″, slim-hipped and broad shouldered, he reminded me a little of the actor Robert Wagner. Bobby had been at an army camp weekend at Fort Ord, California, when he read the Good Friday headlines. As if pledging himself to a rescue mission, he tracked me down and flew to my door as quickly as he could. He never mentioned Good Friday, but he hinted that he felt drawn to me somehow.

As he often pointed out, we shared childhoods of privilege and loneliness. Born in Hollywood and raised by nannies, Bobby was an heir to the Wilshire oil fortune. His parents, who had courted at Ciro's, both met early deaths. Lt. Col. ''Westie'' Westbrook was a famed World War II combat pilot whose P-38 was hit over the Java Sea. When he bailed out at 800 feet, his parachute didn't open fully and he fell to his death. Twelve years later, Bobby's mother was riding in a plane when its two-by-two-foot emergency door flew open and she was sucked into the sky, dropping 20,000 feet into the Atlantic.

Thereafter he was indulged by a favorite aunt and her husband, a portrait painter to stars, for whom Mother and I had both posed. Bobby lived in an old Spanish mansion a hundred feet above Sunset, at the Kings Road corner overlooking Ciro's, and he would soon start receiving half-million-dollar birthday checks. With sporty cars and good looks, Bobby had cut quite a figure at Beverly Hills High School, from which he was being graduated that month. I wanted to fall into his arms, but Gran would not even allow me to take a spin in his car. Jim Discoe overruled her, and that June Bobby and I were soon enjoying daylight-hour dates in record stores and ice cream parlors.

I was buoyed by his compassion, and his flippant sense of humor made me laugh. He was macho, though in a self-mocking way, and he soon made it clear that he wanted to go to bed with me. As much as I liked him, I couldn't go along; my insides had shut down. To my relief, he didn't press. I was in awe of Bobby. Having such a low opinion of myself, I found it hard to believe that a fellow who seemed to have it all would pursue me so ardently.

Late June brought an ordeal we had all been dreading. The next step in the Stompanato family's unlawful death suit required Mother and me to give depositions in a lawyer's office. Having worked so hard to erase Good Friday from my mind, I would now have to relive that night under cross-examination by a hostile attorney.

The suit was being brought on behalf of ten-year-old John Stompanato III of Hammond, Indiana, claiming that he had been deprived of "financial help, the services, assistance, society, comfort, companionship, protection and support of his father." However, this was the first I'd heard of a son; John had never spoken of him.

Asking $500,000 actual damages, $250,000 punitive damages, and $2,500 funeral expenses, the suit contended that any number of facts would support a judgment of wrongful death. The most sensational claim was that the knife had entered John's abdomen while he was lying down. The press had been invited to watch a dramatic reenactment involving a dummy dressed in John's clothes and a stand-in for me; it was meant to show that the blade had entered strangely and traveled an impossible path. The proof that he was lying down when he was stabbed, the suit contended, was that there was no blood below the belt line.

The suit also charged that John might still be alive if Mother had acted faster in calling the police; that, if he had been hit in the stomach, he wouldn't have fallen on his back; that we were all on "the best of terms" only days before; and that Mother had had time to step between John and the knife.

Moreover, the Stompanatos claimed, in light of my "particular predilections and propensities," there was "a great danger" in leaving a butcher knife lying around where I could get it.

"Lana Turner was negligent," the suit concluded, "in that she falsely advised Cheryl that Stompanato had threatened to disfigure or cripple her. Lana Turner otherwise incited Cheryl to inflict the wound."

Even now, some thirty years later, it is not easy for me

to recount these charges. So you can imagine how I felt at the time, being grilled for hours by attorney William Pollack, who had drawn them up. Afterward Pollack gave a press conference in which he made headlines by claiming that Mother and I had given differing stories. Pollack referred to "wide discrepancies," noting in particular that Mother recalled that the slaying had taken place near the door, while I remembered the body lying by the bed. "We believe he could not have fallen that way," said Pollack.

There wasn't anything to the charges, and most everything was refuted in the public record. But the case kept the story alive at a time when we wanted to get it behind us. More important, the headlines helped to rekindle public doubts about whether I had received special handling and if there had been some sort of cover-up—lingering questions that would make things harder for me down the road.

In July Bobby headed off for summer camp at Fort Ord and I retreated to bed. I had come down with mononucleosis, which was then sweeping through America's high schools and colleges. Because it was believed to be transmitted through kissing and coughing, it was known as "the kissing disease." How I caught it was a mystery, for I had not kissed anyone except Bobby, and he was quite healthy. I went to bed and spent much of July there feeling so achy and fatigued that I was unable to sit up. Gran seemed almost relieved that I couldn't move about.

In contrast, Dad was traveling constantly now, planning his restaurant chain, while Mother was filming the most important movie of her career. It was called *Imitation of Life,* and she played the part of a Broadway star who neglects her daughter until the girl competes with her for the love of her boyfriend.

Producer Ross Hunter had come to Mother with his plan to remake the 1934 Claudette Colbert vehicle, which had been based on a Fannie Hurst best-seller. In a Hollywood tending toward comedies and color spectacles, Hunter was known as the last of the great makers of high-glamour "woman's pictures." He had hit the jackpot four years earlier by casting young Rock Hudson opposite veteran

Jane Wyman in *Magnificent Obsession*. Now his shrewd instincts told him that audiences felt sorry for Mother and would run to see her play opposite young John Gavin in a film that mirrored elements of her personal life.

Mother says she hesitated when she considered how close *Imitation of Life* cut to the bone of our lives. But it was a meaty role and, in the end, Mother always opted in favor of her career. To be fair, she didn't have much choice. She was in debt, unemployed, and facing thirty-nine.

Maybe the combination of all these worries began to affect her. Or maybe she had begun to change during the Stompanato affair and I had been too distracted to notice. But it seemed that Mother was now going through an odd sort of personality upheaval. To me, she had always behaved as Mother, while to the world she presented herself as the movie star, that Lana Turner woman. Now she was playing the role of Lana Turner most of the time—even around the house.

It was uncanny the way her personality could switch gears, prompted by something someone said or did, a phone call, something she read, a friend's arrival, some imagined slight by a sales clerk. Suddenly, Mother would metamorphose into the great star. Her back would straighten, her bottom tighten, and her eyebrows float to a level of mild surprise. I would look on amazed as her voice took on more expression and her hands, which were calm and natural a moment before, assumed a sweeping theatricality. This was acting. Didn't she know we could tell?

As it continued and became more common, I came to regard it as part of everyday life. I even gave a nickname to this Lana Turner alter ego. "Here comes L.T.," I'd say under my breath.

That summer, when I visited the set of *Imitation of Life*, I saw the working conditions that encouraged Mother to play L.T. Ross Hunter was famous for the way he massaged the egos of his maturing lady stars, and Mother seemed to purr with delight over the flowers and favors and gifts, the old M-G-M perks such as waiting limousines and music in her dressing room with someone hired to play the records. Since the start of her career, Mother had been known as a good guy on the set and a wisecracker with the crew. Now I winced to see L.T. show up in all her brittleness. Mother indulged this folly of grandeur as a defense mechanism, I believe. L.T. was a role she could slip into to keep people back.

I came to visit one day when they were shooting on location at a boarding school. The scene was the graduation of the Broadway star's daughter. They chose to use my old Town and Country School, and it felt odd to walk around campus, deserted in summer. I sensed I would never be part of any graduation ceremony, mock or real, but there I stood getting my diploma in the person of actress Sandra Dee. Pert, pretty, and blond, she looked more like Mother's daughter than I did.

I was beginning to adore Bobby Westbrook. Corresponding with him was about the only friendship I enjoyed that summer. In the letters we shared our loneliness, his in hectic boot camp, mine in a shuttered house, bedridden, guarded, and watched. The question of where I would attend school in September was still open, and he encouraged me to fight to go to his alma mater, Beverly Hills High School, where he could help pave the way for me. For years Mother had been against my going there on the grounds that it was too sophisticated a place, but now I had a goal. I worked up the chain of command through Gran and Mom to Jim Discoe, who said mildly, "Gee, I don't see why not," and he in turn got Judge Lynch to agree.

Bobby returned in August and we went everywhere together on daylight dates, mostly long drives and soulful talks at Wil Wright's soda fountain.

The rules of visitation permitted Dad to take me out at night if he chose, and, at first, he would take me to Hamburger Hamlet. Soon, however, Bobby and I began to double date with Dad and Helen at old haunts like LaRue's and Mocambo. Later, we would explore the new night scene emerging in little coffeehouses and jazz clubs. As we were returning home early one Sunday evening, Bobby suggested that we stop by his place to play records. His aunt and uncle occupied the vast upper floors of his house, and he had his own bachelor apartment below. It was an adult playroom, really, very much in the *Playboy* style, that looked out on the lights of Hollywood.

I could tell what was coming and I knew what Gidget would have done, but I did not want to resist any longer. If sex meant so much to him, it was okay with me. While everyone else was backing away from me, here was Bobby, helpful and loving, acting as if nothing at all had happened to me four months before. To him I was just an average high school girl. I was not really in love with him, but I did feel love and tremendous gratitude. Besides, he was very good-looking.

"Auntie Kate, I'm home," Bobby yelled up the stairs when we arrived. "I have Cheryl with me. Want to come say hello?" Mercifully, she was busy, so Bobby closed the connecting door, dimmed the lights, and put Pete Seeger on the hi-fi. Anyone listening in would have heard low voices and tinkling Coca-Colas, ending in the thud of falling shoes and the snapping of elastic. "Don't you dare get me pregnant," I whispered urgently.

Bobby was a quick lover. Though he was tender before and after, I still wished he would hurry up. My insides had not awakened yet. The only passion I could feel in those days was a growing anger with Mother. Bobby's joyful love didn't remind me of Lex, the painful memory of whom was locked away in my mind's attic. Nor did I feel guilty about sleeping with Bobby. At the very least, it was a way to defy the court and get around everyone's plan to sit on me.

Although by court order Mother was not supposed to do so, she used Gran to impose her will on me. In the past, Gran had always relished this role of go-between, but there was no longer any fun in the job and she carried an air of mourning about her. She cut off all her friends, took up solitaire, and bit by bit nudged the cocktail hour earlier into the day. On questions of my conduct, Gran invariably sided with her daughter.

But her daughter was now branded before the world as an unfit mother, and as a result Gran was determined to crack down on me with a will. Mother lectured on my sullenness and my clothing. I was still allowed to wear only pastels, flat heels, and no makeup except lipstick. Lights-out was at precisely 10:00 P.M., and on those few occasions I was permitted out of the house, Bobby was the lone, reluctantly approved escort.

None of Mother's strictures had the support of my probation officers, but there was a limit to how often I could run to them for help. I was hoping to build an unblemished record for the court, and reports of never-ending strife between Mother and me would not have looked good. With the stroke of a pen, the court could still consign me to a foster home or state institution. So I mostly knuckled under. Mostly.

Dad showed me around some of the coffeehouses that were sprouting in the UCLA and West Hollywood area, innocent meeting spots that brooked no drugs and sold no liquor, just sweet desserts and cappuccino. On our visits we listened to poetry readings or acoustic guitars, which made me feel very hip at fifteen. But then Mother suddenly decided that she didn't approve, and coffeehouses were placed off limits.

Bobby happened to be taking guitar lessons, and one day he mentioned to me that a guitarist friend of his would be opening at the Ashgrove, a coffeehouse on Melrose Avenue. I seized on the idea of going to the opening night.

"But how are we going to do that?" asked Bobby.

"I think I can sneak out of the house."

"Are you sure? What if your grandmother wakes up?"

"Gran doesn't wake up."

I had tested this. She retired each night around nine o'clock and fell into a deep alcoholic slumber. Shouting her name at close range did not wake her. I was determined to break out of my confinement and, for once, go exactly where I wanted. Bobby was leery, but he agreed.

When the big night came, I stole out of bed, careful not to wake Gran, and retreated to the far side of the house. From her closet I had borrowed a ladylike gray dress that cried out for four-inch heels and acres of petticoats. White gloves added a certain primness, but, checking myself in the mirror, I thought I could pass for at least twenty-three.

At midnight, as arranged, Bobby flashed his headlights

and I darted through the back garden gate. He was known at the Ashgrove, and there was no problem about slipping to a quiet back table at showtime. It was heady stuff to move unnoticed among a college crowd, and all evening I happily clung to Bobby's shoulder. He was my ticket to normalcy.

"Aren't you Cheryl Crane?" someone asked. A thick young man wearing farm clothes stood over our table, weaving unsteadily. "Aren't you the one that killed that gangster?"

Bobby jumped to his feet and swung at the man, sending him sprawling against the wall. Before Bobby could swing again, his guitarist friend grabbed his arms and other friends stepped between. "Go," said one in a loud whisper. I grabbed Bobby's arm and we ducked out the back.

I tiptoed into bed at 3:00 A.M. Gran was snoring with the gusto of a lumberjack, and I felt pretty pleased with myself.

Twenty-nine

There is probably no other public school like Beverly Hills High. Its pale stucco buildings of French Normandy design, all with red tile roofs, sprawl over a lush, manicured campus of palm trees and statues and meandering steps. The giant gym floor rolls back to reveal a swimming pool. A working oil well pumps away on one of the playing fields, and you can see in a glance the difference between the faculty and the student parking lots—the students drive better cars.

Beverly Hills High was just a two-block walk from Gran's apartment, but she insisted on driving me to and from school every day of my sophomore year. Everyone knew that I was coming: it had been in the newspapers. And while the admissions people extended friendly welcomes, my new classmates hurried by in a rush. I kept my eyes on the middle distance. If someone catching my glance happened to smile at me, and some did, I had a hard time smiling back because my cheek muscles quivered.

The first few days, I spoke to no one except for a girl named Suzie who had been assigned by the school to be a kind of big sister to me and to help smooth my arrival. Though Suzie's friends seemed a little snooty, they did help me to find my voice, and by the end of the first week I had been welcomed into another circle of more casual senior girls who ate lunch together. I was sitting with them one warm day on the terraced front mall when a boy's voice carried from a nearby group. "Have you heard the assignment they gave Cheryl Crane?'' he said. "She works in the cafeteria in charge of knives.''

Though I pretended not to hear, I wanted to die. To make matters worse, a well-meaning girl in our group stood up and walked over to the boy. "Why don't you shut up over here?'' she snapped, which set off an exchange of insults.

My new circle and I had a tacit understanding about Good Friday. I knew that they knew and they knew that I knew they knew, but as long as no one pointed it out, the elephant was not standing on my foot. The knife joke was a moment of horror for me, but it passed. I'm told there were several Cheryl jokes going around the student body of 2,000, but none were thrown my way again and before long I sort of melted into the crowd.

Bobby had phoned his friends at school to say that we were going steady and would they please look after me. This gave me a certain status and helped fend off those boys whose corpuscles started racing at the thought of my notoriety.

My name still appeared in the papers once or twice a month as a result of one development or another—Mother and Dad's ongoing custody fight, the unlawful death suit, publicity about *Imitation of Life*, even the settling of Stompanato's estate, which came to $274. A slow week might generate a feature about me as a new public school pupil, always with "the paragraph" recalling Good Friday. One well-meaning, if counterproductive, wire service article quoted my classmates on their feelings about me. "She's so popular," said one boy, "that if you say anything about her, you'd have a hard time getting a date with any girl in the school. She's buddies with lots of girls and they watch out for her.''

Another classmate observed that I usually sat at the back of the room and was "very quiet," which was true. Sitting up front, I could feel eyes on my back. While I had regained the ability to put on a bored face, stand tall, and squeeze that nickel, I still trembled perceptibly.

My routine did not vary much that fall. I spent every day after school with Gran, who had now advanced the cocktail hour to mid-afternoon. "Is it teatime yet?" she'd ask gaily. "Well, what the heck, it's five o'clock in Rangoon."

Gran refused my pleas that she return to her friends and bridge parties. I sat glaring at her endless games of solitaire until one day I threw all the cards on the floor and stomped away to my room. I quickly returned with apologies and we made up with embraces. I could never stay mad at Gran.

One high point in the routine came every Thursday night, when we dined on the famed pot roast and potato pancakes at a nearby restaurant. Another came on Sundays, when I would sit with Dad and Helen at Bar One. We were often still joined by Chief Anderson. "How's school?" he'd ask and say little more.

There was also my regular Thursday "dentist" appointment with Dr. Wahl. He had begun to talk a little by now, coaxing me to tell him everything I could remember of my dreams. I described one that had recurred for years. I'm falling, falling, falling through the center of a cake that is trimmed in yellow roses. I land in a mound of petals and suffocate. Dr. Freud would have noted that yellow roses were Mother's favorite flower.

I would see Mother twice a month. She was in love again, this time with a nice man named Fred May. Fred was a big real estate developer whose first love was breeding racehorses at his Circle M ranch in Chino, California. He was a warm huggy-bear of a man, a rescuer, I think, who was drawn to Mother's tragedy. So reassuring was he that when she unwound on weekends at the ranch, her earthy side came out. In town she was usually L.T., but at the ranch she cleaned out stables, an amazing sight to see.

They were a well-known couple around town at nightclubs and parties, and when Fred escorted her to a major charity dance that December, reports swept Hollywood of an impending marriage. The reports were premature.

That December Dad lost another round in the protracted custody struggle with Mother. The court had let Mother retain legal, though not physical, custody of me. Though Dad wanted both, Mother was still able to tell reporters, "I have complete and legal custody of my daughter. . . .

I see Cheryl a great deal. There are no limitations now.'' Dad vowed to ''fight her tooth and nail.'' In fact, what Judge Lynch had ruled was that I must continue to live with my grandmother ''indefinitely.''

This must have been their sixth or seventh tug-of-war over me. As always, their goal was not to increase their access to me so much as to avoid loss of property. Although the visitation rules had been relaxed by Jim Discoe, neither Dad nor Mother had taken advantage of them.

In what may have been an unconnected event, Helen and Dad officially announced their engagement the day after Judge Lynch's ruling. Flashing a four-carat diamond, Helen made the announcement herself, since Dad was away on a business trip. She said that she, Dad, and I were about to take off on a New Year's holiday to Montreal and New York City. Mother, who strongly opposed the trip, must have burned.

Dad had just signed a major deal with the Sheraton Corporation to re-create the Luau in some of the giant chain's hotels. The pilot restaurant was to open just after Christmas in the Sheraton Montreal, and Dad had been working for months to adapt his designs and set up operations.

Called the Kon Tiki Ports-of-Call, the new place retained much of the flavor of the Luau. The decor of three separate dining rooms evoked the ports of Saigon, Macao, and Papeete, while the bar was fashioned to resemble a giant schooner named ''The Cloud.''

Opening night in Montreal was a great success, the climax of a round of receptions, parties, and even a sleigh ride. With a fiancée on one arm and a daughter on the other, Dad introduced us as ''the two women I love,'' and we almost did look like concubine wives, so similarly were we turned out.

Arriving in New York, we carried the funny illusion further by dashing through Saks and Bergdorf's to buy look-alike outfits. Helen and I decided on pink slipper-satin ball gowns, long gloves, and rhinestone tiaras, while Dad rented twin ermine shrugs to cover our bare shoulders. Out on the town that last night of 1958, we dined at the 21 Club, danced at El Morocco, dropped in on parties, and toasted the new year with late-night jazz at Danny's

Hideaway. Well oiled on champagne, we offered a compelling picture for photographers, something Dad must have considered.

A photo of our smiling, hand-holding trio, which was printed worldwide on January 2, said more than a thousand words. It said that after the shocking events of April, Cheryl Crane had come out happy and normal, that she was close to her father, who was about to remarry a beautiful woman. It said that these three will make a good family.

Though I would have been almost as happy spending that week with Dad and Helen in a snowed-in cabin, New York proved to be delirious fun. We saw *My Fair Lady*, stayed in a hotel penthouse, and were swanned around town by Dad's powerful New York friends. Dad knew that Mother had forbidden me to wear black, but he took me to Bendel's and bought me a basic black wool dress anyway. For me, it simply *made* the trip.

After a week, Dad returned to Montreal, and Helen and I headed back to California. We were at the airport waiting for our plane when reporters spotted us. Mother had taught me to be polite to the press and to say nothing ("I don't know, sir, please ask my mother"), but I was feeling grown up and there was no press agent around to run interference. Fortunately, the reporters' questions were mundane. I chattered about how I loved school, New York, my father, and my future stepmother. Yes, um, I loved my mother, too.

Greeting us at the airport in Los Angeles, Mother beamed a poisonous smile, and one reporter noted that I had played my part well in an "all-girl 'triangle scene' with a former and future Mrs. Steve Crane."

When we got back to Gran's, Mother chewed glass about the New York photos she'd seen in the papers. She instructed me to open my bag and show her the New Year's ball gown. "You don't have room here at Gran's," she said. "I'll take the dress with me and hang it at my house." I surrendered the dress, never to see it again. Still, I chuckled inside because she had missed the treasured black wool dress, which I had packed in another suitcase.

I didn't manage to keep it for long, however. The following month, Mother found me wearing it early one evening at the Ashgrove. I was sitting in the middle of a booth with Helen and some of her friends, when I looked up to see Mother and Fred May heading for our table. I called a breezy hello.

"You will stand up when your mother comes to the table," she said in her best L.T. voice.

"I c-can't stand up," I stammered, struggling in the tight space and sliding back down.

"How dare you sit there!" she snapped. Finally, Fred squeezed her arm and drew her away. I felt her dagger looks from across the room until we left. Helen and I went to Dad's apartment building in West Hollywood, where he retained the two ground-level units while Helen lived in her own upstairs. The phone was ringing when we walked in.

"Where did you get that dress?" demanded Mother. "Your grandmother? Helen? Where?"

"My father . . . in New York."

She began to yell, and I hung up, the first time I'd ever done that. She rang back, and when I refused to speak to her, she told Helen I was forbidden to stay overnight. I called Jim Discoe, and he said, "Relax, go to bed."

Two days later Jim called a summit meeting at Mother's house on Roxbury. His idea was that Mother and I should air our long list of grievances, but, after two hours, no points were yielded and nothing was resolved.

As a peace gesture, I invited Mother and Fred to dine at Gran's apartment, where I would attempt to cook my very first dinner. On the appointed night, it was L.T. who arrived. Though she had already had too much vodka, she sat down in the living room and shared another drink with Fred and Gran. As I fussed in the kitchen over my sauerbraten, Mother rummaged through the record albums in search of something.

"Cheryl," she called, "will you come here?"

"I can't right this second, Mom—hands full."

"When I call you, you come."

"Yes, Mother-r." I appeared at the door.

"Don't take that tone with me, young lady! I want to hear a particular record!"

My plans for a lovely crystal and candlelit dinner party turned into a night on the Titanic. As we sat down at the table, aromas drifting in from the kitchen, Mother objected to the customary presence of my poodle under the table at Gran's feet. "Take her out of here—not while I'm eating," she commanded. As Gran started to pull her away, the dog whimpered and I opened my mouth and said, "Oh, she's not bothering anybody. Leave her alone."

Mother exploded at this impertinence. *"Don't* talk to me that way! Do what I tell you!" We began shouting, until finally I heard myself saying, "Mother, Tinkette has more right to be here than you do. Why don't you get out?"

With that, I ran to my room and slammed the door as Mother shouted oaths and Fred led her away. A moment later, Gran padded softly into my room. "Please, please forgive your mother," she said. "She had too much to drink." It was the first time that Gran had ever mentioned such a problem.

I recount these domestic squabbles to illustrate how competitive Mother and I had become. A woman who was used to controlling everyone around her, she now had a rebellious child on her hands whom she couldn't control. Considering all that she and I had just been through, I suppose our relationship was destined to be like gasoline and matches. I wanted to defy anything she stood for. Circumventing her authority had become a pleasurable end in itself, and I had plenty of help doing it through Dad (via Helen), Jim Discoe, and Judge Lynch.

To make matters worse, Mother was under a lot of pressure. Though *Imitation of Life* had gone well in production and the advance word was positive that spring, she had done the picture for only $2,500 a week, half her Metro salary, accepting deferred income from profits. If the film failed, her career as a star was probably over.

My resentment fed on itself that year as I read the lies being printed about our supposedly rosy relationship. Based on the magazines I saw at the hairdresser's, it was clear that the aftermath of Good Friday had become a topic for inspirational articles. "I believe that today I have a closer relationship with my daughter than ever before in our lives," Mother told *Redbook,* admitting that the "terrible thing that happened" on Good Friday was "partly of my own doing."

"Her father and I see [Cheryl] every day after school and on weekends," she told the *Herald Examiner.* To *Photoplay,* she burbled that when she met Helen and me after our New Year's trip, a trip that she said she had blessed, she thanked Helen "for being so good to my little girl," then laughed and joked with me as we poured over my mementos of the trip.

Dad bought a house on Tower Grove Drive above Benedict Canyon that spring, and Helen moved in with him. Mother was in the throes of Stage One with Fred and lived part of the time at his ranch. These affairs would soon lead to Dad's fifth and Mother's sixth trip up the aisle (counting the two times they had married each other). They had taken so many partners over the years that I began to wonder if their romantic natures might also be throbbing in my veins.

It hardly seemed so. I kept in touch by phone and letter with Bobby Westbrook, who was soldiering in northern California, but our long separations dimmed that great beginning we had. After the coffeehouse incident, when Bobby slugged the man, we had continued to sneak out together at night, and he introduced me to a hipper scene than Dad knew. We toured smoky jazz spots in Redondo Beach and show bars in the valley. But all that was eight months ago.

Although Bobby paid visits every few weeks, he was receding from my mind. Meanwhile, something was missing from my life. Here I was, a child of two great romantics, alone with a brimming heart.

An answer of sorts came one day as I was browsing the spin-around racks of paperback books at Schwab's drugstore in Beverly Hills while Gran waited in her car at the curb. I devoured at least two Gothics or mysteries a week, and my shelves needed replenishing. This time my eye was caught by a book, newly stocked, that looked different. It was a romance novel called *Odd Girl Out* by Ann Bannon. I shrugged and added it to my purchases.

I read it that night. The story started very slowly, and then—oh, my goodness. It told of Laura who goes to New York from her home in the Midwest and gets involved in a world of artists. They live in an exciting place called Greenwich Village, where men and women follow love wherever their hearts lead them. Laura grows fond of Patricia, and by the end of the book they've gotten around to exchanging a very soft kiss.

I was deeply impressed and read it through again. The author described emotions that I recognized, and she pointed to a place on the map where people felt as I did, lots of people. I resolved then and there that when I turned eighteen I was going to Greenwich Village.

Over the next few months, I followed Laura's continuing adventures in other books in the series by Ann Bannon. I also got hooked on a similar series penned by Ann Aldrich (perhaps the same woman writing under a different nom de plume). By today's standards, none of the stories would rate even PG, being utterly without sex or violence, and I treasured them. Seeing no reason to be shy about feelings of love, I tried to interest Gran in reading one. She could not get through it, she said. Later in the great tide of events, she would burn them all.

Imitation of Life was scheduled to open in April, and, for reasons I was unsure of, I was given a prominent place in Mother's publicity. Among other things, I was to escort Mother to the invitation-only preview followed by a supper party at Romanoff's.

A week before the opening, the film was shown in a private screening room at Universal-International for just Mother, Gran, and me. Mother explained that since the film was a "four-handkerchief" tearjerker, seeing it beforehand would enable us to keep our powder dry on opening night. Actually, she wanted to vaccinate me against what otherwise might prove to be an unpleasant surprise. I had not read the Fannie Hurst novel on which the picture was based, and she had never told me what the film was about.

When I saw how badly it exploited us, how much it borrowed from our lives—the amorous star who spoils and ignores her daughter, the pink bedroom, my actual junior high school, the graduation present of a horse—well, it all made me feel used. The film even pandered to the ugly rumors that there had been a romance between Stompanato and me by having the teenage daughter (Sandra Dee) fall jealously in love with her mother's boyfriend.

I felt a shiver of recognition as Sandra Dee spoke the lines, "Oh, Mama, stop *acting*. Stop trying to shift people around as though they were pawns on a stage." And again when she complained that her mother's love had been given only "by telephone, by postcard, by magazine interviews—you've given me everything but yourself."

As the screening ended, Mother, Gran, and I sat in silence, tears running down our cheeks. I think we cried for different reasons.

Thirty

Mother's decision to make *Imitation of Life,* no matter what the personal costs, displayed a shrewd instinct for survival. The picture went on to become the top-grossing movie of her career and was responsible for saving the troubled Universal-International Pictures.

Even if critics didn't love the script's determined sentimentality or the star performance that limned the higher reaches of L.T., the movie was what millions of moviegoers wanted—a peek of sorts into Mother's tangled life of sex and glamour. The film promoted this notion shamelessly. The billboards, for example, showed Sandra Dee saying, "You've given me everything a mother could but the thing I wanted most . . . your love!" Next to her was Mother, exclaiming, "I'll get the things I want out of life . . . one way—or another. From one man—or another!"

The film's publicists wanted to show that Mother and I were loving and united, that I liked the film and was happy to join her in exploiting our problems. That's why my reaction to the film was tested at the private screening.

The premiere was not a formal affair—people came in sportswear—but Mother and I arrived as if we were being presented to the queen. We wore satin, chiffon, ermine, diamonds, and ostrich feathers—all in photogenic white. This was our first public appearance together with me as a grown-up fifteen. Dry-eyed afterward, I told reporters that I loved the movie—it was "so sad" and Mother was "so wonderful." Lacking the self-confidence to refuse to help her to sell the picture, I denied my feelings instead and went along. Truth be told, part of me was pleased to be seen looking halfway sane after all those haggard news photos of me the year before.

In the end, though, *Imitation of Life* hardened my feelings of estrangement toward Mother. Its happy ending made me sneer. Mother was back on top again, the great star, but so what? Hers was an empty life.

The comeback did wonders for Mother's insecurities, in large part because of the windfall it brought. She owned fifty percent of the film's net profits, and it grossed eleven million dollars the first year alone. Though Liz Taylor would make headlines three years later when she was paid a breathtaking one million dollars to make *Cleopatra*, Mother's earnings from *Imitation of Life* handily topped that, and they have continued to this day. Fred May invested much of the money for her in real estate; at one time she had a large holding in the City of Industry, a planned community in Silicon Valley.

Relaxed, reassured, and newly rich that summer, Mother basked in success. As if seeking an oasis of calm, she took Gran and me away on a ten-day lark to Disneyland and the San Diego Zoo. We had fun and no fights, getting by on drive-in hamburgers and low-rent motels, with Gran and me in one bed and her in the other.

When we checked into the first motel, Mother eyed her bed warily and said, "I just know this is going to be hard." She spread out and BAM!—the bed slats collapsed. We all screamed with laughter, Mother the hardest of all. Moments of hilarity like this made me want to laugh and cry at once. I thought of all the wasted years, all the fun she and I might have had.

I would turn sixteen that July, and sweet-sixteen parties being a postpubertal rite of real importance in a certain Beverly Hills set, my parents offered to throw me a bash of any size and design my heart desired. Every girl I knew had had a sweet-sixteen luncheon at the Luau and I was tired of that, so I asked for, and got, a dinner-dance for forty couples at the Bel Air Hotel with Bobby as my escort. I rather enjoyed standing out from the crowd now, and that night I made sure I did by draping myself head-to-toe in lavender.

The night's crowning moment came when Dad gave me his present. He had always promised that when I turned sixteen he would give me any car I wanted, a fact I had never let him forget since I was eight. He had suggested an MG, but I declined, knowing exactly what I wanted. As part of his own small collection, he owned an experimental sports car called a Muntz Jet. It could go from zero to 156 mph in a half mile, and only 127 of them had ever been made. Black and dangerous as a panther, it now sat caged in his garage, up on blocks, and I begged him to keep his promise. "Remember, Dad, *any* car of my choice."

After I blew out my sixteen candles, Dad drew me aside and handed me a small box, saying, "You can open this now." It contained a gold-plated car key inscribed, "Here's your Black Bomb, love, Dad." Mother nearly fell in a faint, but Judge Lynch had approved and there was nothing she could do.

For my sixteenth birthday, the court had eased several restrictions. I was now allowed to go out alone at night as long as I observed the curfew Los Angeles placed on anyone under eighteen not accompanied by an adult. It was 10:00 P.M. on weeknights and midnight on weekends.

Things were looking up for me. Cars were the drugs of the fifties generation, and the Black Bomb put me into orbit. The day after my birthday, I took three girlfriends for a spin and we wound up at a kids' hangout on Wilshire Boulevard called Dolores's Drive-In. I was still wearing lavender nail polish from the night before (I had stopped biting my nails), and as I reached out the car window for a milk shake, the carhop noticed my colorful hands. "Zowie, girl," he remarked, "I dig those."

After he left, one of my friends in the back seat said, "Tom's flirting with you, Cheryl."

"Oh, please," said another girl wearily. "Tom likes guys. Every guy who works here does."

I suddenly thought of *Odd Girl Out.* So people like the ones Laura found in Greenwich Village gathered in Los Angeles, too? I resolved to come back to Dolores's Drive-In another day. That August I became as familiar as a mascot to the boys who hopped cars and worked the counters at Dolores's. I was drawn to their teasing humor and a hands-on friendliness that contained no threats.

One Saturday night after we had visited some clubs, Bobby and I were heading home early in his new red Porsche. Though I knew there were other girls in his life, and our love had mellowed into friendly devotion, Bobby was always sexually ready. "Let's go back to my place," he said with a heavy-lidded glance. I said nothing until he turned the car and headed north to his house above Sunset. "Bob," I said, "I want to go home. You see, there's something I've got to tell you. The truth is, I'm not attracted to you physically. I'm not attracted to guys."

"What do you mean?"

"I prefer girls."

He pulled the car over to the curb and searched my face. "C'mon, you don't mean that," he finally said, beginning to smirk. "I did something, didn't I? What did I do?"

I lit a Marlboro and stared at my long nails. "I mean it, Bob."

Slamming a fist on the dashboard, he exploded. He yelled that I was sick, crazy. I should be locked up and punished. "You goddamn——" He spat out a series of cuss words I had never even heard. I lowered my eyes until he ran out of breath. "Take me home," I said. My neck was snapped back as he hit the gas and knifed into the traffic with tires screeching.

After that, I chewed a nail or two over the loss of Bobby's friendship. It didn't make much sense to me. Would he rather that I had lied to him? This is who I am, Bobby. I already had so much in my life to be shy about, why this too?

When I told Dr. Wahl about it at our next session, his eyebrows flew up and he leaned back, his pipe sending up little puffs of smoke. "I was wondering," he said, "just how long it was going to take you to tell me that." He checked his watch. "Well, we will discuss this next week."

"Not necessarily," I interrupted. I wasn't quite sure I liked how he had put that last remark. It sounded like, "Well, we'll get rid of *that* in short order, young lady."

I decided not to tell anyone else about my feelings for a while.

I did not realize at the time how much sunshine came into my life that summer of 1959. I had freedom. I had my own car, a thirty-dollar-a-week allowance, and permission to come and go as I pleased so long as Gran knew my whereabouts and I observed the city curfew. I rode Rowena on weekends at the ranch in Chino and sometimes dined with Fred and Mother.

Everything was looking up. Mother rented a new house, Dad opened another Kon Tiki, and both enjoyed the happy aches of new love with partners I very much liked. Gran was even playing bridge again.

Nonetheless, amid all this privilege and order, I was still a ward of the court and required to see a probation officer and a psychiatrist every week. It seemed unfair. All I wanted was to be a kid like other kids.

Bobby phoned one day to apologize about our fight, but another date only led to another fight. Dad and Helen fixed me up with some of their young friends, including actor George Hamilton, but there was no romance and I always returned for fun to my loony pals at Dolores's Drive-In. There was one boy in particular, a carhop named Marty Gunn.

Tall, attractively blond, and twenty-two, Marty worked nights behind the counter and dreamed of getting into pictures. Really Bobby McVey from Kansas, he chose his last name from the Peter Gunn television series and combed his pompadour like Fabian. Marty gave me no romantic tingles, but I was drawn to his independence and the ability he had to see things through my eyes. I soon came to love him with all my heart, as a sister.

Since he worked until 10:00 P.M., my bedtime at Gran's, I could only listen in wonder to his tales of West Hollywood nightlife. He and others in the Dolores crowd partied at a round of dark and noisy men's bars on Santa Monica Boulevard, places like the Spotlight and the Four Star. Though it seemed that my father and Bobby had shown me every night spot in town, these clubs were something new and I wanted to see them. In the end, I did, once again sneaking out—this time with Marty—as Gran slept.

Marty started off by taking me to the Four Star, a roisterous dive offering beer and billiards. His friends were especially attentive to me. I was the only female in a friendly sea of well-groomed and well-muscled men, an exhilarating experience. For the next three months, we late-nighted at all the joints, me tiptoeing back to Gran's by 4:00 A.M. This began to affect my alertness, since my school day started at 7:00. That fall, as I cruised my Black Bomb into the student lot, bleary-eyed and tired, I looked a far cry from the shy girl who had been driven to school by her grandmother the previous spring.

Using the Muntz Jet for our midnight tours proved impossible because people crowded around to stare wherever it was parked. Without considering the risk, I borrowed Gran's station wagon as she slept, lifting the car keys from her change purse tucked under the mattress.

Another reason not to use my car in the quiet of the night was that it backfired with the sound of a gun blast. I happened to be driving it along Santa Monica Boulevard on the historic day when Soviet Premier Khrushchev was touring a movie set at Twentieth Century-Fox. The police were everywhere. Gran was beside me, and as we waited for a red light by the studio front gate, I playfully kicked the car in gear, deliberately causing it to backfire with a bang. Police immediately circled with pointed guns. ''Oh, we're going to be shot!'' cried Gran, pulling a sweater up over her head.

Letting me drive the Muntz was like letting a child play with explosives. Fortunately, the mistake eventually corrected itself. I was doing 100 mph on the Hollywood freeway one day when a pin came loose and the engine rocked itself off the motor mount, slamming the generator through the side of the car. After a great crash-bang, the car stopped dead and I steered to the side of the road. My relieved father replaced it with a beige Impala convertible.

The chance I was given that sixteenth summer of mine to exercise some responsibility had a narcotic effect on me. Freedom was heroin, and soon even too much was not enough.

Children raised in normal homes are generally used to a measure of personal liberty by their midteens. They respect limits and know how to take on responsibility. They have learned how to make small decisions. But as a Hollywood princess, I had gone through none of the usual rites of growing up. The good schools and foreign travel to which I had been exposed may have made me precocious in certain ways, but behind the midnight face painted to look twenty-three, I was as immature as a twelve-year-old.

I didn't understand that actions lead to reactions. I still practiced a child's "one-step" thinking, not stopping to consider what might follow from taking that first step. Since I hungered for nightlife, I grabbed at it, never stopping to consider that as a star baby, only recently the object of a murder investigation, I traveled in a spotlight. Nor did I think about the fact that sneaking out at night was a violation of my probation that could get me in serious trouble.

I now also began indulging myself in midnight rendezvous of the heart. It had started as a schoolgirl friendship with a girl named Sally, but after a year, we knew what we felt. We spent long yearning hours on the phone, and some nights I would drive to her family's big Beverly Hills house and creep into her window. One day at school, Jim Discoe appeared in the vice principal's office. He had come to collect me in his car.

"Well, we're in trouble," he said as we headed for his house in Pacific Palisades. "You're going to spend the weekend with me."

"What's up?"

He let out a good-natured sigh. "Sally's father showed up at your grandmother's door today. He was waving a shotgun."

It seemed that Sally's father had gotten suspicious when he found a note I sent her, and he arranged to have her telephone tapped. He listened in horror as the conversation got around to sweet nothings.

Jim Discoe understood the puppy love in my heart and managed to calm the father down, but by Monday Sally had been transferred to a school in Arizona, and the family soon moved away.

I worried what Mother would do about this, but nothing was said. As far as she was concerned, the distasteful matter had never happened. She did find, however, that she now had a lively interest in Marty Gunn and he must come to dinner.

Dad had a very hard time accepting what had happened with Sally. In a wrenching talk in his study, he raged against the psychiatrist for being unable to "cure" me.

Later that week I huddled with Marty in a booth at the drive-in, complaining that happiness would always dance beyond my grasp until I turned eighteen and was free. He listened quietly, then smiled and folded his hands over mine.

"You know," he said, "I think that by law in the state of California if you marry before you turn eighteen, you automatically become a legal adult. If you were married now, your parents wouldn't be able to touch you and neither would Juvenile Court."

"Are you sure?" I asked eagerly.

"Sure." He glanced out the window to the car lot, letting red neon fall across his perfect actor's profile. "You want to get married?"

Hm. What price freedom? I really loved him, and we could always get a divorce afterward.

"Sure, yes, I do."

Marty sent up a whoop that brought Dolores's to a hush. We ducked and giggled in embarrassment. In a moment he leaned close to say, "Now all we've got to do is get your parents' permission."

My joy went thud. Parents' permission? They'd never agree to our marrying outright unless I were pregnant, and I had no desire to become a mother. Maybe if they only suspected I was pregnant. No, they'd call Dr. Mac right away. Well, maybe if they thought we were sleeping together. After the commotion about Sally, that might do the trick.

A few nights later, instead of my sneaking out to meet him, Marty snuck in the back door of Gran's apartment while she slept and joined me in the second bedroom. I wore flannel pajamas and he stripped to his shorts. The idea was for Gran to discover us in bed the next morning and sound the family alarm. We felt surely someone would say, "You kids will have to get married."

We planned to talk through the night to be alert for Gran's waking, but we grew tired and nodded off: She walked in to find a shocking still life of sleeping Eros. "Oh, my God," she said, "get dressed, both of you, and come into the living room!"

The next days brought a flurry of phone calls but little else. Marty and I rushed to Jim's house for his backing, and, while acting noncommittal, Jim turned to Marty and said pointedly, "You realize that if you marry Cheryl, the responsibility will be on you." Then I made the serious mistake of telling him about our late nights in the clubs.

Jim called a summit meeting at Gran's. In attendance were Mother, Dad, Gran, and Jeanette Muhlbach, but not Marty. As though in a witness box, I sat alone on the big empty sofa, very calm, stubborn, and positive. The proceedings took a high bounce that I hadn't expected.

No one seemed to be opposed to the marriage. "Of course, you know, Baby," said Mother, "we think you're too young, but we're not going to stand in the way." She said the meeting's only purpose was to go over what plans Marty and I had made. What would we live on, where, what arrangements for the ceremony, and so on. I offered, plausibly, that we would wed in Las Vegas the following week. They were so agreeable, I was feeling quite happy.

"Of course," said Jim, "this has to have Judge Lynch's blessing, but since your family and probation officers don't object, that's simply a formality." I phoned Marty with the good news.

Jim then rang up to caution Marty and me against doing anything crazy like trying to elope. "Just hang on till I see Lynch," he said, "and I'll have the verdict Monday afternoon."

When the appointed hour finally came, Jim didn't phone. Instead, he and Jeanette appeared at the front door as somber as morticians. "I'm sorry, Cheryl," Jim said, "Lynch

feels you need to be removed from the friends you associate with and placed in a school.''

"A school?"

"It's in the valley. It's called El Retiro.''

I had heard of El Retiro in Juvenile Hall. "But that's
not a school. It's a reformatory.''

"And you must be packed and ready to go right away,''
said Jeanette. "We've come to drive you there.''

I probably should have jumped in my car and raced to
New York, but I went along meekly. Mother and Dad
phoned their regrets and encouragement. There was no
time for good-byes to friends. It was Gran, frail and weeping, who waved farewell to me from the window.

I never heard from Marty again. He told reporters that
he was in no position to marry, but would not discuss it
because he had "been told not to.''

Mother saw it differently. "There is absolutely no truth
that there was ever even any thought of marriage or elopement,'' she said, adding, "The strain is all within
Cheryl.'' She said that her daughter "went willingly because she knows she will receive the proper care and guidance. She was in complete accord with the move.''

During the hour's drive to the San Fernando Valley, I
sank into gloom. *So they think I'm a delinquent? Well, if
I have the name, I might as well have the game. I'll show
them what a delinquent is. I'm going to an institution
where the girls really are bad. I wonder what I'll find out
at El Retiro that I don't already know.*

Thirty-one

My new home was surrounded by a twelve-foot wall and topped by a tangle of barbed wire, making it half as much again higher than Mapletop's. It occurred to me that the month I entered reform school, March 1960, was the twenty-second anniversary of the signing of Mother's first M-G-M contract.

We pulled up to the main gate, where someone had scrawled in chalk over a bell, "EL RETIRO SCHOOL, RING HERE." Kids at Juvenile Hall had said it was a prison, but after we drove inside and were given a look around, I could see it wasn't so bad. There was an apple orchard, a small swimming pool, a tan cinder-block high school, and four houses where girls were locked in only after dark. I was put into a single room in the admissions building.

El Retiro's inmate population consisted of some fifty underprivileged girls, mainly black and Hispanic, most of whom had been running around loose since they were ten. While some had criminal records for prostitution and burglary, others were "incorrigibles" whose families had simply given up on them. I suppose I belonged in this latter slot, but with my background, I was the odd girl out in a tough league.

Inmates were not allowed to develop friendships that might continue after release and not allowed to discuss their families or home addresses, but an official had announced to everyone at lunch the day before that Lana Turner's daughter would be arriving and should be "treated like everybody else." The girls took a vote agreeing to do so.

They were intrigued by me. I knew I had to make a stand and not show any fear. More than half the girls had paired off in affectionate relationships that both prevented loneliness and provided mutual security. There was no opportunity for sex under the watchful eyes of matrons, but young couples hugged, held hands, and "dated" at the movies. (Most of these girls returned to an exclusive preference for boys after release.)

Within the first week, I looked around and made an alliance that offered both safety and status. Donna was a tall, blue-eyed blonde who kept running away from home, but whose confidence and engaging ways made her the campus leader. I took mean pleasure in shocking Mother about Donna when she and Gran drove up for their first Sunday visit.

"Oh yes, Mother," I said, "most of the girls here are couples, and the staff doesn't care. It's quite open."

Her mouth dropped. "I don't believe that," she said, tugging at her gloves, "that it's openly allowed." We were primly sunning ourselves in the orchard while girls and parents strolled by nonchalantly to ogle. Mother was giving a ladylike performance, smiling, straightbacked, and unembarrassed. She had earlier told newsmen that she visited El Retiro personally before approving of it and that it was hardly more than a nice private school for girls "who need that little bit of extra help."

She, Dad, and Gran were going to pretend that I was not behind bars. When I tried to tell them stories about other girls and what had landed them here, they changed the subject. I tried to upset Mother, to make her regret that she had put me in this place, but she had compartmentalized her feelings away.

Discipline was fairly relaxed within El Retiro's walls. If one broke a rule, punishment generally consisted of being put on "restrictions"—being barred from movies, ball games, and the all-girl sock hops for a number of weeks.

One Friday afternoon at the close of my seventh week there, Donna told me she had been put on two weeks' restrictions for some infraction or other. "I'm gonna run," she said. Running meant scaling the outer wall, a routine prank of defiance that at least one inmate attempted each

month, usually to be caught within four hours and returned. Donna had run twice before, but I sensed danger
at the thought of her leaving me alone.

"I wanna go too," chimed in another girl named Mary.

"Well, if you're really both going, I will too," I said,
"but I don't know if I can get over that wall."

It wasn't difficult. A ten-foot service gate offered hinges
for toe holds, and we scrambled over as a matron stood
watching, hands on hips. "Hey, girls, you're making a
mistake," she called.

After we had run a few blocks, Donna thumbed down a
passing car driven by a couple in their twenties. We admitted
we were runaways, who were a familiar sight in the neighborhood, and they laughed. If we promised to move on in
the morning, they said, we could sleep at their place that
night. During the introductions, I called myself "Laura."

We arrived at a tract house with an old garage that
boasted shiny black his and hers motorcycles. The young
woman went off to stock up on groceries. When she returned, her friendly smile had vanished. "You're not
Laura," she said. "You're Lana Turner's daughter. We
heard it on the radio. I don't know if we want you guys
staying here tonight." It took all of Donna's charm to
convince them that they did.

A sleepless night followed our dinner of Cokes and
hamburgers. Wearing just a sleeveless blouse and Capri
pants, I shivered on the floor with only a mattress cover
to use as a blanket. Donna and Mary slept peacefully,
while I jumped at every sound. What was I doing? I was
breaking every rule I'd ever been taught. I had gotten into
a stranger's car and gone to a stranger's house. I didn't
know any of these people, where we were, where we were
headed, or what would happen next. "Oh, shut up," said
Donna when I asked her. "I don't *know* where we're going. I'll figure it out in the morning."

Donna had made a friend at El Retiro who after release
had gone to live in Long Beach. When reached by phone,
the friend said she was willing to take us in. Our Good
Samaritan biker agreed to drive us all the way there. Since
there were now headlines and bulletins about our escape,
Donna made me lie on the floor for the two-hour drive to

Long Beach. When we arrived, she called her friend from a gas station to get local directions. "We're on Pacific Coast Highway," she said, "which way to your place?"

"Don't show up or there'll be trouble!" said the friend and hung up. Donna came running back to the car. "The cops are there!" she yelled. "Go to L.A.!" We quickly headed north. What had happened was that the police had questioned Donna's friend, then staked out her house and tapped her phone.

Perhaps stimulated by the danger, our ever more generous biker friend offered the use of another biker's house, which happened to be vacant for the moment. He dropped us off at a sparsely furnished bungalow in Tarzana that had no radio or television. For the next two days, we desperadoes slept, played cards, and growled at each other, dining exclusively on the only food we could find in the kitchen—beans. The fun was over.

The next Monday, the *Herald-Examiner* printed a letter of appeal from Dad on its front page:

Dear Cheri:

You have all of us who love you so much frantic with worry.

Please, wherever you are, call me.

I love you very much and want to do everything possible for you.

And, if you stop to think, you know that is true or I never would be making this public appeal to you.

Neither your mother nor myself had the slightest idea you were unhappy or dissatisfied at El Retiro.

When I last saw you—one week ago last Wednesday, before I went away—I was very happy because YOU seemed happy and contented.

I am sure you don't realize, Cheri, the danger of being out on your own—almost penniless, as you must be.

I want to help you in any way I can, Cheri. Won't you give me the chance?

Please call me. I haven't left my telephone since you ran away.

Please call me, no matter what time it is, or where
you are, and I will come and get you immediately.
DADDY

Cut off from news, I was unaware of the letter. But it
made no difference. In any emergency, I inevitably flew
to my father's strong arms, and that Monday I phoned him
at the Luau. We arranged to meet at a nearby shopping
mall in order to cover any tracks leading back to the friends
who had helped us on our outlaw trail.

Once again my life escalated into ugly headlines. Amid
lengthy accounts, tabloids ran front-page photos of El Retiro's wall and diagrams of our escape route. The public
was so interested in this next turn in the saga of Lana's
wayward daughter that curiosity overrode reason, and Juvenile authorities felt obliged to remind everyone that
"Cheryl is not a criminal, just a missing juvenile."

Before reporters could reach Mother, she fled to seclusion in Palm Springs. (So I, too, couldn't have reached
her by phone if I had wanted to.)

"Aw, Baby, why?" Dad asked me the afternoon I returned.

"I don't know," I said honestly.

But I had brought this crisis on all by myself. In a reckless moment of one-step thinking, I had grabbed for freedom without stopping to think that the inevitable capture
would likely bring longer confinement.

Maybe I was sinking into a need to punish myself. I
could think of so many reasons to do so, starting with the
fact that I had caused a man's death. Though I had been
pronounced innocent of any criminal intent, here I was,
nonetheless, behind bars. What's more, I still blamed myself for a complicity of silence with Lex Barker. All my
life I had been rejected—by my mother, by so many
schools, by fathers and friends. Even my natural preference for women had almost put me in the path of a shotgun. And finally, why didn't I look more like my mother
instead of being this tall brown mouse?

Five weeks later I leapt the wall again. This time it had
nothing to do with Donna, whom I had stopped seeing, but

rather with something about losing a silly argument. I had
resolved never to run again, and, just an hour before, I had
been keyed up over singing a solo in the school's upcoming
talent show. But after rehearsal, crash, I was downhearted.
This time I was the one who said, "Let's run."

Within fifteen minutes, two other girls and I were riding in
the back seat of a convertible with two high school boys in
T-shirts. "Bet you kids are from the reformatory," they
laughed, and off we went for a bit of harmless joyriding. It
was after midnight when I asked them to leave us off in Beverly Hills, where I knew a place we could stay. Our little trio
soon stood under a lamppost on Charleville Boulevard. I peered
up the street to find Gran's windows dark. There was no response when I knocked at the door and I had no key. Then I
thought of dear Miss Hulley who lived two blocks away.

"What do you want?" she said, squinting through the
peephole.

"Gran's not home, Miss Hulley. Can we come in?"

"Well, uh . . ."

She worked her way through a maze of door chains and
deadbolts before she pulled the door wide enough to let
only me step inside.

"Please, Ma'am," I said, "would you happen to know
where my grandmother—?"

"Y'can't stay here," she said nervously.

"Well, my Gran, I mean, would you—?"

"I have absolutely no idea, Cheryl. It's late. You better
run along."

We returned to the street, and my companions exchanged horror-stricken faces, then looked at me questioningly. "There's a little park at the end of this block," I
said. "We'll hide out there until it gets light."

It was the Roxbury Park of my childhood, where under
Miss Hulley's watchful eye I had played on the swings
and slides. It was a safe and innocent place where I had
toasted hot dogs at cookouts with the Brownies.

But the park's foliage was too skimpy to hide us, and
since our bare arms were stippled with goosebumps, I led
us into the chapellike ladies' room, where we lay down.
The cold, dirty floors were not much fun, but all we had

was $1.10 in coin, and there was nowhere else we could
go until daybreak.

I saw how far I'd fallen and I recognized the bitter expressions of my fellow escapees. "Where to next?" im-
plored Sheila, who was fourteen. Before I could answer,
the door flew open and the room filled up with a troop of
big-shouldered police.

"Okay, girls," I said, deciding to play it El Retiro
tough, "this is it." We were led into squad cars and taken
a few blocks to the Beverly Hills police station where at
6:00 A.M. a handful of photographers stood waiting on the
steps. "Get those goddamn cameras out of here," I
snapped. "Get them away!"

"Oh, shut up, Cheryl," said Sheila, "you'll only make
things worse."

My friend Chief Anderson arrived at the station house soon
after we did. He did not say hello. When I could no longer
avoid his blue eyes, I think I saw in them a mixture of contempt for me and sadness for my father. He watched as one
of his men cuffed my hands behind my back. I had not resisted
arrest, and the cuffs were so tight they hurt. "What are these
for?" I demanded. "I'm not running anyplace."

Someone jerked the cuffs hard to point me in another direction. Hands pulled me roughly this way and that. "Son-
of-a-bitch!" I yelled, "you're hurting me." I darted a look
at the chief. "He's hurting me. I'll do whatever you say.
Please tell them to get their goddamn hands off me!"

Anderson's face became a mask of appalled bafflement.
Try hard as he did to be fair, his department was still being
embarrassed by rumors about me, rumors of special treatment, of sloppy police work, of a cover-up. Was he going
through all this because of the foul-mouthed delinquent
who now sat cursing his men on the station-house bench?

Fred May arrived to find me waiting, shackled and
spent, my head bowed as for a guillotine. He flushed with
anger, throwing curses himself as we were ushered off to
Juvenile Hall. Anderson remarked to newsmen, "This was
a big change from the meek and mild little girl who came
in here on a homicide rap. She's very defiant, antisocial,
and a nonconformist."

I might have behaved even worse if I had known then

what had led to our arrest. Gran was not at her apartment when I knocked at the door because she was spending the night at Mother's. Miss Hulley knew this and had Mother's number, but, instead of phoning Gran, she phoned the police. Gran would no doubt have given my little ragtag trio some tender loving care and driven us quietly back to school in the morning.

El Retiro wasn't entirely sure they wanted me back, although they were "reluctant to give up" on me. "This was probably just one of those crazy impulses young girls have," said director Dorothy Kirby, but she pointed out that her recommendation to Judge Lynch would depend on my attitude when she interviewed me. In the meantime, she directed that I be held at Juvenile Hall.

Unlike two years earlier, when I was kept safe in the gentle infirmary, this time I was put into "general population"—four cell blocks housing a frightening array of society's young castoffs, including teenage hookers and drunks, "throwaway children," devastated rape victims, and girls with records of mayhem and murder.

The inmates greeted my arrival with more than the usual hush. There was a respect for Lana Turner's wild child. I was acquiring something of the dark glamour of a famous criminal, and girls were lightly touching my arm to catch my eye.

Another famous delinquent and I soon gravitated to each other. Beverly Aadland had been at the center of a scandal one year before, when it was revealed that she had been Errol Flynn's mistress since the age of twelve. Flynn was then fifty, and it was charged that Beverly's mother had eagerly blessed the arrangement. Flynn had recently died, and Beverly, now a flaxen-haired Lolita of seventeen, was back in Juvenile Hall on charges of fatally shooting a boyfriend. Hearing her tell her story made me think back. Deirdre and Rory, Errol Flynn's daughters, were almost my age, and I had attended their birthdays. This brought to mind other luckless Hollywood princesses who, unlike me, had managed to stay out of jail, including my dear Stephanie Wanger and Christina Crawford. But while star babies' lives were often star-crossed, that did not excuse the mess I was making of mine.

Rumor had it that I would be sent to the girls' reformatory at Ventura, a terrible place with bars and uniforms. When I had my interview with Mrs. Kirby, I begged her to let me go back to El Retiro. Then one morning, on a special 7:30 A.M. visit, Dad and Sybil Brand came to the rescue.

"What am I going to do with you?" Sybil asked rhetorically with the warm gruffness of a Jewish mother. "Aunt Sybil" took the world to her capacious bosom. She first became recognized nationally in the forties for her progressive work in child welfare. Now she sat sternly on the edge of my bed as I poured out my fear of being sent to Ventura or a foster home and expressed a resolve to straighten out.

"Cheryl, I'm going to say something now," she began. "Maybe I can persuade them to let me personally be your parole officer, but if I continue to take care of you, you've got to promise me something. You will have nothing to do with these other girls or go over the fence again."

"I *promise*."

"Because if you do, I will not work for children anymore. I'll quit."

"Oh, my God, Aunt Sybil, don't do that! I promise I'll do whatever you tell me. I promise." And I meant it.

The question of what to do with me was a vexing one. Gossip columnist Mike Connolly of the *Hollywood Reporter* reviewed the issues faced by the judge at my hearing:

> Hizzoner's dilemma: Cheryl wants to return to El Retiro rather than enter a foster home . . . Lana Turner and Steve Crane are too busy with their acting and restaurant careers, respectively, to suit the judge . . . Cheryl's grandmother can't handle the busting-out-all-over Cheryl . . . Judge doesn't think Cheryl should return to El Retiro: "After all, she IS Lana Turner's daughter, while the other El Retiro girls are mostly from underprivileged families. It would be like sending Tony Curtis or some such star to San Quentin. The cons would either clobber 'em or put 'em on a pedestal. It doesn't work out."

Nevertheless, after sixteen days in Juvenile Hall, I was remanded by the judge back to El Retiro, where I was put on two weeks' restrictions. Aside from one more blot on my record, the only measurable damage done by this second runaway was to my grandmother. A "nervous breakdown" might be overstating it, but she went to pieces, weeping and drinking through the night, mourning for "my tarnished angels."

Gran blamed herself in particular for not being home the night I knocked on her door, and at first she was inconsolable. Mother and Fred took her to the Circle M ranch, where it would take years of quiet and sunshine to restore her strength.

I had vowed not to foul up this time, but I had to figure out how. Who was I supposed to be? Nobody wanted me the way I was. They all saw someone else. Mother wanted back that sweet child who adored her, not this defiant teen. Dad wanted a young sophisticate he could talk shop with and show off. Gran wanted me to worship Mother as she did, to be a prom queen with straight A's and produce three kids. The authorities, of course, just wanted a solid citizen.

As for me, I longed to be wild and free, to look like Helen and be eighteen, to travel Laura's New York journey. But I had to face the fact that there were energies inside me that short-circuited self-control. Given a mere taste of freedom at fifteen, I had gone nuts.

When I passed again through El Retiro's big gates that June, I counted exactly thirteen months before the ultimate goal, my eighteenth birthday. Clearly, in order to earn my emancipation, I would have to be a solid citizen. I set about discovering ways to convince the people who controlled me that I had really changed. I went around to every teacher and asked, "What do I have to do to get an A in this class?" The simple answer seemed to be copywork—copying printed answers into exercise books. While I had actually lost my love of learning some five years before, I now feigned bright interest and copied with a fever. I quickly achieved straight A's. I became a lifeguard at the swimming pool and an organizer of activities. At the same time, I kept my distance from the other girls. Above all, I learned how to give the right answers.

Coached by other inmates who had perfected "the game," I assumed a posture of cheerful resignation and good sense. "Oh, everything's great now," I would tell Mrs. Kirby or Mother or even Dr. Wahl, to whom I was still commuting on Thursdays. "All of you were right not to let me marry Marty. I realize that I was living too fast and heading the wrong way. I really needed this time here." Everyone ate it up.

As I learned the game that summer of 1960, my parents were enjoying huge success. Dad opened his third and fourth Kon-Tikis, and was planning a new brasserie-type place on the Sunset Strip. Mother's *Portrait in Black,* her second film for Ross Hunter, opened to so-so reviews but tremendous business. Mother played a glamorous murderess, while Sandra Dee played her stepdaughter. There were hints of Good Friday in the film's climactic finish, in which Sandra eavesdrops on a quarrel between Mother and her lover (played by Anthony Quinn). When she is discovered listening at the door, a chase begins, leading finally to the lover's accidental death. I saw the film that autumn on a home-release weekend and was left vaguely numb.

The *Hollywood Reporter*'s Mike Connolly was a guest at a post-premiere party at Romanoff's. When he greeted Mother at her table, Fred May jumped up and grabbed his lapels. "I love this girl very much," Fred shouted. "Why do you print such editorials as you did the other day attacking Lana and her upbringing of Cheryl?"

With that, Fred hauled off and swung at Connolly. Glasses spilled and chairs tipped over. The columnist retreated, soon to be followed by most of the guests, while Mother wiped away tears with a napkin. She was furious with Fred for provoking a member of the press, but his fierce loyalty to her, his strength and caring, were more than she could do without, and that November they married.

Two months later, on January 22, 1961, the newspapers were filled with the inauguration of John F. Kennedy. That made it a good day, they thought, to release me from El Retiro after eleven months and let me slip quietly into obscurity.

Thirty-two

On release, I still had six months to go until my eighteenth birthday. That glittering prize was so important to me that I named it "Free Day" and marked off the days remaining on a wallet calendar. Before release, a probation official had asked me if I didn't really prefer to remain in the secure surroundings of El Retiro until Free Day. "You might face pressures you haven't figured on in these next six months," he said. He was right.

While I was a solid citizen on the surface, inside I still smoldered with a low sense of self and the same old guilts. And in some clash of needs that I didn't understand, I both yearned to be in control and to *be* controlled.

As it happened, Mother would be my main control for the next 184 days. The court had awarded her custody after Dad had withdrawn from the field and "Aunt Sybil" had again helped to shelve the idea of putting me into a foster home. I was scheduled to return to Beverly Hills High School and live in Mother's house on Tower Road, but as a result of a foul-up having to do with school-district boundaries, I had to move into her new Malibu beach house.

Having sold the Circle M, Mother and Fred had bought a ranch in Malibu and rented a gigantic Moorish palazzo on the Pacific Coast Highway. I moved into a separate apartment above the garage but resolved never to use its private entrance, always the front door. Mother gave me a turquoise 1956 Thunderbird, and I felt buoyant the day

I sped off to register at the new school that "Aunt Sybil" had recommended.

Santa Monica High School had a student body of 8,000 drawn from every stratum of life. Some pupils returned each night to modest homes above family stores, others to beachfront movie-mogul mansions. I recognized girls from El Retiro and Juvenile Hall, and waved at them blandly.

By taking extra courses at El Retiro, I had already earned enough high school credits to graduate, but everyone thought I would be better occupied in school, so I enrolled lackadaisically in easy courses in art and dramatics.

Living on the Pacific Ocean with almost nothing to do and plenty of time to do it, I got into my sunglasses and T-bird to explore the two worlds that were waiting for me. It was a twenty-minute drive down to Muscle Beach and the kind of folks that, in a way, I had come to be most comfortable with—rebels and people with a past. There, I hung out with a body-builder crowd and was soon promoted to the girl on top of the pyramid. I spent long afternoons in beachside cafes with friends, people-watching, gazing at the ocean, and drinking coffee spiked with scotch.

Dad had been helping me to develop a cultured palate for wines and liquors since I was fifteen, when he first discreetly pushed his wineglass between us to share. "Honey, this is a brut, very dry," he'd say. "An okay year, '52, but notice there's no side taste." By now, with my grown-up looks, the only restaurant in town that wouldn't serve me liquor when I was escorted by Dad was the Luau.

The second world I began to explore that Malibu spring of 1961 was Dad's. In something of a minirevival of the Golden Era, Hollywood nightlife was coming back strong in different forms. Up and down the Sunset Strip, establishment clubs like Ciro's and Trocadero had closed their shutters, while hip showplaces like Crescendo and the Interlude were catering to the more easygoing style of a so-called New Hollywood. It was new in the sense that a crop of new stars like Marlon Brando and Audrey Hepburn were making movies with grittier styles and franker themes. Network television production had centered in Los Angeles, and America's perception of urban nightlife was increasingly based on the Hollywood model. One of the Strip's best known clubs was Dino's; named after Dean Martin, it served as the setting for the hit TV series *77 Sunset Strip*.

I was becoming a frequent flyer now at Dino's, Crescendo, and the others, sometimes in the company of Dad and Helen, but often with the young boulevardiers to whom they introduced me. One such young man, Max Baer, Jr., became a steady date of mine that spring. Max was a big, nice-looking galoot who could feather-stroke my moods and always make me laugh. Dad had known his father, the late world heavyweight boxing champ, since the days when he had owned a Cuban lightweight. Max Jr., who went on to play Jethro for nine years in *The Beverly Hillbillies* and become a movie producer, was then a hopeful actor, and we did all the clubs and special movie-industry events together.

Though I thought I was biding my time until Free Day, I was living fast again, and it was being noted on my record. I got tickets for speeding. I cut classes. (My acting teacher thought I had talent enough for the La Jolla Playhouse, but I knew about actors' lives.) I twice got caught violating the city's 10:00 P.M. curfew.

The first time the police picked me up, I was driving by myself after hours in the spooky wilds of Tuna Canyon. I liked to turn the dust along the canyon's narrow roads at night and think. The second time, I was sitting with friends in a Hollywood coffeehouse and my watch said 10:12 P.M. I looked up to see two plainclothes vice cops at the door coming to check ID cards for people under eighteen. I suspect they had seen my turquoise T-bird in the lot, a car well known to most officers in the area.

"Okay, Cheryl," one of them said without even asking for my ID, "I guess you're coming in." I got into the squad car to find I had a companion, another underage girl who was hysterical with fear. I sat calmly shaking my head—what next? A cop in the front seat spun around. "Will you *please* shut up," he barked at her.

"But my parents will kill me!" she cried.

"Look," he said, "the kid next to you is in a hell of a

lot more trouble than you are for this, and she's not bawling.''

The final infraction on my record came when I was found to have associated with a friend from El Retiro. Her name was Mickey, and she had invited me to her eighteenth birthday party, which was supposed to be held with a splash in Malibu. It sounded so respectable that I accepted. A few days before the event, she phoned to ask if Mother and I could put her up for a night. Without thinking, we obliged.

In the morning, Mother found police at our door looking for Mickey. Mickey was a runaway; the party was a hoax.

I didn't see much of Mother and Fred that spring. Unlike Dad, they didn't often take me out. Fred worked in an office in Malibu, and Mother was making two movies back to back. In *By Love Possessed* she played a nymphomaniacal dipsomaniac, but, to my surprise, she had no wayward daughter. This film was followed by a comedy with Bob Hope, and both roles were smaller than those she was used to.

Though Fred had been able to calm Mother down a bit, she and I still had our moments. She complained that I went out too much with Max or Dad or Helen, that I raced around Tuna Canyon or vanished into disreputable bars. ''I don't even know where you are nights,'' she once said to me over lunch. ''I hear you're running around and into and out of every club on the Strip.''

''Well, what's wrong with that? I'm with adults.''

''You're going to get a reputation, young lady.''

''Mother,'' I protested, ''by eighteen you were already the 'Nightclub Queen.' ''

She arched her back and fixed me with a baleful stare. ''But I was paying the *bills,*'' she replied.

Though the court still required me to see Dr. Wahl every week and report to probation, I often drove out to Pacific Palisades and visited Jim Discoe as a friend. Our chats were lighthearted until I got into the scrape with the El Retiro runaway. Then Jim sat me down for a talk. ''Hang on,'' he said. ''In just two months, when you're released, nobody will have any say about your life. In the mean-

time, you're being watched for every little single thing you
do.''

"But I'm not *doing* anything."

"I know. Look, if you were Jane Doe, none of these
things would matter, but you're not. You've got the eye
of the court, the police, and the newspapers, and all those
movie people who like your mother or who do not like
your mother. And then there may be millions of people
who think that there was hanky-panky about the investigation and that you're being treated with kid gloves and
all that stuff. Cheryl, why don't you just lock yourself in
your room and read books for the next two months?''

I trusted Jim almost more than I trusted Dad, and I
resolved to really watch it until July 25—no more flirting
with self-destruction.

The following month I was enjoying a hamburger one evening with friends at Coffee Dan's, a quiet teen hangout on
Hollywood Boulevard. At around nine o'clock, I excused
myself to drive back home to the beach, but, as I was
leaving the restaurant, I spotted Gail, one of my chums
back at El Retiro. We said our hellos and I sat down with
her for a moment. I could see she was tipsy. She introduced the girl beside her as Rachael. While Gail was a
fragile pastel redhead, Rachael looked like a cute young
boy. With her short hair, jacket, and slacks, she seemed
like one of Ann Bannon's Greenwich Village girls, and I
was curious.

They were leaving for a club and insisted I join them.
I paused. It would be fun to talk, but it was nearing curfew
and I knew Gail from the reformatory. I remembered that
Gran's empty apartment was ten minutes away and I had
a key. We would be in a quiet, private place before 10:00
P.M. What could be safer?

When we got there, I offered them something from
Gran's bar cart. (Nothing for me, thank you.) After just
one vodka, Gail jumped up and started to sing dirty lim-
ericks, swaggering like a music hall dandy. This wasn't
as much fun as I thought. "How are you going to get her
home in this condition?" I said to Rachael.

Suddenly the bell rang. I sprang to the curtains and

looked out to see a pair of Beverly Hills squad cars. I drew the girls back to the rear bedroom. "Not a sound now," I pleaded and returned to the front door.

"We've had complaints about prowlers here," said the cop. "Some disturbance?"

"Well," I said, "I'm alone here. What disturbance? This is my grandmother's place and I have permission to use it."

"The neighbor said she saw boys coming in here, and there has obviously been drinking. We'll have to search."

I hadn't seen enough movies to know about search warrants, so I could only stall for a minute. Gail appeared behind me. "What's going on?" she asked in a bleary voice, and it was all over. After they found Rachael hiding in a closet, we were hustled off to the Beverly Hills police station. "You'll really be sent away this time," a detective said with obvious delight.

I was booked on charges of lacking parental supervision and of being in danger of leading a "lewd and immoral life." The other girls faced lesser charges. (Rachael, who was eighteen, later drew probation, while Gail went free.)

Mother couldn't face coming down to the station, so I was released in the custody of my stepfather, who lashed out at the police about the stiff charges. They instructed Fred to return me to the police station the very next day for a hearing with the County Probation Department and Chief Anderson.

I writhed in my bed back in Malibu. Fool that I was, I had handed my detractors the gun with which to shoot me. Everyone could now show how tough they were, and I would probably wind up in Ventura maximum security, where I could be held until the age of twenty-five. There were only forty-four days to Free Day. Could I hide out until then? At El Retiro you learn how to drop from sight without leaving a trail.

I got out of bed, packed a bag, and wrote Mother a note: "I've gone away to think things over. Don't worry. I'm with a friend." I left my car in the garage and at daybreak waited on the highway for a lift I had lined up. The lift dropped me off in North Hollywood, near where

I knew of a runaway who was hiding at her boyfriend's apartment. I knocked on the door. Could I stay? Sure.

For the next few days I did not leave the apartment except to call Jim Discoe by pay phone. I turned into a couch potato, sleeping and reading and watching TV, the safe routine I should have started earlier.

The newspapers said I had been ordered to appear at a special hearing on Friday, June 23, which was only a few days away. Mother and Dad issued appeals for my return, and a probation official warned, "Come home—before it's too late," adding: "If she waits much longer, it could be very bad. Very bad."

It seemed they were out to get me, although Jim Discoe was reassuring on the phone. "I can almost give you my word," he said, "that they won't send you to Ventura if you'll just come home. So can I come pick you up?"

"I'll call you back."

After a week in the apartment, I had overstayed my welcome. The girl's boyfriend worked nights at an FM radio station, and while I paid the food bills, it made them nervous to have me around. I decided to write to Judge Lynch, stating my case in a six-page letter. It closed with, "If I show up for the hearing, I hope you'll consider my side of the story."

As I waited through the days on that battered sofa, twilight time was the worst. I stared at the dying light and I thought of Mapletop and my stomach began to ache again with a child's loneliness. Here I was on the run for the fourth time, and there was no one to go to. I began to think that maybe it would be better to go home than to face this uncertainty in a strange place. But where was home? Finally, after nine days, I phoned Gran in Malibu, asking her to please come take me to the ranch, the only family house that wasn't staked out by the press.

Jim called a secret summit meeting of the family to discuss a deal he was trying to work out with Judge Lynch and the police. I had no idea what was coming. Everyone seemed to agree, he said, that I needed to be removed from the pressures I faced in Los Angeles during this last crucial month before my birthday. "There's a place," he said, "in Hartford, Connecticut, a mental hospital—"

"Not really a *mental* hospital, dear," said Mother, jumping in. "It's a very nice place."

"And if you agree to sign yourself in there for a few weeks," he continued, "to have a chance to talk with some doctors and let things die down here until you turn eighteen, well, there won't be any question of sending you anyplace else."

I was plain tired. And that didn't sound so bad to me.

The Institute for Living in Hartford is one of those luxurious asylums for the rich whose emotional problems do not make them dangerous to others. A medieval castle with cottages, tennis courts, a pool, and a nine-hole golf course, it is set on a square city block of rolling green lawns edged by a fence and gatehouse.

There were then 300 patients at the institute, each paying some $100 a day for the privilege of going about in their own nice clothes while zonked on mood controllers. They ranged in age from thirty to sixty. I believe I was the only teenager there, one of just a dozen patients under thirty, and I quickly responded to being treated as a grownup.

Some patients were drying out or managing serious depression, while others, mere eccentrics, seemed to be turning inward from the world. Every patient carried some vivid background of abuse or tragedy, a lobotomy or an exasperated family who shut them away because of their oddness. One sweet old lady, heir to a fortune, had supposedly been committed thirty years earlier by scheming relatives. She could have easily signed herself out, but the institute's pleasantness bred complaisance and she was happy playing bridge every day and smacking her lips around hot fudge sundaes.

I was assigned to a sunny room with twin upholstered chairs and leaded windows with diamond-shaped panes. Mother and Fred had delivered me there, then continued on for a holiday in New York. Before long Dad arrived, on his way to a new Kon Tiki in Boston, bearing my eighteenth-birthday present, a blond mink stole. He signed me out that evening and we dined at the best restaurant in Hartford.

He explained by candlelight that he and Helen were adopting a son, a four-year-old who came from an under-privileged family of eight children. They had renamed the boy J. Stephen Crane IV. A few years earlier this news might have shaken me, made me wonder if I would now have to compete for his love, but these days my mind was running on automatic—to say nothing of three-times-daily Thorazine shots. I thought only of the freedom my birth-day would bring in just seventeen days.

I did think of one thing. "Dad," I said, "how do you think he's going to react when kids at school ask him about me and the, you know, the . . ."

"I wouldn't worry about that, dear. When he's older I'll explain that you had to defend your mother."

"But Dad, kids can be cruel—"

"Don't *worry* about it. Just put it out of your head."

I told him I had decided that, after my release, I wanted to get a job in New York. Though he had spoken of my going to college, his reaction was similar to Mother's when I told her. They both nodded sadly and smiled.

I soon fell into the institute's routine of mental tests, pot-tery classes, and bridge. The only problem I had was in dealing with my assigned psychiatrist, a young black-haired New England preppy who knew how good-looking he was and spoke in a confident way. "Let's see here, Miss Crane," he began, swinging his legs on the desk. "Let's start by talking about this Stompanato thing. Do you have a problem about that?"

"I have no problem with it because I don't discuss it."

"Well, we'll see about that. We are going to discuss *every*thing."

"You and I aren't going to discuss a thing."

"Miss Crane, until you start talking, you're not getting moved anywhere."

"Fine. I'll sit right here until I'm eighteen."

After that, all our sessions began with me shaking my head and staring out the window while he busied himself with papers. "I'll be here when you want to talk," he'd say. Maybe, if he had taken a gentler tack or not been so smug, I would have opened up a little. But we butted heads and no good ever came of it, and I didn't care.

After years of yearning and counting, Free Day finally arrived. That morning of July 25, 1961, I awakened like a lark instead of a crow and set about handling the formalities. As a legal adult no longer a ward of the court, I could sign the release papers myself. I asked a nurse to bring the forms. A moment later my white-coated psychiatrist appeared in the door, flaps flying. "Miss Crane, you are certainly not ready to sign yourself out," he said.

"Doctor, I have every legal right. I need the forms and my suitcases too." There was a short waiting period, but I wanted to pack right away. He looked nonplussed and fled down the hall.

The nurse reappeared in a while to say there was a call for me on the pay phone. It was Mother.

"Oh, darling . . . oh, darling," she said plaintively. "I don't know how to tell you this. You're not free. Not yet. Judge Lynch hasn't released you."

"He has to. I'm eighteen."

"No, dear, he doesn't. Not until he feels you've been there long enough to get some help. You won't talk to your doctor, so the court has extended your wardship. If you try to leave there, he can send you right to Ventura."

"Oh, Mother, you're just trying to keep me here!"

"I wouldn't lie to you."

"Yes, you would. They can't do this. It's illegal! I'm calling Jim Discoe."

"Well, dear, if you must," she said, and clicked off.

When I reached him at the office there was a hollowness in his voice. "I'm afraid it's true, Cheryl," said Jim. "The court has extended your wardship another year." I could barely hear him over telephone static and institutional noise in the background. "What?" I asked. *"What?"*

"Well, I'm afraid your mother is right," he said, speaking up. "You really should give that place a chance. We'll talk in a month or so. Maybe things will be different."

"I will never speak to you again!" I screamed, and ran back to my room.

I smashed both fists into the mirror while shrieking a wordless babble. Bloody shards stuck from my palms as I held them before me and ran at the window. The iron mullions broke my run. I was too big to fly out, so I punched my hands through the diamond panes and impaled my arms. Strong hands lifted me back, and I whimpered after feeling the prick of syringes.

When I awoke I found I was tied to a bed. I floated in timelessness as people shot me with drugs and liquid food, put me into a bath or a straitjacket, helped me onto a scale or a toilet. An ever vigilant nurse sat observing me under the glare of a ceiling light that never went out.

I was under a round-the-clock suicide watch, and I drifted in a narcotic haze for a period I can't guess at. One day a nurse said, "I'll untie you if you promise not to break anything," and the restraints fell away. Then my psychiatrist came in and said, "I have a paper here for you to sign."

"No no. Go away. I'm not signing anything."

Later another doctor sat on my bed, a tall, tweedy Scotsman in his fifties with enormous hands and a soft voice. He introduced himself as Dr. McCauley and said that since there had been a little problem with my doctor, he would be taking over. "I thought it might make you feel better if he's not on your case anymore," he said. "And if sometime you'd like to talk, I'm here. First of all, I'd like to get you into a more comfortable room, okay?" In his Scottish burr I heard the reassuring sound of Nana, and I quite suddenly gave him my trust.

Over the next few months McCauley started progressing me through wards that involved less and less restraint. The first ward reminded me of scenes from Hieronymus Bosch, with people screaming in the night, wandering in trances, laughing wildly, or giving orations to unseen throngs.

We lived in the perpetual twilight of a half basement, padding along linoleum floors at bedtime to line up for our sleeping potions. We all drank blue liquid phenobarbital from wax cups, then opened our mouths and wiggled our tongues to prove we had swallowed our medicine.

I begged McCauley to reduce my medication, but as the Thorazine level came down, trembling returned to my mouth, hands, arms, legs, and stomach. Months drifted by, filled with days when breakfast seemed to be followed suddenly by dinner. I went nowhere on the ward without my arms being held by two nurses. I received no mail except letters from my family, which I wouldn't read. I spoke to no one but McCauley. I had given up. I was beaten, whipped. Let them do with me what they would. I didn't care about being locked up. Had I been able to, I would have taken my life. Suicide or not, I knew that if they forced me to endure enough of this, I would die anyway.

A long time passed before I felt any hint of my old spirit coming back. McCauley trod carefully around the subject of Stompanato, as if he had forever to dig it out, and I gave ground by inches.

By late autumn I was moved to a locked coeducational ward in which patients enjoyed access to normal services. I had the beautician dye my hair Vampira black and indulged myself on books and magazines from the newsstand. One day I was thumbing through *Confidential* magazine when I came upon a full-length photo of myself being arrested with Gail and Rachael. The article said that, before being locked up for psychiatric treatment, I was seen in the company of mannish women. Mother had often been a target of that tabloid. Now it seemed it was my turn. I shrugged.

The Institute for Living prided itself on its discreet treatment of famous people. Actress Gene Tierney had been helped there, and when I was promoted to a minimum-security ward I fell into a friendship with comedian Jonathan Winters. Jonathan's nerves had collapsed from overwork two years before while he was appearing at the Hungry i in San Francisco.

On stage one night he began to mumble, and the next day at Fisherman's Wharf he swung from the yardarm of a sailing ship, declaring himself to be a man from outer space. Jonathan was at the institute for a rest, but, to the dismay of his doctors, he could not stop doing his standup routines for the inmates, even to an audience of one.

"Pal, we've got to stick together," he said to me, his arm around my shoulder. "We come from a crazy world, Hollywood, but neither of us belongs in this nuthouse. You and I know it's all a dream anyway." He grinned and flapped his eyebrows. "As long as we keep laughing, they can't get us."

In art class, he painted a picture of a giant fish about to swallow a school of little fish. In the caption below, two other fish are looking on, and one says to the other, "You see, Lamar Jean, that's what happens to conformists."

Jonathan's friendship was a great help in my struggle to regain some sense of myself. "Kid, you can't let them do this to you," he'd say. "You've got to figure your way out of here."

When Mother and Gran came to visit me at Christmas, I fired the opening shot in my campaign to get out. I said I would indeed go crazy if I had to associate much longer with all those odd people. Mother explained that the court would not release me until Dr. McCauley thought I was ready. She would, however, ask him to grant me more privileges.

She, Gran, and I made a sad little trio that Christmas in their hotel suite, gathered around a tiny tree the chauffeur had arranged. As her present to me, Mother opened a charge account at G. Fox, Hartford's biggest department store, where I ran up a $3,000 bill that week. I gave Gran some dressing-table boxes I'd made in ceramics class. I gave Mother an oil painting I'd spent long hours on. It showed a great golden lioness, beautiful and fearsome, whose paws held the tiniest cub.

Mother had news to share that Christmas, none of it good. Fred had not accompanied her east because they were estranged. I got the feeling that L.T. had cleaned out one stable too many.

Sadder still, Dad and Helen were drifting apart. If they divorced, Dad intended to retain custody of Stephen IV. It was clear that Mother had been appalled by the adoption, seeing it as a veiled rejection of me and an act of spite against her.

To add to my distress, Mother had agreed to settle the Stompanato family's damage suit with a $20,000 payment to the son. "Call it peace money," she said wearily. It made me feel as if my innocence had been bartered.

Sometime after Christmas, Dr. McCauley moved me to

the nicest ward, Ward A, where one's days floated by in a pleasant parody of country-club living.

It wasn't long before I could see me giving myself over to thirty years of hot fudge sundaes. I had every freedom that could be enjoyed by a pampered adolescent except the privilege of venturing unescorted beyond the asylum's front gate—that was still withheld for reasons McCauley never made clear.

I stepped up my campaign for release. "I like it *too much* here," I kept telling Mother. "I'm sure they'll be glad to keep me forever as long as you're paying the bills."

When Mother arrived for a one-week stay in April, I moved into her hotel suite and intensified the arm-twisting. She finally gave in and signed me out.

Thirty-three

We flew back to Los Angeles on April 8, 1962. An hour before the plane touched down, Dad told the press that he and Helen were separated. She had already gone to Alabama, where she was asking for a quick divorce in order to marry Ronnie Burns, the actor son of George Burns and Gracie Allen.

I settled in at the ranch with a newly reconciled Mother and Fred, took the Thunderbird out of storage, and exercised the still high-spirited Rowena. Feeling rather lobotomized, I went back to things that were easy and familiar, like riding, driving, and reading. I got in touch with a few friends from both Muscle Beach and Dad's celebrity world. It seemed utterly humiliating to have just spent ten months in a mental hospital.

Soon after returning to Los Angeles, I drove out to visit Jim Discoe filled with nagging questions. There was one in particular—How could he have let the court extend its control over me after I had turned eighteen?—that had to be answered.

"Jim," I said, "those next seven months nearly killed me. How could that have been legal?"

"Cheryl," he began slowly, "this has been weighing on my mind. I've never done something like this before, and I want to tell you how sorry I am. I lied to you. Your doctors wanted to keep you there, so I agreed to back up your mother and say the wardship had been extended. Actually, you could have signed yourself out at any time."

So many people had lied to me. *And now you, too, Jim?*

I thought. I was too exhausted, too beaten, too pumped full of tranquilizers, to react. I just sat there, stunned.

I didn't speak to Jim again for six years.

Before long Mother was once more hectoring me about clothes and makeup and too many evenings out somewhere. L.T. was coming back, and it drove Fred wild. He could not get used to a woman's needing six hours to dress for a restaurant dinner. For her part, Mother seemed to be growing a little bored by solid Fred. He may not have been sexy and dangerous enough. Whatever the reasons, and though he was surely the best husband she had ever had, she divorced him that October.

To make Mother's state of mind worse, her last picture, a comedy called *Bachelor in Paradise* in which she'd co-starred with Bob Hope, hadn't done well. Currently she was working on an even more lackluster comedy with Dean Martin, with whom she had little rapport.

Dad's career, on the other hand, was booming. Long since a millionaire, he could now boast six Kon Tikis, while the expanded Luau had become a Hollywood landmark. People loved to tell stories about the place, including those about the night Eartha Kitt smashed an Easter Island lamp over someone's head, and the time Gordon Scott, a movie Tarzan, stripped naked and jumped in the lagoon. A giant 500-pound sculptured Samoan head stood at the Luau's front door, and one night, before the big football game against UCLA, USC fans stole the head and planted it on the stadium fifty-yard line.

At forty-five, Dad was in his prime. His adopted namesake, Stephen IV, lived at the Tower Grove house. I just couldn't resist the little round-eyed boy's energy. In the years ahead, we would develop into conspiratorial friends.

After Hartford, I lacked the ability to make plans for my life. Going off to the unknowns of college or New York seemed frightening to me now, but I had to do something. Dad couldn't hire me as a hostess at the Luau because I was under the drinking age of twenty-one, but he had another idea. He phoned Alfred Bloomingdale, his Malibu roommate at the time he first met Mother. The New York department store heir had founded Diners Club since then, and, yes, there was an entry-level job there for me.

The job involved phoning past-due customers and twisting their arms to pay up. Sitting in a Kafkaesque room filled with badgering bill collectors, I pleaded all day for money. I was awful at it, falling for every excuse, even weeping over sad stories. "Oh ple-ease," I'd beg, "if you could just send a little something on account, maybe I could talk to them about it here." After a month of torture, both administered and received, I quit.

I had moved into Gran's apartment to be near the Diners Club. Now, with nothing to do, I took up the pastimes of a Hollywood brat. I shopped. I took long lunches at La Scala and crashed the guests-only pool at the Beverly Hills Hotel. My cohorts on such adventures were usually two new chums, a onetime roommate of mine at Sacred Heart Academy named Diane Lewis and her friend Bobbie Gentry, a would-be actress who would go on to record the hit single *Ode to Billy Joe*. Our idea of style was cruising up and down the Strip in Dad's Lincoln Continental making calls on his phone and looking very bored.

One day Bobbie came up with a job idea. A nightclub on the Strip named the Summit was about to start holding lunchtime fashion shows, and they were auditioning for models. I jumped at the chance. To our surprise, all three of us were hired.

We showed up bright-eyed at the dress rehearsal the day before the opening. The Summit was a big dark place with chrome chairs, sticky floors, and black-and-white striped walls. A low runway cut through the tables.

It was going to be a businessman's lunch type of thing, the manager explained, and the fashions we had to wear were created by Frederick's of Hollywood. Diane, Bobbie, and I laughed as we struggled into skimpy swimsuits and playsuits, satin short-shorts and halters. We were not being asked to model lingerie, and nothing bare or see-through, thank goodness. If we had been, the three of us would have left.

Heads held high, we paraded as statuesquely as we could to the loud strains of Bobby Darin singing "Mack the Knife." The rehearsal was going well when a crowd of photographers and reporters suddenly began to appear at the front door. "Okay girls," said the manager with two waves of his hand. "We got here a little publicity to do— just keep rolling."

The photographers got out their Graflexes and TV cameras, the reporters opened their notebooks, and everyone went to work. When the rehearsal was over, they drew me aside. I told them I was proud to have landed a modeling job by myself. One reporter asked if my mother had approved my new job. "Gee," I said, "I know the odds are sort of against me, but give me a chance."

Later that day I excitedly phoned Dad to say I thought I might be on the evening news. "Oh, I can't tell you why, Daddy," I said. "It's a surprise."

That night he sat in his favorite chair with me curled at his knee as the news came on. There I was—swanking along the runway in a black bathing suit. "Cheryl Crane is back in the spotlight," read the announcer. "A nightclub spotlight. The eighteen-year-old daughter of Lana Turner, who four years ago killed her mother's gangster boyfriend Johnny Stompanato, will be modeling hot pants and swimsuits at a nightspot on the Strip. Cheryl has just returned from a year of psychiatric therapy at a New England—"

Dad knocked back his drink and glared at the rug. "Bastards," he said. "I know those guys who are opening that joint. It's a pickup spot, Cheryl. Don't worry. I'll get you out of it."

"But I signed a contract."

"Oh, I'll fix this one fast."

And so he did. A letter from his attorney the next morning prevented the club from even opening that day.

I was a little girl again, getting into trouble and being rescued by my daddy. He didn't ask my opinion. He wasn't mad at me. He just killed it. My friends and I believed that we had landed the job solely on our looks and talent. How could I have been so naive?

Again my confidence plunged. I vowed that the Summit fiasco would mark the last public appearance of Cheryl Crane. I would have to reinvent myself as someone else, to make a break from my family's emotional and financial old. But now at least, instead of running away, I could go off quietly and legally.

I thought of a girl I'd just met who had a bungalow on Hawthorne Avenue in a working-class section of Hollywood. Her name was Diana, and she worked at Stan's Drive-In, which was across the street from the Olympic Stadium where Dad and I had sometimes gone to watch the boxing matches of his Cuban prizefighter. One day, while she was serving me a milk shake, we got to talking and wound up exchanging phone numbers. When I called, she said there was room in the bungalow for me.

I guess Diana and I saw ourselves as a pair of lost souls who were better off together in a perilous world. She had been deeply depressed since her father's suicide and kept a chilly distance from her mother, a nurse in Beverly Hills.

I packed my car and phoned Gran to say I was moving in with a friend. I didn't know the phone number, but I'd call her when I did.

"Well, where is it?"

"Gran," I said softly, "I don't want anyone to know the address. I'll be fine. Don't worry."

Stan's had an opening, and I took it. It was in a dangerous neighborhood, but I owed Diana money and her work looked rather like fun. Having served briefly as a stockroom helper, a bill collector, and a runway cutie, I now donned the proud uniform of a carhop. I worked three nights a week until midnight. I dropped a lot of trays at first, but I learned, and the tips some nights could run to sixty dollars. One flirty salesman gave me five dollars for a coffee.

The name tag on my jacket read "Cheryl." I had considered using "Laura," but my roommate had let my past identity seep out to friends without noticeable effect. Besides, I seemed to have assumed the protective coloring of my surroundings. Who would have thought in the lowdown depths of Los Angeles that this Vampira bringing your burger was a movie star's daughter?

I called Mother and Dad that autumn but refused to give my number or address. I told them that my new life was no song, but I was getting by.

That October a novel entitled *Where Love Has Gone* appeared on the best-seller list. Author Harold Robbins had taken the story of Good Friday and written a flat-out *roman à clef*, exercising care to alter just enough details to avoid any chance of a libel action. Mother was portrayed as a world-famous sculptress who had stabbed her lover with a sculptor's chisel, but whose daughter took the blame for the killing. This, of course, pandered to the most widely held notion of what "really" happened that night, a notion that lingers to this day.

I never even thought of reading the novel. Mother did, and refused comment to the press. No reporter tracked me down or even realized that I was missing, because Mother and Dad glossed over my whereabouts. My name did surface when Mother's divorce from Fred was announced amid speculation that trouble between Fred and me was to blame for the breakup. Fred gave heated denials. Poor man, he tried so hard.

That winter, in order to numb the return of my twilight reveries, I began to drink seriously. Having managed to acquire a false ID card, I could go into a bar and knock back scotch, usually with a group of Diana's friends but sometimes on my own. Many nights, by closing time I couldn't drive the car.

I finally told my parents where I lived after Mother threatened to hire a detective to find me. At first they were shocked, then hurt, then vaguely detached about my new lifestyle. Two people who wrapped themselves in glamour had bred a child who chose the gutter. They never came to visit.

That Christmas, while Mother was entertaining the troops in Korea, Dad tried to involve me in his world again, inviting me to his third annual New Year's Day Hangover Party at his house up on Tower Grove. It was a lavish all-day-and-night blast for hundreds of guests, who were encouraged to wear costumes. Dad hosted in the black brocade of a Mississippi gambler.

The gaiety of the party only added to a depression that now clung to me like overweight. I saw in glaring contrast the wretchedness of the life I had chosen on Hawthorn Avenue.

One listless afternoon, Diana invited a couple of friends in for drinks. One of them had smuggled a few bottles of absinthe from Paris. Repelled by the taste, I only sipped at it, while everyone proceeded to drink it down and pass out. I studied their faces as they lay sprawled unconscious across the furniture, eyes slightly parted, their labored snoring obscene. The room was cramped with depression furniture, overflowing ashtrays, and clutter. Everything was bathed in the lonely glow of twilight.

When I tried to shake Diana awake, she wouldn't stir. I pushed myself unsteadily to my feet and wandered through the bungalow's warren of rooms. Each looked unhappy. Sleeves of sweaters hung from drawers like the arms of accident victims. Mousetraps waited in corners to pounce on balls of dust, and clothing was piled everywhere for mending or washing. I drifted into the bathroom and rested my elbows against the mirror to study my face.

After spending nearly two years behind bars, how free was I now—now that I was free? I had gone to some of the best schools, and how had I chosen to use my mind? I had been raised in mansions, and now where was I?

I absently opened the mirror cabinet and saw all those sleeping pills. Why not? Anything would feel less painful than this loneliness. I went to the kitchen, poured water into a glass, and downed a handful of pills. More water. More pills. More water, more pills. Then, throwing the bottles in the trash, I washed the glass and turned it upside down on the drain.

Seeing that my companions had not moved and would probably be unconscious until morning, I went to a far bedroom, where I curled up in a blanket to close my eyes, hoping to die.

The pain was excruciating. I felt bandages everywhere and my eyes wouldn't open. A woman's voice was saying, "She's got acute gastritis, poor thing. You can tell from her terrible breath that she hasn't been able to eat in days."

I was in Beverly Hills again, lying in Doctors' Hospital under Dr. McDonald's care. It was the day after I had gobbled fifty Seconals. Diana had awakened late that night to find me nearly comatose, and she phoned her mother in panic. By some discreet arrangement that avoided tipping off the police, Diana rushed me by car to a private clinic, where my stomach was pumped. Then, while still unconscious, I was moved to Doctors' Hospital and admitted for severe gastrointestinal blockage. I was also badly lacerated from a fall I'd taken on the sidewalk as Diana struggled to walk me into the emergency room.

Refusing to see anyone, especially Mother, I stayed in the hospital and pondered. I was so grateful to be alive. I wanted to live now, to do something with what I had been given. I saw that the answer was not in death, which was a waste, nor in seeking a wanton existence in which I was worthless and nobody around me was any better.

Suddenly—and I don't know why—I decided that I had talents to work with. With all my advantages of nature and nurture, I could expect more of myself.

After a week, I telephoned Mother at the new house that she had bought since divorcing Fred. It was on the beach in a gated enclave known as the Malibu Colony. I apologized for the fright I'd caused and then I opened myself to Mother as I had never done before. I laid bare my vulnerability. After taking a deep breath, I explained that while I was now stabilized again on Librium, I was still very unhappy and had been thinking things over. "I want to make real changes in my life," I said. "Will you help me?"

"My God, I'll do anything in the world!" she said. "What? What do you need? Shall I come get you?"

"No, Mother, thank you. What I want is to get away from the people I've been around and not fall back on you. I want to find a job somewhere and get my own apartment. I need time to be by myself and on my own. The hitch is, I don't have much money, so, frankly, will you help me get an apartment? I hope it's the last thing I'll ask."

She wanted to do much more, but I declined beyond accepting part of the rent deposit and a loan of furniture.

My parting from Diana was resolute. "We're not good for each other," I said, "and, forgive me, but if I were you, I'd get out of here, too." As it turned out, she moved back to live with her mother and two years later took her own life.

* * *

That spring I found a tiny three-room apartment on Stanley Street in a lower-middle-class section of West Hollywood. It was good therapy running a tiny household, making my meals, and paying the bills. I soon discovered the joys of having one's own private space, things like the freedom to sleep till noon or cook while naked.

I returned at first to my old job at Diners Club. I had bumped into a former coworker while making the rounds of employment agencies, and he urged me to come back. It seemed safe and steady and boring—just what I needed. But I never did manage to toughen my heart for nonpaying customers.

The next eighteen months were stabilizing. Though I ignored my inner problems, I was getting my social legs, moving around with a set of young people on their way up in something other than the entertainment industry. I made friends with shopkeepers, decorators, doctors, bi-coastal New Yorkers in finance. It was a real eye-opener to see young women my age with good jobs and gorgeous apartments.

I began to think that I might have a flair for making living spaces attractive, and I began to try my hand at it, decorating three new apartments during the next eighteen months. I slimmed down to a size six (112 pounds at 5'9") and started runway modeling for a smart women's store on Rodeo Drive.

I had swallowed so many of my problems that to deal with the tension that was gnawing inside, I used Librium and Seconal (plus Escatrol to stay a size six). My system was overloaded, and I became a victim of unexplainable fainting spells. Without warning, my pulse would race, I would get dizzy, tremble, and black out. Dr. Mac and his experts ran every test imaginable, and they could conclude only that I had a condition known as shallow breathing. Their remedy: when starting to feel dizzy, I should breathe into a paper bag. I began to carry one in my purse.

New York was increasingly on my mind. I almost felt strong enough to try it. When I submitted fashion photos to the exclusive Ford model agency in Manhattan, they expressed interest and invited me to come for an interview. I tried the idea on Dad. "Give me some time," he said. "Let me see what I can come up with."

It may have struck almost everyone as a miracle that I had managed to survive to see my twenty-first birthday, but Mother made sure no one missed the fact. That July, she gave me a big party at the Galaxy, a nightclub on the Strip. Mother, escorted by Fred May, ordered a cake that stood four feet high, and some seventy-five couples wiggled the watusi until 2:00 A.M. "For weeks I've been working on every tiny detail," Mother told reporters. "The flowers, the buffet, the entertainment. I even invited every guest by telephone. I woke up this morning and wondered if I could finally live through it."

Jim Discoe sent me a huge sportsman's trophy inscribed, "To a Winner. You made it to 21. Love, Jim." Frank Sinatra dropped in to give me a gold and diamond St. Christopher's medal. "How does it feel," he asked, "to be a twenty-one-year-old broad?"

Having survived three institutions, seven schools, six governesses, fourteen homes, and five stepparents, I really did feel like an old broad. "Oh, just wonderful, Frank," I said.

The best present came after the party from Dad. "Honey, you're of age now," he said. "Why don't you come work at the Luau. If you don't like it, then try New York, but give me six months, okay?"

I wound up giving him fifteen years.

VIII

JOSH

Thirty-four

began my illustrious career at the Luau working as a "seater," that smiling person to whom the captain hands you over, saying, "Miss Crane will seat you now."

I enjoyed the job, once I got over my shyness, and before long the New York daydreams drifted away. Among the Luau's 200 or so employees I was known, not as Lana Turner's daughter, but as the daughter of the president of Stephen Crane Associates (SCA), a company whose restaurants and licenses were then bringing in some $10 million a year. It was the first time in my life that I was identified mainly as my father's daughter rather than my mother's, and though I was proud of my connection to a screen star, I felt gratified that Dad was finally getting equal time.

After a year at the Luau, Dad put me in charge of daytime operations at a new Italian restaurant that he had opened on the Strip. He had named the place Stefanino's, after himself.

I grew to enjoy most everything about the restaurant business—especially its theatricality. In a sense, running a restaurant is like running a theater. You have a kitchen backstage, a cast of cooks and waiters, and an audience out front. The food's the thing, of course, to which you add lights, settings, costumes, and music in an effort to create the most inviting fantasy possible.

Deciding to make a career of it, I took a year off to attend the noted hotel and restaurant-management school at Cornell University. Thereafter I worked closely with

Dad to expand SCA's operations. Before long we had nine Kon Tikis in the Sheraton chain and six other restaurants with varying themes in and around Los Angeles. In the process, I rose to become executive vice president of SCA, Dad's Number Two. He and I ended most every workday together, drinks in hand, mulling over business and the day's events.

Mother and I settled into a relationship that was strained but cordial. We would run into each other at clubs, and every once in a while one of us would ring up the other to arrange an evening out together at a disco. Her conversation sparkled in such public settings, and we never spoke of anything that mattered. I viewed her now with a certain detachment, one adult observing another. The tie of blood had never been broken—we still loved each other as mother and daughter—but somehow it was easier to hold each other's hand than to talk.

By the spring of 1969 I was doing well enough to buy a new three-story Spanish-style house in the western suburb of Calabasas Park. It had a swimming pool and fronted on a large manmade lake, on the other side of which was our newest restaurant, the Californian.

Dad married his fifth wife that year, an attractive divorcee named Leslie Deeb. Mother, meanwhile, divorced her sixth husband, a would-be film producer ten years her junior, and promptly married her seventh, a nightclub hypnotist who did not last out the year.

Mother's career was clearly on the decline. Now in her late forties, she had outlasted Ava, Rita, and Betty. Just the same, after five forgettable pictures in a row, her future as a screen goddess was looking decidedly dim. On the positive side, she and Dad seemed finally to have reached some sort of modus vivendi. Throughout the 1960s and 1970s Mother often dined at the Luau. Dad always welcomed her as a guest of the house, and she always wowed the room with a classic star entrance.

Despite a sixty-hour work week, I managed to enjoy my share of nightlife. Indeed, I was playing nearly as hard as I was working. When I wasn't out dancing at the Daisy, the Candy Store, or the Whiskey a Go Go, I was giving

or attending parties on the movie colony circuit. Well-
known around town, I seemed to be welcome everywhere.
I think I radiated what I was feeling, which was that I
liked myself, was proud of my work, and was determined
to have a good time. I was discovering a profound truth:
when you accept yourself, people accept you.

What I was doing was reconstructing myself from the
outside in: building a career, exploring new interests,
learning to be an adult, developing my own style. Having
spent most of my childhood rebelling against my parents,
I had a very strong sense of what I didn't like—namely,
just about everything that they valued. The trouble was, I
had never really developed any positive idea of what I did
like. Now I was finally giving myself a chance to find out.

Not surprisingly, there was a lot of my parents in me.
I found that I enjoyed entertaining, giving dinner parties
with good silver and china. I enjoyed being well turned
out, dressing stylishly, and speaking softly. I stopped trying to look the complete opposite of L.T. I might have
been tall and thin rather than small and buxom, but Mother
and I had the same coloring and there was no denying that,
just like her, I looked better as a blonde. If I sometimes
drove too fast, sometimes drank too much, sometimes took
too many tranquilizers, this was the life I wanted.

As I began to come into my own, began to get the ex-
ternals sorted out, I found myself feeling an internal emptiness. I was happy and successful, but I was alone. It
soon dawned on me that I was finally ready for a real
relationship.

Late one February evening in 1968, I had gone to a party
given by my friend Wally Cox. A well-known star of early
television, Wally had made his mark as the lovable science
teacher in the hit series *Mr. Peepers*. Although playing
the wimp was his stock-in-trade professionally, Wally was
in reality a forceful man whose slender frame bulged with
well-developed muscles. His best weight-lifting buddy was
Marlon Brando, and together they formed the hub of a
show-business circle that hung around Wally's Laurel
Canyon ranch house.

The party was already in full swing when I arrived.

Brando, I noticed, had retreated from the commotion by crawling under a pool table, where he was deep in conversation with a beautiful girl. When they finally surfaced, I recognized the girl—a tall, raven-haired beauty—as a well-known model and star on the celebrity amateur tennis circuit who had dated actors John Derek and Ron Ely. Last I had heard, she was Peter Lawford's girlfriend.

Though we had met before, I couldn't remember her name. She remembered mine, however, and introduced herself as Josh. (Her real name, I eventually learned, was Joyce LeRoy; as a model, and to her friends, she was known simply as Josh.) Poised and determined, with a quick wit and an easy laugh, she looked into my eyes as if she were examining my soul. She wore a fresh gardenia in the lapel of her jacket—her trademark—and she took my breath away.

We talked for a while, and she seemed to like me. But though I knew she was bisexual, I dismissed the thought that she might have any serious interest in me.

Over the next two years, we kept running into each other around town. Then, one afternoon in April 1970, when I was home in bed in Calabasas recovering from some oral surgery, Gran, who was playing nursemaid, announced that I had a visitor. A moment later Josh appeared in the doorway laughing and struggling with an antique picnic hamper filled with cans of Campbell soup. She had been thinking of me being laid up in a sickbed and didn't want me to starve, she explained, so she brought me every flavor Campbell's made except one. "They didn't have chicken," she said with a frown. Suddenly I loved her.

We talked the afternoon away. She had long since parted from Peter Lawford. Currently, she was acting in commercials and modeling fashions at a Beverly Hills department store. When she finally went on her way that evening, she paused at the door and smiled at me. "You might not believe this, Cheryl," she said, "but someday we'll be together."

We saw each other every day that April. In some ways, we had much in common. Like me, she had been an only child; like me, she was strong-willed and independent. Raised in Los Angeles, she had gone through school with the children of Bob Hope, John Wayne, and Ronald Reagan, so my star-baby background didn't impress her. But we were different, too. Where I had had six stepfathers, four stepmothers, and no end of childhood trauma, she came from a stable, loving family. Where I had inherited Mother's and Gran's preference for ignoring awkward realities—their belief that the best way to deal with unpleasantness was to pretend it never happened—she was an uncompromising realist who insisted on tackling problems head on.

A strange thing began to happen to me as our relationship deepened. For years, the subject of Stompanato had been securely locked away in my mental attic, along with Lex and my time in the institutions. I never worried about it, I never thought about it. Suddenly, however, it was on my mind. What did Josh think about "the paragraph," about what had happened that Good Friday night? There was, I decided, no way she could love a person who had killed someone. I would have to make up a story. I would have to tell her that someone else had been holding the knife.

We were sipping martinis in Booth One at Stefanino's one evening early in May when I decided that the time had come. I had never even mentioned Stompanato to Josh—the topic had never come up—but during a pause in the conversation we traded a glance, and I knew she could tell what I was thinking. It was now or never.

"You know," I began, "I didn't do it."

She didn't react. I would have to try again.

"I love you so much more than anyone before in my life, Josh, that I don't want you to think I could do a terrible thing like that."

Her perceptive eyes surveyed the room before coming finally to rest on mine. "Cheryl," she said simply, "I think it was a very brave and noble thing to go to your mother's defense."

I blinked in surprise. No one had ever said anything like that to me before. No one had ever said that what I had done could have been anything but monstrous. No one had ever said that it might actually have been in some way creditable. Certainly I had never looked at it like that. For all these years, I had lived with the terrible knowledge that I had killed a human being. It was a notion so overwhelmingly horrible that I had had to shut the door on it, bury it away out of sight, in order to be able to get on with my life. The idea of dispassionately considering the whys and wherefores of the deed, no less of concluding that it was anything but deplorable, was simply beyond me.

"As a matter of fact," Josh continued, "our friends all feel the same way I do. It was a tragic accident, and something you will have to live with the rest of your life." She paused. "Now you have someone to share it with."

In that moment, while sitting in a candlelit booth in a Sunset Strip restaurant, my life changed.

Over the next few weeks, Josh encouraged me to speak the name Stompanato until the sting went out of it. She even got me to talk about Lex and Mother and what Good Friday had been like. According to Josh, I began to undergo a subtle physical change. It was as if I had had a minifacelift. Frown lines faded and my smile brightened. I could feel the tightness in my body drain away, to be replaced by a feeling of buoyancy. I began to exult in living. I didn't drive as fast or drink as hard as I had before. I stopped taking pills. I began looking forward to the future—with Josh.

A few months later, I asked Josh to come live with me at Calabasas. Suddenly, it was her turn to wrestle with doubt. I had long been open about the fact that I preferred women (and had surely done so since the days at St. Paul's Academy when I had clung to Charlene's skirt). It was different for Josh. True, she had discreetly been seeing women as well as men for the last couple of years. But that was hardly the same as committing herself to living in a suburban house with another woman—and with Cheryl Crane, at that. By moving in with me, she would be making a statement that would be hard to take back if things didn't work out.

I had made my statement, such as it was, back in 1964, when I first started working at the Luau. For all my insecurities, I knew that, as an attractive restaurant hostess, I was sure to be asked out by men. The challenge was, how to deal with it? Even in the cosmopolitan world in which my parents and I lived, homosexuals were expected to keep their preferences to themselves, to be discreet. But I was fed up with the lies of my childhood, the stifled emotions, the covered-up violence, the games I'd had to play to survive the juvenile justice system. Now that I was discovering Cheryl Crane the woman, and was certain about my sexual preference, I couldn't bear the thought of any more deceit.

Anyway, what was there to hide? There was nothing wrong with being gay—not that I had been taught, at any rate. It's just the way some people are. And I had been brought up to take people as you found them. For all its other problems, my family had never shown any prejudice. I had never heard either of my parents put anyone down because of race, religion, or sexual preference. And I was certainly not about to put myself down. I was the offspring of very proud people. "No matter what they print about you," Gran would say to me, "always hold your head up high."

In any case, the juvenile justice system had only winked at such matters. And my parents, who had long known the truth about me, had always been supportive.

My course was clear. I had no choice but to be honest about myself and let the chips fall where they would.

The first test came my first week at the Luau, when a customer, an actor I knew, asked me for a date. "Thanks very much," I said, "but no."

"Are you going out with someone?" he persisted, leaning on my desk.

"No," I replied nervously. "I just don't date."

"What?" He was genuinely puzzled.

"Well, I like you a lot, and I hope you'll be my friend, but the fact is, I prefer girls."

He straightened up, then shook his head skeptically and retreated. A little while later he came back. "Thanks for your honesty," he said, clearly meaning it.

That became the pattern when men asked me out. They were astounded at first by my frankness, then charmed when they thought about it. Most wound up as friends, becoming brotherly and protective—especially, I noticed, when other men were around.

In the fall of 1970, Josh finally decided to cast her lot with me. I vowed to myself never to let her down. We would blend our lives and our families.

We were joined the next year by Gran, still feisty and fun, but too frail now to live by herself. Josh and I converted our ground floor into a private apartment for her.

That same year, Mother launched a successful stage career in dinner theater. Her fans having moved to the suburbs, she found she could command as much as $25,000 a week in ten-week tours of romantic comedies such as *Forty Carats*. It was a bizarre life, living out of twenty suitcases, pressing the flesh every night with fans, and getting star treatment wherever she went. She did not cope with it well. "I'm sorry," she told me much later. "I just don't remember a lot of the seventies."

The end of that decade brought changes for all of us. In 1978 an Iranian consortium offered Dad $4.1 million for the Luau. The Rodeo Drive lot on which the restaurant stood was in the middle of what had become the prime block of one of the most fashionable shopping streets in the world. The Iranians wanted to tear the Luau down and replace it with a two-level complex of designer boutiques.

Now sixty-one, Dad was inclined to sell. Both he and SCA (which was now grossing upward of $20 million a year) were in good health. But he had just gone through a messy divorce from Leslie Deeb, a close friend of his had died, and he lacked the fire inside to push on. Though I could see what was coming, I was powerless to dissuade him. In January 1979 the Luau was razed right down to the subbasement.

Josh and I weighed our options and decided to move to Hawaii. We had fallen in love with the islands on a series of vacations, and we decided that a fresh start in the land of blue lagoons and powdered white sand was just what we needed.

Gran temporarily moved to a retirement complex on Sunset Boulevard, and in April 1979 Josh and I flew off to Honolulu. We immediately set about looking for a house that realtors call a "fixer-upper," one that a little love, sweat, and artful remodeling could turn into a showplace ready for quick resale. Before long, we found a large colonial in the middle of an Oahu rain forest. It was faded but sound of beam, so we bought it and went to work.

We hired contractors for the heavy work, but did almost everything else ourselves. Josh turned out to be handy with a hammer, while I have the patience of a painter. We completed the job in three months, then took a little while to furnish the place completely before showing it to prospective buyers. The look we went for was light and airy, lots of plants, pictures, and flowers, fluffy pillows and sofas you sank into. We then added a fair but sizable markup to our investment, and put it on the market. We had a buyer in less than a week.

We promptly repeated the process with another house twice the size and cost of the first. By the end of the year, we were well and truly launched. Acquiring real estate licenses, we branched out as agents, specializing in those million-dollar oceanfront palaces everyone dreams about, while still offering our fixer-upper skills as a separate service.

We seemed to be blessed with success. At the same time, we found ourselves welcomed into Oahu society. Though Josh and I were usually the only female couple at their glittering parties and sit-down dinners for twenty-four, no one ever made a fuss, least of all us. We have always preferred the company of married couples.

Mother paid us a visit our first Thanksgiving in Hawaii. She was in a terrible state, shaken by a violent quarrel with a personal secretary she had just let go and suffering from an inner-ear infection that affected her balance and made travel difficult for her. After some tension and several flare-ups, she cut the trip short and returned to Los Angeles. It would be eighteen months before we saw each other again, though we stayed in touch via monthly telephone calls.

The following spring, in the middle of a casual phone conversation, Gran let slip some shocking news. Mother was writing her autobiography. I couldn't believe it. "Gran," I said, "she always preached and preached to us about keeping secrets. Our lives are private, she said. Don't talk to reporters. How could she *do* this?''

I had made a new life for myself on an island paradise with a partner I loved and work I was good at. I was respected. I had friends. If my name turned up in the newspapers, it was in the society column or the real estate section. But now, it seemed, Mother was trying to exploit our story.

Frightened by the thought of her book, I decided to discuss it with her the next time we spoke on the phone.

"I hear you're writing a book," I began casually.

"Yes," she replied, "and you will be handled beautifully."

She explained that a well-known film critic named Hollis Alpert had approached her for help on a biography he was writing about her. After sitting down with him for several long, probing interviews, she decided to make the book her own. Would I agree, she asked me, to be interviewed by Alpert? I would not.

The next year Josh and I moved into a big Victorian house in Kahala just a block from the beach. We brought Gran out from Los Angeles to live with us, and she arrived with happy tales of how Mother seemed to be in much better shape. With the help of a doctor, she had sworn off liquor and pills. Intrigued and hopeful, we decided to invite Mother to Hawaii for my thirty-seventh birthday.

We didn't know what to expect that July afternoon in 1981 when she finally arrived. As it turned out, the Lana Turner who stepped off the plane in Hawaii was no one we knew. She was so easygoing and good-natured that, after an exchange of sly smiles, Josh and I stopped calling her "Mother." That was much too formal. She was now "Mom."

We checked her into a hotel suite, where she doffed her jewelry and severe black L.T. traveling outfit, replacing it with an informal new look that she maintained the rest of her time on the islands—clogs, a muu-muu over a bathing suit, and (if she was going out for a hamburger) a strand of good pearls. Off came all the makeup except for lipstick and eyebrows. Gone was the archness of L.T., the sternness of Mother. There were no deep-breathing *Peyton Place* stares, no dramatic pauses as if she were shooting a close-up. This nice lady, Mom, displayed the bounce she had shown the world at seventeen in *Love Finds Andy Hardy*. She spoke straight from the shoulder. She even laughed at herself. Her long fingers with their Fu Manchu nails would soon be peeling potatoes and pushing a dust mop. I was astonished.

When we sat down to dinner that night and started to catch up, she explained her transformation. Not only had she given up liquor and pills, she had discovered religion, taken up celibacy, and gained thirteen well-needed pounds.

Most striking of all was her new independent way. While Josh and I were at work, this woman—who, for most of her life, had expected an entourage of family and retainers to take care of her—would trudge off to the beach by herself and sit happily alone in the sun. She struck up friendships with fans and strangers, and even began to go around with a lively circle of islanders she'd met.

It was on this visit that our old, strained relationship began to turn into one of friendship and understanding. Deep down, I had always loved my mother, even been obsessed by her. Now, for the first time, I could like her. We became a real family that summer, Mom, Gran, Josh, and I. Not only did I fall in love with her all over again, but she took to calling Josh her "second daughter."

Not long after she arrived, Mom asked me to help her find an apartment retreat in Honolulu. I wound up getting her a nice penthouse co-op at the Colony Surf Hotel on Diamond Head beach. She moved in that autumn, and used it periodically for the next three years.

Mom had arrived just in time to help us cope with a family crisis. Gran had long been fighting a losing battle against emphysema, and she finally reached the point where she needed round-the-clock care in a nursing home. I had always promised my grandmother that I would never leave her side (just as she had promised me), and I shrank from breaking the awful news. Mother insisted it was her duty. But because her relationship with Gran was so complicated, I feared that she might mishandle the moment. (Several years before, in a press interview that touched on what Mom had called her and Gran's "strange" early years together, she said: "I knew she loved me, and she was a warm and giving mother, but I never felt close to her.")

It turned out to be one of the most heartbreaking moments of my life. Dear Gran, perched in her wheelchair, as wary as a caged bird, listened intently as Mom cheerily explained that a nearby luxury nursing home would be the very best thing for everyone. Mom was at once strong and delicate, promising Gran our faithful love and attention, her velvet voice calm and reassuring. She was warm and mature and magnificent.

Gran's reaction careened through suspicion, skepticism, defiance, doubt, and finally, with tiny sniffles, resignation. In the end, Mom and I sank to our knees, enfolding Gran in a loving embrace. I found it hard to look Mom in the eye at such close range. To me, this had been her finest hour, and my old feelings of adoration were stirring once again.

Gran died in the nursing home four months later. Her last words to me were, "Cheryl, take care of your mother." We scattered her ashes in Hawaii.

Thirty-five

For years I had been nurturing a dream. After working at Dad's side for so long, I wanted to run a restaurant of my own. Now was the time. With our real estate operations flourishing, Josh and I decided to branch out and give Oahu its first top-notch Spanish-Mexican restaurant. Dad thought we were out of our minds. "You're doing so well," he pleaded. "Don't give up your real estate to get back in this crazy business."

We ignored his advice, and in June 1982 opened the Por Favor in a swank suburb of Honolulu. It was a big hit.

That fall *Lana: The Lady, The Legend, The Truth* by Lana Turner appeared in bookstores. Spot-checking its most sensitive sections, I was relieved to find that Mom had kept her word about matters involving me.

I was also relieved to find that my friends and associates in Hawaii were too sophisticated to care much about what the book did or did not reveal. But the resulting commotion (*Lana* quickly became a best-seller) did make a whole new generation aware of what was being called "one of Hollywood's greatest scandals." Of course, they didn't always get the story straight. I remember one of the teenage busboys at Por Favor coming up to me and saying, "Miss Crane, I hear that your mother is famous." When I confirmed that she was, he added: "But I'm not quite sure—is it Lana Turner . . . or Tina Turner?"

As a result of the book, the press began clamoring to write update articles about me. The phone rang constantly. When it came to my unhappy past, I had always avoided publicity, refusing ever to be interviewed about Good Friday or anything associated with my personal life, and now, more than ever, I wanted to maintain my privacy. I managed to duck all the reporters except one. He was a disarming Englishman who said he was researching a business article for a European newspaper about the Hawaiian real estate boom. I had cooperated with this sort of coverage in the past, so I agreed to talk to him. A few weeks later I found my remarks splashed across the *National Enquirer.*

"AFTER KILLING MOM'S GANGSTER BOYFRIEND AT AGE 14," the headline screamed, "LANA TURNER'S DAUGHTER NOW A MULTIMILLIONAIRE BUSINESS WOMAN." The paper quoted a competitor of mine, who described me as one of Hawaii's "top three brokers," with a net worth of "at least" $2 million and a client list of tycoons and Hollywood stars. It was true that we had done work for the likes of Dolly Parton and Barry Manilow, but we were not rich and not looking for publicity. As a result of the article, I received about 1,500 letters over the next year, some asking for money, autographs, and advice, others offering love, snapshots, and congratulations. Despite my fears, there was not one hate letter in the bunch. Someone even sent me a six-foot-high floral display.

I had been exposed in my paradise hideaway, and I had survived. Still, when Mom's agent asked me to sign a release so my story could be used in a movie version of *Lana,* I said no. I was still a bit fragile, and I knew what a Hollywood treatment might mean.

Since the movie could not proceed without my permission, Mom phoned me one day to apply a little pressure. I listened to her in silence, then asked simply: "Mom, how would you like to see your daughter on the big screen stabbing somebody?"

There was a crackling pause on the transpacific line. "Oh, darling," she said after a moment, genuinely chagrined, "I never thought of that. Forget signing the release. Please, just forget I ever asked."

In fact, just such a stabbing scene had already been filmed—though not for *Lana.* Two months later, a totally unrelated production called *Hollywood's Greatest Myster-*

ies was broadcast on NBC. An hour-long special, it dealt
with three still controversial deaths in Hollywood: the
suicide of Marilyn Monroe, the unsolved murder of silent
film director William Desmond Taylor, and the Stompanato stabbing.

Although it left me feeling battered, I found I had the
strength to weather it. Watching in horror as actors re-
created in gritty docudrama style the events of Good Friday, 1958, I realized that what had happened that terrible
night happened to the child I was—not to the adult I had
become.

We closed the Por Favor in the spring of 1983, reopening
it with a new look and more elegant cuisine as the Cafe
Kahala. To act as manager, we brought in Dad's old friend
Patrick Terrail, the man behind Hollywood's trendy Ma
Maison restaurant. I often phoned Dad, ostensibly to ask
his advice, but really to flatter him and help keep up his
spirits. After closing the Luau five years earlier, he had
glumly shut himself into a hotel suite in Westwood, the
latest best-seller in one hand, a bottle of scotch in the
other. He had put his house in order, he said, and had no
desire to live to be an old man. As a result of too much
lonely drinking, he developed cirrhosis. The combination
of that and a rare blood disorder was too much for him.
Soon he had wasted away to 137 pounds and his doctor
was urging us to have him declared incompetent and committed to a hospital.

His ex-wife, and my old role model, Helen DeMaree,
wound up coming to the rescue. Divorced from her third
husband, actor Doug McClure, Helen was doing social
work at an Indian reservation near San Diego. Still friendly
with Dad, she took loving care of him in her home that
winter and spring, trying to wean him away from alcohol
and watching in despair as he sank into melancholy.

Dad knew that his glory days were gone, never to return. The new movie stars were all on diets, didn't drink,
and had never heard of him. The studios were now owned
by soft-drink conglomerates. The old gossip columns
hardly mattered anymore, and Ciro's had been turned into
a comedy club. Where the Luau had flourished there now

stood a chrome and marble shopper's paradise called "The Rodeo Collection."

Dad died on February 6, 1985. At his request, he was buried back home in Crawfordsville, Indiana. Though the local paper carried a funeral announcement and he still had a few friends in the area, there were only seven mourners at his grave. "He wasn't a Hoosier anymore," explained Uncle Bill.

Among the belongings he left me was a trunk filled with scrapbooks containing articles and pictures of him and Mom from the 1940s. Of all the newspaper articles in which he had been mentioned over the years, he had saved only these. Mom, I think, had been the love of his life, and this was his way of telling me.

A month later the Cafe Kahala was sold. It had had a glorious beginning, with private parties for patrons such as Clare Boothe Luce and Adnan Khashoggi, but it was time to move on. Josh and I had both been working at top speed for more than twenty years. It was time to smell the roses. We decided to move to San Francisco, where we took a hilltop terraced flat in the Pacific Heights section.

We're still there. The apartment is a fantasy of flowers and white walls, of sunny morning views of the park and lavender twilights across the bay. I love to garden and decorate, while Josh enjoys cooking and entertaining. When we aren't traveling, we tend our investments.

We have an interesting and varied social life that, I have to admit, owes at least something to Mom's fame and my notoriety. People are often curious to meet me, and I've long since come to terms with the fact that, with new people at least, my past can seem to be the most interesting thing about me.

I talk on the phone with Mother twice a week, and we visit each other once every six weeks or so. Mom has come to look to me for companionship; among other things, I suspect she's drawn to the stability of the life I lead. Indeed, I have chosen a conventional life, centered around my home and a devotion to one partner for nearly eighteen years. Mom's life, with its caravan of husbands and lovers, its almost constant strife and upheaval, was something else, and I think she gets a kick out of being a central part of my well-ordered existence.

I decided to write this book not because of anything my mother did or didn't do, but as a result of discovering that so many people still had mistaken notions of what happened that Good Friday in 1958. In discussing Stompanato with one of my closest friends recently, it came out that he thought I had been found guilty. Others continue to cling to the myth that there was something illicit going on between Stompanato and me, or that I have been covering up all these years for a crime that Mom actually committed. Even though this tale has been written about and filmed nearly a dozen times over the years, with and without disguise, the fact is, the whole truth has never before been told.

This book also marks the first time I've publicly discussed the abuse, sexual and otherwise, that I suffered as a child. Digging it out of my memory, not to mention committing it to paper, wasn't an easy process. But with the passing of time, and through the eyes of happiness, I have been able to look back without bitterness. When I heard on the radio some years ago that Lex Barker had died (of a heart attack on a Manhattan sidewalk), I felt no joy, no relief, not even any anger. What he had done to me was history.

What strikes me now as I look back at that unhappy episode is how often, out of the best of intentions, we treat abused children in a way that only adds to their trauma. Why is it that, at a moment when a child's greatest need is to feel loved and not blamed, he or she is so often ostracized or sent away? Why is it that, at a time when a child is desperate to understand what has happened, when he or she should be encouraged to talk with someone he or she loves and trusts, the child is so often told to forget about the experience, to put it out of his or her mind? The fact is, without the right kind of attention, the abused child will continue to live on inside an apparently happy and well-adjusted adolescent and adult. Unless that abused child is recognized and embraced, its cries will never be stilled.

Though it wasn't easy to tell Mom I was writing this book, the act of doing so opened a door that had been shut between us for many years. When I brought up the subject, I began by telling her the things I intended to write about. Among them, I said, was my relationship with Josh.

Mom looked at me with alarm. "Are you sure you two know what you're letting yourselves in for?" she asked.

"Yes," I said, "we've considered it carefully. If I'm going to be honest about my life, I have to be truthful about this part also. Anyway, there are so many misconceptions about it. I mean, I've known I was gay since I was six—"

"You have?" Mom interrupted.

"Actually, I believe we're born this way. I think it's innate."

Mom looked astonished. "You mean it wasn't my fault? It was nothing I did? It wasn't . . ." She paused dramatically. ". . . environmental?"

"Of course not."

She looked so relieved that I almost laughed.

"Look," I said, "I wouldn't change anything about myself if I could. I'm happy. You know that."

Mom still looked stunned—stunned and relieved. "Well, darling," she finally said, "I feel you have every right to tell your story. I'm sure it will be rough at times, but I'm behind you one hundred percent."

Thus began a series of intimate mother-daughter chats such as we had never enjoyed before. With Josh sitting beside us, we would become engrossed in self-revelation. By the glow of after-dinner firesides, Mom and I swept cobwebs from the most painful of subjects, helping each other recollect the most minute details. "So *that's* how you felt," we kept saying to each other. "So *that's* what you meant."

Our chats proved a cleansing way to draw closer, even if the process came thirty years late. There was plenty of soul-baring, the most difficult of all involving Lex. When Mom told me what had happened when she returned to Mapleton from Gran's that night after learning from me of Lex's abuse, it struck me for the first time that his actions had represented an assault upon her as well as on me.

Perhaps the most important watershed came on Thanksgiving Day, 1986. Mom was celebrating the holiday with us in San Francisco, and we were relaxing in our apartment with champagne and caviar while the turkey slowly cooked in the oven. I knew she was curious about how the book was going. I also knew that she would never dare ask, so I began to describe the first few chapters. When I got to the stabbing, Josh interrupted. "Lana," she said, "it's so difficult to talk about the taking of someone's life, but I've always told Cheryl how noble I thought it was. I know you agree with me that for any child to go to the defense of her mother—"

"My God," Mom broke in, "of course!" She slid from the couch to kneel at my side, taking my hand in hers. "Cheryl, have I never told you how much I appreciated what you did for me? How you saved my life? Gran's life? Your own life? How, if it wasn't for you, I wouldn't be here today? Didn't I ever let you know how grateful I was?"

It was hard for me to speak. "You never told me in words," I finally managed to say, "but I sort of felt I knew. It's just that no one until Josh ever actually told me whether I had done a good thing or a bad thing. I was never punished or rewarded."

"Of *course* that's how you must have felt!" Mom exclaimed. "How could we have let that happen?"

"Gran would never speak of it," I replied softly. "Dad would change the subject. And you and I never talked."

At that moment, having heard her express it in words, I realized that I had sensed her gratitude all along. We embraced, dabbing our eyes with tissues, then started to laugh, which made us fall into each other's arms all over again.

I have no regrets about my childhood. I think everything happens for a reason, and life is seldom fair. I was blessed with great advantages, and, despite everything, I wouldn't change my parents if I could. The outrageous privilege and travail of my early years strike me now as a distant adventure, a detour that I was able to survive with only the tiniest scars to show for it.

The fact is, I've come through, and while it's true that I grew up before my mother did, she has caught up by leaps and bounds. It's good she's here to share with Josh and me what is flowering into the happiest time of our lives.